Modern DUTCH Grammar

Modern Dutch Grammar: A Practical Guide is an innovative reference guide to Dutch, combining traditional and function-based grammar in a single volume. With a strong emphasis on contemporary usage, all grammar points and functions are richly illustrated with examples.

The *Grammar* is divided into two parts. Part I covers traditional grammatical categories such as nouns and verbs. Part II is carefully organized around language functions and contexts such as:

- giving and seeking information;
- describing processes and results;
- expressing attitudes, mental states, and emotions;
- registers and style;
- formal and informal communication, e.g., youth talk.

Main features of the *Grammar* include:

- clear, succinct and jargon-free explanations;
- extensive cross-referencing between the different sections;
- emphasis on areas of particular difficulty for learners of Dutch.

This is the ideal reference grammar for learners of Dutch at all levels, from elementary to advanced; no prior knowledge of grammatical terminology is assumed and it provides indexes of grammatical terms and functions. This *Grammar* is complemented by a companion website at www.routledge.com/cw/oosterhoff featuring related exercises and activities to reinforce learning.

Jenneke Oosterhoff is Senior Lecturer in the Department of German, Scandinavian and Dutch at the University of Minnesota. She has taught both German and Dutch.

Routledge Modern Grammars
Series concept and development – Sarah Butler

Other books in the series
Modern Mandarin Chinese Grammar
Modern Mandarin Chinese Grammar Workbook

Modern French Grammar, Second Edition
Modern French Grammar Workbook, Second Edition

Modern German Grammar, Second Edition
Modern German Grammar Workbook, Second Edition

Modern Italian Grammar, Third Edition
Modern Italian Grammar Workbook, Second Edition

Modern Japanese Grammar
Modern Japanese Grammar Workbook

Modern Brazilian Portuguese Grammar
Modern Brazilian Portuguese Grammar Workbook

Modern Russian Grammar
Modern Russian Grammar Workbook

Modern Spanish Grammar, Third Edition
Modern Spanish Grammar Workbook, Third Edition

Modern DUTCH Grammar

A Practical Guide

Jenneke Oosterhoff

Routledge
Taylor & Francis Group
LONDON AND NEW YORK

First published 2015
by Routledge
2 Park Square, Milton Park, Abingdon, Oxon OX14 4RN

and by Routledge
711 Third Avenue, New York, NY 10017

Routledge is an imprint of the Taylor & Francis Group, an informa business

British Library Cataloguing in Publication Data
A catalogue record for this book is available from the British Library

Library of Congress Cataloging in Publication Data
Oosterhoff, Jenneke A., author.
Modern Dutch grammar : a practical guide / Jenneke Oosterhoff.
pages cm. – (Routledge Modern grammars)
Includes bibliographical references and index.
1. Dutch language–Textbooks for foreign speakers–English. 2. Dutch language–Grammar–Problems, exercises, etc. I. Title.
PF112.O67 2014
439.318′2421–dc23

2014020169

ISBN: 978-0-415-82840-6 (hbk)
ISBN: 978-0-415-82841-3 (pbk)
ISBN: 978-1-315-74343-1 (ebk)

Typeset in Times New Roman
by Graphicraft Limited, Hong Kong

MIX
Paper from responsible sources
FSC
www.fsc.org
FSC® C013604

Printed and bound by CPI Group (UK) Ltd, Croydon, CR0 4YY

Contents

Acknowledgements

While writing this book, I consulted excellent reference grammars such as the online *Algemene Nederlandse Spraakkunst* (Nijhoff, 1997), *De Regels van het Nederlands* (Wolters Noordhoff, 1994) and *Nederlandse Grammatica voor Anderstaligen* (Utrecht, 1985). I thank the people at taaladvies.net for promptly sending me answers to complex grammatical questions. I especially thank my colleagues Wijnie de Groot and Inez Hollander for proofreading my chapters, helping me with translations, giving me ideas and supporting me with good humor along the way. Special thanks also to Michel van der Hoek for proofreading and commenting on my chapters on pronunciation, spelling, and sounds. I also want to thank Paulien Detailleur for reviewing my chapters as well as my anonymous reviewer who gave me invaluable advice for improving the manuscript. I also thank my students at the University of Minnesota for giving me ideas for this book. Lastly, I thank the College of Liberal Arts at the University of Minnesota for granting me a leave of absence to finish this book.

Introduction

Modern Dutch Grammar: A Practical Guide is a practical reference grammar designed with a modern, communicative approach for students learning and teachers teaching Dutch as a foreign language. This book differs from traditional grammars in that it combines detailed explanations of grammatical structures in Part I with a functional approach to the language in Part II. In Part II, learners of Dutch can find the specific uses of language in particular situations such as introducing oneself and others, talking about likes and dislikes, agreeing and disagreeing, expressing belief and disbelief, and many more. Part II aims to illustrate how we use the structures as explained in Part I to form statements, questions, hypotheses, conditions, observations, descriptions, opinions, and commands and to express attitudes and emotions. In Part II therefore, particular attention is paid to idiomatic use of the language and register. Register refers to the different vocabulary and grammar structures speakers use when talking or writing to different people, taking into account the status, age, and the relationship they have with other people, and whether the situation demands a formal or an informal level of speech. And so for each situation described, examples are given in formal as well as informal or colloquial contexts. By offering frequent cross-references, the book illustrates the interdependence of structures and functions. The functions illustrate how the grammatical structures are applied. For instance, one cannot give commands without knowing the imperative, just as one cannot describe and compare objects without the proper use of adjectival endings. Furthermore, the book points out particular language pitfalls, i.e., situations where native speakers of English are tempted to translate literally while the Dutch expression is totally different. Some examples of this are **Hoe ben je?** for 'How are you?' where it should be **Hoe gaat het met je?** which always automatically prompts the answer **Ik ben goed** for 'I'm fine/good' where it should be **Het gaat goed met me**. Another mistake that is often made is **Ik ben vervelend** for 'I am bored' where it should be **Ik verveel me**. The book offers many examples of such pitfalls.

This book is intended for learners who already have a basic knowledge of the Dutch language. While the grammatical structures are explained in a way that is also easy to understand for beginner learners, the functions in Part II would require a student to have reached the level of A2 or B1 as defined by the Common European Framework of Reference for Language Learning or Intermediate-Mid according to the ACTFL proficiency guidelines. The book will be a useful reference tool for undergraduate students taking Dutch to fulfill a language requirement or as a major or minor part of their four-year college program. It will also be a helpful reference tool for students of Dutch in secondary schools and adult education classes. University students as well as self-learners in an academic, non-academic, or postgraduate environment will find this book a welcome addition to my other two Dutch grammar books: *Basic Dutch: A Grammar and Workbook* and *Intermediate Dutch: A Grammar and Workbook*, also published by Routledge in 2009. Finally, teachers of Dutch will find this an invaluable resource in planning syllabi and teaching Dutch courses.

Exercises are an essential part in language learning. This textbook is accompanied by a companion website with exercises for both Part I and Part II. Students can also use my *Basic Dutch: A Grammar and Workbook* and *Intermediate Dutch: A Grammar and Workbook*, which both have a number of exercises for each grammar topic.

How to use this book

Modern Dutch Grammar: A Practical Guide is divided into two parts. Part I – Structures, is a reference guide to the grammatical structures of Dutch, organized in four parts: noun groups, verb groups, word order and sentence structure, and letters and sounds. In some cases, tables are used to illustrate forms and patterns, for example verb conjugation and subject and object pronouns. Part I, therefore, offers the reader quick and easy-to-locate reminders of adjectival endings, prepositions, the passive, and so on. An appendix with the most common strong and irregular verbs, organized according to their stem vowel change, is located at the back of the book. Part II – Functions, shows how the structures are used to express communicative functions in particular contexts and situations. The functions are organized in seven main categories: social contact, basic communication strategies, factual information, the wider context, transactions, attitudes and mental states, emotions. In the table of contents, the reader can find the contents of each category in more detail; most of the chapters each have ten sections.

While the detailed table of contents and the frequent cross-references facilitate navigating this book, two indexes, one on grammatical terminology, and one on functions, will allow the reader to look up exactly the grammatical or functional detail that he or she needs for a particular purpose. The index of grammatical terms includes examples in Dutch. The index of functions contains key words such as 'availability,' under which the different functions with which one can express the availability of something or someone are listed, for example 'through borrowing/rental,' 'through purchase,' 'at hand,' 'available to meet,' etc. When the learner has located the function, he or she will find examples in different contexts and registers.

Throughout the book, the reader will find cross-references to further information on, for instance, a particular grammatical structure or to other examples of a particular function.

The translations of the examples are kept as close to the Dutch as possible. But if one takes into consideration that the purpose of this book is to show that literal translations from English to Dutch are best avoided, one will understand that the translations sometimes have their own English wording, just as Dutch has its own way of expressing things and using particular idioms that may differ from English idioms.

Part I

Structures

A

Noun groups

1

Nouns

1.1 Articles and nouns

Dutch has two definite articles, **de** 'the' for masculine and feminine (or common) nouns, and **het** 'the' for neuter nouns. Examples are **de tafel** 'the table,' **de stoel** 'the chair,' and **het bed** 'the bed.' When we use indefinite nouns, we use **een** 'a' or no article. Examples are **een huis** 'a house' and **melk** 'milk.' **Melk** is an uncountable noun, and while all nouns, countable or uncountable, can appear with a definite article, the indefinite article **een** only appears with countable nouns in the singular. Uncountable indefinite nouns as well as countable indefinite nouns in the plural appear without article. All definite nouns in the plural appear with the article **de**. Examples:

	Definite		*Indefinite*	
	Countable	*Uncountable*	*Countable*	*Uncountable*
Singular	**de tafel**	**de melk**	**een tafel**	**- melk**
Plural	**de tafels**	**-**	**- tafels**	**-**
Singular	**het bed**	**het ijs**	**een bed**	**- ijs**
Plural	**de bedden**	**-**	**- bedden**	**-**

General uses of the article

Indefinite articles are used to introduce a subject or object that is not known to the listener or to use nouns in a general, categorical or abstract meaning. Definite articles are used to talk about subjects and objects that are known to the listener (often as abstract concepts) or to further specify or qualify an indefinite noun that has been introduced. The examples show the similarity to English.

Ik heb *een* tafel gekocht. *De* tafel staat nu in de eetkamer.
I bought a table. The table is now in the dining room.

Ik wou melk in de koffie doen, maar *de* melk was zuur.
I wanted to put milk in my coffee, but the milk was sour.

Er ligt ijs op het water. *Het* ijs is nog niet dik genoeg om te schaatsen.
There is ice on the water. The ice is not yet thick enough to skate.

***Een* poes is minder werk dan *een* hond, want je hoeft hem niet uit te laten.**
A cat is less work than a dog, because you don't have to walk it.

***De* meeste mensen denken dat *de* gloeilamp door Edison werd uitgevonden.**
Most people think the light bulb was invented by Edison.

***De* krant wordt 's morgens bezorgd.**
The newspaper is delivered in the morning.

Names of people, countries and cities

These categories have no article, but take a definite article when a specific qualification or distinction is added. Note the difference in the following examples:

Mondriaan schilderde vooral abstracte schilderijen. Maar ken je *de* Mondriaan van de figuratieve schilderijen?
Mondriaan painted primarily abstract paintings. But do you know the Mondriaan of the figurative paintings?

Ik woon al heel lang in Amsterdam. Ik hield vooral van *het* Amsterdam van de 70er jaren. *Het* Amsterdam van nu vind ik vreselijk.
I have lived in Amsterdam for a long time. I loved the Amsterdam of the 1970s. I think today's Amsterdam is terrible.

Names of languages

Similarly, names of languages that one knows, speaks, or learns do not take an article.

Peter spreekt goed Duits en Engels. Hij leert nu ook Frans.
Peter speaks German and English well. He is also learning French now.

However, when talking about a certain kind of a specific language, the indefinite article is added.

In Baden spreken ze *een* Duits dat ik niet versta.
In Baden, they speak a German that I don't understand.

Note that contrary to English, in the following cases, the name of a language takes the definite article.

Karel heeft drie boeken in *het* Engels vertaald.
Carl has translated three books into English.

Annemarie bestudeert de geschiedenis van *het* Nederlands.
Annemarie is doing research on the history of Dutch.

Other cases in which Dutch often differs from English

There are some cases in which the use of the article differs from English. For example, when talking about one's profession, function, or hobby, one's affiliation with a country, a city, or a religion, we do not use the indefinite article.

Johan is advocaat.
John is a lawyer.

Stephan is Duitser.
Stephan is a German.

Veel kinderen willen brandweerman worden.
Many kids want to become a firefighter.

Hij is manager in een groot bedrijf.
He is a manager in a big company.

Karin en Minnie spelen piano.
Karin and Minnie play the piano.

Joop is lid van de tennisvereniging.
Joop is a member of the tennis club.

Professions, functions, nouns in a general meaning with the conjunction **als** (meaning 'as a') also do not take the indefinite article.

Als leraar heb je veel correctiewerk.
As a teacher, one has a lot of grading to do.

Als Moslim mag je geen alcohol drinken.
As a Muslim, one is not allowed to drink alcohol.

Een oude klomp kan je ook als plantenbakje gebruiken.
You can use an old clog as a plant pot.

However, similar to English, when an adjective or any other qualifying notion is added, or when **als** means 'in the manner of' to indicate a stereotype, we use the indefinite article. Also, when talking about affiliations in a general sense, Dutch uses the indefinite article.

André Hazes was *een* echte Amsterdammer.
André Hazes was a real Amsterdammer.

In dat zwarte pak zie je eruit als *een* begrafenisondernemer.
In that black suit you look like an undertaker.

***Een* manager heeft veel verantwoordelijkheid.**
A manager has a lot of responsibility.

Seasons and wind directions

These categories are generally used with the definite article.

Margrieten bloeien midden in *de* zomer.
Daisies bloom in the middle of summer.

***Het* voorjaar begon dit jaar heel vroeg.**
Spring started very early this year.

Ron en Lisa wonen nu in *het* noorden van het land.
Ron and Lisa now live in the north of the country.

Note, however, the following examples for names of seasons in which an indefinite article or no article is used.

Het was *een* prachtige zomer.
It was a beautiful summer.

Het wordt binnenkort weer winter.
Winter is coming soon.

Other important differences to English

Time expressions involving a meal take the definite article in Dutch.

We gaan na *het* eten naar oma.
After dinner, we go to grandma's.

Laten we dit nog even voor *de* lunch afmaken.
Let's finish this before lunch.

Similarly, names of streets, places, parks and many buildings take the definite article.

Pieter woont in *de* Raadhuisstraat.
Pieter lives on Raadhuisstreet.

Ik heb meer zin om naar *het* Vondelpark te gaan.
I'd rather go to Vondel Park.

We gaan vanmiddag *de* stad in.
We are going to town this afternoon.

Ik moet naar *het* Centraal Station.
I have to go to Central Station.

Ga je mee naar *de* kerk?
Do you want to come along to church?

Note also that there are many abstract, familiar concepts and phenomena where Dutch uses the definite article, while English does not.

***Het* leven is niet altijd makkelijk.**
Life is not always easy.

***De* dood speelt een belangrijke rol in dit boek.**
Death plays an important role in this book.

***De* tijd vliegt.**
Time flies.

Ik wandel graag in *de* natuur.
I like walking in nature.

Wat weet jij over *het* boeddhisme?
What do you know about Buddhism?

Similarly, Dutch puts the definite article in front of nouns in a very general meaning, words that are not further specified. Examples:

Peter gaat met *de* trein (de bus, de tram, de fiets) naar z'n werk.
Peter goes to work by train (bus, light rail, bike).

Jan moet naar *het* ziekenhuis.
Jan has to go to hospital.

Ik stuur dit pakje met *de* post.
I'm sending this parcel by mail.

Fixed combinations

Many fixed combinations of preposition and noun appear without article.

Opa en oma komen *op bezoek*.
Grandpa and grandma are coming to visit.

In augustus gaan alle kinderen weer *naar school*.
In August, all the children go back to school.

***Na gebruik* van deze pijnstiller kun je beter niet autorijden.**
After using this painkiller, it is better not to drive.

Ik ben *van plan* om m'n huis te verkopen.
I'm planning to sell my house.

Je moet nooit *zonder rijbewijs* in de auto stappen.
You should never get into your car without a driver's license.

Ik heb dat kopje *per ongeluk* gebroken.
I broke that cup by accident.

Similarly, Dutch has idiomatic or generic sentence parts involving two nouns that do not take an article.

Je kunt hier *dag en nacht* parkeren.
You can park here around the clock.

De kat heeft die muis *met huid en haar* opgegeten.
The cat devoured that mouse completely, the whole thing.

De politie vond een foto met *naam en adres* erop.
The police found a photograph with a name and an address.

And lastly, the article is also omitted in many fixed combinations of noun and verb. I am including certain bodily sensations such as hunger, thirst, and pain in this group.

Heb jij *moeite* met wakker worden?
Do you have difficulty waking up?

We moeten even *rekening* houden met het weer.
We need to take the weather into consideration.

Ik heb *honger*. Heb jij ook *zin* in een broodje?
I'm hungry. Would you also like a sandwich?

Jan is met *hoofdpijn* naar huis gegaan.
Jan went home with a headache.

Thuis bleek dat hij *koorts* had. Hij heeft *griep*.
At home, he appeared to have a fever. He has the flu.

1.2 The gender of nouns

Roughly 75% of Dutch nouns are **de**-words, and 25% are **het**-words. There are also some nouns that can have either **de** or **het**. Noun gender can be determined either by the meaning of the word or by its derivation from other words. This section will focus on gender by meaning only, while subsequent sections will focus on gender by derivation.

Nouns with the article '*de*'

Names of persons such as family names and professions are **de**-words. Note, however, that **kind** 'child' is a **het**-word.

de mens person, **de vader** father, **de moeder** mother, **de zoon** son,
de dochter daughter, **de bakker** baker, **de musicus** musician, **de onderwijzer** teacher

Names of most animals are also **de**-words.

de poes cat, **de hond** dog, **de ooievaar** stork, **de koe** cow, **de tijger** tiger

Names of flowers, trees, and fruits are also **de**-words. Note, however, that **fruit** 'fruit' itself is a **het**-word.

de dahlia dahlia, **de tulp** tulip, **de eik** oak, **de beuk** beech, **de aardbei** strawberry,
de appel apple

Names of seasons are **de**-words:

de lente spring, **de zomer** summer, **de herfst** fall, **de winter** winter

Names of numbers, letters and music notes are **de**-words.

de drie three, **de a** a, **de f** f, **de gis** g sharp

Lastly, most musical instruments are **de**-words. However, instruments with keyboards, except **piano** 'piano,' are **het**-words.

de viool violin, **de fluit** flute, **de cello** cello, **de trompet** trumpet, **de gitaar** guitar

► See **1.4** for gender of noun derivations with suffixes.

Nouns with the article '*het*'

In the previous section, we learned that most animal names are **de**-words. However, the names of cattle are **het**-words. Only **big** 'piglet' is a **de**-word.

> **het paard** horse, **het veulen** foal, **het hoen** hen, **het kuiken** chick, **het varken** pig, **het zwijn** swine, **het schaap** sheep, **het lam** lamb, **het rund** cow, **het kalf** calf

While most musical instruments are **de**-words, most keyboard instruments are **het**-words, including the word for keyboard itself.

> **het klavier** keyboard, **het klavecimbel** clavichord, **het harmonium** chamber organ, **het spinet** spinet, **het orgel** organ

Names of wind directions are **het**-words.

> **het westen** west, **het oosten** east, **het noorden** north, **het zuiden** south, **het noordwesten** northwest

Names of sports and games are also **het**-words.

> **het voetbal** soccer, **het hockey** hockey, **het monopoly** monopoly, **het mens-erger-je-niet** Sorry!

Names of metals are **het**-words as well.

> **het zilver** silver, **het goud** gold, **het brons** bronze, **het ijzer** iron

Lastly, names of countries, cities, and languages belong in this group.

> **het Nederland van de jaren zestig** the Netherlands of the sixties, **het Amsterdam van mijn jeugd** the Amsterdam of my youth, **het Frans** French, **het Duits** German, **het Engels** English

Nouns with '*de*' or '*het*'

There are many nouns that can appear with either the article **de** or with **het**. The meaning of the word changes with the gender. For example, **de bal** is a round object for playing a game, while **het bal** is an event at which people dance a waltz or a foxtrot. Other such examples are, to name but a few, **de bos** 'bunch' vs. **het bos** 'forest,' **de jacht** 'hunt' vs. **het jacht** 'yacht,' **de pad** 'toad' vs. **het pad** 'path,' and **de was** 'laundry' vs. **het was** 'wax.'

In the following sections, note how word derivation often determines the gender of the noun.

1.3 Compound nouns

Most of the time, compound nouns are formed by simply putting two words together, for example, **de koffie** 'coffee' and **de pot** 'pot' together form the noun **de koffiepot** 'coffeepot.' Note that the gender of the compound noun is determined by the gender of the second noun, and therefore **de post** 'post' and **het kantoor** 'office' together form the word **het postkantoor** 'post office.' While many English compound nouns are written separate (fish tank, bank account), Dutch compound nouns are always written as one word: **het huiswerk** 'homework,' **het tafelkleed** 'tablecloth,' **de aardappelsalade** 'potato salad,' **de avondjurk** 'evening dress.'

In some cases, nouns change their gender when forming a compound noun with another word. A few examples of these are **de blik** 'glance' vs. **het ogenblik** 'moment,' **de doek** 'cloth' vs. **het spandoek** 'banner,' **de hof** 'garden' vs. **het kerkhof** 'graveyard,' and **het sap** 'juice' vs. **de bessensap** 'currant juice.'

Some nouns take a '**tussenklank**,' an 'in-between sound,' to form compound nouns. There are four of these **tussenklanken**: **-en-** or **-e-**, **-s-**, and **-er-**. Examples:

-en-	**pannenkoek** pancake, **boekenkast** bookcase, **hondenweer** bad weather
-e-	**zonneschijn** sunshine, **Koninginnedag** Queen's Day
-s-	**bedrijfsarts** company physician, **groepswerk** group work
-er-	**kinderkamer** nursery, **eierdoosje** egg carton

Compound nouns are formed with **-en-** if the plural of the first noun ends in **-en**, and not in **-es**:

de pan – de pannen	⇒	**de pannenkoek** pancake
het boek – de boeken	⇒	**de boekenkast** bookcase
de zaak – de zaken	⇒	**de zakenreis** business trip

Compound nouns are formed with **-e-** if the plural of the noun doesn't exist (as in the example with **rijst**), if it isn't used much (as in the example with **zon**), or if the noun ends in unstressed **-e** and its plural form ends in **-s** or **-n** or both. Examples of these are **asperge**, **garage**, **weide**, **groente**.

de asperge – de asperges	⇒	**de aspergesoep**
de weide – de weiden	⇒	**het weidelandschap**
de groente – de groentes/en	⇒	**de groentewinkel**

It is much more difficult to give a rule for the **tussenklank -s-**. Compound nouns are written with **-s-** if the **-s-** can be heard in the pronunciation. We use the **-s-** when it makes more sense in how the noun is spoken. This means that there are regional differences, and sometimes two forms of a compound noun exist, either with or without **-s-**, for example **tijdverschil** and **tijdsverschil** 'time difference,' or **drugbeleid** and **drugsbeleid** 'drug policy,' and also **doodkist** and **doodskist** 'coffin.' However, some Dutch suffixes almost always ask for a **tussenklank -s-**: **-heid**, **-iteit**, **-ing**, and **-schap**. Examples for these are **schoonheidsspecialiste** 'beautician,' **elektriciteitskabel** 'power cable,' **verzekeringsmaatschappij** 'insurance company,' and **zwangerschapstest** 'pregnancy test.'

Lastly, the **tussenklank -er-** is used in only a few cases, when the plural of a noun ends in **-eren**, such as **kinderen** 'children,' **eieren** 'eggs.' Examples of compound nouns with these are **kinderboek** 'children's book' and **eiersalade** 'egg salad.'

So far we have discussed compound nouns formed with nouns only. There are also compound nouns formed with verb stems, adjectives, and adverbs and prepositions. Compound nouns with verb stems are formed by putting the stem of a verb in front of another noun:

lezen (lees) + bril	⇒	**de leesbril** reading glasses
schrijven (schrijf) + fout	⇒	**de schrijffout** spelling mistake
slapen (slaap) + pil	⇒	**de slaappil** sleeping pill

Similarly, adjectives can be the first part of a compound noun:

klein + geld	⇒	**het kleingeld** change
snel + restaurant	⇒	**het snelrestaurant** fast-food restaurant
laag + bouw	⇒	**de laagbouw** low-rise building

Lastly, prepositions and adverbs can form the first part of a compound noun:

voor + deur	⇒	**de voordeur** front door
bij + werking	⇒	**de bijwerking** side effect
boven + verdieping	⇒	**de bovenverdieping** upper floor

1.4 Noun derivation

Noun derivation from verbs

The following is a closer look at other forms of noun formation and derivation. As pointed out above, verb stems can be the first part of a compound word. But nouns can be derived from verbs in various other ways. For example, the verb infinitive itself can be a noun. Such nouns take the definite article **het**. Examples:

> ***Het koken* van risotto vergt een beetje tijd en inspanning.**
> Cooking risotto demands a little time and effort.

> ***Het fotograferen* van kolibri's is heel moeilijk.**
> Taking photographs of humming birds is very difficult.

Many other nouns are derived from verbs. In some, it is easier to recognize a verb stem than in others. A number of irregular verbs, for example, have corresponding nouns that show only a vague resemblance to the original verb stem. Note that most of these nouns are **de**-words.

> ***breken* – Door een *breuk* in het bovenbeen was de atleet lang geblesseerd.**
> Because of a fracture in the upper leg, the athlete was injured for a long time.

> ***grijpen* – De jongen deed een *greep* in het zakje snoep.**
> The boy grabbed from the bag of candy.

> ***slaan* – Die opmerking was een *slag* in m'n gezicht.**
> The remark was a slap in my face.

> ***rijden* – Wat kostte die *rit* naar het centrum van de stad?**
> How much was the ride to the center of the city?

Other nouns are directly derived from the verb stem, and identical with it.

> ***duiken* – Ik heb zin in een frisse *duik* in de rivier.**
> I'm feeling like a fresh dive into the river.

> ***vallen* – De *val* van de Muur is alweer meer dan 20 jaar geleden.**
> The fall of the Berlin Wall is now more than 20 years ago.

> ***spelen* – Politiek is soms net een *spel*, vind je niet?**
> Sometimes, politics is like a game, don't you agree?

> ***lopen* – In de *loop* van de tijd ging hij harder praten.**
> In the course of time, he began to speak louder.

When the prefix **ge-** is put in front of a verb stem, this expresses that the action of the verb is presently going on, conscious or unconscious to the subject of the action, and in many cases it is somewhat annoying or disturbing. Many verbs that can form a noun with this prefix are emotional or physical expressions. Note that all nouns with the prefix **ge-** take the article **het**.

> **gezeur/gemopper/gezanik/gezeik** nagging, whining
> **gejank/gejammer/gehuil/geblaf** whining, crying, barking
> **geschreeuw/geroep/gejuich/geraas/getier** screaming, yelling, raging and ranting
> **gepraat/geroddel/gefluister** talking, gossiping, whispering
> **geloop/gestamp/getrommel/getik/gedonder** walking, stomping, drumming, ticking, thundering

Examples in context with these verbs show irritation of the speaker:

> **Hou op met dat getrommel op de tafel!**
> Stop drumming on the table.

Ik word gek van het geroddel van mijn buurvrouw.
My neighbor's gossip drives me nuts.

Moet ik al die formulieren invullen? Wat een gedoe!
Do I have to fill out all those forms? What a fuss!

Ik hoorde gestamp op de overloop.
I heard stomping on the landing.

Similarly, the suffix **-ing** is added to verb stems to form nouns. All nouns ending in **-ing** take the article **de**.

***wandelen* – Zullen we vanmiddag een *wandeling* maken?**
Shall we go out for a walk this afternoon?

***rekenen* – Ik moet deze *rekening* nog betalen.**
I still need to pay this bill.

***openen* – Na de *opening* is er een receptie.**
After the opening, there is a reception.

The suffix **-atie** is added to many verbs on stressed **-eren** such as **present*eren***, **confront*eren***, **felicit*eren***. Such nouns denote abstract concepts and take the article **de**.

Wat is de *negatie* van werkwoorden?
What is the negation of verbs?

Dag, ik kom voor de *installatie* van uw nieuwe boiler.
Hi, I'm here to install the new water heater.

Another group of verbs on stressed **-eren**, mostly loan words such as **mass*eren***, **spion*eren***, **chant*eren***, take the suffix **-age** to form nouns denoting abstract concepts. Occasionally, this ending is added to other verb stems and nouns. Most of these are **de**-words.

Heb je nu alweer een *tatoeage* laten maken?!
Did you have yet another tattoo made?!

Wat vind je van deze *filmmontage*?
How do you like this film editing?

Another group of verb stems form nouns with the ending **-st**. These are **de**-words.

***dienen* – Dank u wel. Tot uw *dienst*.**
Thank you. At your service (you're welcome).

***komen* – De ouders wachten op de *komst* van hun eerste kind.**
The parents are awaiting the arrival of their first child.

***winnen* – De bedrijfsleider schonk een deel van de *winst* aan een goed doel.**
The CEO gave a part of the profits to charity.

Nouns formed from verb stems by adding the suffix **-sel** denote the product or end result of the verb action, often in the context of cooking or other forms of handiwork. Note that most of these nouns are **het**-words, but **deksel** 'lid' appears with either **het** or **de**.

***bakken* – Hij haalde een verbrand *baksel* uit de oven.**
He pulled a burnt piece of bakery out of the oven.

***mengen* – Met dit *mengsel* besmeer je de bovenkant van de taart.**
With this mixture, you cover the top of the cake.

***dekken* – Doe even het *deksel* op de pan.**
Put the cover on the pot, please.

Noun derivation from adjectives

Another group of nouns is derived from adjectives. Some nouns are identical with the adjective. A few of these are descriptions of persons. Another group of these are the colors. Names of languages also belong in this group. Examples in context:

geheim **– Wat is het *geheim* van de kok?**
What is the cook's secret?

jong **– Het *jong* van de koe kon al meteen staan.**
The calf could stand right away.

zout **– Mag ik even het *zout*?**
Can I have the salt, please?

crimineel **– Hebben ze die *crimineel* al opgepakt?**
Have they arrested that criminal yet?

rood **– Zij ging helemaal in het *rood* naar dat feest.**
She went to the party all in red.

Frans **– Zij beheerst het *Frans* alsof het haar moedertaal is.**
She masters French as if it were her native language.

Many adjectives, and this group includes present and past participles, take the ending **-e** to form nouns. Most of these nouns are abstract concepts or nouns denoting a person.

vervelend **– Het *vervelende* van deze schaar is dat hij helemaal stomp is.**
The annoying thing about these scissors is that they are completely blunt.

weinig **– Nu neem je me het *weinige* dat ik nog had ook nog weg.**
Now you take what little I had away from me.

ziek **– De *zieke* moet een paar dagen in bed blijven.**
The patient must stay in bed a few days.

dood **– Bij het ongeluk viel een *dode*.**
The accident caused one casualty.

slapend **– Hij stond naar de *slapende* te kijken.**
He was watching the sleeping person.

geleerd **– De *geleerde* kreeg een prijs voor zijn laatste boek.**
The scholar received a prize for his latest book.

In addition, we use the suffix **-heid** to form nouns from many adjectives and adverbs. These nouns all take the article **de** and are equivalent to English nouns on -ness or -(it)y. This suffix is occasionally added to a noun. Examples:

Dit gedicht gaat over de *schoonheid* van de natuur.
This poem is about the beauty of nature.

Heb jij een *gelegenheid* gehad die brief te beantwoorden?
Did you have a chance to answer that letter?

Similar to nouns on **-heid**, we use the suffix **-te** to form nouns from adjectives. Many of these nouns denote a dimension. The ending is equivalent to English -th or -ness. These nouns are **de**-words.

Geef me even de *lengte*, de *breedte* en de *hoogte* van die kast?
Can you give me the length, width and height of that cabinet?

Na die opmerking van de voorzitter viel er even een *stilte*.
After that remark by the chairman, there was a brief silence.

Note, however, that most nouns with the prefix **ge-** as well as the suffix **-te**, derived from other nouns, are **het**-words.

vogel – **Ik zocht naar een recept voor ge*vogel*te.**
I was looking for a recipe for poultry.

berg – **Hoe heet het ge*berg*te tussen Frankrijk en Spanje?**
What's the name of the mountain range between France and Spain?

The suffix **-iteit** is used to form nouns denoting abstract concepts derived also from adjectives, mostly from loan words on **-eel**, **-aal**, **-iel**, **-ief**, **-iem**, **-air**. Nouns on **-iteit** are **de**-words.

aktueel – **Laten we even naar dat *aktualiteiten*programma kijken.**
Let's watch this news program.

legaal – **Ik twijfel aan de *legaliteit* van deze handeling.**
I doubt that this action is legal.

populair – **De *populariteit* van deze rapgroep is verbazend.**
The popularity of this rap group is astonishing.

Noun derivation with other suffixes

Many other suffixes are used to form nouns. They can be added to adjectives, verb stems, and nouns. The following is an overview of the most common suffixes.

-schap Many nouns with this suffix are derived from other nouns and form collective terms similar to some words in English on -ship: **lidmaatschap** 'membership,' **gezelschap** 'company,' **leraarschap** 'the teaching profession.' Some are derived from adjectives: **beterschap** 'get well,' **zwangerschap** 'pregnancy'; and some from verbs: **weddenschap** 'bet,' **wetenschap** 'science.'

-nis This suffix is used to form nouns from verb stems and adjectives such as **kennis** (from **kennen**) 'knowledge,' **erfenis** (from **erven**) 'inheritance,' **vuilnis** 'trash,' and **duisternis** 'darkness.'

-theek Nouns ending in **-theek** usually refer to places: **discotheek** 'disco,' **bibliotheek** 'library,' **apotheek** 'pharmacy.' Note that words on **-theek** are **de**-words.

-ij This particular group also includes nouns on **-dij**, **-enij**, **-nij**, **-erij** and **-arij**, and **-derij**. They are derived from verb stems and nouns and often denote a company or institution. Examples are **boerderij** 'farm,' **slijterij** 'liquor store,' **bakkerij** 'bakery,' **makelaardij** 'real estate agency,' **drogisterij** 'drug store.' Words on **-ij** are all **de**-words.

-dom The unstressed suffix **-dom** is used to denote territories and judicial districts such as **heiligdom** 'sanctuary,' **eigendom** 'property,' **aartsbisdom** 'diocese.' Most nouns on **-dom** are **het**-words, but some abstract concepts are **de**-words, such as **rijkdom** 'wealth,' **ouderdom** 'old age.'

-isme Nouns with this suffix denote ideologies, cultural phenomena, and movements, such as **kapitalisme** 'capitalism,' **calvinisme** 'Calvinism,' **toerisme** 'tourism.' All nouns on **-isme** are **het**-words.

Common suffixes for nouns describing persons

There are a number of suffixes that are used to form nouns to describe what a person is or does. Such nouns can be derived from verbs, adjectives, or other nouns, including the names of places. Note that all nouns describing persons are **de**-words.

-aar/-er/-der

The suffix **-aar** is used after **l**, **n**, and **r** preceded by unstressed **e**: **leugenaar** 'liar,' **Texelaar** 'someone from Texel,' **luisteraar** 'listener.' Others end in **-er**: **tiener** 'teenager,' **aannemer** 'contractor.' Verb stems with vowels other than unstressed **e** and ending in **-r** will add a **-d-** to the suffix: **bestuurder** 'driver,' **aanvoerder** 'leader.'

-aard/-erd

Often pejorative: **luiaard** 'lazy person,' **rijkaard** 'rich guy,' **stommerd** 'fool.'

-ant/-ent/-ator/-ateur/-eur

Nouns derived from verbs ending in stressed **-eren**: **sollicitant** 'applicant,' **dirigent** 'conductor,' **illustrator** 'illustrator,' **restaurateur** 'restorer,' **monteur** 'mechanic.'

-icus

Mostly on words ending in **-iek** such as **muziek – musicus**, **politiek – politicus**.

-ier

These are male denominators that point to a profession or occupation. The suffix is stressed. Examples: **kruiden*ier*** 'grocer,' **tuin*ier*** 'gardener,' **avontur*ier*** 'adventurer.'

-ist

This suffix forms nouns denoting a male person's profession, function, or his affiliation with a group or belief: **bloemist** 'florist,' **fluitist** 'flute player,' **telefonist** 'operator,' **socialist** 'socialist,' **anarchist** 'anarchist.'

-ling, -eling

The unstressed **e** is added when **-ling** is added to words ending in **p**, **k**, **p**, **d**, **ng**, **m**, **w**, **f**, and **t**. Note that **f** changes into **v**: **lie*f*** – **lie*v*eling** 'darling.' Other examples are **stom – stommeling** 'fool,' **stad – stedeling** 'urbanite,' **vreemd – vreemdeling** 'stranger.' Many of these nouns are derived from verbs: **beginnen – beginneling** 'beginner,' **zuigen – zuigeling** 'infant,' **volgen – volgeling** 'follower.'

-oog

From numerous loan words on **-ogie**: **dermatologie – dermatoloog** 'dermatologist.'

To form nouns for female descriptions, the following suffixes are needed.

-e

Unstressed **-e** is used to derive female from male descriptions. Many of these are loan words with multiple syllables with stressed endings such as **advoc*aat*** – **advocat*e*** 'lawyer,' **biol*oog*** – **biolog*e*** 'biologist,' **schol*ier*** – **scholier*e*** 'pupil.'

-es, -esse

Stressed **-es** and **-esse** are also used to derive female from male descriptions: **leraar – lerar*es*** 'teacher,' **zanger – zanger*es*** 'singer,' **baron – baron*es*** 'baroness.' Stressed **-esse** forms the counterpart for male denominators ending in **-is**: **bibliothecaris – bibliothecar*esse*** 'librarian,' **secretaris – secretar*esse*** 'secretary.'

-euse

Used to form female counterparts to some loan words on **-eur** such as **masseur – masseuse**, **chauffeur – chauffeuse**.

-in

Commonly used to form many female from male descriptions: **vriend – vriendin** 'friend,' **boer – boerin** 'farmer,' **waard – waardin** 'innkeeper,' **leeuw – leeuwin** 'lion.'

-se

When **-er** is used to describe where a person comes from, **-se** is used to form the female counterpart: **Duitser – Duitse**, **Nederlander – Nederlandse**, **Amsterdammer – Amsterdamse**, and so on.

-ster

Primarily used to form the female counterparts to some male descriptions on **-aar** and **-ier**: **gijzelaarster** 'hostage,' **bankierster** 'banker'; and also used to derive female denominators from many verbs: **serveren – serveerster** 'waitress,' **naaien – naaister** 'seamstress,' **werken – werkster** 'cleaning lady.'

-trice

Used to form the female pendant to many words on **-teur**: **directeur – directrice** 'director,' **conducteur – conductrice** 'railway guard.'

Noun derivation with prefixes that carry meaning

Many nouns are formed with a prefix. Nouns with prefixes can be derivations, such as ***on*kruid** 'weeds,' or compound nouns, such as ***mis*daad** 'crime.' Prefixes can make the meaning of a noun negative, incomplete or bad, or stronger. The following is a brief overview of some common prefixes.

on-, non-, niet-

These prefixes give the noun to which they are affixed a negative meaning. Examples are **ontrouw** 'infidelity,' **onzin** 'nonsense,' **non-beleid** 'bad policy,' **non-conformisme** 'non-conformism,' **niet-roker** 'non-smoker,' **niet-vakman** 'not a specialist.'

mis-, wan-

To express that the action of the noun has gone wrong or is simply bad: **miskoop** 'waste of money,' **misverstand** 'misunderstanding,' **wandaad** 'misdeed,' **wanorde** 'chaos.'

anti-, contra-, pro-

Similar to English: **antidrugsbeleid** 'policy against drugs,' **antiroosshampoo** 'anti-dandruff shampoo,' **contrarevolutie** 'contra-revolution,' **pro-Duitsland** 'pro Germany.'

aarts-, hyper-, super-, ultra-

These prefixes can make the meaning of the noun to which they are affixed much stronger, and sometimes in a negative way: **aartsleugenaar** 'terrible liar,' **hypercorrectie** 'hyper-correction,' **supermacht** 'super-power,' **ultramarathon** 'ultra-marathon.' Note that **aarts-** can also mean "highest in rank," such as in **aartsbisschop** 'archbishop,' **aartsengel** 'archangel.'

ex-, oud-

To express that the person named by the noun is no longer in this capacity or function: **ex-minister** 'ex-minister,' **ex-man** 'ex-husband,' **oud-leerling** 'former student,' **oud-strijder** 'former soldier.'

her-, oer-

The prefix **her-** is used to express that the action of the noun (derived from a verb) will be repeated: **herexamen** 'makeup test,' **heruitgave** 'new edition.' The prefix **oer-** is used to express that what the noun describes is the original, the very first of something: **oerbewoner** 'native,' **oerknal** 'big bang.'

1.5 The diminutive

A special form of noun derivation is the diminutive. This noun ending is extremely widely used, and not just to say that an object is literally small. Oftentimes, a diminutive expresses an attitude: positive or negative, endearment, sarcasm, or contempt. The diminutive appears in many proverbs and idiomatic expressions. Some words are used only in the diminutive, and there is no non-diminutive counterpart to them. Examples:

We hebben een *zomerhuisje* aan zee gehuurd.
We've rented a summer house on the sea.

Ik heb toch zo'n lekker *wijntje* voor vanavond gekoeld.
I have cooled such a delicious (little) wine for tonight.

Jij hebt daar een heel schunnig *boekje* geschreven.
You've written a dirty little book there.

Is dat jouw *dochtertje*? Wat een *snoesje*.
Is that your daughter? What a cutie.

Die buurjongen van ons is een vreselijk *ettertje*.
That neighbor's kid is a nasty little boy.

Vroeger at ik graag Haagse *hopjes*.
I used to love Haagse hopjes (type of candy).

Ze stonden over *koetjes* en *kalfjes* te praten.
They were engaged in small talk.

De tuin staat vol met *madeliefjes*.
The garden is full of daisies.

All diminutives are neuter, with the article **het** in singular and **de** in plural. There are different forms of the diminutive ending, depending on the last letter(s) of the noun to which it is affixed.

-je

Most common diminutive ending, in words such as **huisje** 'little house,' **boekje** 'little book,' **straatje** 'little street,' **aapje** 'little monkey,' **bordje** 'little plate, sign.'

-tje

This ending is affixed to nouns ending in single vowels and diphthongs. Note that in the diminutive, the vowels **a**, **o**, **u**, **é** are doubled (in which case the acute accent is dropped from the **é**), and **i** becomes **ie**: **chocolaatje** 'little chocolate,' **autootje** 'little car,' **parapluutje** 'small umbrella,' **cafeetje** 'small café,' **taxietje** 'little taxi,' **koetje** 'little cow,' **eitje** 'little egg.' Second, this ending is added to nouns with a long vowel or diphthong ending in **n**, **l**, **r**, and **rn**: **boontje** 'little bean,' **paaltje** 'little pole,' **deurtje** 'little door,' **hoorntje** 'little horn.' It is also added to nouns ending in unstressed **-en**, **-el**, **-er**: **wagentje** 'little wagon,' **nageltje** 'little nail,' **bekertje** 'little cup.' Nouns ending in **(u)w** also belong in this group: **vrouwtje** 'little woman,' **meeuwtje** 'little seagull,' **duwtje** 'little push.' Finally, some nouns ending in unstressed **-e** (schwa), also have the diminutive ending **-tje**: **anekdotetje** 'little anecdote.'

-etje

This ending is added to nouns with a short vowel ending in **-m**, **-n**, **-ng**, **-l**, and **-r**: **kammetje** 'little comb,' **bonnetje** 'little receipt,' **ringetje** 'little ring,' **balletje** 'little ball,' **sterretje** 'little star.' There are also a few words ending in **p**, **b**, and **g** that have diminutive forms in **-etje**: **kippetje** 'little chicken,' **ribbetje** 'little rib,' **biggetje** 'little pig'; and some have an alternative form in **-je**: **poppetje/popje** 'little doll,' **bruggetje/brugje** 'little bridge,' **slabbetje/slabje** 'little bib.'

-kje

This ending is affixed to nouns ending in unstressed **-ing**: **woninkje** 'small dwelling.' Note that the **g** of **-ing** is dropped. When the vowel of the preceding syllable is also unstressed, the diminutive is formed with **-etje**. Compare ***ha*ring – harinkje** with ***re*kening – rekeningetje**. In **rekening**, the second syllable is unstressed. However, nouns for persons ending in **-ling** always form their diminutive with **-etje**: **leerlingetje** 'little pupil.'

-pje

This ending is added to nouns ending in **-m** after a long vowel, unstressed **-e-**, a diphtong, **-l** or **-r**: **raampje** 'little window,' **bezempje** 'little broom,' **geheimpje** 'little secret,' **filmpje** 'little film,' **armpje** 'little arm.' Also, nouns in unstressed **-um** take this ending: **museumpje** 'small museum.' Note that **bloempje** 'little flower' also has the alternative form **bloemetje**, as in the expression **een bloemetje meebrengen** 'to bring flowers as a gift.'

-ie

Often used in the west of the Netherlands, as a rather colloquial alternative to the ending **-je** in certain words: **jochie** 'boy,' **boompie** 'small tree,' **sjekkie** 'shag cigarette.'

-ke/-ske/-eke

Used in the south of the Netherlands and Belgium: **manneke** 'little man,' **pakske** 'small present,' **huiske** 'small house.'

Irregular forms of the diminutive

Some nouns have irregular diminutive forms, such as those that double or change their vowel:

blad – blaadje leaf, **gat – gaatje** hole, **glas – glaasje** glass, **lot – lootje** lottery ticket, **pad – paadje** path, **schip – scheepje** ship, **staf – staafje** rod, **rad – raadje** wheel, **vat – vaatje** barrel

Loan words ending in **-y** and **-u** (pronounce **oe**) have an apostrophe:

baby'tje little baby, **tiramisu'tje** little tiramisu

Some Francophone words with unpronounced endings change the spelling in the diminutive or take a Dutch ending:

diner – dineetje diner, **depot – depootje** depot, **enveloppe – envelopje** envelope, **enclave – enclaafje** enclave, **parachute – parachuutje** parachute

Uses of the *diminutiva tantum*

As mentioned in the beginning, diminutives are very common in the Dutch language. Some nouns only exist in the diminutive form. For these, there is no non-diminutive equivalent. Many of these are plants, animals, persons, and objects that are small by definition.

meisje young girl, **sprookje** fairy tale, **poffertje** small pancake, **kaakje** type of cookie, **koolwitje** cabbage white butterfly, **herderstasje** shepherd's purse, **roodborstje** robin, **nachtkastje** nightstand, **zeepbakje** soap-dish

Some diminutives for which there is no non-diminutive equivalent are derived from unflexed adjectives or from a verb stem:

blondje blond woman (derogatory), **dubbeltje** ten-cent coin, **zuurtje** type of candy, **dutje** nap, **praatje** chat, **kijkje** peek

There are many *diminutiva tantum* that do have a non-diminutive counterpart, but the diminutive has its own specific meaning, often appreciative, endearing, or the opposite, belittling or relativizing. The list of these is endless. Some examples in context:

een cola met een *rietje* coke with a straw, **thee met een *suikerklontje*** tea with a sugar cube, **een *standje* geven** give a reprimand, **een *telefoontje* krijgen** to receive a phone call, **een *vuiltje* in het oog** a speck of dust in the eye, ***touwtje* springen** jump rope, **een *ijsje* eten** eat ice cream, **een *etentje* geven** give a dinner party

Lastly, there are many fixed expressions and proverbs that use *diminutiva tantum.*

een *oogje* in het zeil houden keep an eye on things, **een *appeltje* met iemand te schillen hebben** to have a bone to pick with someone, **iets op je *duimpje* kennen** know something by heart, **de *bloemetjes* buiten zetten** have a great time

1.6 The plural of nouns

There are two endings for plural: **-en** and **-s**. The definite article for all plurals is **de**. Indefinite plurals do not have an article.

The plural ending *-en*

The majority of Dutch nouns take the plural ending **-en**:

kaarten cards, **honden** dogs, **mouwen** sleeves, **boeken** books, **woorden** words

When forming the plural, bear in mind the spelling rules for closed and open syllables as explained in Chapter 11.

In nouns ending in voiceless **f** and **s** preceded by a long vowel or a diphthong, the plural ending turns these voiceless sounds into voiced **v** and **z**. The same rule applies to nouns ending in **-lf**, **-rf**, **-ls**, **-ms**, **-ns**, **-rs**:

> **druif – druiven** grape, **prijs – prijzen** price, **wolf – wolven** wolf,
> **scherf – scherven** fragment, **hals – halzen** neck, **gems – gemzen** mountain goat,
> **gans – ganzen** goose, **laars – laarzen** boot

Note, however, that there are a substantial number of exceptions to this rule. The voiceless **f** is maintained in words ending in **-graaf** and **-soof** and, for instance, in **elfen** 'elves.' Also, a number of words ending in **-s**, **-ls**, **-ns**, and **-rs** maintain the voiceless **-s-** in the plural. A selection:

> **fotografen** photographers, **filosofen** philosophers, **eisen** demands, **polsen** wrists, **kousen** stockings, **kruisen** crosses, **walsen** waltzes, **dansen** dances, **kansen** chances, **mensen** people, **wensen** wishes, **kaarsen** candles, **kersen** cherries, **marsen** marches, **koersen** exchange rates

Next, some nouns ending in stressed **-ie** with the plural ending **-en** receive a diaeresis (Dutch **trema**) on the second **-e-**:

> **melod*ie* – melodieën** melody, **kn*ie* – knieën** knee, **epidemie – epidemieën** epidemic

If, however, the **-ie** ending is unstressed, the plural ending is **-n**, and the diaeresis comes on the **-e-**:

> **ko*lo*nie – koloniën** colonies, **bac*te*rie – bacteriën** bacteria, ***po*rie – poriën** pores

Note also that in the plural of nouns ending in **-ij**, **-ei**, **-ui**, and **-ee**, a **-j-** can be heard in the pronunciation. In the plural of **vlo** 'flea' and **koe** 'cow,' this **-j-** sound is spelled **-i-**. Plurals of nouns ending in **-ee** receive a diaeresis. Examples:

> **rijen** rows, **keien** boulders, **uien** onions, **vlooien** fleas, **koeien** cows, **zeeën** seas

As for many rules, there are exceptions. Some nouns with short vowels **a**, **o**, and **e** followed by a single consonant do not double the consonant in the plural. Instead, the vowel becomes long in an open syllable. Some examples are:

> **bad – baden** bath, **dag – dagen** day, **gat – gaten** hole, **glas – glazen** glass,
> **graf – graven** grave, **vat – vaten** barrel, **bevel – bevelen** command, **gebed – gebeden** prayer, **spel – spelen** game, **weg – wegen** road, **gebod – geboden** commandment,
> **hol – holen** cave, **lot – loten** lottery ticket, **slot – sloten** lock

The plural of nouns ending in the suffix **-heid** is formed with the suffix **-heden**:

> **schoonheid – schoonheden** beauty, **mogelijkheid – mogelijkheden** possibility

Note also the irregular plural forms of some words with the short vowel **-i-**:

> **lid – leden** member, **schip – schepen** ship, **smid – smeden** blacksmith

And lastly, the plural of **stad** 'city' is also irregular: **stad – steden**.

The plural ending *-s*

The majority of nouns ending in a vowel form the plural with **-s**. Note that an apostrophe is added in words ending in **-a**, **-o**, **-u**, **-i**, and **-y**.

> **agenda's** calendars, **auto's** cars, **paraplu's** umbrellas, **taxi's** cabs, **baby's** babies,
> **cafés** cafés, **garages** garages, **vakanties** vacations

Note that most nouns ending in unstressed **-e** take the plural ending **-s**, except nouns for persons derived from participles and adjectives.

de groten en de kleinen the big ones and the small ones, **de overledenen** the deceased, **nieuws voor doven en slechthorenden** news for the deaf and the hearing impaired

Next, nouns ending in unstressed **-el**, **-em**, **-en**, and **-er** form the plural with **-s**.

lepels spoons, **bezems** brooms, **keukens** kitchens, **kamers** rooms

All diminutives take the plural ending **-s**.

boekjes little books, **truitjes** little sweaters, **boompjes** little trees, **harinkjes** little herrings, **pannetjes** little pots

Most nouns of foreign origin also take the plural ending **-s**.

bureaus offices, **etuis** pen-cases, **films** films, **perrons** platforms, **tanks** tanks

Most nouns for persons ending in **-ier** form the plural with **-s**, but nouns for objects ending in **-ier** take the plural ending **-en**. Examples:

winkeliers shopkeepers, **bankiers** bankers, **portiers** doormen, **formulieren** forms, **rivieren** rivers, **papieren** papers

Many nouns for persons ending in **-eur** take the plural ending **-s**, while some can have either ending, **-s** or **-en**.

amateurs amateurs, **collaborateurs** collaborators, **directeurs/-en** directors, **redacteurs/-en** editors, **administrateurs/-en** administrators

Nouns (mostly names for persons) ending in **-aar** are a similarly mixed group. Most form the plural with **-s**, but some can have either ending. Note that the ending **-en** is used more in the Netherlands, while **-s** is typically Flemish.

adelaars eagles, **metselaars** masons, **schakelaars** switch, **gijzelaars** hostages, **leraars/-aren** teachers, **ambtenaars/-aren** white-collar workers, **Brusselaars/-aren** people from Brussels, **Texelaars/-aren** people from Texel

Many loan words ending in **-or** can also either take **-s** or **-en**.

professors/-oren, **projectors/-oren**, **ventilators/-oren**, **radiators/-oren**

Lastly, letters and acronyms form their plural with apostrophe **-s**, except the letters **s** and **x**, and acronyms ending in **s**.

a's, b's, k's, cd's, dvd's, BV's, s'en, x'en, PS'en

Other plural endings

Some nouns form their plural with the ending **-eren**.

kinderen children, **kalveren** calves, **eieren** eggs, **goederen** goods, **liederen** songs, **lammeren** lambs, **runderen** cows, **bladeren** leaves

Sometimes, loan words ending in **-um** can be seen with either the ending **-s** or **-a**.

museums/musea, **criteriums/criteria**, **centrums/centra**

Finally, loan words ending in **-us** might appear with the ending **-en** or **-i**. Note, however, that some nouns can only have the ending **-i**, and some have only the Dutch ending **-en**.

catalogussen/-ogi catalogs, **doctorandussen/-andi** masters of science, **musici** musicians, **historici** historians, **virussen** viruses, **cursussen** courses

1.7 The negation of nouns

Nouns are negated with either **geen** 'no, not a' or **niet** 'not.' Dutch uses **geen** for indefinite nouns, i.e., nouns with the indefinite article **een** 'a' or without article, and **niet** for nouns with a definite article. Examples:

geen

> **Ik heb geen tijd.**
> I have no time.
>
> **Jan heeft vandaag geen horloge om.**
> Jan isn't wearing a watch today.
>
> **Dit zijn geen verse bloemen.**
> These are not fresh flowers.
>
> **De ober bracht geen koffie.**
> The waiter didn't bring coffee.

niet

> **De ober bracht de koffie niet.**
> The waiter didn't bring the coffee.
>
> **Mieke en Johan kopen het huis niet.**
> Mieke and Johan are not buying the house.
>
> **Dit is niet het juiste lokaal.**
> This isn't the right classroom.
>
> **Ernie gaf Bert niet het grote, maar het kleinere stuk appeltaart.**
> Ernie gave Bert not the big, but the smaller piece of apple pie.

Note the difference between **De ober bracht geen koffie** and **De ober bracht de koffie niet**. In the sentence with **geen**, the waiter didn't bring coffee, but maybe something else, or he didn't bring anything at all. In the sentence with **niet**, the waiter didn't bring the coffee that was ordered.

▶ See **3.4** and **9.8** for more information on negation.

2

Pronouns

2.1 Personal pronouns

Subject forms

Personal pronouns refer to persons and things. When addressing someone, the Dutch distinguish between formal and informal forms of address. In informal situations, they use **je** and **jij** (in spoken Flemish **ge** and **gij**) 'you,' and in formal situations, they address someone with **u** 'you.' The informal pronoun **jij** is used with emphasis, and to mark difference. Note how, in the following examples, the pronouns in italics need to be spoken with emphasis.

Ik heb een heerlijke vakantie gehad. En *jij*?
I've had a great vacation. And *you*?

Zal *ik* vanavond koken of doe *jij* het?
Shall *I* cook tonight, or will *you* do it?

The formal pronoun **u** is used for singular and plural, but the corresponding verb form is always in singular. The informal form for second person plural is **jullie**. The corresponding verb form is in the plural.

Dokter de Graaff, kunt u even aan de telefoon komen?
Doctor de Graaff, could you come to the phone, please?

Dames en heren, kijkt u allemaal even naar het scherm.
Ladies and gentlemen, please look at the screen for a minute.

Jongens, geven jullie de proefwerken even door naar voren?
Guys, will you pass the tests to the front please?

► See **12.1** for more information on formal and informal address.

The following is an overview of Dutch personal pronouns in the subject form.

	Singular		*Plural*	
1st person	**ik**	I	**wij/we**	we
2nd person	**jij/je** (informal), **u** (formal)	you	**jullie**	you
3rd person	**hij** (m), **zij/ze** (f), **het** (n)	he, she, it	**zij/ze**	they

The third person pronouns **hij** (masculine), **zij/ze** (feminine), and **het** (neuter) refer to persons as well as things, preserving the gender and number of the nouns to which they refer. In reference to objects, the subject pronoun **hij** is used for masculine and feminine nouns (**de**-words), **het** is used for nouns in the singular that are neuter (**het**-words), and **zij/ze** is used for nouns in the plural. The Dutch only seldom use feminine **zij/ze** in reference to objects. Examples:

Ik vind die jas erg mooi, maar hij is wel ontzettend duur.
I think that coat is beautiful, but it is very expensive.

Ik zocht m'n woordenboek, maar het ligt waarschijnlijk op m'n kantoor.
I looked for my dictionary, but it is probably in my office.

We wilden witte asperges kopen, maar ze zagen er niet zo vers uit.
We wanted to buy white asparagus, but they didn't look very fresh.

Note that there are unstressed, reduced forms of **ik**, **hij**, and **het**: **'k**, **-ie**, and **'t**. These often appear in informal speech. At the beginning of a sentence, **'k** and **'t** are followed by a capital letter.

'k Heb vanavond geen tijd om naar de film te gaan.
I don't have time to go to the movies tonight.

Heeft-ie de deur weer open laten staan?
Did he leave the door open again?

't Is een uitstekende dag om iets leuks te gaan doen.
It's a perfect day to do something fun.

Object forms

Similarly, the object forms of personal pronouns refer to persons and things. For an overview of the object forms, see the table below.

	Singular		*Plural*	
1st person	**me**	me	**ons**	us
2nd person	**jou/je** (informal), **u** (formal)	you	**jullie**	you
3rd person	**hem** (m), **haar** (f), **het** (n)	him, her, it	**hen, hun, ze**	them

The pronouns **hem** (masculine) and **haar** (feminine) refer to people. In reference to things, the object pronoun **hem** is used for masculine and feminine nouns, **het** is used for neuter nouns, and **ze** is used for nouns in the plural.

Erik zou hier om 8 uur zijn, maar ik heb hem nog niet gezien.
Erik would be here at 8 o'clock, but I have not seen him yet.

Geef mij je jas maar, ik hang hem wel even in de gang.
Give me your coat, I'll hang it in the hall.

Mag ik even je boek lenen? Je krijgt het meteen terug.
Can I borrow your book for a minute? You'll get it back right away.

De schoenen zijn te klein, ik ga ze ruilen.
The shoes are too small, I'm going to exchange them.

Note that when **hem** is used to refer to an object, it cannot be at the beginning of the sentence. In that case, **hem** must be replaced by **die**.

A: Waar is mijn zwarte spijkerbroek?
B: Die heb ik in de was gedaan.
A: Where are my black jeans?
B: Those I've put in the laundry.

The object forms of first- and second-person singular have unstressed forms **me** and **je**. When to use stressed versus unstressed forms depends on what one wants to emphasize. The stressed forms indicate difference. In the examples, the emphasis is on the words in italics.

De pizza is voor *mij* en de pasta is voor *jou*.
The pizza is for *me* and the pasta is for *you*.

Geef me even het *zout*, alsjeblieft.
Pass the *salt*, please.

Johan, er iemand voor je aan de *telefoon*.
Johan, someone on the *phone* for you.

There are unstressed, reduced forms of third-person singular **hem**, **haar**, and **het**. These forms, **'m**, **d'r** (also **'r**), and **'t**, are colloquial and appear in informal speech and literary texts.

Joop is jarig, stuur 'm even een kaartje.
It's Joop's birthday, send him a card.

Note that there are three forms for third-person plural, **hen**, **hun**, and **ze**. The form **hen** is used for persons as direct objects and after a preposition, while **hun** is used for persons as direct objects without a preposition. The form **ze** is commonly used for persons and things. However, at the beginning of a sentence, **ze** must be replaced by **die**.

Mijn gasten staan op het station, ik ga hen (ze) even halen.
My guests are at the station, I am going to pick them up.

We gaan vanavond met hen (ze) uit eten.
We are going out for dinner with them tonight.

We geven hun kaartjes voor het Rijksmuseum.
We'll give them tickets for the Rijksmuseum.

Die heb ik vorige week al gekocht/Ik heb ze vorige week al gekocht.
I bought them last week.

Note, however, that speakers of Dutch don't always adhere to the rules for the use of **hen** and **hun**. In spoken Dutch, **hun** seems to have preference over **hen**, and **ze** is commonly used as an alternative for both.

The pronoun **zelf** 'self' can be connected to the subject and object forms of personal pronouns to emphasize 'self' in contrast to 'other.' Note that subject forms are often separated from **zelf**.

Ikzelf blijf thuis/Ik blijf zelf thuis, maar mijn ouders gaan op wintersport.
I myself am staying home, but my parents are going on a skiing vacation.

Hijzelf komt niet/Hij komt zelf niet, maar z'n vrouw wel.
He is not coming, but his wife is.

Dit boek is voor mezelf, het is geen cadeautje.
This book is for myself; it isn't a present.

Volgens mij mag het niet van papa, vraag het hemzelf maar even.
I don't think dad will allow you, so you should go ask him.

▶ See also **2.3** and **2.5** for more information on the uses of **zelf**.

Personal pronouns in a general meaning

The personal pronouns **men**, **je**, **ze**, and **we** are used to make general statements, similar to English 'they.' The pronoun **men** can only take the subject position, and the verb form is singular.

Men zegt dat het een koele zomer wordt.
They say it's going to be a cool summer.

In deze gebouwen mag men niet roken.
One cannot smoke in these buildings.

The unstressed pronoun **je** in general statements can take the subject as well as the object position. While statements with **men** are rather formal, **je** is commonly used in informal speech. Note that the emphasized form **jij** cannot be used in this way.

Bij Lee Yang krijg je de lekkerste loempia's.
You can get the finest spring rolls from Lee Yang.

Ze geven je er twee gratis als je er tien koopt.
If you buy ten of them, you get two free.

Note that general statements with unstressed **je** are not possible in every context. To avoid confusion with the usual meaning of the personal pronoun **je**, one can also make general statements with informal **ze**. In this case, the verb form is in the plural.

Ze zeggen dat de benzine weer duurder gaat worden.
They are saying that the fuel prices will go up again.

Finally, we also use **we** to make general statements. Similar to **je**, it includes speaker and listener, and is more personal than **men** or **ze**.

In Nederland eten we allerlei soorten stamppot.
In the Netherlands, we eat all sorts of dishes with mashed potatoes.

2.2 Interrogative pronouns

The pronouns **wie** 'who,' **welk(e)** 'which,' **wat** 'what,' and **wat voor een** 'what sort of' can all be used independently, while **welk(e)** and **wat voor (een)** can also be used with a noun.

Independent	asking about people	**wie, welk(e), wat voor (een)**
	asking about objects	**wat, welk(e), wat voor (een)**
with a noun	singular: **het**-words	**welk, wat voor (een)**
	singular: **de**-words	**welke, wat voor (een)**
	plural	**welke, wat voor**

The interrogative **wie** 'who' asks for the identification of persons. When the interrogative is used as a subject, the corresponding verb form is in the singular, unless it is clear that a group of people is meant, or when the subject of the sentence is in the plural.

Wie is die man naast je op de foto?
Who is that man next to you in the picture?

Wie heeft die laatste dropjes opgegeten?
Who ate those last licorice drops?

Wie zijn jouw beste vrienden?
Who are your best friends?

Wie spelen er in het nationale elftal?
Who are playing in the national team?

There is a (now rather formal) genitive form of **wie** that is used to express a question about relationships that indicate possession. The masculine form of this pronoun is **wiens** 'whose' and the feminine and plural form is **wier** 'whose.'

Wiens boek gebruik jij daar?
Whose book are you using there?

Dames, mag ik even vragen wier mantel dit is?
Ladies, may I ask whose coat this is?

In speech, we avoid these genitive forms of **wie** by using the preposition **van** or other possessives.

Jongens, van wie zijn deze handschoenen?
Guys, whose gloves are these?

Wie z'n handschoenen liggen hier?
Whose gloves are these?

▶ See **2.4** and **14.9** for more information on possessives.

The pronoun **welk(e)** can stand by itself or with a noun. It asks for an identification of persons or objects. In the singular, **welk** refers to **het**-words, while **welke** refers to **de**-words and plural forms.

Welk bier vind je lekkerder, Heineken of Amstel?
Which beer do you prefer, Heineken or Amstel?

Welke film wil je vanavond zien?
Which movie do you want to see tonight?

Ik moet een studierichting kiezen, maar ik weet nog niet welke.
I have to choose a major, but I don't know which one yet.

Welk van deze twee boeken zullen we aan Opa geven?
Which of these two books do we give to grandfather?

Het zijn allebei leuke jongens, maar met welke ga je nou eigenlijk?
They are both nice guys, but which one are you actually dating?

The pronoun **wat** can be used in a question to identify anything that isn't a person. It can refer to objects, thoughts, situations, and the like.

Wat koop jij deze week van je zakgeld?
What will you buy with your allowance this week?

Wat vind je van deze rok?
What do you think about this skirt?

Wat is er gebeurd?
What happened?

In combination with a preposition, **wat** becomes **waar**. So instead of **voor wat**, Dutch uses **waarvoor**. In speech, this pronoun is often separated. In an interrogative, the preposition **met** becomes **mee**, and **tot** becomes **toe**.

Waar hebben jullie het over?
What are you talking about?

Waarmee kan ik u van dienst zijn?
How (With what) can I help you?

Waartoe dient dit apparaat?
What do you use this tool for?

The interrogative **wat voor (een)** can be used in a question about people and things, and it can stand alone or be combined with a noun. In the plural, **een** is left out.

Wat voor (een) groente wil je bij de vis?
What sort of vegetable would you like with your fish?

Ik zoek een lamp, maar ik weet niet wat voor een.
I'm looking for a lamp, but I don't know what kind.

Wat voor mensen zijn die buren van jou?
What kind of people are your neighbors?

► See **9.2** and **14.1** for more information about asking questions.

2.3 Demonstrative pronouns

Demonstrative pronouns correspond in gender and number to the nouns to which they refer. The form also depends on how close to or how far away from the subject or object the speaker is, as illustrated in the table below.

	dichtbij, hier	close by, here	**ver weg, daar**	far away, there
de-words	**deze lamp**	this lamp	**die lamp**	that lamp
Plural	**deze lampen**	these lamps	**die lampen**	those lamps
het-words	**dit boek**	this book	**dat boek**	that book
Plural	**deze boeken**	these books	**die boeken**	those books

Demonstrative pronouns can appear with the noun to which they refer (first example) or alone in which case the object is implied (second example) or the pronoun refers to a noun that was mentioned earlier (third example). Sometimes the pronoun refers to an entire sentence (fourth example).

Dit boek is heel mooi, heb je het al gelezen?
This book is really beautiful, have you read it yet?

Wil je deze sokken vandaag aan of die?
Do you want to wear these socks today or those?

A: Waar is m'n leesbril nou weer?
B: Die ligt op je bureau.
A: Where the heck are my reading glasses?
B: They are on your desk.

A: Wist jij dat Joop volgend jaar met pensioen gaat?
B: Nee, dat wist ik niet.
A: Did you know that Joop is retiring next year?
B: No, I did not know that.

Note also that the demonstrative pronouns **dit** and **dat** can introduce a subject with a linking verb such as **zijn** 'to be,' **worden** 'to become,' **lijken** 'to appear.' When the subject is in the plural, the linking verb is also in the plural. However, **dit** and **dat** stay singular. Note the difference from English, where it changes to 'those.'

Dit wordt een mooie dag.
This will be a nice day.

Dat zijn mooie schoenen.
Those are nice shoes.

Dit is mijn nichtje Lida.
This is my niece, Lida.

The demonstrative pronouns **die** and **dat** are used with the preposition **van** and the object form of a personal pronoun or a name to express possessive relations. Examples:

We kregen allebei een pop van Sinterklaas en die van mij kan huilen.
We both got a doll from Santa Claus and mine can cry.

Mijn boek ziet er nog piekfijn uit maar dat van Peter zit vol vlekken.
My book still looks great but Peter's is full of stains.

▶ See **2.4** and **14.9** for more on possessives.

The demonstratives **zo'n** 'such a,' **zulk** 'such,' and **zulke** 'such' have a classifying meaning, because they make a noun a noun of a particular kind. In combination with an adjective, they make the meaning of that adjective much stronger.

The pronoun **zo'n** (abbreviated from **zo een**) appears with countable **de**-words and **het**-words in singular.

Ik wil voor mijn verjaardag ook zo'n horloge.
I want a watch just like that one for my birthday.

Zullen we voor de logeerkamer zo'n slaapbankje kopen?
Shall we buy one of those sleeper sofas for the guest room?

Jaap en Greet hebben zo'n mooi huis gekocht!
Jaap and Greet have bought such a beautiful house!

The pronoun **zulk** appears with uncountable **het**-words in singular.

Bakker de Boer verkoopt zulk lekker volkorenbrood!
Bakery de Boer sells such delicious multigrain bread.

Zulk hout is hier moeilijk te krijgen.
It is hard to find that kind of wood here.

The pronoun **zulke** appears with uncountable **de**-words in singular and with all plurals.

Ik drink niet graag zulke sterke koffie.
I don't like to drink such strong coffee.

Jan en Ina hebben zulke leuke buren!
Jan and Ina have such nice neighbors!

The pronouns **zo'n**, **zulk**, and **zulke** are often used to compare things with one another, using **net . . . als** to say that things are similar, and **niet . . . als** to express difference.

Het is vandaag net zo'n mooie dag als gisteren.
Today is just as beautiful as yesterday.

Vorige week was het niet zulk mooi weer als deze week.
Last week the weather wasn't as good as it is this week.

Mick heeft net zulke voetbalschoenen gekocht als Freddy.
Mick has bought exactly the same soccer shoes as Freddy.

Other demonstratives are **degene die**, **diegene die** 'the one who' and **datgene wat** 'that which.' They are independent and always followed by a relative sentence. **Degene** and **diegene** refer to people, while **datgene** refers to things. These demonstratives, however, are only used in more formal contexts.

Wil degene die het propje gegooid heeft, zich nu direct melden?
The person who threw the paper wad, please report immediately.

Diegenen die zich nog niet ingeschreven hebben, moeten dat nu gauw doen.
Those who have not yet registered should do it soon.

Ik ben het niet eens met datgene wat u in de vorige vergadering hebt voorgesteld.
I do not agree with what you proposed in the last meeting.

▶ See **2.7** for more information on relative pronouns.

Finally, the demonstrative pronoun **zelf** 'self' can be added to nouns and pronouns to emphasize contrast to 'other.'

Ik heb wel de film gezien, maar het boek zelf heb ik nooit gelezen.
I have seen the movie, but I have never read the book itself.

Zij had die bruidstaart zelf gemaakt.
She had made the wedding cake herself.

▶ See **2.1** and **2.5** for more information on the uses of **zelf**.

2.4 Possessive pronouns

	Personal pronoun	Subject	Possessive pronoun	
Singular	**ik**	I	**mijn/m'n**	my
	jij/je	you	**jouw/je**	your
	u	you (formal)	**uw**	your (formal)
	hij, zij/ze, het	he, she, it	**zijn/z'n, haar/d'r**	his, her
Plural	**wij/we**	we	**onze (de), ons (het)**	our
	jullie	you	**jullie/je**	your
	u	you (formal)	**uw**	your (formal)
	zij/ze	they	**hun**	their

As illustrated in the table, there are stressed and unstressed reduced forms of the possessive pronoun. The stressed form **jouw**, for instance, is only used to indicate contrast, whereas the unstressed form **je** is much more common. Note the emphasis in the following examples:

Gaan we met *mijn* auto of met *jouw* auto naar het feestje?
Are we taking *my* car or *your* car to the party?

Vergeet je *autosleutels* niet.
Don't forget your *car keys*.

The reduced forms **m'n**, **z'n**, and **d'r** are mostly colloquial and commonly used in speech and literary texts. In very informal speech, they sometimes appear after a name or a noun or the interrogative **wie**.

Ik heb m'n telefoon ergens laten liggen.
I left my phone somewhere.

Wie z'n omelet staat hier koud te worden?
Whose omelet is getting cold here?

Karin d'r fiets is alweer gestolen.
Karin's bike was stolen again.

Note that **onze** is used with **de**-words and plurals, while **ons** is used with **het**-words.

Onze ouders gaan ons huis volgend jaar verkopen.
Our parents are going to sell our house next year.

The possessive pronoun **uw** is for both singular and plural. For second person plural, the possessive pronoun is **jullie** or **je**. When the subject of the sentence is **jullie**, the preferred possessive pronoun is **je** to avoid repetition of **jullie**.

Dames en heren, uw tafel is gereed.
Ladies and gentlemen, your table is ready.

Breng morgen jullie atlassen even mee naar de les.
Please bring your atlases to class tomorrow.

Ik zou graag willen dat jullie je atlassen morgen mee naar de les brengen.
I would ask you to bring your atlases to class tomorrow.

Possessive pronouns are used as nouns in constructions in which the article relative to the noun is combined with the stressed form of the possessive, to which the ending **-e** is added: **het mijne** 'mine,' **het jouwe** 'yours,' **de zijne** 'his,' **de onze** 'ours,' etc. The only possessive pronoun that doesn't allow this form is **jullie**. For **jullie**, we use **die van jullie**. Examples:

Gaan we met mijn auto naar het feest of met de jouwe?
Are we taking my car to the party or yours?

Het huis van de buren is veel groter dan het onze.
The neighbors' house is much bigger than ours.

Onze tuin ziet er dit jaar droog uit, hoe komt die van jullie zo mooi?
Our garden looks dry this year. How come yours is so beautiful?

Finally, in combination with a cardinal number in the plural or the diminutive plural, possessive pronouns express the number of people involved in the action of the verb. An exception is the number **een** 'one,' which is used only in the diminutive singular. Note the **trema** 'diaresis' in numbers ending in stressed **-e** such as **twee**, **drie**.

Ik moest in m'n eentje naar dat feest van Johan.
I had to go to Johan's party all by myself.

We gaan deze zomer met ons tweetjes op vakantie, zonder de kinderen.
This summer, we are going on vacation just the two of us.

Ze gingen met hun/z'n drieën zwemmen.
The three of them went swimming.

▶ See **14.9** for more information about possessive relations.

2.5 Reflexive and reciprocal pronouns

Reflexive pronouns

In sentences with reflexive verbs, the subject is also the object of the action described by the verb. The position of the object is taken by the reflexive pronoun. Typical Dutch reflexive verbs are daily routines such as **zich wassen** 'wash oneself,' **zich scheren** 'shave,' **zich aankleden** 'get dressed,' and certain expressions of mental states such as **zich schamen** 'to be ashamed,' **zich vervelen** 'to be bored,' **zich herinneren** 'remember.' The pronoun **zich** in the verb infinitive is third-person singular and plural. Below is an overview of all reflexive pronouns in the verb **zich wassen** 'to wash oneself.'

ik was me	myself	**wij wassen ons**	ourselves
jij wast je	yourself	**jullie wassen je**	yourselves
u wast zich/u	yourself	**u wast zich/u**	yourselves
hij, zij/ze, het wast zich	him/her/itself	**zij/ze wassen zich**	themselves

There are two forms for second-person formal: **u** or **zich**. In the imperative, if the reflexive pronoun is the only pronoun, it must be **u**. In all other cases, either **u** or **zich** is accepted, but **zich** is more common. Examples:

Haast u!
Hurry!

Haast u zich!
Hurry!

U moet u/zich haasten, als u nog op tijd wilt komen.
You have to hurry, if you want to be on time.

True reflexive verbs are those of which there is no non-reflexive form. Examples:

Ik wil me niet met jouw zaken bemoeien.
I don't want to interfere with your business.

Je hebt je vergist, hier moet een komma staan.
You made a mistake; there should be a comma here.

Some reflexive verbs also have non-reflexive forms that don't differ much in meaning. Sometimes, however, the true reflexive verb has an entirely different meaning from the non-reflexive form. Examples of each:

Ik herinner me m'n eerste schooldag niet.
I don't remember my first day at school.

Kun jij Hans even aan die vergadering herinneren?
Can you remind Hans of that meeting?

Karel stelt zich idioot aan als hij teveel op heeft.
Karel makes a fool of himself when he's had too much to drink.

Karel stelde gisteren een nieuwe medewerker aan.
Karel hired a new co-worker yesterday.

Note also that some normally non-reflexive verbs can be combined with reflexive pronouns in certain fixed expressions: **zich dood schrikken** 'be scared to death,' **zich slap lachen** 'laugh one's head off,' **zich kapot werken** 'work oneself to death.'

The suffix **-zelf** can be added to reflexive pronouns: **mezelf**, **jezelf**, **uzelf**, **zichzelf**, **onszelf**, **jezelf**, **uzelf**, **zichzelf**. The forms with **-zelf** are used with both true reflexive and non-reflexive verbs to emphasize 'self' as opposed to 'other.'

Ik kleedde eerst mezelf en daarna de baby aan.
I dressed first myself and then the baby.

Hij schonk alleen zichzelf een glas wijn in.
He poured only himself a glass of wine.

Geef jezelf maar een schouderklopje.
Give yourself a pat on the shoulder.

Reflexive pronouns with **-zelf** are often used as part of a prepositional object. They are spoken with emphasis.

Ik heb dat boek voor mezelf gekocht.
I bought that book for myself.

Hoe lang woon jij al op jezelf?
How long have you lived alone?

Dat heeft hij aan zichzelf te danken.
He only has himself to blame for that.

De kat ging uit zichzelf op de kattebak.
The cat didn't need to be trained to use the litterbox.

In some fixed expressions, only the reflexive pronoun with **-zelf** is possible.

Hij was buiten zichzelf van woede.
He was beside himself with rage.

Na enkele minuten kwam hij weer tot zichzelf.
After a few minutes, he came to himself.

Ik ben mezelf niet meer.
I am not quite myself.

Reciprocal pronoun

Dutch has one reciprocal pronoun, **elkaar**, of which there is an informal (spoken) variation, **mekaar**, and a formal equivalent, **elkander**. The reciprocal pronoun **elkaar** is an independent object form that refers to an antecedent at the beginning of the sentence. The reciprocal possessive pronoun **elkaars** works like an adjective. Examples:

Dirk en Liesbeth geven elkaar dit jaar nieuwe skikleren voor Sinterklaas.
Dirk and Liesbeth give each other ski outfits for Christmas this year.

Paul en Peter geven elkaars kinderen videospelletjes voor Sinterklaas.
Paul and Peter give each other's kids video games for Christmas.

Martin en Sander zitten elkaar altijd te pesten.
Martin and Sander are always bullying each other.

De tweelingen dragen elkaars kleren.
The twins wear each other's clothes.

In certain fixed combinations with a preposition, the reciprocal relationship in **elkaar** is not as obvious. Sometimes, there is no such relationship at all. Examples:

In deze groep zitten de leerlingen achter elkaar.
In this group, the students sit behind each other.

Karel zette het modelbouwvliegtuigje in drie minuten in elkaar.
Karel put the model airplane together in three minutes.

De kleren lagen door elkaar op bed.
The clothes were spread around on the bed.

De begroting is eindelijk voor elkaar.
The budget is finally finished.

Hij zit achter mekaar door aan die tekening te werken.
He is working non-stop on that drawing.

In the last two examples, we are dealing with idioms. There is no obvious reciprocal relationship in these forms of **elkaar**.

2.6 Indefinite pronouns

The most commonly used indefinite pronouns in Dutch are as follows:

al all, **alle(n)** all, **alles** everything, **allemaal** all
iemand someone, **niemand** no one, **iets/wat** something, **niets/niks** nothing
elk(e) each, **ieder(e)** every, **iedereen** everyone

Other pronouns that express the indeterminate character of people and things are:

de/het een of ander some . . . or other
(een) zeker(e) a certain
deze en/of gene this or that
de/het eerste de/het beste . . . just any

Al, alle(n), alles, allemaal

The pronouns **al**, **alle(n)**, **alles**, and **allemaal** have a similar meaning 'all,' however, they differ in their grammatical use. The pronoun **al** appears with uncountable **het**-nouns, demonstrative pronouns, and possessive pronouns.

Al het ijs is in een paar nachten gesmolten.
All the ice has melted in a few nights.

Wat doen al die mensen hier?
What are all those people doing here?

Ik heb al mijn huiswerk af.
I have finished all my homework.

The indefinite pronoun **alle** appears with uncountable and abstract **de**-nouns in the singular, countable nouns in the plural, and numbers.

Alle suiker is in de appeltaart gegaan.
All the sugar went into the apple pie.

Ik wil vandaag alle bedden verschonen.
I want to put fresh sheets on all the beds today.

Alle vier onze kinderen gaan nu naar de middelbare school.
All four of our children are now going to high school.

When referring to a group of people, the Dutch use the pronoun **allen**. Note, however, that **allen** is rather formal.

U bent allen uitgenodigd voor de receptie na de dienst.
You are all invited to the reception after the service.

Ze gingen allen naar buiten om naar het vuurwerk te kijken.
They all went outside to watch the fireworks.

In more informal speech, one would use **iedereen** or **allemaal** in these situations. Note that **iedereen** and **allemaal** are discussed further below as well.

U bent allemaal uitgenodigd voor de receptie na de dienst.
You are all invited to the reception after the service.

Iedereen ging naar buiten om naar het vuurwerk te kijken.
Everyone went outside to watch the fireworks.

The pronoun **alles** refers to a collective of things, not to persons. It is the opposite of **niets**. If **alles** is followed by a relative sentence, this sentence begins with **wat**.

Is alles ingepakt? Dan kunnen de koffers dicht.
Is everything packed? Then the suitcases can be closed.

Alles wat hier verder nog rondslingert kan de kast weer in.
Everything else that is lying around here can go back into the closet.

Zet hem op, jongens, vandaag is het alles of niets.
Go get 'em, boys, today it is everything or nothing.

If **alles** is part of a prepositional object, it can be replaced (but doesn't have to be) by **overal**, followed by the preposition.

Jij klaagt over alles or **Jij klaagt overal over.**
You complain about everything.

Karin heeft voor alles gezorgd or **Karin heeft overal voor gezorgd.**
Karin has taken care of everything.

Next, **allemaal** can refer to a collective of things as well as persons. The position of **allemaal** is after the noun or pronoun to which it refers and after the finite verb.

Ze hebben de koekjes allemaal achter elkaar opgegeten.
They ate the cookies all at once.

De studenten zijn allemaal voor het examen geslaagd.
All students passed the test.

Ik kan dat allemaal nu even niet doen.
I can't do all that right now.

Iemand, niemand, iets, niets

The pronoun **iemand** and its negation **niemand** refer to persons.

Kan iemand me even met die koffer helpen?
Can someone help me with that suitcase?

Ik heb nog niemand voor die functie gevonden.
I have not yet found anyone for that position.

Next, **iets** and **niets** refer to things. A more informal form for **iets** is **wat**, and a more informal form for **niets** is **niks**. Note, however, that **wat** cannot replace **iets** at the beginning of the sentence, before **niet**, or with a preposition.

Wil je wat drinken? Koffie met iets erbij?
Would you like to drink something? Coffee with something to eat?

Ik heb dit weekend niets/niks te doen.
I don't have anything to do this weekend.

Elk(e), ieder(e), iedereen

The pronouns **elk** and **ieder** can be used independently and as attributive adjectives. As adjectives, they appear with countable nouns. Independently, **ieder** refers to persons, and **elk** can refer to persons as well as things.

Mia gaat elke/iedere week naar de sportschool.
Mia goes to the gym every week.

In iedere/elke boom in deze straat zit een nest.
There is a nest in every tree in this street.

De kinderen krijgen ieder/elk een beker chocolademelk.
The children will each get a cup of cocoa.

Op elk van deze huizen komen rode dakpannen.
Each of these houses will have red roof tiles.

As mentioned in a previous example, **iedereen** refers to a group of people. The corresponding verb form, however, is in the singular.

Tante Julia had voor iedereen een geschenk meegebracht.
Aunt Julia had brought a gift for everyone.

Iedereen was naar de jaarvergadering gekomen.
Everyone had come to the annual meeting.

Other indefinite pronouns

Finally, the pronouns **de/het een of/en ander** 'some . . . or/and other,' **deze en/of gene** 'this and/or that (person),' **de/het eerste de/het beste . . .** 'just any, the first available' can all be used as attributive adjectives or independently, while **(een) zeker(e)** 'a certain' works like an adjective.

De een of andere onverlaat heeft z'n fiets in het trappenhuis laten liggen.
Some idiot has left his bike lying in the stairwell.

Er werd op de vergadering het een en ander besproken.
At the meeting, a few things were discussed.

Ik heb op het feestje met deze en gene een paar woorden gewisseld.
I had a chat with a few people at the party.

Hij greep de eerste de beste kans om naar het buitenland te gaan.
He took the first available chance to go abroad.

Er heeft een zekere meneer Pappelendam voor je gebeld.
Some person called Pappelendam called for you.

▶ See **5.3** for indefinite numbers.

2.7 Relative pronouns

Relative sentences begin with relative pronouns. The relative pronouns refer to a noun, pronoun, or noun phrase in the main sentence. The relative pronouns correspond in gender and number with their antecedent, as illustrated in the table below.

Relative pronoun	*Antecedent*
die	**de**-words in singular, all nouns in plural
dat	**het**-words in singular
wie	1) persons preceded by a preposition, 2) no explicit antecedent
waar + preposition	objects preceded by a preposition
wat	1) no explicit antecedent, 2) complete sentence, 3) indefinite pronoun, 4) adjectives in the superlative with **het**
hetgeen	in formal speech, complete sentence (usually replaced by **wat**)

Most relative sentences begin with **die** or **dat**.

Laat me die jurk eens zien die je gisteren hebt gekocht.
Show me the dress that you bought yesterday.

We zijn erg tevreden met het werk dat hij voor ons doet.
We are very satisfied with the work he does for us.

When referring to a person, **die** must be either the subject or the direct object of the relative clause.

Ik had een gesprek met de man die dat hotel heeft ontworpen.
I had a conversation with the man who designed that hotel.

Hoe heet die vrouw die je op vakantie hebt ontmoet?
What is the name of the woman whom you met on vacation?

If the relative pronoun refers to a person, but is not the subject or the direct object of the relative clause, but an object with a preposition, it cannot be **die**, but must be **wie**. This is also the case when there is no explicit antecedent in the sentence.

Daar staat de nieuwe medewerker over wie ik je verteld heb.
That's the new co-worker about whom I have told you.

Wie de petitie nog niet ondertekend heeft, kan dat nu nog doen.
Whoever has not yet signed the petition can do that now.

However, when the object with preposition is not a person but a thing, then the relative pronoun must be **waar + preposition**. This is often the case in fixed combinations of verb and preposition: **denken aan**, **praten over**, **besteden aan**, **zorgen voor**, and so on. Note that **met** changes to **mee**, and **tot** changes to **toe**.

Ik heb nu een bril waarmee ik beter kan lezen.
I now have glasses with which I can read better.

De kinderen willen het computerspelletje waarover iedereen praat.
The children want the computer game everyone is talking about.

Note that in speech, the relative pronoun **waar + preposition** often gets separated.

> **Dit is de nieuwe snelkookpan waar ik een vermogen aan besteed heb.**
> This is the new pressure cooker on which I spent a fortune.

The relative pronoun **wat** is used when there is no explicit antecedent in the relative sentence, in reference to a complete sentence, after an indefinite pronoun such as **alles**, **iets**, **niets**, **weinig**, **veel**, and after superlatives with **het** in a general meaning.

> **Wat je niet opeet, geef ik aan de hond.**
> Whatever you don't eat, I'll give to the dog.

> **De buurman ruimde alle sneeuw van m'n stoep, wat ik ontzettend aardig vond.**
> The neighbor cleared all the snow from my steps, something I really appreciated.

> **Er is maar weinig wat hij nog niet heeft uitgeprobeerd.**
> There isn't much that he has not yet tried out.

> **Die bergtocht was het mooiste wat ik op die vakantie heb beleefd.**
> That mountain hike was the most beautiful thing I experienced during that vacation.

Finally, the pronoun **hetgeen** is used in formal speech, and it refers to a complete sentence. In more informal speech, we would use **wat** here.

> **Uw zoon heeft van een medeleerling gestolen, hetgeen wij zeer betreuren.**
> Your son has stolen from a fellow student, something we deeply deplore.

► For relative sentences after **degene**, **diegene**, and **datgene**, see **2.3**.

3

Adjectives and adverbs

3.1 The adjective

Adjectives are used to describe nouns and pronouns. They can appear before or after the noun they describe. Attributive adjectives appear before the noun, and predicative adjectives usually follow a linking verb such as **zijn** 'to be,' **worden** 'to become,' **blijven** 'to stay,' **heten** 'to be called.' Examples, first attributive, then predicative:

> **We zagen op onze wandeling een grote buizerd.**
> On our hike, we saw a big buzzard.
>
> **De wandeling was lang en vermoeiend.**
> The hike was long and tiresome.

Predicative adjectives do not decline; they never have an ending. Attributive adjectives have the ending **-e** most of the time, except in one case: a **het**-word preceded by an indefinite article or in an otherwise indefinite context. Examples:

> **We hebben gisteren een lange film gezien. De film was prachtig.**
> We saw a long movie yesterday. The film was beautiful.
>
> **Karel woont in een groot huis. Het kleine huis ernaast staat momenteel leeg.**
> Karel lives in a big house. The small house next door to it is unoccupied right now.
>
> **Onze leraar corrigeert ieder klein foutje in onze opstellen.**
> Our teacher corrects every little mistake in our essays.

In a table, adjective endings can be organized as follows:

Definite		*Indefinite*	
Singular	**de lange film**	Singular	**een lange film**
	het goede boek		**een *goed* boek**
Plural	**de lange films**	Plural	**– lange films**
	de goede boeken		**– goede boeken**

Note the one case (in italics) in which the adjective does not get the ending **-e**: **een goed boek**. This also happens when a **het**-word appears in a different indefinite context, for example when there is no article, with the negation **geen** 'no' or with words such as **ieder** 'every,' **elk** 'each,' **veel** 'much,' **weinig** 'little,' **meer** 'more,' **minder** 'less,' and **welk** 'which.'

> **We hadden een dag geen warm water want de geiser was kapot.**
> We had a day without warm water because the boiler was broken.
>
> **Er stond lekker koud bier voor ons klaar na de wedstrijd.**
> There was delicious cold beer for us after the match.
>
> **De bakker heeft vandaag te weinig wit brood.**
> The bakery has too little white bread today.

After possessive pronouns and demonstrative pronouns, attributive adjectives with **het**-words and **de**-words always have the ending **-e**, in singular and plural.

Piet staat z'n blauwe overhemd te strijken.
Piet is ironing his blue shirt.

Heb jij dat nieuwe boek van Connie Palmen al uit?
Have you finished Connie Palmen's new book?

Je ziet er belachelijk uit met die malle hoed.
You look ridiculous with that silly hat.

Adjectives that do not decline

Adjectives ending in **-en** do not decline. Two main groups belong in this category: adjectives derived from strong past participles, and adjectives derived from materials such as **wol** 'wool,' **zilver** 'silver,' **goud** 'gold,' **zijde** 'silk,' the **stofadjectieven**.

We eten vanavond een gebakken visje.
We are having fried fish tonight.

Ze gingen naar het monument voor de gevallen soldaten.
They went to the monument for the fallen soldiers.

Monika droeg een gouden armband.
Monika was wearing a golden bracelet.

Zijden sjaals blijven altijd in de mode.
Silk scarfs always stay in fashion.

Adjectives derived from loan words such as **rayon**, **platina**, and **nylon**, and adjectives ending in **-e** and **-a**, such as **oranje** 'orange' and **lila** 'lilac,' do not decline.

Een rayon jurk kun je wel in de wasmachine gooien.
A rayon dress can be thrown into the washing machine.

Ze droeg een oranje rok met een lila bloes. Vreselijke combinatie.
She wore an orange skirt and a purple blouse. Terrible combination.

Adjectives after indefinite pronouns

After **iets**, **niets**, **veel**, **weinig**, **meer**, **minder**, **genoeg**, **voldoende**, **wat**, **wat voor**, **zoiets**, and **allerlei**, the adjective has the ending **-s**.

Ga je dit weekend iets leuks doen?
Are you going to do something nice this weekend?

Ik heb niets interessants over die vulkaanuitbarsting gevonden.
I didn't find anything interesting about that volcanic eruption.

Ik heb weinig goeds over die film gehoord.
I didn't hear a lot of good things about that film.

After **iets**, **niets**, and **wat**, this can also be an adjective in the comparative.

Kunnen jullie niets leukers bedenken om te doen dan kikkers vangen?
Can't you think of something nicer to do than catch frogs?

Note the spelling in adjectives. Double vowels in a closed syllable become single when an **-e** is added (**groot** 'big' ⇒ **grote**), **s** becomes **z** (**vies** 'dirty' ⇒ **vieze**), and **f** turns into **v** (**doof** 'deaf' ⇒ **dove**).

3.2

The adjective in comparison

To compare objects, the adjective has the ending **-er** in the comparative and **-st** in the superlative: **groot** 'big,' **groter** 'bigger,' **grootst** 'biggest.' While English uses 'more' and 'most' for adjectives longer than one syllable, Dutch generally uses the comparative and superlative endings for both short and long adjectives: **interessanter** 'more interesting,' **belangrijker** 'more important,' **interessantst** 'most interesting,' **belangrijkst** 'most important.' Adjectives ending in **-r** receive an extra **-d-** in the comparative ending: **duur** 'expensive' ⇒ **duurder**, **zwaar** 'heavy' ⇒ **zwaarder**, and so on. Overview:

Basic	*Comparative*	*Superlative*
groot 'big'	**groter**	**(het) grootst(e)**
leuk 'nice'	**leuker**	**(het) leukst(e)**
duur 'expensive'	**duurder**	**(het) duurst(e)**
mooi 'beautiful'	**mooier**	**(het) mooist(e)**
vies 'dirty'	**viezer**	**(het) viest(e)**
lief 'sweet, cute'	**liever**	**(het) liefst(e)**
dik 'thick, fat'	**dikker**	**(het) dikst(e)**

Note the spelling rules. Double vowels become single when the comparative ending is added (**groot** ⇒ **groter**), and single consonants are doubled (**dik** ⇒ **dikker**). Again, **f** turns into **v** (**lief** ⇒ **liever**), and **s** turns into **z** (**vies** ⇒ **viezer**). Adjectives ending in **-s** only get **-t** in the superlative (**vies** ⇒ **viest**).

Irregular endings

Some adjectives have irregular endings in the comparative and superlative:

goed good	**beter** better	**best** best
veel much	**meer** more	**meest** most
weinig little/few	**minder** less	**minst** least
graag readily/gladly	**liever** preferably	**het liefst** most desired

Note that **graag** is an adverb that can be added to verbs that express what one likes to do, eat, drink, etc. Added to such verbs, **liever** and **het liefst** express what one prefers and what one likes most.

Mia speelt graag tennis, maar ze gaat liever langs het strand hardlopen.
Mia likes to play tennis, but she prefers to go for a run along the beach.

Jos houdt van kip en rundvlees, maar het liefst eet hij vis bij de warme maaltijd.
Jos likes chicken and beef, but he prefers to eat fish for dinner.

Attributive adjectives

Attributive adjectives in the comparative follow the same declination rules as attributive adjectives in their basic form. All forms have the ending **-e**, except **het**-words with an indefinite article or pronoun, or without such a determiner.

De buren hebben een grotere auto dan wij.
The neighbors have a bigger car than we have.

De duurdere jas is natuurlijk wel veel mooier dan die goedkopere.
It's true that the more expensive coat is more beautiful than the cheaper one.

Erik en Lydia gaan in een kleiner huis wonen.
Erik and Lydia are going to live in a smaller house.

Attributive adjectives in the superlative always have the ending **-e**, because nouns with an adjective in the superlative never have an indefinite article or pronoun.

Wat is nou de mooiste film die jij ooit gezien hebt?
What is the most beautiful movie you have ever seen?

Katja is het meisje met het langste haar in onze klas.
Katja is the girl with the longest hair in our class.

Predicative adjectives

Predicate adjectives in the comparative behave just like adjectives in their basic form. Besides the comparative ending **-er**, they do not decline.

De nieuwste roman van deze schrijver is saaier dan zijn eerdere werk.
The newest novel by this author is more boring than his earlier work.

Hm, deze koffiemelk is veel romiger dan die van Friese Vlag.
Hmm, this coffee cream is much creamier than the one from Friese Vlag.

In the superlative, predicative adjectives are preceded by **het**. The ending **-e** is optional, and used mostly in speech.

De beste zitplaatsen in het theater zijn het duurst(e).
The best seats in the theatre are the most expensive.

Welke appel wil je? Deze is het grootst(e).
Which apple do you want? This is the biggest.

Note that adjectives ending in **-e** receive an **-r** in the comparative, and the superlative is circumscribed with **meest** 'most.' For adjectives ending in **-s** we also often use a superlative with **meest**.

Dat is wel het meest stupide voorstel dat ik ooit heb gehoord.
That's got to be the most stupid suggestion I have ever heard.

Gooi de meest vieze kleren maar meteen in de was.
Just throw the most dirty clothes into the laundry right away.

Comparing things

To compare objects that are different, we use the comparative ending **-er** and **dan** 'than': **groter dan** 'bigger than,' **mooier dan** 'more beautiful than,' etc. Another way to compare things that are different, is to use **niet zo . . . als** 'not as . . . as.'

Ik vind dit overhemd leuker dan dat met die strepen.
I think this shirt is nicer than the one with the stripes.

Echt? Nou, ik vind dat overhemd niet zo leuk als dit hoor.
Really? Well, I think that shirt isn't as nice as this one.

To compare things that are similar, we use **even . . . als** 'just as . . . as,' **net zo . . . als** 'just as . . . as,' or simply **even . . .** 'equally . . .'

De kinderen van onze buurman zijn even oud als die van ons.
Our neighbor's kids are the same age as our kids.

Ik vind zoute drop net zo lekker als zoete drop.
I think salty licorice is just as good as sweet licorice.

A: Neem jij nu het grotere stuk taart?
B: Zeur niet, ze zijn even groot.
A: Are you taking the bigger piece of cake?
B: Shut up, they are the same size.

To show a positive correlation between two entities, similar to English 'the more . . . the more . . . ,' Dutch uses **hoe . . . des te . . .** or **hoe . . . hoe . . .** and the adjective or adverb in the comparative.

Hoe groter de porties, des te dikker word je/je wordt.
The bigger the portions, the fatter you get.

Hoe ouder het kind is, hoe later het naar bed mag.
The older the kid, the later he or she can go to bed.

Note that the sentences beginning with **hoe** are subordinated sentences. Sentences beginning with **des te** can be subordinated sentences or coordinated sentences with inverted word order. The combination **hoe . . . hoe . . .** can also be part of one sentence, and then it means 'more and more.'

Dat boek wordt hoe langer hoe saaier.
That book is becoming more and more boring.

► For more information on coordinated and subordinated sentences, see Chapter **9**.

3.3 Adverbs

Adverbs are used to modify a verb (first example), an adjective (second example), or another adverb (third example).

Peter speelt goed piano.
Peter plays the piano well.

Ik heb een heel leuk restaurant gevonden.
I've found a very nice restaurant.

We hebben erg lang moeten wachten.
We had to wait for a very long time.

Adverbs usually follow the verb. They can also be placed at the beginning of the sentence, in which case subject and verb are inverted, and note that there is *no comma* after the adverb.

De krant komt misschien/Misschien komt de krant wat later dan normaal.
Maybe the paper comes a bit later than normal.

Functions of adverbs

Adverbs can be classified in groups according to their function. *Adverbs of manner*, for instance, give answer to the question how something happens. Some examples:

Peter speelt goed/slecht/snel/langzaam/mooi piano.
Peter plays the piano well/badly/quickly/slowly/beautifully.

Next, *adverbs of modality* express the reality value of the utterance, i.e., the speaker's attitude to what is said in the sentence.

Het gaat misschien/waarschijnlijk/helaas/ongetwijfeld regenen.
It's probably/possibly/unfortunately/undoubtedly going to rain.

Karel slaagt hopelijk/natuurlijk/zeker/echt/gelukkig voor z'n examen.
Karel will hopefully/naturally/certainly/really/fortunately pass the exam.

► See also Chapters **15** and **17** for the use of these adverbs.

Adverbs of degree express the degree or intensity of an adjective (first example), another adverb (second example), or a verb phrase (third example). Many of these are so-called quantifying adverbs.

Ik vond de film hartstikke/heel/erg/vrij goed.
I thought the film was utterly/very/very/rather good.

We gaan vrij/redelijk/nogal/te/erg vaak uit eten.
We go out for dinner rather/reasonably/somewhat/too/very often.

Ik had m'n schoolboeken bijna/totaal/helemaal/volkomen vergeten.
I had almost/totally/completely/entirely forgotten my school books.

A very large group of adverbs are **adverbs of time and frequency**. Within this group, we can distinguish a few sub-groups: parts of the week (first example), order of events (second example), and frequency (third example).

Ben je vandaag of gisteren naar Amsterdam geweest? Of ga je morgen pas?
Did you go to Amsterdam today or yesterday? Or are you going tomorrow?

Ik ga eerst sporten, dan naar college en daarna nog even naar de kroeg.
I'm going to work out first, then to school, and after that to the pub for a bit.

Sommigen ontbijten nooit, anderen zelden, maar de meesten ontbijten altijd.
Some people never eat breakfast, others rarely, but most people always do.

Many adverbs of time cannot be categorized in any particular sub-group. Some are each other's synonym (or very similar in meaning), and some have more than one meaning.

We gaan straks/dadelijk/gauw/binnenkort/zo naar de ijsbaan.
We are going to the ice rink later/in a moment/soon/soon/in a minute.

Het begon ineens/plotseling te regenen.
It started to rain suddenly.

Niet met vieze schoenen binnenkomen, ik heb net/pas gedweild.
Don't enter with dirty shoes. I just mopped.

Ik ga pas weer met de fiets naar school als het niet meer vriest.
I'm not biking to school again until it stops freezing.

Note also how, similar to particles, adverbs of time often appear in combinations of two or more.

We moeten gauw weer eens een dagje naar Amsterdam.
We should soon again take a day trip to Amsterdam.

Ben je nu pas/nu al/nu alweer thuis?
You're home this late/already/already again?

Ik heb die film pas nog/pas weer/net weer gezien.
I saw that film (only) just recently.

Frequent combinations are made with the adverbs **weer**, **meer**, and **nog** to slightly alter the meaning of adverbs of time: **nooit weer** 'never again,' **nooit meer** 'never anymore,' **alweer** 'already again,' **nog nooit** 'not yet ever,' **nog eens** 'again,' **nog even** 'a little while longer,' **pas nog** 'only recently,' **net nog** 'just a minute ago,' **nog net** 'just barely,' and so on. Some examples:

Waar ligt m'n bril nou? Ik zag hem net nog.
Where are my glasses? I only just saw them.

Ik heb de trein nog net gehaald.
I just barely made my train.

Doe dat alsjeblieft nooit weer.
Please don't ever do that again.

Ik ga nooit meer naar Schotland op vakantie.
I'm never going to Scotland again for vacation.

► See **14.8** for adverbs of time and frequency.

Another large group of adverbs are those that indicate **place and direction**. The examples in the table below are organized as each other's opposite:

thuis	at home	**naar huis**	(going) home
binnen	inside	**buiten**	outside
ergens, overal	somewhere, everywhere	**nergens**	nowhere
beneden	downstairs	**boven**	upstairs
daar	there	**hier**	here
links(af)	to the left	**rechts(af)**	to the right
heen, naartoe	to	**vandaan**	from

Some of these commonly used adverbs of place can be used with **naar** 'to' to change from place to direction: **naar boven** 'going upstairs,' **naar rechts** 'to the right,' **naar buiten** 'going outside,' etc. The adverbs **heen** and **naartoe** do this as well: **ergens heen** 'going somewhere,' **hiernaartoe** 'coming here.' The adverb **vandaan** is combined with other adverbs to express motion from somewhere: **overal vandaan** 'from everywhere,' **daarvandaan** 'from there.' Lastly, **heen**, **naartoe**, and **vandaan** can also form question words with **waar**:

Waar komt u vandaan?
Where are you from?

Waar gaat deze trein naartoe/heen?
Where is this train going?

► See **14.7** for adverbs of place and direction in context.

3.4 Negation of adjectives and adverbs

Predicative adjectives are negated with **niet** 'not.' The negation precedes the adjective.

Wat een avond. Het orkest was niet goed en de koffie was niet lekker.
What an evening. The orchestra wasn't good and the coffee wasn't tasty.

Attributive adjectives in an indefinite context are negated with **geen** 'no.'

Wat een avond. Het was geen goed orkest en ze verkochten geen lekkere koffie.
What an evening. It wasn't a good orchestra and they didn't sell tasty coffee.

Adjectives can also be negated with prefixes that indicate the opposite of what the adjective means. Examples of these prefixes are **on-**, **in-** (also **il-**, **ir-**, **im-**), **non-**, **a-**, and **niet-**.

Ik vind dit een onbelangrijk thema.
I think this is an unimportant topic.

Hé, deze puzzel is incompleet!
Hey, this puzzle is incomplete.

Asymmetrische kapsels waren een tijdje in de mode.
Asymmetric haircuts were fashionable for a while.

Adverbs are negated with **niet**. The position of **niet** is at the back of the sentence, but before verb groups that take the end position of the sentence, such as participles and verb infinitives.

Harry heeft gisteren niet gewerkt.
Harry didn't work yesterday.

Je hoeft vandaag niet te oefenen.
You don't have to practice today.

Niet precedes adverbs of manner such as **mooi**, **hard**, and **langzaam**.

De pianist speelde niet mooi.
The pianist didn't play beautifully.

De trein reed niet langzamer door het station.
The train didn't slow down through the station.

The negation also precedes adverbs of time such as **altijd**, **vroeg**, **laat**, **vaak**, **zelden**, **gauw**, and adverbs of place such as **thuis**, **binnen**, **buiten**, **beneden**, **boven**, **links**, **rechts**.

Ik wil morgen niet vroeg beginnen.
I don't want to start early tomorrow.

Jan en Minnie gaan niet vaak uit eten.
Jan and Minnie don't often go out for dinner.

We zijn vanavond niet thuis.
We're not at home tonight.

The negation follows adverbs such as **er**, **daar**, and **hier**. However, in contrast situations, the adverb can also precede **daar** and **hier**. This is also the case with other adverbs that are usually followed by **niet**. Some examples:

Je bril ligt niet hier bij de tv, maar daar op tafel, bij de krant.
Your glasses aren't here near the TV, but there, on the table, near the paper.

We gaan niet morgen naar de film, maar overmorgen.
We are not going to the film tomorrow, but the day after tomorrow.

The negation follows adverbs of modality such as **misschien**, **waarschijnlijk**, **hopelijk**. It also follows certain adverbs of time, namely **vandaag**, **(eer)gisteren**, and **(over)morgen**.

Het regent morgen hopelijk niet.
Hopefully, it doesn't rain tomorrow.

Karel komt ongetwijfeld niet naar het feest.
Undoubtedly, Karel isn't coming to the party.

▶ See **9.8** on the position of **niet**.

3.5 Conjunctional adverbs

Many adverbs can function as conjunctions creating a meaningful relationship between two main sentences. Conjunctional adverbs usually appear at the beginning of the second sentence, thus putting the subject in third place (inversion). They can also follow the verb or follow a direct object.

▶ For information on word order and conjunctions, see Chapter **9**.

A conjunctional adverb links a sentence to the previous sentence, creating a relationship of time, cause and effect, contrast, or conclusion.

Time

Conjunctional adverbs of time are **daarna** 'after that,' **daarvoor** 'before that,' **dan** 'then,' and **toen** 'then.' Examples:

Pim gaat sporten. Daarna moet hij een paar boodschappen doen.
Pim is going to work out. After that, he has to run a few errands.

Vroeger schreven we echte brieven. Je had toen nog geen email.
We used to write real letters. There wasn't any email then.

Note that there is no comma after the conjunctional adverb. Note also that **toen** is only for events in the past, while dan can be used for past and present. When used for the past, **dan** describes recurrent events. Example:

We gingen op zondag eerst naar de kerk. Dan kwam er koffie op tafel.
We first went to church on Sundays. After that, there would be coffee.

Cause and effect

Conjunctional adverbs of cause and effect are **daarom** 'therefore,' **daardoor** 'because of that, thus,' **dus** 'so, thus.'

> **Het had gesneeuwd. Daardoor lag het hele treinverkeer stil.**
> It had snowed. Because of that, the entire train traffic was shut down.

> **Ze krijgen een natte zomer in Engeland. We gaan dus maar naar Frankrijk.**
> England is going to get a rainy summer. And so we'll just go to France.

Note the flexibility of **dus**; it allows regular word order as well as inversion, and it can follow the verb: **Dus we gaan/Dus gaan we/We gaan dus . . .**

Contrast

Conjunctional adverbs of contrast are **daarentegen** 'on the other hand,' **echter/evenwel** 'however, though,' **niettemin** 'nevertheless,' **desondanks** 'notwithstanding, in spite of,' **integendeel** 'on the contrary,' and **toch** 'nevertheless, anyway.'

> **Het sneeuwde geweldig. Desondanks kwam de bus op tijd.**
> It snowed heavily. In spite of that, the bus was on time.

> **Jeroentje pest nooit. Integendeel, hij is een voorbeeldig joch.**
> Jeroentje doesn't ever bully. On the contrary, he is a real good kid.

> **Ik weet dat je niet graag vroeg opstaat, maar je zult er toch aan moeten wennen.**
> I know you don't like getting up early, but you'll have to get used to it anyway.

Note that **echter** and **evenwel** usually follow the verb or a direct object. They should preferably not be at the beginning of the sentence.

> **U kunt op het terras roken. In het restaurant is roken echter verboden.**
> You can smoke on the terrace. In the restaurant, however, smoking is prohibited.

Other commonly used conjunctional adverbs are **althans/tenminste** 'that is to say, at least,' **trouwens/overigens** 'by the way, apart from that,' **immers** 'after all,' and **bovendien** 'besides, what's more.' At the beginning of the sentence, all of these except **bovendien** are separated with a comma. They can, however, also follow the verb.

> **Maarten komt vanavond. Althans, dat heeft hij gezegd.**
> Maarten is coming tonight. At least, that's what he said.

> **Het is te ver om te fietsen. Bovendien is het licht van m'n fiets kapot.**
> It's too far to bike. Besides, the light on my bike is broken.

> **Jij moet dat artikel maar schrijven. Jij hebt immers met de minister gesproken.**
> You should write that article. After all, you spoke to the minister.

3.6 The adverb *er*

A particular case is the adverb **er**. It is used a lot in Dutch, and it has many functions.

Existential *er*

The function most similar to English is when **er** introduces an indefinite subject.

> **Er is een stukje appeltaart voor je als je nog trek hebt.**
> There is a slice of apple pie for you if you're still hungry.

> **Er zijn geen paperclips meer. Kun je nieuwe bestellen?**
> There are no more paperclips. Can you order new ones?

In combination with the verb **zijn**, **er** indicates that something simply exists. Therefore, we call this the existential **er**. As a preliminary subject, **er** can also be combined with other verbs: **staan**, **lopen**, **liggen**, **zitten**, **komen**, **blijven**, **wonen**, **gaan**, etc.

Er liggen duizenden woonboten in de grachten van Amsterdam.
There are thousands of boat houses in the canals of Amsterdam.

Er komen vanavond twintig mensen naar het feest.
Twenty people will come to the party tonight.

Wie blijven er slapen, denk je?
Who do you think will stay the night?

Existential **er** can only be used with an indefinite subject. It often appears in combination with indefinite pronouns such as **iemand** 'someone,' **niemand** 'nobody,' **iets** 'something,' **niets** 'nothing':

Er staat iemand op je te wachten.
Somebody's waiting for you.

Er is vanavond niets op de televisie.
There's nothing on TV tonight.

Existential **er** also appears in questions with **wie** 'who,' **wat** 'what,' **welke/wat voor** 'which/what kind,' **hoeveel** 'how much/how many':

Wat is er aan de hand?
What's wrong?

Hoeveel tomaten zitten er in een pond?
How many tomatoes are there in a pound?

Quantitative *er*

Building on the previous, **er** can also indicate how much or how many of something exist. We call this the quantitative function of **er**. In the answer to the question **Hoeveel boeken heb je bij je?**, **er** replaces **boeken**, and a number is added:

Ik heb er drie bij me.
I have three (of them).

Note that quantitative **er** can be used with cardinal numbers and also with indefinite numbers such as **veel** 'much,' **weinig** 'few,' **een paar** 'a couple,' **genoeg** 'enough,' **voldoende** 'enough,' **geen** 'none.'

A: Hoeveel koekjes kreeg je bij de thee?
B: O, ik kreeg er een paar.
A: How many cookies did you get with your tea?
B: Oh, I got a couple.

Menno wilde mij een zakdoekje geven maar hij had er geen bij zich.
Menno wanted to give me a tissue but he didn't have any with him.

The existential and the quantitative **er** often appear in a sentence together. See B:

A: Er komen vanavond twintig mensen naar het feest. Hoeveel blijven er slapen?
B: Er blijven er vier slapen.
A: Twenty people are coming to the party tonight. How many will spend the night?
B: Four (of them) will spend the night.

Place indicator

A commonly used third function of the adverb **er** is as a place indicator. This is also called the locative **er**. In this function, it refers to a place that was either mentioned in a previous sentence and is therefore known to the speaker, or it talks about a place in a general meaning. Examples:

A: Ben jij wel eens in Egypte geweest?
B: Ja, ik ben er twee keer geweest.
A: Have you ever been to Egypt?
B: Yes, I was there twice.

A: Is Kees er vandaag niet?
B: Nee, hij is er niet.
A: Is Kees not here today?
B: No, he isn't here.

In the first example, **er** replaces **in Egypte**. In this function, **er** works the same way as **daar**. However, because **er** is unstressed, it cannot be at the beginning of the sentence, while **daar** (and also **hier**) can be both at the beginning and after the verb:

Ja, daar ben ik twee keer geweest./Ja, ik ben daar twee keer geweest.
Yes, I was there twice.

However, when we talk about a place in a general sense, such as in the second example, we prefer to use the unstressed **er** rather than **hier**.

Kijk, de paperclips zijn er al. Snel hè?
Look, the paperclips are already here. That was quick, wasn't it?

Er in passive sentences

Finally, **er** is a common adverb to begin passive sentences. Passive sentences with **er** place the emphasis on the action described by the verb, not necessarily on the subject who is involved in the action. Such sentences appear a lot in newspaper language, when the subject of the action is not (yet) known or not important. Passive sentences with **er** are also used when we talk about actions in a very general sense (second example).

Er was gisteren een feestje bij de buren. Er werd erg veel gedronken.
There was a party at the neighbors' place. There was a lot of drinking going on.

Er wordt tegenwoordig niet meer veel in Nederland geschaatst.
People don't skate a lot in the Netherlands anymore.

Er werden door de demonstranten vier auto's in brand gezet.
Four cars were set on fire by the demonstrators.

▶ For more information on the passive, see **8.3**.

3.7 Pronominal adverbs

Pronominal adverbs are used to refer to things when the verb or the object in the sentence take a preposition. This happens often in fixed combinations of verb and preposition such as **denken aan** 'think about,' **praten over** 'talk about,' **zich interesseren voor** 'be interested in,' etc. Pronominal adverbs are formed with **er** when the object to which it refers is not emphasized, and with **hier** or **daar** when we want to put emphasis on it. Examples:

A: Denk je aan die afspraak met Jansen?
B: Ja hoor, ik zal eraan denken.
A: Remember that appointment with Jansen?
B: Yes, I'll remember it.

A: Wilt u een stuk van die kaas daar?
B: Nee, ik wil liever een stuk hiervan.
A: Do you want a piece of this cheese?
B: No, I would like a piece of this one.

Mijn problemen op het werk? Nou, daarover wil ik liever niet praten.
My problems at work? Well, I'd rather not talk about those.

Most of the time, and especially in speech, the pronominal adverb is separated by other elements in the sentence: adverbial phrases of time and place, negations, direct and indirect objects.

Ik moet een scriptie schrijven, maar ik denk er nu even niet aan.
I have to write an essay, but I don't think about it for now.

Dat treinongeluk? O ja, daar heb ik in de krant een artikel over gelezen.
That train accident? Oh yes, I read an article about it in the newspaper.

In fixed combinations of an adjective, a linking verb, and a preposition, separation of the pronominal adverb is mandatory.

A: Ben je bang voor spinnen?
B: Ja, ik ben er vreselijk bang voor.
A: Are you afraid of spiders?
B: Yes, I'm terribly afraid of them.

Pronominal adverbs with **er-** can never be at the beginning of the sentence. Those with **hier** and **daar**, however, can begin a sentence, separated or unseparated.

Daaraan heb ik nog nooit gedacht/Daar heb ik nooit aan gedacht.
I have never thought about that.

Hieraan kun je zien dat ik geen avontuurlijk mens ben.
This tells you that I am not an adventurous person.

Pronominal adverbs can also begin a question. In a question, the combination **wat** + preposition is changed into **waar** + preposition. Note that, again, in most cases the pronominal adverb as question word is separated in speech. The preposition **met** changes into **mee**, and the preposition **tot** changes into **toe**. Note that some prepositions (**zonder**, **tijdens**, **sinds**, **behalve**, **volgens**, **wegens**) cannot be used to form a pronominal adverb.

Waarover praten jullie?/Waar praten jullie over?
What are you talking about?

Waarmee maak ik dit open?/Waar maak ik dit mee open?
With what/How do I open this?

Pronominal adverbs with **waar-** can be used as relative pronouns when the relative sentence refers to an object with a preposition. In speech, these relative pronouns with **waar-** are separated most of the time.

Wat was die film waar jullie gisteren de hele avond over praatten?
What was that movie that you talked about all last night?

Dit is een keukenapparaat waarmee je wafels kan bakken.
This is a kitchen tool with which you can bake waffles.

Note that pronominal adverbs with **er-** and **waar-** are only used for objects, not for persons. For persons, we use the preposition and **wie** 'who.'

Wie was die man met wie je daar stond te praten?
Who was the man you were talking to?

Lastly, the adverbs **er**, **hier**, **daar**, and **waar** are combined with **heen**, **naartoe**, or **vandaan** when the verb in the sentence expresses motion to or from a place. Again, they can be separated by other sentence elements.

> **Moet ik alweer naar de bakker?? Ik kom er net vandaan!**
> Do I have to go to the bakery again? I just came from there!

> **Kom je straks hierheen? Of wil je dat ik daarnaartoe kom?**
> Are you coming here later? Or do you want me to come over there?

> **Gaan jullie morgen naar het strand? Leuk, wij gaan er ook heen.**
> Are you going to the beach tomorrow? Fun, we're going there, too.

▶ For more information on relative pronouns and sentences, see **2.7** and **9.6**.

3.8 Forming adjectives and adverbs

One can form adjectives from other words such as nouns, verbs, names, and the like. For example, past and present participles can be used as adjectives.

> **De kok maakte gebakken aardappels.**
> The cook made fried potatoes.

> **Hij gooide de aardappelplakjes in de spetterende boter.**
> He tossed the potato slices into the splashing butter.

> **Daarna deed hij er nog wat stukjes gerookt spek bij.**
> After that he added some pieces of smoked bacon.

Prefixes can give an adjective or an adverb a different meaning. As mentioned in a previous section, the prefixes **on-**, **in-** (**il-**, **ir-**, **im-**), **niet-/non-**, and **a-** give the adjective a negative meaning.

> **Dat was een onbeleefde opmerking.**
> That was a rude remark.

> **Hij werd gearresteerd wegens illegaal wapenbezit.**
> He was arrested for illegal possession of guns.

Prefixes such as **aarts-**, **oer-**, **door-**, **in-**, **hyper-**, and **over-** give the adjective a much stronger and reinforcing meaning.

> **Hij is niet alleen aartslui, hij is ook nog oerdom.**
> He is not only very lazy, but also really stupid.

> **De jongens kwamen doornat van hun fietstocht terug.**
> The boys came back soaking wet from their bike trip.

> **Die moeder is altijd overbezorgd om haar kinderen.**
> That mother worries way too much about her kids.

There are also many suffixes to form adjectives. The suffixes **-aal**, **-eel**, **-achtig**, **-ief**, **-iek**, **-ig**, **-erig**, **-isch**, **-lijk**, **-matig**, and **-s** all have a similar meaning: of a certain nature, characteristic, manner, in a certain way. Examples are **muzikaal** 'musical,' **cultureel** 'cultural,' **stormachtig** 'stormy,' **primitief** 'primitive,' **energiek** 'energetic,' **kattig** 'catty,' **plagerig** 'teasingly,' **tragisch** 'tragic,' **gevaarlijk** 'dangerous,' **gevoelsmatig** 'intuitive,' **zomers** 'summerlike.'

> **Het was een regenachtige dag.**
> It was a rainy day.

> **We moeten dit stelselmatig veranderen.**
> We have to systematically change this.

The suffixes **-baar** and **-zaam** are often added to verb stems, and they express that something can be done. Example: **buigzaam** 'can be bent, is flexible.'

Deze instrumenten zijn van buigzaam hout gemaakt.
These instruments were made of flexible wood.

We hadden vroeger een draagbare televisie.
We used to have a portable TV.

The suffix **-loos**, finally, means 'without.' For example, **stijlloos** means 'without style.'

Wat hadden we in de zeventiger jaren toch stijlloze inrichtingen.
Didn't we have tasteless furnishings in the seventies?

Mijn oma moest jarenlang zoutloos eten.
My grandmother had to eat saltless food for years.

3.9 Particles

Particles are adverbs that often seem to have no particular meaning and are therefore difficult for non-speakers of Dutch to learn. They are often organized into three groups: focus particles, modal particles, and discourse particles or discourse markers.

Focus particles

The function of focus particles is literally to focus on particular sentence parts, to place these in the foreground. Examples of such particles are **alleen** 'only,' **zelfs** 'even,' **vooral** 'especially,' **met name** 'in particular,' **ook** 'also,' **niet eens** 'not even,' **maar** 'just, only,' **slechts** 'just, only,' **juist** 'just, particularly.' Note how these particles can change the meaning of a sentence.

Het was een vreselijke film. Zelfs Brad Pitt speelde slecht.
It was a terrible movie. Even Brad Pitt played badly.

Het was een vreselijke film. Vooral Brad Pitt speelde slecht.
It was a terrible movie. Especially Brad Pitt played badly.

Ik ben echt platzak. Ik heb maar één euro bij me.
I'm really broke. I only have one euro on me.

Ik ben echt platzak. Ik heb niet eens één euro bij me.
I'm really broke. I don't even have one euro on me.

Time

A sub-group of the focus particles are particles expressing time. These include **net** 'just,' **pas** 'only, not until,' **al** 'already,' **nog** 'still, yet,' **weer** 'again,' **eerst** 'first.' Note again the slight differences between the sentences.

Karin is net binnengekomen.
Karin just came in.

Karin is weer binnengekomen.
Karin came in again.

Karin is al binnengekomen.
Karin has already come in.

Modal particles

Modal particles are very difficult to learn because they don't always seem to have any particular meaning. We see them used a lot in the imperative, the command form. They don't focus on a particular sentence part, but instead they give the whole sentence a slightly different character. They make statements or commands friendlier or more polite, or they express impatience, or they show that the speaker is somewhat annoyed or that he or she is hesitant, and so on. Examples are **maar**, **even**, **eens**, **nou**, **toch**, **dan**.

> **Doe jij het raam maar open** (friendly, encouraging).
> Go ahead and open the window.

> **Doe jij het raam nou open** (with impatience).
> Open the window, please.

> **We moeten die oude tent maar wegdoen** (with a kind of resignation).
> We should just pitch that old tent.

> **We moeten die oude tent eens wegdoen** (as if saying: it's about time).
> We should finally get rid of that old tent.

► For more on modal particles, see **13.8**.

Discourse particles

Some particles are not strictly part of the sentence, but function more like interjections. They merely shape the conversation. They can be used to get someone's attention, for instance, or to ask someone to agree, or to summarize what was said in the previous sentences. Some examples are **hé** 'hey,' **hè** 'right,' **hoor** 'mind, you know, okay,' **luister** 'listen,' **kijk** 'look,' **joh** 'hey,' **enfin** 'anyway,' **kortom** 'in short, anyway.'

> **Hé, zit je te slapen of zo? Let eens op.**
> Hey, are you sleeping, or what? Pay attention, will you?

> **Wat was dat een gezellige avond, hè?**
> Wasn't that a nice evening?

> **Je moet niet naar die man luisteren, hoor.**
> You shouldn't listen to that man, okay?

> **Kortom, ik wil het er niet meer over hebben.**
> Anyway, I don't want to talk about it anymore.

► For more on discourse particles, see **13.8**.

4

Prepositions

4.1 Prepositions expressing time

binnen within	**Je moet dat werk binnen een week klaar hebben.** You have to finish the work within a week.
in in	**Joost is in 1965 geboren.** Joost was born in 1965.
met with	**Met de jaren ging ze krommer lopen.** As the years went by, she started walking more bent over.
na after	**Na het eten loop ik even met de hond.** After dinner, I walk the dog.
om at	**Kom je vanavond om acht uur even langs?** Will you stop by tonight at eight?
onder during	**Onder het eten wil ik niet gebeld worden.** I don't want to get phone calls during dinner.
op on	**Op vrijdag krijg ik m'n nieuwe computer.** On Friday, I'll get my new computer.
over in	**De trein vertrekt over tien minuten.** The train leaves in ten minutes.
per per	**De thuiszorg komt drie keer per week.** The home-care comes three times a week.
rond around	**De post wordt bij ons rond het middaguur bezorgd.** They deliver our mail around noon.
sinds since	**Sinds die tijd gaan we niet meer op vakantie.** Ever since then we have not gone on vacation.
tegen just before	**Ik kom tegen zessen even die cd ophalen.** I'll come and get that CD right before six.
tijdens during	**Wilt u tijdens de voorstelling uw mobieltjes uitdoen?** Can you turn off your mobile phones during the show?
tot until	**Ik werk tot vijf uur en geen minuut langer.** I work until five and not a minute longer.
tussen between	**Tussen twaalf en één is de winkel gesloten.** The store is closed between noon and one.
van(af) from	**Van maandag tot vrijdag zijn wij op vakantie.** From Monday until Friday, we are on vacation. **Vanaf 1 juni is het openluchtbad weer open.** Beginning on June 1, the outdoor pool is open again.

voor before — **Ik eet voor de training een lichte maaltijd.**
I eat a light meal before training.

Note that **om** is for clock-time, and **op** is for days of the week.

Ik heb op maandag om 3 uur autorijles.
I have driving lessons on Monday at 3.

Speakers of English often confuse **sinds** with 'because.' Note, however, that it means 'ever since.'

Sinds hij op dieet is, voelt Johan zich een stuk fitter.
Ever since he has been on a diet, Johan has been feeling a lot fitter.

Note also that **in** is also used for centuries, seasons, and months; **in de zeventiende eeuw** 'in the seventeenth century,' **in de winter** 'in winter,' **in januari** 'in January.'

4.2 Prepositions expressing place

This is a large group of prepositions. It is impossible to show all possible contexts. Here, I will give examples of motion, direction, location, and those that have a more figurative meaning.

aan on, at, by — **Karin zit aan een lage tafel.**
Karin sits at a low table.

Laten we die foto aan de muur hangen.
Let's hang that photo on the wall.

Mieke studeert aan de Universiteit van Amsterdam.
Mieke studies at the University of Amsterdam.

achter behind — **Ik reed de hele tijd achter een vrachtwagen.**
I was driving behind a truck the whole time.

Zet de vuilnisbak maar achter het huis.
Put the trash can behind the house.

beneden below — **Beneden ons woonde vroeger een zanger.**
A singer used to live below us.

Die scriptie is beneden de maat.
That thesis is subpar.

bij to, near, at — **Hoe kom ik het snelst bij het station?**
What's the fastest way to the station?

Kom even bij me zitten.
Come sit with me for a minute.

Henk werkt al jaren bij Siemens.
Henk has been working at Siemens for years.

Peter woont nog bij z'n ouders.
Peter still lives with his parents.

binnen within — **Hij had altijd sigaretten binnen handbereik.**
He always had cigarettes within reach.

Hou die hond binnen het hek.
Keep that dog within the fence.

boven above — **Boven de deur hing een plaatje met een spreekwoord.**
Above the door, there was a picture with a proverb.

Een directeur staat boven een projectleider.
A director is a step above a project manager.

buiten outside	**Mijn flat is buiten het centrum.** My flat is outside the center.
	De patiënt is buiten levensgevaar. The patient is no longer in critical condition.
door through	**U loopt door het park en dan is het museum aan uw rechterhand.** You walk through the park and then the museum is on your right.
	Probeer de draad maar door de naald te steken. Try to put the thread through the needle.
in in	**Hij is in Utrecht/in z'n flat/in de trein/in een winkel.** He is in Utrecht/in his flat/in the train/in a store.
langs alongside	**Op weg naar m'n werk fiets ik langs een moskee.** On the way to work, I bike past a mosque.
	Er staan prachtige populieren langs het water. There are beautiful poplars along the water.
naar to	**Ik fiets naar Utrecht/naar school/naar werk/naar oma.** I bike to Utrecht/to school/to work/to grandma.
naast next to	**We wonen naast een pianist.** We live next door to a pianist.
	Ik zit op school naast Joost. At school, I sit next to Joost.
	Zet die boekenkast maar naast het buro. Put the bookcase next to the desk.
	Naast m'n werk heb ik heel veel hobby's. Besides work, I have a lot of hobbies.
om around	**De winkel is om de hoek.** The shop is around the corner.
	Wikkel jij de ham maar even om de asperges. You wrap the asparagus in the ham.
	We graven een geul om het zandkasteel. We dig a trench around the sandcastle.
onder under	**De kat ligt onder de burolamp.** The cat is lying under the desk-lamp.
	James Bond legt het pistool onder z'n kussen. James Bond puts the gun under his pillow.
op on	**Er moeten nieuwe pannen op het dak.** We need new tiles on the roof.
	De kinderen zijn op school. The children are at school.
	Lucy zit op tennis. Lucy takes tennis lessons.
over over	**We konden niet over de brug.** We couldn't go over the bridge.
	We rijden over Osnabrück naar Berlijn. We're driving to Berlin via Osnabrück.

rond(om) around	**De commissie zat rond(om) de tafel.** The committee sat around the table.
tegen against	**De auto reed tegen een boom.** The car drove against a tree.
	Wat zei hij tegen jou? What did he say to you?
tegenover across	**Tegenover de kerk is een bruin café.** There is a pub across from the church.
tot up to	**We lopen tot het pleintje en dan terug, okee?** We walk to the square and then back, okay?
tussen between	**Tussen de twee hoge ramen hing een schilderij.** A painting was hanging between the two tall windows.
	Hij kwam tussen mij en mijn partner. He came between me and my partner.
van off, from	**Haal die spullen maar van tafel, we gaan eten.** Take those things off the table, we're going to eat.
	Ik kom net van de kapper. I just came from the hairdresser.
	Die auto kwam van links, hij had geen voorrang. That car came from the left, it didn't have the right of way.
via via, through	**We gaan via de snackbar naar huis.** We'll pass the snackbar on the way home.
voor in front of	**Er staat een prachtige eik voor ons huis.** There's a beautiful oak tree in front of our house.
voorbij past	**Even voorbij de supermarkt is een drogist.** Just past the supermarket, there is a drug store.
uit out	**Ik zag jou net uit de bibliotheek komen.** I just saw you coming out of the library.
	Hij haalde de brief uit de envelop. He took the letter from the envelope.

4.3 Double prepositions

Many of the prepositions from **4.2** combine to double prepositions expressing motion and direction. In a double preposition, the first preposition is placed before the noun or pronoun, and the second is placed after. Some common examples are:

achter . . . aan following behind	**De politie ging achter de dief aan.** The police went after the thief.
	De collecte komt achter de preek aan. The collection follows the sermon.
door . . . heen all the way through	**Na tien keer wassen kon je door de stof heen zien.** After ten washes, you could see right through the fabric.
naar . . . toe towards	**Ik wil naar huis toe.** I want to go home.

onder . . . door under and through — **De vrachtwagen kon niet onder het viadukt door.**
The truck couldn't go underneath the overpass.

over . . . heen (getting) over — **De buurman smeet een rotte appel over de schutting heen.**
The neighbor tossed a rotten apple over the fence.

Ze kwam niet over die longontsteking heen.
She couldn't get over the pneumonia.

tegen . . . aan (leaning) against — **Zet je fiets niet tegen de etalage aan.**
Don't put your bike up against the shop window.

tussen . . . door in between — **We liepen tussen de geparkeerde auto's door.**
We walked between the parked cars.

Tussen mijn twee colleges door eet ik een appel.
In between my two lecture classes, I eat an apple.

4.4 Prepositions expressing cause and reason

aan (because) of — **De patiënt is aan kanker overleden.**
The patient died of cancer.

door because of — **Door het slechte weer had de trein vertraging.**
The train was delayed because of bad weather.

om because of — **Hij deed het alleen maar om het geld.**
He only did it because of the money.

van from — **Zijn gezicht was rood van woede.**
His face was red with anger.

vanwege because of — **Vanwege de regen was de wedstrijd afgelast.**
Because of the rain, the match was cancelled.

uit out of — **Uit verlegenheid keek hij een andere kant uit.**
Out of shyness, he looked away.

wegens because of — **Wegens omstandigheden is dit loket gesloten.**
Because of circumstances, this counter is closed.

4.5 Other prepositions

Prepositions expressing bringing or coming into possession:

van of — **Dat boek is van mij.**
That book is mine.

voor for — **Is deze pizza voor u, meneer?**
Is this pizza for you, sir?

Prepositions expressing opinion:

tegen against — **Veel caféhouders zijn tegen het rookverbod.**
Many pub-owners are against the smoking ban.

volgens according to — **Volgens mij kun je maar beter met dat medicijn stoppen.**
I think you'd better stop taking that medication.

voor for — **Ik ben voor het voorstel van de commissie.**
I am for the proposal of the committee.

Preposition expressing the agent of an action:

door by	**Dat boek is door Harry Mulisch geschreven.** That book was written by Harry Muslisch.

Preposition expressing a topic:

over about	**De professor gaf een lezing over euthanasie.** The professor gave a talk about euthanasia.

Preposition expressing by means of:

met with	**We gaan met de fiets naar het strand.** We're going to the beach by bike.
	Je moet die splinter er met een pincet uit halen. You have to take that splinter out with tweezers.

Preposition expressing lack of something:

zonder without	**Na de storm zaten we zonder stroom.** After the storm, we were without power.
	Zonder aarzelen stemde hij toe. He agreed without hesitation.
	Ga je zonder jas naar buiten? Are you going out without a coat?

4.6 Postpositions

Some prepositions with verbs expressing motion and direction are placed after the noun and are therefore called postpositions. In the following group, all postpositions can also be prepositions, except **af**.

af down	**Hij liep de trap af naar de toiletten.** He walked down the stairs to the restrooms.
door through	**Je fietst het park door en dan kom je bij het museum.** You bike through the park and then you get to the museum.
in into	**De kat kwam met een muis de kamer in.** The cat came into the room with a mouse.
langs along	**We liepen de gracht langs in de richting van het plein.** We walked along the canal towards the square.
om around	**De auto reed de hoek om en verdween uit het zicht.** The car drove around the corner and disappeared from sight.
op onto, up	**Hij rende de trap op naar z'n kamer.** He ran up the stairs to his room.
over over	**U gaat hier de brug over en dan naar links.** You go over the bridge here, and then left.
rond around	**Tijdens de test liep de leraar de klas rond.** During the test, the teacher walked around the classroom.
uit out of, from	**De kerkgangers kwamen de kerk uit.** The churchgoers came out of the church.
voorbij past	**Sinterklaas, rijd ons huisje niet voorbij.** Santa Claus, don't ride past our little house.

4.7 Common verbs, adverbs, and nouns with prepositions

There are many fixed combinations of verb, adverb or noun with preposition. The following is just a sample of such combinations. For every preposition, there is, where possible, an example with a verb, one with an adverb, and one with a noun.

aan **Denk je veel aan de toekomst?**
Do you think about the future a lot?

Karina is verslaafd aan zachte nougat.
Karina is addicted to soft nougat.

Ik heb een hekel aan schreeuwende kinderen.
I can't stand screaming kids.

bij **Deze oorbellen horen bij die ketting.**
These earrings belong to that necklace.

Ik heb geen belang bij een nieuwe computer.
I'm not interested in a new computer.

in **Hij gaat helemaal op in zijn werk.**
He is absorbed in his work.

Karin is teleurgesteld in haar nieuwe baan.
Karin is disappointed in her new job.

We hebben niet veel vertrouwen in het verloop van de wedstrijd.
We don't really have a lot of confidence in the outcome of the game.

met **Bemoei je niet met mijn zaken.**
Mind your own business.

Ina is tevreden met haar nieuwe salaris.
Ina is satisfied with her new salary.

Houdt u rekening met vertraging.
Please expect delays.

naar **Kijk je veel naar voetbal?**
Do you watch soccer a lot?

Ik ben heel benieuwd naar je nieuwe vriend.
I'm excited to meet your new boyfriend.

om **De vrouw naast me vroeg om een vuurtje.**
The lady next to me asked for a light.

Zij is heel bezorgd om haar oude kat.
She worries a lot about her old cat.

op **Peter lijkt op z'n vader.**
Peter looks like his father.

Joop is verliefd op Tineke.
Joop is in love with Tineke.

Ik heb even geen antwoord op die vraag.
I don't have an answer to that question right now.

over **Anna klaagt over hoofdpijn.**
Anna complains about headaches.

Ik was verbaasd over die testresultaten.
I was surprised about those test results.

tegen **De studenten protesteren tegen het verhoogde collegegeld.**
The students are protesting the higher tuition rates.

De professor was heel aardig tegen me.
The professor was very nice to me.

Ik zoek een middeltje tegen de hoest.
I'm looking for a remedy for a cough.

tot **Ze hebben hem tot een bekentenis gedwongen.**
They forced him to confess.

uit **Dit boek bestaat uit drie delen.**
This book consists of three parts.

Je hebt de keuze uit vier verschillende menu's.
You have the choice between four different menus.

van **Hij droomt van een grote toekomst.**
He is dreaming of a great future.

Deze economie is heel afhankelijk van de handel met het buitenland.
This economy is very dependent on foreign trade.

Heb jij verstand van computers?
Do you know anything about computers?

voor **Interesseer je je voor moderne kunst?**
Are you interested in modern art?

Wie is verantwoordelijk voor die fout?
Who is responsible for that mistake?

Ik heb grote bewondering voor die zanger.
I really admire that singer.

4.8 Common fixed expressions with prepositions

Finally, there are also many word groups that together function as one preposition. Here are a few commonly used examples of such word groups.

aan de hand van on the basis of
Aan de hand van deze gegevens kunnen we de oorzaak van de ziekte vinden.
On the basis of these data, we can find the cause of the illness.

bij wijze van by way of
Bij wijze van uitzondering mocht ik het examen overdoen.
By way of exception, I was allowed to do the exam again.

door middel van by means of
Door middel van een infuus werd het medicijn toegediend.
The medication was administered by means of an infusion.

in geval van in the case of
In geval van brand gaan de sproeiers automatisch aan.
In the case of a fire, the sprinklers will come on automatically.

in verband met in connection with, on account of
In verband met de pensionering van de voorzitter is er een receptie.
On account of the chairman's retirement, there is a reception.

in verhouding tot in relation to

In verhouding tot het werk dat hij moet doen verdient hij weinig.
He doesn't make much money in relation to the work that he has to do.

met behulp van with the help of

Met behulp van de buurman haalden we de oude eik uit de tuin.
With the help of the neighbor, we pulled the old oak from the garden.

na verloop van after

Na verloop van tijd ging het litteken weg.
After a while, the scar disappeared.

naar aanleiding van on account of, on the basis of, as a result of

Naar aanleiding van het gesprek werd het volgende besloten.
On account of the conversation, they made the following decision.

onder leiding van under the direction of

Het orkest stond onder leiding van een Poolse dirigent.
The orchestra was directed by a Polish director.

op basis van on the basis of

Ik maak het liefst soep op basis van bouillon.
I prefer to make soup with a bouillon cube.

op grond van on account of

Op grond van uw beperkte kwalificatie kunnen wij u niet aanstellen.
On account of your limited qualification, we cannot hire you.

op verzoek van at the request of

Op verzoek van de studenten werd het examen uitgesteld.
At the request of the students, the exam was postponed.

ten koste van at the cost of

Dat harde werken gaat ten koste van je gezondheid.
Working so hard is going to come at the cost of your health.

ter gelegenheid van on the occasion of

Ter gelegenheid van het huwelijk van de prins waren alle straten versierd.
On the occasion of the prince's wedding, all the streets were decorated.

This is just a brief impression. Expressions such as these are best learned and memorized in context.

5

Numbers and measures

5.1 Cardinal numbers

1 *één*	11 elf	21 eenentwintig	40 veertig, 50 vijftig, 60 zestig . . .
2 twee	12 twaalf	22 *tweeëntwintig*	80 *tachtig*
3 drie	13 *dertien*	23 *drieëntwintig*	100 *honderd*
4 vier	14 *veertien*	24 vierentwintig	200 tweehonderd, 300 driehonderd . . .
5 vijf	15 vijftien	25 vijfentwintig	1.000 duizend
6 zes	16 zestien	26 zesentwintig	10.000 tienduizend
7 zeven	17 zeventien	27 zevenentwintig	100.000 honderdduizend
8 acht	18 achttien	28 achtentwintig	1.000.000 één miljoen
9 negen	19 negentien	29 negenentwintig	1.000.000.000 één miljard
10 tien	20 twintig	30 dertig	0 nul

In the table above, note the accents on **één**. This is to make sure there is no confusion between the cardinal number one and the indefinite article **een** 'a.' Also, pay attention to the irregular spelling of 13 ***der*tien**, 14 ***veer*tien**, 30 ***der*tig**, 40 ***veer*tig**, and 80 ***t*achtig**. Also note the dieresis (Dutch **trema**) on the unstressed **e** at the beginning of a new syllable in numbers such as 22 **tweeëntwintig** and 23 **drieëntwintig**.

All compound cardinal numbers up to 100 **honderd** are written as one word: 17 **zeventien**, 35 **vijfendertig**, 89 **negenentachtig**, and so on. Also, all multiples of 100 **honderd** and 1.000 **duizend** that are formed with a cardinal number up to 100 **honderd** or with a multiple of 100 **honderd** are written as one word: 500 **vijfhonderd**, 1.800 **achttienhonderd**, 4.500 **vijfenveertighonderd**, 7.000 **zevenduizend**, 86.000 **zesentachtigduizend**, 300.000 **driehonderdduizend**, etc.

However, all compound cardinal numbers above 100 **honderd** (except multiples) are written as separate words: 102 **honderd twee**, 345 **driehonderd vijfenveertig**, 1.975 **negentienhonderd vijfenzeventig**, 18.614 **achttienduizend zeshonderd veertien** and so on. Similarly, multiples of 1.000 **duizend** that are formed with other compound cardinal numbers such as the ones above are written separate: 105.000 **honderd vijf duizend**, 436.000 **vierhonderd zesendertig duizend**. And lastly, all multiples of **een miljoen**, **een miljard**, etc., are written separate: **eenendertig miljoen, vijfenveertig miljard**, and so on.

There are alternate ways to write and say four digit numbers such as 5.345. For instance, one can say **vijfduizend driehonderd vijfenveertig** or **drieënvijftighonderd vijfenveertig**. However, the second digit cannot be pronounced as a zero. There is therefore no alternate way to say, for instance, 3.086 **drieduizend zesentachtig**.

In Dutch, dates are written and spoken as follows:

June 2, 2013	**Twee juni tweeduizend dertien.**
September 7, 1975	**Zeven september negentien(honderd) vijfenzeventig.**

Note the preposition **in** 'in' for years and the preposition **op** 'on' for days.

Jacob is in 2011 afgestudeerd.
Jacob graduated in 2011.

Minna is op 3 februari 1983 geboren.
Minna was born on February 3, 1983.

The numbers **beide, beiden, allebei/alle twee** 'both' are also considered to be cardinal numbers. **Beide** can be used as an adjective or independently. As an adjective, it can refer to people and things. Independently, it refers to things only. Examples:

Beide ouders van John zijn overleden.
Both of John's parents have died.

Je moet beide boeken voor het examen lezen.
You need to read both books for the exam.

Die broeken kunnen beide in de was.
Both those pants can go in the laundry.

Note that **beiden** refers only to people. It is used independently.

Karin en Nico zijn beiden voor het examen geslaagd.
Karin and Nico both passed the exam.

Allebei and **alle twee** refer to both people and things. They follow the noun or pronoun to which they refer.

Jullie moeten allebei bij de rector komen.
Both of you have to come to the principal.

Die katjes zijn lief, hè? Zullen we ze alle twee nemen?
Those kittens are sweet, aren't they? Shall we take them both?

5.2 Ordinal numbers

In Dutch, ordinal numbers from 1 to 19 are written with the ending **-de**, and those from 20 and up have the ending **-ste**. Note, however, the exceptions **eerste** 'first' and **achtste** 'eighth.' Note also the irregular spelling of **derde** 'third.'

1–19 ⇒ -de		*20 and up ⇒ -ste*
1e ***eerste***	**11e elfde**	**20e twintigste**
2e tweede	**12e twaalfde**	**21e eenentwintigste**
3e ***derde***	**13e dertiende**	**30e dertigste, 40e veertigste . . .**
4e vierde	**14e veertiende**	**67e zevenenzestigste**
5e vijfde	**15e vijftiende**	**135e honderd vijfendertigste**
6e zesde	**16e zestiende**	**450e vierhonderd vijfendertigste**
7e zevende	**17e zeventiende**	**1000e duizendste**
8e ***achtste***	**18e achttiende**	**100.000e honderdduizendste**
9e negende	**19e negentiende**	**1.000.000e een miljoenste**
10e tiende		**1.000.000.000e een miljardste**

Compound ordinal numbers are written the same way as compound cardinal numbers.

Ordinal numbers indicate a certain order of things and events.

M'n fiets is gestolen. Dat is nou al de derde keer dit jaar.
My bike was stolen. That's the third time this year.

Jij was mijn honderdste vriend op Facebook.
You were my hundredth friend on Facebook.

Ordinal numbers are frequently used in dates.

Vandaag is het de vierde juni.
Today is the fourth of June.

Karin is op de zestiende augustus geboren.
Karin was born on the sixteenth of August.

Note that fractions are also formed with the endings of ordinal numbers, **-de** and **-ste**. $^1/_3$ is **een derde**, $^1/_4$ is **een vierde**, $^2/_5$ is **twee vijfde**, and so on. $^1/_8$ is **een achtste**, $^1/_{100}$ is **een honderdste**. The only one that is different is $^1/_2$: **(een) half**. $1^1/_2$ is **anderhalf**. The noun for **half/halve** is **de helft**.

We kregen ieder een halve reep chocola.
Each of us got a half bar of chocolate.

Door de sneeuw was de helft van de klas te laat.
Because of the snow, half of the class was late.

5.3 Indefinite numbers

veel many, much	**verscheidene** various	**enig(e)** some	**genoeg** enough
weinig few, little	**verschillende** various	**menig(e)** many	**voldoende** enough
een paar a few, a pair	**sommige** some	**enkele** a few	**wat** some

Indefinite numbers are used to denote an unspecified number of things or people. Examples:

Er waren veel demonstranten op straat.
There were many demonstrators on the street.

Ik heb hier nog enige/enkele modellen van vorig jaar.
I still have a few of last year's models.

Heb je genoeg/voldoende mensen voor dat project?
Do you have enough people for that project?

Ik heb verscheidene keren geprobeerd je te bellen.
I tried to call you several times.

Note that **veel**, **weinig**, **genoeg**, **voldoende**, and **wat** can be used with nouns in the singular or plural: **veel geld** 'much money,' **veel bloemen** 'many flowers,' **weinig animo** 'little interest,' **weinig mensen** 'few people,' **genoeg/voldoende eten** 'enough food,' **genoeg/voldoende pizza's** 'enough pizzas,' **wat snoep** 'some candy,' **wat broodjes** 'some sandwiches' (informal).

Note also that **een paar** can mean a few or a pair of.

Ik heb een paar foto's gemaakt.
I took a few pictures.

Joost krijgt dit jaar een nieuw paar ski's.
Joost will get a new pair of skis this year.

An **-n** added to indefinite numbers such as **vele**, **sommige**, and **enkele** indicates that they refer to people only.

Voor velen was het examen te moeilijk.
For many, the exam was too difficult.

Sommigen bleven maar een uurtje op het feestje.
Some only stayed an hour at the party.

Ik wil enkelen van u vragen even na te blijven.
I'd like to ask some of you to stay on for a moment.

5.4 Clock time

Clock time in Dutch is expressed as follows:

Time	*How we say it in daily interaction:*	*Alternate way to say it:*
3:00	**Het is drie uur.**	
3:05	**Het is vijf over drie.**	**Het is drie uur vijf.**
3:10	**Het is tien over drie.**	**Het is drie uur tien.**
3:15	**Het is kwart over drie.**	**Het is drie uur vijftien.**
3:20	**Het is twintig over drie/tien voor half vier.**	**Het is drie uur twintig.**
3:25	**Het is vijf voor half vier.**	**Het is drie uur vijfentwintig.**
3:30	**Het is half vier.**	**Het is drie uur dertig.**
3:35	**Het is vijf over half vier.**	**Het is drie uur vijfendertig.**
3:40	**Het is twintig voor vier/tien over half vier.**	**Het is drie uur veertig.**
3:45	**Het is kwart voor vier.**	**Het is drie uur vijfenveertig.**
3:50	**Het is tien voor vier.**	**Het is drie uur vijftig.**
3:55	**Het is vijf voor vier.**	**Het is drie uur vijfenvijftig.**
4:00	**Het is vier uur.**	

To inquire about and give information about clock time, the Dutch say:

A: Hoe laat is het?
B: Het is kwart over drie.
A: What time is it?
B: It is a quarter past three.

A: Hoe laat is het?
B: Het is twaalf uur.
A: What time is it?
B: It is twelve o'clock.

Note that in the answer, we use **uur** only on the exact hour; **twaalf uur**, **vier uur**, **negen uur**, and so on. In all other cases, **uur** is left out; **tien voor half vijf**, **kwart voor zes**, etc.

The preposition **om** is used to express at what time something is happening.

A: Hoe laat begint het college van professor Jansen?
B: Het begint om 4 uur.
A: At what time does Professor Jansen's class start?
B: It starts at 4 o'clock.

► See **4.1** and **14.8** for more on time expressions.

5.5 Measures

The Dutch use the metric system. Size and distance are therefore measured in meters, centimeters, and millimeters, and weight is measured in kilos, pounds, and grams.

1 kilo (kg)	**1.000 gram (gr)**	**1 kilometer (km)**	**1.000 meter**
1 pond	**500 gram**	**1 meter (m)**	**100 centimeter**
1 ons	**100 gram**	**1 centimeter (cm)**	**10 millimeter (mm)**
1 liter	**10 deciliter (dl)**	**1 m^2**	**1 vierkante meter**

Note that after a cardinal number and after **hoeveel** 'how much/many,' **zoveel** 'so much/many,' and **een paar** 'a few,' measure units are used in singular. Examples:

Ik wil graag 2 kilo appels/3 pond oude kaas/2 ons champignons.
I would like 2 kilos of apples/3 pounds of old cheese/2 ounces of mushrooms.

Voor dit recept heb je 2 deciliter slagroom nodig.
You need 2 deciliters of heavy whipping cream for this recipe.

Mijn kamer in de studentenflat is 16 vierkante meter (m^2).
My room in the dorm is 16 square meters.

Hoeveel kilo appels wilde u?
How many kilos of apples did you want?

However, when a measure unit is used with emphasis or as an object in itself, it appears in the plural. Examples:

Ik ben in de vakantie kilo's aangekomen!
I gained kilo after kilo during my vacation!

We hebben gisteren kilometers gefietst.
We biked miles and miles yesterday.

The Dutch currency unit is the euro (€). There are bills of 500, 200, 100, 50, 20, 10 and 5 euros. There are coins of 2 euros, 1 euro, 50, 20, 10, 5, and 2 euro cents and 1 euro cent. Note the punctuation in decimals; the Dutch use commas instead of points; 2,5 is **twee komma vijf**. Note also that euro and cent preceded by a cardinal number are used in the singular. Examples:

€ 2,75	**Twee vijfenzeventig** (informal).
	Twee euro vijfenzeventig (more formal).
	Twee euro en vijfenzeventig cent (very formal).
€ 385,95	**Driehonderd vijfentachtig vijfennegentig** (informal).
	Driehonderd vijfentachtig euro vijfennegentig (more formal).
	Driehonderd vijfentachtig euro en vijfennegentig cent (very formal).

Note the difference between the two sentences below:

Hij legde drie euro op de toonbank.
He put (an amount of) 3 euros on the counter.

Hij legde 3 euro's op de toonbank.
He put 3 euro coins on the counter.

In the first sentence, we are talking about the amount of money, in the second sentence, the emphasis is on the coins.

► See **14.3** for numbers and measures in describing objects.

B

Verb groups

6

Verbs

6.1 Verb conjugation

Verb conjugation in the present tense works as shown in the overview below. The personal pronouns are listed as follows: 1 sg) **ik**, 2 sg) **jij**, **je**, inv) inversion of second-person subject and verb, formal) **u**, 3 sg) **hij**, **zij/ze**, **het**, 1 pl) **wij**, **we**, 2 pl) **jullie**, 3 pl) **zij**, **ze**. The letters a, b, c, etc., refer to my comments after the overview.

► For personal pronouns, see also **2.1**.

	werken *work (a)*	***zetten*** *put (b)*	***leiden*** *lead (c)*	***zeggen*** *say (d)*	***nemen*** *take (e)*	***geven*** *give (f)*	***lezen*** *read (g)*
ik	**werk**	**zet**	**leid**	**zeg**	**neem**	**geef**	**lees**
jij, je	**werk*t***	**zet**	**leidt**	**zegt**	**neemt**	**geeft**	**leest**
inverted	**werk je**	**zet je**	**leid je**	**zeg je**	**neem je**	**geef je**	**lees je**
u	**werk*t***	**zet**	**leidt**	**zegt**	**neemt**	**geeft**	**leest**
hij, zij, het	**werk*t***	**zet**	**leidt**	**zegt**	**neemt**	**geeft**	**leest**
wij, we	**werk*en***	**zetten**	**leiden**	**zeggen**	**nemen**	**geven**	**lezen**
jullie	**werk*en***	**zetten**	**leiden**	**zeggen**	**nemen**	**geven**	**lezen**
zij, ze	**werk*en***	**zetten**	**leiden**	**zeggen**	**nemen**	**geven**	**lezen**

a) In verb conjugation in present tense, the infinitive (**werken**) loses its ending **-en**, which is replaced by the appropriate ending (italics in the table) for each person. The form for first-person singular is the same as the verb stem (**werk-**). Note that when verb and subject are inverted in second-person singular, the verb loses its ending **-t**. Examples:

> **Werk je vanavond laat?**
> Are you working late tonight?
>
> **Op zaterdag krijg je je zakgeld.**
> You will get your allowance on Saturday.

The verb ending for formal **u** is always **-t**, in singular and plural.
b) When a verb stem ends in **-t**, we do not add the verb ending **-t** in second- and third-person singular. Thus, all singular forms are the same.
c) When a verb stem ends in **-d**, we do add the ending **-t** in second- and third-person singular.
d) Verbs with a double consonant in the infinitive (**zeggen** 'say,' **pakken** 'grab,' **zwemmen** 'swim,' etc.) lose one consonant in all singular verb forms.
e) Verbs with a single, long vowel in the verb stem (**spelen** 'play,' **nemen** 'take,' **laten** 'let,' etc.) double this vowel in all singular verb forms.
f) In verbs with a **-v-** in the verb stem, **-v-** changes to **-f-** in all singular verb forms.
g) In verbs with a **-z-** in the verb stem, **-z-** changes to **-s-** in all singular verb forms.

► See also **11.1** for more information on spelling rules.

The verbs **hebben** 'to have,' **zijn** 'to be,' and some other unusual verb forms such as **gaan** 'to go,' **zien** 'to see,' and **doen** 'to do' are conjugated as follows:

	hebben	*zijn*	*gaan*	*zien*	*doen*
ik	**heb**	**ben**	**ga**	**zie**	**doe**
jij, je	**hebt/heb je**	**bent/ben je**	**gaat/ga je**	**ziet/zie je**	**doet/doe je**
u	**hebt/heeft**	**bent**	**gaat**	**ziet**	**doet**
hij, zij/ze, het	**heeft**	**is**	**gaat**	**ziet**	**doet**
wij, we	**hebben**	**zijn**	**gaan**	**zien**	**doen**
jullie	**hebben**	**zijn**	**gaan**	**zien**	**doen**
zij, ze	**hebben**	**zijn**	**gaan**	**zien**	**doen**

6.2 Modal auxiliary verbs

Modal verbs have the function to modify the mood or modality of the main verb in the sentence. They can express what one can (**kunnen**), must (**moeten**), may (**mogen**), wants to (**willen**), and proposes to or shall (**zullen**) do. They are conjugated as follows:

	kunnen *(a)*	***moeten*** *(b)*	***mogen*** *(c)*	***willen*** *(d)*	***zullen*** *(e)*
ik	***kan***	***moet***	***mag***	***wil***	***zal***
jij, je	**kunt/kan**	**moet**	**mag**	**wilt/wil**	**zult/zal**
	kun/kan je	**moet je**	**mag je**	**wil je**	**zul/zal je**
u	**kunt/kan**	**moet**	**mag**	**wilt**	**zult/zal**
hij, zij/ze, het	***kan***	***moet***	***mag***	***wil***	***zal***
wij, we	**kunnen**	**moeten**	**mogen**	**willen**	**zullen**
jullie	**kunnen**	**moeten**	**mogen**	**willen**	**zullen**
zij, ze	**kunnen**	**moeten**	**mogen**	**willen**	**zullen**

a) In all modal verbs, note that first- and third-person singular are the same (in italics). Also, in second-person singular, there are two forms for **kunnen** and **zullen**. The first is more formal, and the second is more informal or colloquial (and certainly less accepted in formal speech).
b) In **moeten** as well as **mogen**, there are strictly only two forms, one for singular and one for plural.
c) Note the vowel change in singular in **mogen** and also in **kunnen** and **zullen**.
d) English-speaking students of Dutch often confuse **willen** with 'will' in English. Remember that **willen** is 'to want to.'
e) Note that when used as a form of the future tense, **zullen** means 'shall, will.'

Kunnen

The verb **kunnen** is used to say what one can do, but also for polite requests. In addition, it is used to express possibilities.

> **Maarten kan goed pianospelen.**
> Maarten can play the piano very well.
>
> **Kun je even het raam voor me openen?**
> Can you open the window for me?
>
> **Er kan vanavond een bui vallen.**
> Showers are possible tonight.

Moeten

The verb **moeten** is used to say what one must do. Also, one can express an assumption with some certainty with this verb.

We moeten voor morgen twee hoofdstukken geschiedenis lezen.
We have to read two chapters of history for tomorrow.

Dat moet een zoon van Nico zijn, hij lijkt sprekend op hem.
That must be one of Nico's sons, he looks just like him.

Note that the negation of **moeten** is **niet hoeven te**.

Je hoeft je huiswerk niet te maken.
You don't have to do your homework.

Mogen

The verb **mogen** expresses what one is allowed to do. One can also express a certain doubt with it.

Mag ik een koekje uit de trommel nemen?
May I take a cookie from the tin?

Hij mag dan een goede baas op het werk zijn, thuis is hij een bruut.
He may be a good boss at work, but at home he is a bully.

Willen

As mentioned above, **willen** denotes what one wants. It can also express a possibility.

Ik wil niet dat jij vanavond naar dat feest gaat.
I don't want you to go to that party tonight.

Het wil nog wel eens sneeuwen in april.
Snow can happen in April.

Zullen

Finally, **zullen** has many different usages. It expresses things that happen in the future. Also, one can make promises, proposals and suggestions with this verb. In addition, one can ask polite questions in the conditional with **zou**. And one can express possibilities and assumptions.

De economie zal vogend jaar weer sterker zijn.
The economy will be stronger again next year.

Ik zal die hond niet meer alleen laten.
I won't leave that dog alone anymore.

Zul je me elke avond bellen?
Promise to call me every evening.

Zullen we dinsdag samen naar de markt gaan?
Shall we go to the market together on Tuesday?

Zou je me even met die tuinstoelen willen helpen?
Could you help me with those garden chairs for a moment?

Wat een lawaai. De buurman zal wel weer aan het klussen zijn.
What a racket. The neighbor must be working on something again.

► See also **15.3**, **15.6**, **15.7**, and **15.8** for more examples of modal verbs.

Word order with modal verbs

Most of the time, modal verbs take second position in the sentence, while the main verb is moved to the end of the sentence.

Ik kan dat aanbod niet aannemen.
I can't accept that offer.

We moeten die mensen helpen.
We have to help those people.

Sometimes, however, the main verb is left out, or simply implied. In the following sentences, the verbs in brackets are implied.

Wil je een koekje (eten)?
Do you want a cookie?

Moet je nu al naar school (gaan)?
Do you have to go to school right now?

Ik mag niet alleen naar het zwembad (gaan, fietsen, rijden, lopen).
I may not go (bike, drive, walk) to the swimming pool by myself.

Mogen, moeten van

The verbs **mogen** and **moeten** are often used with the preposition **van**. The preposition refers to the person who allows (or doesn't) or gives an order to do something. The negative form of moeten is **niet hoeven te**, which is also used this way. Examples:

Ik mag van m'n vader niet roken.
My father doesn't allow me to smoke.

We moeten van de meester een foto van een huisdier meebrengen naar school.
The teacher told us to bring a picture of a pet to school.

Ik hoef van m'n moeder m'n bed nooit op te maken.
My mom never tells me to make my bed.

Other auxiliary verbs

The verbs described above are true modal verbs. Then there are some verbs that can be used as either a main or a modal auxiliary verb. As an auxiliary verb, they stand in second position in the sentence. Such verbs are **blijven** 'stay,' **gaan** 'go,' **komen** 'come,' **laten** 'let,' and the verbs of the senses **horen** 'hear,' **voelen** 'feel,' and **zien** 'see.' Examples:

Karin blijft vanavond eten.
Karin stays for dinner tonight.

Ik ga een paar croissantjes halen.
I'm going to get a few croissants.

Patrick komt me straks met mijn huiswerk helpen.
Patrick is coming over to help me with my homework later.

Laat jij je haar nog steeds door Melinda knippen?
Are you still having your hair cut by Melinda?

Ik hoor de buurvrouw pianospelen.
I can hear the neighbor play the piano.

We voelden een storm opkomen.
We sensed a storm coming.

Ik zag een kat de boom in klimmen.
I saw a cat climbing up a tree.

Even the verb **zijn** is sporadically used as a modal verb.

A: Waar is Siem?
B: Die is vissen.
A: Where is Siem?
B: He has gone fishing.

A: Zijn de kinderen niet thuis?
B: Nee, ze zijn fietsen.
A: Are the kids not at home?
B: No, they're biking.

6.3 Verbs with infinitive + *te*

In Dutch, many verbs are combined with an infinitive with **te**. They work similar to English, **proberen te** 'try to,' **vergeten te** 'forget to.' The most common verbs with **te** are **beginnen** 'begin,' **beloven** 'promise,' **besluiten** 'decide,' **durven** 'dare,' **hopen** 'hope,' **proberen** 'try,' **verbieden** 'forbid,' **vergeten** 'forget,' **weigeren** 'refuse.' Examples:

We hebben besloten een huis te kopen.
We have decided to buy a house.

Durf jij een spin aan te raken?
Do you dare to touch a spider?

Ik weiger die rekening te betalen.
I refuse to pay that bill.

Note that when the main verb is a separable verb, **te** comes between the separable prefix and the stem.

Het kind probeerde een kaars aan te steken.
The child tried to light a candle.

Ik ben vergeten de buren uit te nodigen.
I forgot to invite the neighbors.

Five verbs are used to form "durative constructions": **zitten** 'sit,' **staan** 'stand,' **liggen** 'lay,' **lopen** 'walk,' and **hangen** 'hang.' When combined with an infinitive and **te**, they express that someone is doing something while actually sitting, standing, laying or walking. They are closest to the English -ing form.

Maarten zit huiswerk te maken.
Maarten is doing his homework.

De studenten stonden buiten een sigaret te roken.
The students were smoking a cigarette outside.

▶ See also **6.7** for more information on durative constructions.

The verbs **schijnen** 'appear, seem,' **lijken** 'seem,' and **blijken** 'appear, turn out' also take an infinitive with **te**.

Die film schijnt/lijkt heel goed te zijn.
That film is apparently really good.

De film bleek ontzettend slecht te zijn.
The film turned out to be incredibly bad.

In the first sentence, the speaker expresses uncertainty because the information is based on hearsay. In the second sentence, the information has proven to be wrong.

The verbs **leren** 'learn, teach' and **helpen** 'help' can take an infinitive with or without **te**. When the sentence is longer, however, because of a direct object or other sentence elements, there is a preference for **te**. Note the difference between the shorter and longer sentences.

Marina leert breien.
Marina is learning to knit.

Karin leert Marina een sok te breien.
Karin teaches Marina to knit a sock.

Help me even dragen.
Help me carry (this stuff).

Help me even de boodschappen naar binnen te dragen.
Help me carry the groceries inside.

Lastly, an infinitive construction with **om . . . te . . .** is used when 1) there is a clear sense of purpose to the action, 2) to express for what purpose an object is used, and 3) after an adjective with **te** 'too.' Examples of each:

Ik ga even naar de apotheek om dat medicijn af te halen.
I'm going to the pharmacy to pick up that medication.

Je gebruikt dit mesje om een mango te schillen.
You use this knife to peel a mango.

Het is vandaag te koud om buiten te zitten.
It's too cold today to sit outside.

► See also **9.7** for word order in infinitive constructions.

6.4 Separable and inseparable verbs

Separable verbs

Separable verbs consist of a verb and a separable prefix. The emphasis in speech lies on the prefix: ***op*****bellen** 'call,' ***af*****spreken** 'agree, make an appointment,' ***uit*****nodigen** 'invite,' and so on. In a sentence in present or simple past tense, the separable prefix goes to the end of the sentence.

Ik bel vanavond m'n ouders op.
I'll call my parents tonight.

Hij nodigde mij voor een etentje uit.
He invited me to dinner.

In a sentence in present or past perfect, the helping verb **hebben** or **zijn** takes second position, while the past participle goes to the end of the sentence. The past participle of the separable verb is divided by **-ge-**.

Ik heb m'n avondjurk aangetrokken.
I have put on my evening gown.

Het kind was de straat overgestoken.
The child had crossed the street.

In a sentence with a modal verb, the modal verb takes second position, and the separable infinitive goes to the end of the sentence.

We moeten gauw weer eens iets afspreken.
We should get together again soon.

In a sentence in present or past perfect with a modal verb, the separable verb and the modal verb (both infinitives) go to the end of the sentence. However, the modal verb may split the separable verb as shown in the examples.

Ik heb niet alle examens kunnen nakijken/Ik heb niet alle examens na kunnen kijken.
I couldn't grade all the exams.

Je had met hem moeten meegaan/Je had met hem mee moeten gaan.
You should have gone with him.

Inseparable verbs

Inseparable verbs, on the other hand, are characterized by the following unstressed, inseparable prefixes: **be-**, **er-**, **ge-**, **her-**, **ont-**, and **ver-**. The emphasis of these verbs lies on the second syllable. In the examples, this is illustrated with italics: **be*ta*len** 'pay,' **er*va*ren** 'experience,' **ge*lo*ven** 'believe,' **her*ken*nen** 'recognize,' **ont*moe*ten** 'meet,' **ver*tel*len** 'tell.' In present and simple past tense, they follow normal conjugation rules:

Erik be*taalt* de boodschappen met contant geld.
Erik pays for the groceries with cash.

Sara ont*moet*te haar man in Griekenland.
Sara met her husband in Greece.

Note, however, that in present and past perfect, the past participle is not formed with **ge-**.

Ze zijn met de bouw van ons huis be*gon*nen.
They've started building our house.

Ik heb hem op straat niet her*kend*.
I didn't recognize him on the street.

Johan heeft z'n leesbril ver*ge*ten.
Johan has forgotten his reading glasses.

Most inseparable prefixes carry meaning. The prefix **be-**, for instance, turns an intransitive verb with a preposition into a transitive verb: **kijken naar** 'look at' versus **bekijken** 'view,' **spreken over** 'talk about' versus **bespreken** 'discuss.' The prefix **her-** means that something is done again: **herhalen** 'repeat,' **herschrijven** 'rewrite.' The prefix **ont-** indicates that something is being undone: **ontdekken** 'discover, uncover,' **ontwrichten** 'derange.' And the prefix **ver-** indicates a change in state or condition: **veranderen** 'change,' **vergroten** 'enlarge.'

6.5 Reflexive verbs

Reflexive verbs express that the action of the verb happens upon the subject him- or herself. They are followed by a reflexive pronoun matching the subject.

ik scheer me myself	**wij/we scheren ons** ourselves
jij/je scheert je yourself	**jullie scheren jullie** yourselves
u scheert zich/u yourself	**u scheert zich/u** yourselves
hij, zij/ze scheert zich him/herself	**zij/ze scheren zich** themselves

► For true reflexive versus not necessarily reflexive verbs, see also **2.5**.

In a coordinated sentence, the reflexive pronoun follows the verb.

Joost haast zich naar het station.
Joost hurries to the station.

Wij ergeren ons aan de hond van de buren.
We are annoyed by our neighbor's dog.

De student gedroeg zich als een idioot.
The student behaved like an idiot.

Note the word order in inverted forms such as questions and the imperative.

Schaam je je niet voor je slechte cijfers?
Aren't you ashamed about your bad grades?

Bemoei je niet met mijn zaken.
Mind your own business.

In a subordinated sentence, the reflexive pronoun follows the subject.

Ik vraag me af of de kinderen zich vervelen.
I wonder if the children are bored.

De baas zei dat ik me in de datum had vergist.
The boss said I was wrong about the date.

▶ For more on coordinated and subordinated sentences, see Chapter **9**.

As illustrated in section **2.5**, some verbs can be reflexive or not. Examples of such not necessarily reflexive verbs are **(zich) wassen**, **(zich) aankleden**, **(zich) vervelen**. Note the differences in each sentence pair.

De moeder wast zich vs. **De moeder wast de baby.**
The mother washes herself vs. The mother washes the baby.

Het kind kleedt zich aan vs. **Het kind kleedt haar pop aan.**
The child gets dressed vs. The child dresses her doll.

Ik verveelde me tijdens de film vs. **De film verveelde me.**
I was bored during the movie vs. The film was boring to me.

In all of these examples, the verbs mean mostly the same, whether they are reflexive or not. Some verbs, however, change their meaning completely when a reflexive pronoun is added.

De manager stelde een nieuwe werknemer aan.
The manager hired a new employee.

De manager stelde zich vreselijk aan op het feestje.
The manager made a fool of himself during the party.

6.6 Verbs of action and result

Verbs of action express movement to a location, while verbs of result express the result of that movement. Action verbs are transitive (they have a direct object) and verbs of result are intransitive (they don't have a direct object).

Verbs of action (transitive)		*Verbs of result (intransitive)*	
zetten	put	**staan**	stand
leggen	lay	**liggen**	lie
stoppen/steken	put, stick, stuff	**zitten**	sit
hangen	hang	**hangen**	hang

Zetten, staan

The verb **zetten** is used to say that an object is being placed somewhere which then stands in an upright position. The verb **staan** is used for that upright position.

Ik zet de pannen op tafel. De pannen staan op tafel.
I put the pots on the table. The pots are (standing) on the table.

We zetten de boeken in de kast. Multatuli staat op de vierde plank.
We put the books in the bookcase. Multatuli is on the fourth shelf.

Leggen, liggen

The verb **leggen** is used to say that one lays something in a horizontal position. The verb **liggen** expresses the result of that action.

> **Hij legde drie briefjes van tien op de toonbank.**
> He put three ten euro notes on the counter.

> **Je schone was ligt op je bed.**
> Your clean laundry lies on your bed.

Note that **zetten** and **leggen** are often used with the separable prefix **neer** 'down.'

> **Ze hebben hier in een week drie huizen neergezet.**
> They put three houses down here in one week.

> **Leg die kranten hier maar neer.**
> Put those papers down here.

Stoppen, steken, zitten

The verbs **stoppen** and **steken** express that something is being put in a small, confined space like a bag or a pocket. The verb **zitten** expresses the result of that action.

> **Ik heb een paar mandarijnen in je schooltas gestopt.**
> I put a few mandarins in your school bag.

> **De gastprofessor stak zijn lezing in een mapje.**
> The guest professor put the lecture in a folder.

> **M'n sleutels zitten niet in mijn tas. Heb jij ze gezien?**
> My keys are not in my bag. Have you seen them?

> **Misschien heb je ze in je jaszak gestoken.**
> Maybe you put them in your coat pocket.

Hangen

The verb **hangen** is used to say that something is being hung. The same verb is used for the result of that action. Note that **hangen** is often used with the separable prefix **op-**.

> **Laten we het schilderij aan die muur daar hangen. Daar hangt het heel mooi.**
> Let's hang this painting on that wall there. It hangs beautifully there.

> **Wil jij even de was ophangen?**
> Could you hang the laundry?

To change the verbs **zitten**, **liggen**, and **staan** into action verbs for people rather than objects, we simply add the verb **gaan** 'to go.'

> **Kom binnen. Ga even zitten.**
> Come in. Sit down for a moment.

> **Karin ging even op de bank liggen om een dutje te doen.**
> Karin lay down on the sofa to take a nap.

> **De gemeente ging voor het slotlied staan.**
> The congregation rose for the closing hymn.

The verb **hangen** is almost never used for people, except in **(zich) ophangen** 'to hang (oneself)' and in certain contexts when it means to lounge, to hang around.

> **De kinderen hangen veel te lang voor de televisie.**
> The children are watching TV for way too long.

Een groepje jongens hing op het plein bij de fontein rond.
Some boys were hanging around the square by the fountain.

6.7 Durative constructions

Section **6.3** explained durative constructions with the verbs **zitten**, **liggen**, **staan**, **lopen**, and **hangen**. In combination with **te** and a verb infinitive, these verbs express that one is actually sitting, lying, standing, or walking while doing something (**hangen** is only used for objects).

Hij zit op de bank een boek te lezen.
He is sitting on the sofa reading a book.

De gasten stonden in de tuin te praten.
The guests were talking in the garden.

Durative constructions with these verbs in the present perfect are formed with the helping verb **hebben** and two infinitives at the end. These can be separated by **te** or not.

Ze heeft daar heel lang zitten (te) lezen.
She sat there reading for a long time.

Ze hebben nog een lange tijd staan (te) praten.
They stood talking for a long time.

Note that the order of the infinitives is not arbitrary. The infinitive which expresses the main action (**lezen**, **praten**) comes last.

Separable verbs in durative constructions in the present perfect can be separated by **zitten**, **liggen**, **staan**, and **lopen** or not. In speech, the separated form is often preferred.

Hij heeft de hele dag formulieren zitten invullen/in zitten vullen.
He was filling in forms all day.

Another durative construction very similar to English -ing is formed with **zijn** 'to be' in combination with **aan het** + infinitive. The question **Wat ben je aan het doen?** 'What are you doing?', for instance, could be answered as follows:

Ik ben een cake aan het bakken.
I'm baking a cake.

Ik ben een opstel aan het schrijven.
I'm writing an essay.

The past tense of this construction is formed with the simple past of **zijn**.

Karel was net nog aan het telefoneren.
Karel was just talking on the phone.

Lastly, another durative construction is formed with **bezig zijn te** or **bezig zijn met**. The first takes an infinitive and the second a noun. Note the difference:

De docent is bezig proefwerken na te kijken.
The teacher is (in the process of) grading tests.

De docent is met proefwerken bezig.
The teacher is working on tests.

These durative constructions can either be used in the simple past or in present perfect.

De docent was bezig proefwerken na te kijken.
The teacher was grading tests.

De docent is bezig geweest proefwerken na te kijken.
The teacher was grading tests.

7

Verb tenses

7.1 The present tense and its uses

► For an overview of verb conjugation in present tense, see **6.1**.

The present tense is used for events happening in the present.

Karel kijkt naar een spannende film.
Karel is watching a suspense movie.

Het verhaal speelt zich af in Londen.
The story takes place in London.

These events can be in the present moment, or they may have lasted for longer than just the present moment. They may happen on a regular basis, and they may also repeat themselves in the future. Examples:

We wonen hier al een jaar.
We've lived here for a year.

Hans drinkt 's morgens koffie bij het ontbijt.
Every morning, Hans drinks coffee with his breakfast.

Ik koop regelmatig een Libelle.
I buy a *Libelle* magazine regularly.

The present tense is also used for general statements, scientific truths and facts.

Nederlanders praten altijd over het weer.
Dutch people always talk about the weather.

Water kookt bij een temperatuur van 100 graden.
Water boils at 100 degrees C.

In addition, the present tense is used for future events. In most cases, the future is indicated with an adverb that expresses future time. Another way to talk about the future is to use the verb **gaan** 'go' with an infinitive. Here, we also often add an adverb expressing future.

Peter komt met de fiets.
Peter is coming by bike.

Ik begin deze week met een nieuw schilderij.
I'm starting a new painting this week.

Jaap gaat economie studeren.
Jaap is going to study economics.

Native speakers of English often use the present perfect mistakenly in Dutch when it needs to be the present tense. For events that have been going on for a while in sentences such as 'I have worked here for 20 years' and 'I have known him for three months,' one must use present tense in Dutch. We add adverbs such as **al** 'already' or **nu** 'now.'

Ik werk hier al 20 jaar.
I have worked here for 20 years.

Ik ken hem nu drie maanden.
I have known him for three months.

Occasionally, the present tense is used for an event that actually happened in the past. We see this in texts on history, and sometimes in spoken Dutch it is used to give a story a sense of actuality. In speech, it can happen that we hear the past and present tense in one sentence.

In 1940 breekt de tweede wereldoorlog uit.
In 1940, the Second World War breaks out.

Vanmorgen om zeven uur gaat de bel. Ik denk: Wie belt er nou zo vroeg?
This morning at seven the doorbell rings. I think: Who calls this early?

Ik zag Cora in Amsterdam en ik zeg tegen haar: Goh, wat doe jij hier nou?
I saw Cora in Amsterdam and I say to her: Geez, what are you doing here?

7.2 The simple past tense and its uses

The simple past tense of regular or weak verbs is formed by adding the ending **-te** or **-de** to the stem of the verb. The ending **-te** is added to verb stems ending in t, f, k, s, ch, and p (building the word **'t fokschaap** 'the breeding sheep'), while the ending **-de** is added to all stems ending in a soft consonant. There are only two forms, one for singular, and one for plural. Here are the simple past forms of **werken** 'work' and **spelen** 'play.'

	ik	*jij/je, u*	*hij, zij/ze, het*	*wij/we*	*jullie*	*zij/ze*
werken	**werkte**	**werkte**	**werkte**	**werkten**	**werkten**	**werkten**
spelen	**speelde**	**speelde**	**speelde**	**speelden**	**speelden**	**speelden**

Note that long single vowels in an open syllable double in the conjugated simple past form: **maken** 'make' ⇒ **maakte**; **roken** 'smoke' ⇒ **rookte**; **spelen** 'play' ⇒ **speelde**. The stem consonants **v** and **z** become voiceless with the ending **-te** or **-de**: **reizen** 'travel' ⇒ **reisde**; **leven** 'live' ⇒ **leefde**. Single or double **t** or **d** in the stem are doubled in the simple past: **praten** 'talk' ⇒ **praatte**; **zetten** 'put' ⇒ **zette**; **antwoorden** 'answer' ⇒ **antwoordde**; **redden** 'save' ⇒ **redde**. Double consonants in the stem become single in the simple past: **bakken** 'bake' ⇒ **bakte**; **rollen** 'roll' ⇒ **rolde**; **rennen** 'run' ⇒ **rende**, and so on.

The simple past of strong verbs involves a vowel change. While one must memorize these forms, one thing that helps is that many verbs with the same stem vowel follow the same vowel change pattern. For example, **ij** changes to **e**, **i** to **a** or **o**, **e** to **a** or **o**, **ie** to **oo**, **ui** to **oo**, and **a** to **ie** or **oe**. Examples:

blijven stay, **schrijven** write ⇒ **bleef/bleven, schreef/schreven**
liggen lie, **zitten** sit ⇒ **lag/lagen, zat/zaten**
drinken drink, **vinden** find ⇒ **dronk/dronken, vond/vonden**
nemen take, **geven** give ⇒ **nam/namen, gaf/gaven**
trekken pull, **zwemmen** swim ⇒ **trok/trokken, zwom/zwommen**
bieden offer, **gieten** pour ⇒ **bood/boden, goot/goten**
spuiten spray, **ruiken** smell ⇒ **spoot/spoten, rook/roken**
laten let, **slapen** sleep ⇒ **liet/lieten, sliep/sliepen**
dragen carry, **varen** sail ⇒ **droeg/droegen, voer/voeren**

▶ See the **appendix** in the back of this book for the most common strong verbs.

The verbs **hebben** and **zijn** each also have a singular and a plural form for the simple past: **had** and **hadden** for **hebben** and **was** and **waren** for **zijn**.

We hadden vroeger twee honden thuis, een boxer en een collie.
We used to have two dogs at home, a boxer and a collie.

Ze waren heel lief, maar de boxer was heel ongehoorzaam.
They were real sweet, but the boxer was very disobedient.

The modal auxiliary verbs also have a singular and a plural form for the simple past:

kunnen	*mogen*	*moeten*	*zullen*	*willen*	*laten*
kon	**mocht**	**moest**	**zou**	**wilde/wou**	**liet**
konden	**mochten**	**moesten**	**zouden**	**wilden/wouden**	**lieten**

Note that **willen** has two forms, of which **wilde** is preferred, while **wou** is more colloquial.

> **Hij wilde/wou graag mee naar de bioscoop, maar hij mocht niet van zijn moeder, want hij moest zijn huiswerk nog maken.**
> He wanted to come along to the cinema, but his mom didn't let him, because he still had to do his homework.

> **Anton zou me met schilderen helpen, maar hij kon niet vroeger van z'n werk wegkomen.**
> Anton was going to help me paint, but he couldn't get away from work earlier.

The simple past of separable and inseparable verbs follows the rules for weak and strong verbs. The separable and inseparable prefixes have no influence on the formation of the simple past form.

> **Johan dronk snel zijn koffie op en betaalde de ober.**
> Johan quickly finished his coffee and paid the waiter.

> **Karin vergat op te letten en stapte bij de verkeerde halte uit.**
> Karin forgot to pay attention and got off at the wrong stop.

The simple past or imperfect tense is used primarily to narrate a series of events in the far or recent past or things that happened on a regular basis. Needless to say, the simple past is the typical tense form for narrative texts such as in storytelling and literature.

> **We woonden vroeger tegenover een bakker. We werkten soms op zaterdag een paar uur in de tuin van m'n moeder en met het geld dat we daarvoor kregen gingen we dan meteen bij die bakker snoep kopen. Ik kocht meestal drop.**
> We used to live across from a bakery. We would sometimes work a few hours on a Saturday in my mother's garden, and with the money we earned, we would go and buy sweets at this bakery. I usually bought licorice.

> **Alex kwam thuis, gooide zijn jas op een stoel, pakte een biertje uit de koelkast en zette de tv aan. Zodra hij zat, sprong de kat op zijn schoot.**
> Alex came home, tossed his coat on a chair, grabbed a beer from the fridge and turned the TV on. As soon as he sat down, the cat jumped in his lap.

> **Er was eens een arme houthakker. Hij woonde met zijn vrouw en twee kinderen in een klein huisje in het bos.**
> Once upon a time there was a poor lumberjack. He and his wife and two children lived in a small house in the forest.

In many cases, the narrated past event is introduced with a sentence in the present perfect tense (see also the next section), after which the event itself is described in sentences in the simple past.

> **Ik ben gisteren naar een voorstelling van *De kersentuin* geweest. Het was een fantastische avond. De zaal was uitverkocht en het stuk werd meesterlijk gespeeld. Carine Crutzen speelde de hoofdrol. Ze deed het prima. In de pauze trof ik Peter met wie ik een kop koffie dronk.**
> Yesterday, I went to a performance of *The Cherry Orchard*. It was a fantastic evening. The theater was sold out and the performance of the play was magnificent. Carine Crutzen played the main character. She did a fine job. In the intermission, I met Peter and had coffee with him.

The simple past tense is also used to talk about imaginary situations in the future.

Als je je huiswerk wat eerder maakte, kon je na het eten nog even buiten spelen.
If you did your homework a little earlier, you could play outside for a bit after dinner.

Als ik tijd had, ging ik met je mee naar de markt.
If I had time, I would go to the market with you.

▶ See also **8.2** and **15.7** for more on the conditional.

Finally, the simple past can be used for wishful thinking. In this case, the order of subject and verb is reversed. Note also the use of particles such as **maar** and **nou**.

Was ik maar een topatleet.
If only I were a top athlete.

Had ik maar een betere auto.
If only I had a better car.

Zei hij nou maar iets.
I wish he'd say something.

▶ See also **18.1** for expressing wishes and **3.9** for particles.

7.3 The present perfect tense and its uses

The present perfect tense is formed with an auxiliary verb, **hebben** or **zijn**, and a past participle at the end of the sentence.

Karin heeft gisteren de hele dag in de tuin gewerkt.
Karin worked in the garden the whole day yesterday.

Heb je je tabletten vandaag al genomen?
Have you taken your pills today?

Past participles are formed with the prefix **ge-**. Participles of weak verbs end in **-t** or **-d**. If the stem of a weak verb ends in any of the letters t, f, k, s, ch, and p, (building the mnemonic **'t fokschaap** 'breeding sheep'), the past participle ends in **-t**. If the stem ends in a soft consonant, the participle ends in **-d**. Examples:

maken make ⇒ **gemaakt**
stoffen dust ⇒ **gestoft**
rapen pick up ⇒ **geraapt**
spelen play ⇒ **gespeeld**
kammen comb ⇒ **gekamd**
leggen lay ⇒ **gelegd**

Participles of strong verbs end in **-en**. Participles of most strong verbs change their stem vowel.

nemen take ⇒ **genomen**
drinken drink ⇒ **gedronken**
rijden drive ⇒ **gereden**

The most frequent vowel changes are as follows:

e ⇒ **o**: **nemen** take ⇒ **genomen**; **helpen** help ⇒ **geholpen**
i ⇒ **e**: **liggen** lie ⇒ **gelegen**; **zitten** sit ⇒ **gezeten**
i ⇒ **o**: **drinken** drink ⇒ **gedronken**; **vinden** find ⇒ **gevonden**
ie ⇒ **o**: **bieden** offer ⇒ **geboden**; **vliegen** fly ⇒ **gevlogen**
ij ⇒ **e**: **schrijven** write ⇒ **geschreven**; **blijven** stay ⇒ **gebleven**
ui ⇒ **o**: **ruiken** smell ⇒ **geroken**; **buigen** bend ⇒ **gebogen**

▶ There are more examples in the **appendix** in the back of this book.

Verbs that express motion from one place to another or a change of condition or substance take **zijn** instead of **hebben** as the auxiliary verb. Such verbs are **gaan** 'go,' **komen** 'come,' **rijden** 'drive,' **vliegen** 'fly,' **lopen** 'walk' (motion), **smelten** 'melt,' **veranderen** 'change,' **worden** 'become' (change of condition). Examples:

René is gisteren naar de bioscoop gegaan en laat thuisgekomen.
René went to the movies yesterday and came home late.

We zijn van Amsterdam naar Johannesburg gevlogen.
We flew from Amsterdam to Johannesburg.

Wat is dit dorp in de laatste tien jaar veranderd.
How this village has changed in the last ten years.

Het schilderij is mooi geworden.
The painting turned out beautifully.

Note that some verbs also take the auxiliary verb **zijn**, even though they don't express motion or a change of condition: **beginnen** 'begin,' **gebeuren** 'happen,' **blijven** 'stay,' **stoppen** 'stop,' **ophouden** 'stop.'

The present perfect of **hebben** is **heeft gehad** and of **zijn** it is **is geweest**.

We zijn gisteren met de kinderen naar Artis geweest.
We went to Artis with the kids yesterday.

We hebben een heerlijke dag gehad.
We had a wonderful day.

Separable verbs form the past participle by inserting **ge-** between prefix and verb stem.

Heb je dat formulier al ingevuld?
Have you filled in that form yet?

Sanne heeft me met haar geklep van m'n werk afgeleid.
Sanne's chatting distracted me from work.

Inseparable verbs, on the other hand, don't have **ge-** in the past participle.

Ik heb gisteren de nieuwe vriendin van Kees ontmoet.
I met Kees's new girlfriend yesterday.

Meneer, u heeft nog niet voor uw koffie betaald.
Sir, you haven't paid for your coffee yet.

► See also **6.4** for more information on separable and inseparable verbs.

The present perfect of modal verbs is formed with the auxiliary **hebben**. The modal verb and the main verb move to the end of the sentence, both in their infinitive form. The main verb follows the modal verb, as it carries the main information.

Ze hebben dat huis moeten afbreken.
They had to tear down that house.

De politie heeft de dader niet kunnen vinden.
The police couldn't find the suspect.

Note, however, that the present perfect of modal verbs is not often used. Especially in speech, we prefer to use the simple past.

Ze moesten dat huis afbreken.
They had to tear down that house.

De politie kon de dader niet vinden.
The police couldn't find the suspect.

Only modal verbs that can be used independently have a past participle: **moeten – gemoeten**, **kunnen – gekund**, **willen – gewild**, **mogen – gemogen**.

Ik heb hem nooit gemogen.
I've never liked him.

Hij wil dat ik die braamstruik weghaal, maar ik heb het nooit gekund.
He wants me to get rid of that blackberry bush, but I've never been able to do it.

While sentences in the simple past take the listener into the past, sentences in the present perfect are expressed from the perspective of the present. The present perfect is used to describe isolated events in the past that carry a certain relevance for the present. It talks about completed actions with lasting effect in the present. Example:

Ik heb mijn man ontmoet, toen ik in Utrecht studeerde.
I met my husband when I studied in Utrecht.

Ik heb mijn man ontmoet describes an isolated event in the past, while **toen ik in Utrecht studeerde** describes a longer, more clearly defined period in the past. Sentences introduced with **toen** are therefore preferably in the simple past.

Ik heb gisteren de hele dag gestudeerd. Ik ben klaar voor het examen.
I studied all day yesterday. I'm ready for the exam.

Ik heb de hele zomer gefietst. Ik voel me superfit.
I biked all summer. I feel super-fit.

The first sentence in each pair describes an isolated, completed, and very recent event. The second sentence is the effect of the first sentence.

Ik heb alle boeken van Harry Mulisch gelezen.
I read all Harry Mulisch's books.

Tijdens mijn studie las ik alle boeken van Harry Mulisch.
During my studies, I read all of Harry Mulisch's books.

The first sentence is told from the perspective of the present. It is possible that the speaker just finished reading the last of Mulisch's books. The second sentence takes the listener into a more clearly defined period in the past when the speaker read all Mulisch's books.

Ik ben bij de dokter geweest. Het is gelukkig geen longontsteking.
I was at the doctor's. Fortunately it is not pneumonia.

A: Waar was je gisteren?
B: Ik was bij de dokter.
A: Where were you yesterday?
B: I was at the doctor's.

Again, the first sentence pair describes a past moment from the perspective of the present. The second pair describes the past while taking the speaker and listener into the past.

The present perfect can also be used to talk about the future. The sentence in the present perfect is about an event or action that must be completed before the action of the main sentence can take place. It is a form of the conditional:

Je mag naar buiten als je je huiswerk hebt afgemaakt.
You can go outside when you have finished your homework.

Zodra de gasten zich wat hebben opgefrist, gaan we aan tafel.
As soon as the guests have refreshed themselves a little, we'll sit down for dinner.

7.4 The past perfect tense and its uses

The past perfect tense is formed with the simple past of **hebben** or **zijn** and a past participle at the end of the sentence.

Ik had die nieuwe televisie gekocht.
I had bought that new television.

Karel was naar het feest gekomen.
Karel had come to the party.

Nina had nog nooit een beer in het wild gezien.
Nina had never seen a bear in the wild.

Rob vertelde dat hij al een paar keer in New York was geweest.
Rob said that he had been in New York a few times.

The past perfect is used to talk about a past event from the perspective of another past event.

Toen hij zijn scriptie afgemaakt had, opende Sander een fles whiskey.
After finishing his thesis, Sander opened a bottle of whiskey.

The different tenses in the sentence above create a certain chronology of events. What happened before the event in the simple past (**opende Sander een fles whiskey**) must be in the past perfect (**Toen hij zijn scriptie afgemaakt had**).

Nadat hij met zijn mentor had gesproken, ging Jasper meteen naar de bibliotheek.
After he talked to his mentor, Jasper went straight to the library.

Voordat Maarten er ging studeren, had hij nog niets van Amerika gezien.
Before Maarten went to study there, he had not seen anything of the US.

Jeroen trof een oude vriend in de stad. Die was net uit India teruggekomen.
Jeroen met an old friend in the city. He had just returned from India.

The past perfect is also used to reflect on events that could have happened, but never did.

Als het mooi weer was geweest, hadden we een wandeling kunnen maken.
If the weather had been nice, we could have taken a walk.

Had nou maar naar me geluisterd in plaats van maar te doen wat je wilt.
You should have listened to me instead of just doing what you want.

▶ See **8.2** for more examples of the conditional.

The past perfect is used to reflect on events that should not have happened, but did.

Je had die Volvo nooit moeten kopen.
You shouldn't have bought that Volvo.

Dat kind was nooit in het water gevallen als er iemand op gelet had.
That child wouldn't have fallen into the water if someone had paid attention.

Finally, the past perfect tense is used for wishful thinking. In this case, the order of subject and verb is reversed. Again, note the use of particles.

Was ik nou maar niet naar dat feest gegaan.
I wish I had not gone to that party.

Had ik haar die dure schoenen maar niet gegeven.
If only I had not given her those expensive shoes.

▶ See also **18.1** for expressing wishes and **3.9** for particles.

7.5 The future tense and its uses

Strictly speaking, there is no future tense in Dutch. We use different forms that can, however, also have other functions. The most common form is the present tense with an adverb or time expression added to the sentence that indicates future time.

Morgen komt de glazenwasser.
Tomorrow, the window washer will come.

Volgende week behandel ik het perfectum in de les.
Next week, I discuss the present perfect in class.

We eten over vijf minuten.
We eat in five minutes.

Another common way to talk about the future is to use a form of **gaan** 'go' with an infinitive at the end of the sentence. We often add an adverb that expresses future time.

Ik ga een nieuwe fiets kopen.
I'm going to buy a new bike.

Morgen gaan we met een nieuw hoofdstuk beginnen.
Tomorrow, we'll start a new chapter.

Wat gaan jullie dit jaar met vakantie doen?
What are you doing for vacation this year?

A less common way to talk about the future is to use a form of **zullen** 'shall, will' with an infinitive at the end of the sentence.

De directeur zal de avond openen.
The director will open the evening.

Morgen zal ik de garage opruimen.
Tomorrow I'll clean up the garage.

Wat zal het nieuwe jaar brengen?
What will the new year bring?

However, this form is not entirely uncomplicated, because in many cases, one cannot clearly tell whether someone is just talking about a future intention or making an actual promise. The sentence **Morgen zal ik de garage opruimen** could also be read as a promise.

The "futurum exactum," a form of **zullen** in combination with the main verb in the present perfect, is used to talk about (often important) events that one expects to be completed at a specific point in the future.

Over drie maanden zal ik mijn studie afgesloten hebben.
In three months, I'll have graduated.

Volgend jaar zullen we ons huis helemaal verbouwd hebben.
Next year, we will have remodeled our entire house.

Donderdag over een week zal de boerderij verkocht zijn.
Thursday in a week, the farm will be sold.

7.6 The present participle

The present participle is formed with a verb infinitive + **-d**: **werkend** 'working,' **lachend** 'smiling,' **roepend** 'calling,' **etend en drinkend** 'eating and drinking.' It can be used as an adjective or independently, as an adverb. Note the following sentence pair:

De lachende jongen duwde zijn vriend in het zwembad.
The laughing boy pushed his friend into the pool.

Lachend duwde de jongen zijn vriend in het zwembad.
Laughing, the boy pushed his friend into the pool.

In the first sentence, the present participle is used as an adjective, and in the second, it is used as an adverb.

When used as an adjective, all rules for adjectives as described in Chapter 3 apply. The present participle can take additional sentence elements such as adverbs, objects and prepositional phrases. Note that these sentences are difficult to translate without using more sentences in English.

Op straat liep een blaffende hond.
A barking dog walked in the street.

Op straat liep een luid blaffende hond.
A dog walked in the street, barking loudly.

Op straat liep een luid tegen een voorbijganger blaffende hond.
A dog walked in the street, barking loudly at a passerby.

When used independently as an adverb, the present participle usually appears in its basic form: verb infinitive + **-d**.

Lachend legde hij het boek weg.
He laughed while he put the book away.

Schreeuwend renden de kinderen de school uit.
The kids ran out of the school screaming.

Een liedje neuriënd kwam zij de kamer binnen.
She came into the room humming a tune.

As an adverb, the present participle can also have other sentence elements.

Heftig over het thema van de les discussiërend kwamen de studenten de zaal uit.
In a heated discussion about the topic of the class, the students exited the hall.

In some fixed expressions, and when preceded by the word **al**, the present participle appears with the ending **-e**.

Al doende leert men.
You learn it by doing it.

Al pratende schonk ze de kopjes koffie vol.
Talking and talking, she filled the coffee cups.

8

Verb modes and voices

8.1 The imperative

The imperative is the command form. Most of the time, it is used without a subject. The basic form is the stem of the verb. Note that the separable part of separable verbs goes to the end of the sentence.

Kom binnen, ga zitten.
Come in, sit down.

Doe de deur achter je dicht.
Close the door behind you.

Laat die hond met rust.
Leave that dog alone.

Voeg de inhoud van het zakje aan het kokende water toe.
Add the contents of the bag to the boiling water.

Hang jullie jassen daar maar op.
Please hang your coats there.

Because the imperative form without a subject can sometimes come across as rude or impolite, a subject form is often added, especially in formal situations. When a subject is added, the verb conjugation follows the personal pronoun. In informal situations, **jij** or **jullie** is added, and in formal situations, we add **u**. Note that **u** can be used for a single person or for a group.

Komt u binnen, gaat u zitten.
Come in, sit down.

Zegt u het maar.
Please say what you would like (or: How can I help you?).

Ruim jij de tafel even op.
Please clear the table, will you.

Zet jij die vuilnisbak even aan de straat.
Please put the trash bin on the curb.

Komen jullie snel aan tafel, alsjeblieft.
Please come to the table quickly.

Leggen jullie je pennen nu neer.
Please put down your pens now.

Note that the imperative form of **zijn** is irregular, **wees** in singular, and **weest** in the plural.

Wees beleefd als je met de rector spreekt.
Be polite when you speak to the principal.

Weest u gerust, er is niets aan de hand.
Please don't worry, there's nothing wrong.

▶ For shaping the imperative with particles, see **3.9** and **13.8**.

Another way to form the imperative is with the verb infinitive. This form is often used in the negative, to say that something is prohibited. It is also used in recipes.

Doorlopen!	**Niet roken.**	**Afblijven!**
Keep walking!	Don't smoke.	Hands off!

Aardappels schillen, in dunne plakjes snijden en in olie goudbruin bakken.
Peel and cut the potatoes in thin slices and fry in oil until golden brown.

The past participle is also sometimes used to form the imperative.

Opgelet nu, we gaan beginnen.
Pay attention now, we're starting.

Niet getreurd, Sinterklaas komt volgend jaar weer.
Don't be sad, Santa will come back again next year.

Ingerukt, je hebt hier niets te zoeken.
Get lost, you have no business being here.

Further, when one wants to admonish someone about a situation in the past, and in particular to express one's disapproval, a form of the imperative in the past perfect (without subject) can be used. The past perfect indicates that the situation cannot be changed.

Had die auto nou maar niet gekocht.
You shouldn't have bought that car.

Was nou maar op tijd gekomen.
You should have come on time.

Had even gewacht, dan was ik met je meegegaan.
If you had waited for a minute, I'd have gone with you.

Finally, if the sentence in the imperative is followed by a sentence beginning with **en** or **of**, the sentence in the imperative can sound like a condition.

Zeg dat nog eens en je krijgt een pats om de oren.
Say that again and you'll get slapped.

Ruim je kamer op of je komt straks niet aan tafel.
Clean up your room or you won't come to dinner later.

▶ For more on giving commands and orders, see **16.1**.

8.2 The subjunctive or conditional

Conditionals

Conditional sentences are used to express a condition that must be fulfilled in order for something else to be possible. Typical conjunctions that introduce such sentences are **als** 'if,' 'when,' **tenzij** 'unless, except,' **mits** 'unless, on condition that, as long as.' Depending on what tense is used, the fulfillment of the condition is more or less likely. In sentences in present tense, for instance, the condition is likely to be fulfilled. In such sentences, **als** can mean 'if' or 'when.'

Als ik vanavond tijd heb, kom ik even bij je langs.
If I have time tonight, I'll stop by at your place.

Als Nico er is, kunnen we beginnen.
When Nico is here, we can start.

Het feest zal buiten plaatsvinden, tenzij het regent.
The party will take place outside, unless it rains.

U kunt het artikel ruilen, mits u de bon nog heeft.
You can exchange the item as long as you still have the receipt.

When using the simple past, the speaker indicates that the condition is less likely to be fulfilled, or that it is merely a fantasy or daydream.

Als ik jou was, ging ik niet naar die house party.
If I were you, I wouldn't go to that house party.

Als ik geld had, kocht ik een nieuwe auto.
If I had money, I'd buy a new car.

Sentences with **als** in the simple past, however, can also describe regularly recurring events in the past. Note that these are not conditional sentences.

Als oma op bezoek kwam, kregen we een reep chocola.
Every time grandma came to visit, we'd get a bar of chocolate.

Als dominee op de preekstoel klom, kwamen de pepermuntjes tevoorschijn.
When the vicar climbed on to the pulpit, the peppermints would appear.

To avoid confusion of a conditional sentence with a recurring event, we use, in at least one of the two sentences and sometimes in both, the simple past of **zullen**, **zou**, in combination with an infinitive at the end of the sentence. Examples:

Als oma op bezoek zou komen, zouden we een reep chocola krijgen.
If grandma came to visit, we'd get a bar of chocolate.

Als die jurk niet zo duur was, zou ik hem kopen.
If that dress wasn't so expensive, I'd buy it.

Als het zou regenen, bleef ik hier lekker op de bank een boek lezen.
If it rained, I'd happily stay here on the sofa and read a book.

Note that these sentences express wishes, dreams, and conditions less likely to be fulfilled. If, from the perspective of the speaker, the condition was not fulfilled and will never be fulfilled, we use conditional sentences in the past perfect. These describe situations that cannot be changed anymore.

Als ik geweten had dat je zou komen, was ik vanmorgen thuisgebleven.
If I had known that you would come, I would have stayed at home this morning.

Ik had het examen gehaald als het niet zo moeilijk was geweest.
I would have passed the exam if it hadn't been so difficult.

Als je me had verteld dat je vegetariër bent, had ik iets anders gekookt.
If you had told me that you are a vegetarian, I would have cooked something different.

Conditional sentences with modal verbs are formed either with the modal verb in simple past tense or with **zou** and two infinitives at the end of the sentence. The verb carrying the main information follows the modal verb infinitive.

Als ik er verstand van had, kon ik je met die computer helpen.
If I knew anything about it, I could help you with that computer.

Als ik er verstand van had, zou ik je met die computer kunnen helpen.
If I knew anything about it, I could help you with that computer.

Als het je niets kon schelen, wou ik die opdracht wel aannemen.
If it didn't matter to you, I'd like to take that assignment.

Als het je niets kon schelen, zou ik die opdracht wel willen aannemen.
If it didn't matter to you, I'd like to take that assignment.

Again, to avoid confusion with regularly recurring events, the form with **zou** is more common in the conditional.

Als m'n fiets kapot was, moest ik naar school lopen.
If/When my bike was broken, I had to walk to school.

Als m'n fiets kapot zou zijn, zou ik naar school moeten lopen.
If my bike was broken, I'd have to walk to school.

Conditional sentences with modal verbs in past perfect are formed with the past perfect of the modal verb, for which one needs two infinitives, or one can use **zou** with three infinitives: the past perfect helping verb **hebben** or **zijn**, the modal verb and the main verb.

Als ik toen beter geïnvesteerd had, had ik nu met pensioen kunnen gaan.
If I had made better investments then, I could have retired now.

Als ik toen beter geïnvesteerd had, zou ik nu met pensioen hebben kunnen gaan.
If I had made better investments then, I could have retired now.

Zonder een legitimatiebewijs had je geen rekening kunnen openen.
Without an ID, you couldn't have opened an account.

Zonder een legitimatiebewijs zou je geen rekening hebben kunnen openen.
Without an ID, you couldn't have opened an account.

Polite questions

A form of the conditional with **zou** and the modal verbs **mogen**, **willen**, and **kunnen** is also used to form very polite and formal questions.

Zou ik je pen even mogen lenen?
Could I borrow your pen, please?

Zou je die brieven even op de bus kunnen doen?
Could you mail those letters, please?

Zou je me even met die zware koffers kunnen helpen?
Could you help me with those heavy suitcases, please?

Note that separable verbs in such sentences can be separated by the modal verb or not.

Zou je die pannen even kunnen afwassen?
Could you wash those pots, please?
Alternative: **Zou je die pannen even af kunnen wassen?**

Friendly advice

Conditional sentences (with or without modal verbs) are also used to give friendly advice.

Je zou eens wat vaker moeten sporten.
You should exercise more often.

Jullie zouden de nieuwe woorden uit het hoofd moeten leren.
You should memorize the new vocabulary.

Je zou op dieet kunnen gaan.
You could go on a diet.

Ik zou die auto niet kopen.
I wouldn't buy that car.

Zou je nu wel in de auto stappen met je dronken kop?
Should you really get into that car, drunk as you are?

► See also **16.2** for giving advice.

Hypotheses

Conditional sentences are also used to express hypotheses and uncertainties. Note that sentences in the present express uncertainties about future events, while the past tense indicates something that happened before the moment in which the hypothesis is uttered.

Het zou wel eens kunnen gaan regenen.
It could rain.

Zou Karin komen, denk je?
Do you think Karin is coming?

Zou Peter dat dossier hebben meegenomen?
Is it possible that Peter took that dossier?

Zouden de buren al zijn vertrokken?
Do you think the neighbors have already left?

News reports

The conditional in the past tense is often used in news reports. It indicates that the reporter doesn't know if what happened is actually true or just a rumor. He or she is reporting what he/she has heard.

Bij de aanslag zouden vier mensen om het leven gekomen zijn.
Four people are believed to have died in the attack.

De bankrovers zouden in een zwarte Mercedes op de vlucht zijn geslagen.
The bank robbers are believed to have fled in a black Mercedes.

8.3 The passive

Passive sentences are used when the emphasis lies more on the action of the statement than on the agent.

Deze huizen zijn in 1965 gebouwd.
These houses were built in 1965.

De patiënt wordt morgen geopereerd.
The patient will have surgery tomorrow.

Gisteren werd de nieuwe bibliotheek geopend.
The new library was opened yesterday.

If the agent of such actions is of special importance, a construction with **door** 'by' and the agent is used.

Dit huis werd in 1965 door de bekende architect Ger Roelofs ontworpen.
This house was designed in 1965 by the well-known architect Ger Roelofs.

De patiënt wordt morgen door dokter van Balen geopereerd.
The patient will be operated by doctor van Balen tomorrow.

Gisteren werd de nieuwe bibliotheek door de burgemeester geopend.
Yesterday, the new library was opened by the mayor.

The form of the passive in present tense is made with the helping verb **worden** 'become' and the past participle of the main verb (called the passive participle) at the end of the sentence.

Klompen worden niet meer met de hand gemaakt.
Clogs are not made by hand anymore.

De koeien worden elke morgen gemolken.
The cows are milked every morning.

De krant wordt bij ons heel vroeg in de morgen bezorgd.
Our paper is delivered very early in the morning.

To make the passive form in the simple past (imperfect), one puts the helping verb **worden** in the simple past.

De voorzitter werd gevraagd, het woord te doen.
The chairman was asked to do the honors.

De pannenkoeken werden binnen een half uur opgegeten.
The pancakes were eaten within a half-hour.

Het voorstel werd meteen aangenomen.
The proposal was accepted right away.

The present and past perfect of the passive form is made with the helping verb **zijn** 'to be.'

De auto is gerepareerd.
The car is fixed.

Deze trui is met angorawol gebreid.
The sweater was knitted with angora wool.

De politie ontdekte dat de safe opengebroken was.
The police discovered that the safe had been broken into.

Het huis was al verkocht voordat de advertentie in de krant verscheen.
The house had been sold before the ad appeared in the paper.

In the examples above, the object of the action has emphasis, and so the object becomes the *subject* of the passive sentence. When, however, the object of the action is indefinite, or when the action doesn't have an explicit object, the passive sentence begins with **er** (sometimes **hier** or **daar**), and the indefinite subject follows the verb or other sentence parts. In the following examples, the indefinite subject appears in italics.

Er werd dit jaar *meer vuurwerk* verkocht dan vorig jaar.
This year, more fireworks were sold than last year.

Er wordt in onze straat *een Chinees restaurant* geopend.
They are opening a Chinese restaurant in our street.

Often, there is no object to the action at all. What matters is only the action itself. Note that many other sentence parts can stand between the passive helping verb and the passive participle at the end of the sentence.

Er werd gedanst en gedronken.
There was dancing and drinking.

Er werd de hele avond op het feest gedanst en gedronken.
They danced and drank the whole evening at the party.

When the sentence has a modal or auxiliary verb, this verb is the finite verb, in second place, and the passive verb **worden** goes to the end of the sentence, where it can appear on either side of the passive participle.

Deze kleren moeten gewassen worden/worden gewassen.
These clothes need to be washed.

In dit gebouw mag niet gerookt worden/worden gerookt.
Smoking is prohibited in this building.

Na 12 uur kan de scriptie niet meer ingeleverd worden/worden ingeleverd.
After 12 noon, the paper cannot be handed in anymore.

Note that the auxiliary verb **zullen** is used to make the future form of the passive as well as the conditional with **zou**.

> **De nieuwe treinen zullen volgend jaar in gebruik worden genomen/genomen worden.**
> They will start using the new trains next year.

> **Ik zou graag door de baas zelf worden geholpen/geholpen worden.**
> I would like to be served by the boss himself.

▶ For more on the conditional, see **8.2**.

When passive sentences appear with subordinating conjunctions, either the passive participle or the helping passive verb can be at the end of the sentence.

> **Karel vertelde dat zijn moeder gisteren is geopereerd/geopereerd is.**
> Karel said that his mother had surgery yesterday.

> **Nienke vroeg waarom de kerstboom pas morgen versierd wordt/wordt versierd.**
> Nienke asked why the Christmas tree won't be decorated until tomorrow.

> **Terwijl de verdachte verhoord werd/werd verhoord, maakte een agent proces-verbaal op.**
> While the suspect was interrogated, an officer drew up a statement.

▶ For more on subordinating conjunctions, see **9.4**.

In complex passive constructions with a modal or other auxiliary verb, the verb group at the end of the subordinated sentence can have alternative word orders as well.

> **De arts zei dat de tumor niet bestraald kon worden/kon worden bestraald.**
> The doctor said that the tumor could not be treated with radiation.

> **Denk je dat die wet zal worden aangenomen/aangenomen zal worden?**
> Do you think that law will be passed?

▶ For more on modal auxiliary verbs, see **6.2**. For more on sentence structure, see Chapter **9**.

C

Word order and sentence structure

9

Word order

9.1 Basic sentence structure

In a main sentence (Dutch **hoofdzin**), the conjugated verb takes second position. The word order for the elements after the verb consistently follows the model *time, manner, place*. When a different sentence element such as a time expression takes the first position, the subject moves to third place. This is called *inversion* of subject and verb. Examples:

> **Karin gaat vandaag met de trein naar Amsterdam.**
> Karin is going to Amsterdam by train today.

> **Vandaag gaat Karin met de trein naar Amsterdam.**
> Today, Karin is going to Amsterdam by train.

In a yes/no question and in the imperative, the verb takes first position.

> **Gaat Karin vandaag met de trein naar Amsterdam?**
> Is Karin going to Amsterdam by train today?

> **Ga vandaag maar met de trein naar Amsterdam.**
> Take the train to Amsterdam today.

► See **8.1** for more on the imperative.

Auxiliary verbs

In sentences with auxiliary verbs, the auxiliary verb (the conjugated verb) takes second place in the sentence and any other verb, infinitives, or participles, go to the end of the sentence.

> **Petra moet haar zoon van school ophalen.**
> Petra has to pick up her son from school.

> **De leerlingen hebben allemaal hun huiswerk gemaakt.**
> The students have all done their homework.

► See also **6.2** on modal auxiliary verbs. See Chapter **7** for verb tenses.

Transitive verbs

In sentences with transitive verbs (verbs that can have a direct object), the direct object is placed after the indirect object. In the following sentence, **zijn vrouw** is the indirect object.

> **Peter geeft zijn vrouw een halsketting voor haar verjaardag.**
> Peter gives his wife a necklace for her birthday.

However, when the indirect object is preceded by a preposition, it follows the direct object.

> **Peter geeft een halsketting aan zijn vrouw.**
> Peter gives his wife a necklace.

Note that when the direct object is reduced to the personal pronoun **het** 'it,' the word order is inverted. The direct object precedes the indirect object.

Ik vertel mijn zoon het verhaal. ⇒ **Ik vertel het mijn zoon.**
I tell my son the story. ⇒ I tell it to my son.

Ik geef jou het boek. ⇒ **Ik geef het jou.**
I give you the book. ⇒ I give it to you.

Overview

To summarize, a main sentence can contain six different slots. Position one and two are held by subject and verb (sometimes inverted). Position three is taken by the subject when it is not in first place or by a reflexive or object pronoun. Position four is the middle part that contains objects and elements that follow the time-manner-place rule, position five holds the verb group (infinitives, past participles), and position six has elements such as infinitive constructions with **om . . . te** or prepositional phrases.

1) Subject/Other	*2) Verb*	*3) Subject/Other*	*4) Middle*	*5) Verb group*	*6) Final*
Maarten	drinkt		altijd koffie		bij het ontbijt
	Drink	jij	graag koffie		op het werk?
Peter	geeft	mij	elke zaterdag bloemen		
Op maandag	gaat	Sylvia	met de trein naar Parijs		
Maarten	is		een week in Londen	geweest	
Simon	heeft		niet al zijn huiswerk	kunnen maken	
Nico	ging		even naar de kantine		om te eten
	Kom		vanavond lekker bij ons	kaarten	
Philip	zat		gisteren in de trein	te praten	met een man
Hij	was		heel lang met die man	aan het praten	
Hij	kan	zich	zijn naam niet	herinneren	

There is some flexibility with position six. The prepositional phrases could also be taken into the middle part. In speech, however, they are usually placed at the end, especially when they are long. Example:

Annie zat gisteren in de trein met een leuke man uit Berlijn te praten.

or

Annie zat gisteren in de trein te praten met een leuke man uit Berlijn.
Annie was talking on the train yesterday with a nice guy from Berlin.

▶ For the position of **er**, **daar**, and **hier**, see **9.9**.

9.2 Questions

In a closed question (or yes/no question), the word order of subject and verb is inverted. The sentence begins with the verb and ends with a question mark. Note that the verb in second person singular drops the **-t**.

Komt Harmen ook naar het feest?
Is Harmen also coming to the party?

Koop je die trui nou wel of niet?
Are you buying that sweater, yes or no?

In an open question, the sentence begins with a question word such as **wie** 'who,' **wat** 'what,' **waar** 'where,' **welk(e)** 'which,' **hoe** 'how,' and the order of subject and verb is inverted.

Wat is het thema van de lezing vandaag?
What is the topic of today's lecture?

Hoe kom ik het snelst aan een tweedehands fiets?
How do I get a used bike the quickest?

Note that question words formed with **waar** + preposition may be separated in the sentence. The preposition moves to the end of the sentence, except when the sentence has a modal verb and an infinitive at the end, or when the sentence is in present or past perfect.

Waaraan denk je?/Waar denk je aan?
What are you thinking about?

Waaraan wil je niet meer denken?/Waar wil je niet meer aan denken?
What is it that you don't want to think about anymore?

Waarover hebben jullie gepraat?/Waar hebben jullie over gepraat?
What did you talk about?

▶ For word order in indirect questions, see **9.5**. For interrogative pronouns, see **2.2**.

9.3 Conjunctions with coordinated sentences

Conjunctions link clauses together. Conjunctions that link main clauses together in which the conjugated verb is in second place, are **en** 'and,' **maar** 'but,' **of** 'or,' and **want** 'because.' These conjunctions take the so-called zero position.

Ik moet de was nog doen en ik wil even naar de markt.
I have yet to do the laundry and I want to go to the market.

Peter rende naar de bushalte maar de bus reed net weg.
Peter ran to the bus stop, but the bus just drove off.

Zullen we vanavond lekker thuisblijven of wil je liever uit eten?
Shall we stay in tonight or do you want to eat out?

We gaan ons huis sneller afbetalen want de rente is nu laag.
We're going to pay off our house quicker because the interest is low now.

9.4 Conjunctions with subordinated sentences

In subordinated sentences, the conjugated verb goes to the end of the sentence.

Marco zegt dat hij morgen met een nieuwe baan begint.
Marco says he's starting a new job tomorrow.

When the sentence contains an auxiliary verb, the conjugated auxiliary verb can be on either side of the infinitive of the main verb, but it is much more common to put it in front of the infinitive.

Ik bel je even omdat ik morgen niet kan komen/komen kan.
I'm calling you because I cannot come tomorrow.

Similarly, in sentences in present or past perfect, the word order of auxiliary verb and past participle can be two ways. It is more common to put the auxiliary verb before the participle.

Mam wil weten of jullie al hebben gegeten/gegeten hebben.
Mom wants to know if you have eaten already.

When the conjugated verb is part of a verb group with a series of infinitives, the conjugated auxiliary verb comes first, then a verb (sometimes more than one) that can function as an auxiliary verb and lastly the main verb, because this carries the main information.

Ik geloof dat we de piano eens moeten laten stemmen.
I believe we need to have the piano tuned.

Hij snauwde tegen me dat hij niet langer kon blijven staan wachten.
He snapped at me that he couldn't stand there waiting any longer.

When the verb in the subordinated sentence is separable, the auxiliary verb can separate the prefix from the main verb.

Vind je niet ook dat we je moeder weer eens moeten opbellen/op moeten bellen?
Don't you agree that we should call your mother again?

► See **8.3** for word order of passive sentences.

Subordinating conjunctions expressing time

als	when, if	**nadat**	after
nu	now that	**sinds**	ever since
terwijl	while, during	**toen**	when
tot/totdat	until	**voordat**	before
wanneer	when	**zodra**	as soon as
zolang	as long as		

Note the difference between **als**, **toen**, and **wanneer**. **Als** is used for events happening in the present and recurring events in the past.

Als het mooi weer is, kunnen we vandaag gaan wandelen.
When/If the weather is nice, we can go for a hike today.

Als we van school thuiskwamen, stond er altijd thee klaar.
Tea was always ready when we came home from school.

Toen is used for non-recurring, more specific, sometimes longer-lasting past events, while **wanneer** should only be used to introduce an indirect question.

Toen Peter op de basisschool zat, ging hij 's middags naar de naschoolse opvang.
When Peter was in grade school, he went to an after-school program in the afternoons.

Toen ik gisteren in de stad was, liep ik Anton tegen het lijf.
When I was in town yesterday, I ran into Anton.

Weet jij wanneer de repetities weer beginnen?
Do you know when the rehearsals start again?

Note also that sentences with **nadat** can only occur in present perfect or past perfect tense. If the sentence with **nadat** is in the present perfect, the main sentence is in the present, and the speaker is looking into the future. If it is in the past perfect, the main sentence is in the simple past, and the speaker is looking back on the past.

Nadat ik dit ontwerp afgemaakt heb, kan het naar de drukker.
After I have finished this draft, it can go to the printer.

Nadat we gegeten hadden, liepen we nog even het strand op.
After we had dinner, we walked out on the beach for a little.

Note also that **sinds** should not be confused with English 'since' in the meaning of 'because.' It is strictly a time expression.

Sinds Karin een auto heeft, gaat ze nooit meer met de bus naar kantoor.
Ever since Karin has had a car, she doesn't take the bus to the office anymore.

The other conjunctions expressing time do not pose any problems. In the following, there is an example for each.

Nu het eindelijk warm weer is, kunnen de tuinstoelen naar buiten.
Now that the weather is finally warm, the garden chairs can go outside.

Erik zit een puzzel te maken terwijl Annelies televisie kijkt.
Erik is doing a jigsaw puzzle while Annelies is watching TV.

Ik blijf op kantoor tot/totdat ik deze rekeningen afgewerkt heb.
I'm staying at the office until I have finished these bills.

Raadpleeg uw arts voordat u dit medicijn neemt.
Consult your doctor before taking this medication.

Ik kom je helpen zodra ik met deze email klaar ben.
I will come and help you as soon as I have finished this email.

Zolang je allemaal onvoldoendes haalt, kom je 's avonds de deur niet uit.
For as long as you're getting failing grades, you are not to go out in the evenings.

▶ For more on time expressions, see **4.1**, **5.4**, and **14.8**.

Subordinating conjunctions expressing cause, reason, and effect

aangezien	as, since, given that	**omdat**	because
daar	because, due to	**zodat**	in order, so that
doordat	as a result of, because of		

While **aangezien**, **daar**, and **omdat** are nearly identical in meaning (note that **omdat** is most commonly used), **doordat** gives a cause of a more instrumental or mechanical nature.

Aangezien u na drie aanmaningen nog niet heeft betaald, storneren wij uw abonnement.
Given that after three reminders you still have not paid, we cancel your subscription.

Daar er een fout in de berekening zit, kan de levering pas volgende week plaatsvinden.
Because there is an error in the calculation, the delivery can't take place until next week.

Doordat er ergens een bliksem insloeg, hadden wij drie dagen geen stroom.
Because lightning struck somewhere, we were out of power for three days.

De treinen hadden vertraging omdat het hard sneeuwde.
The trains were delayed because it snowed a lot.

Ik haal de keukenkastjes leeg zodat de werkster ze morgen kan schoonmaken.
I'm emptying the kitchen cabinets so that the cleaner can clean them tomorrow.

▶ See also **4.4** and **15.1** for talking about cause and effect.

Subordinating conjunctions expressing a condition

als	if	**indien**	if
mits	on condition that	**tenzij**	unless

Note that **als** and **indien** are identical in meaning, but **indien** is more formal. Sometimes, it is hard to distinguish between 'if' and 'when' in a sentence with **als**.

Als je met je huiswerk klaar bent, mag je nog even tv kijken.
If (When) you are finished with your homework, you may watch TV for a little bit.

Indien u van de sauna gebruik wenst te maken, kunt u zich bij de receptie aanmelden.
If you would like to use the sauna, you can register at the reception desk.

Honden zijn toegestaan in dit park, mits ze zijn aangelijnd.
Dogs are allowed in this park, on condition that they are leashed.

U kunt dit artikel binnen acht dagen ruilen, tenzij u de bon niet meer hebt.
You can exchange this item within eight days, unless you no longer have the receipt.

▶ For more on the conditional, see **8.2**. For more on expressing conditions, see **15.7**.

Subordinating conjunctions expressing contrast

hoewel, alhoewel	although	**ofschoon**	although
ondanks (dat)	despite	**terwijl**	while, even though

Note that **hoewel** and **ofschoon** are identical in meaning, but **hoewel** is more common.

Hij bleef op het perron staan, hoewel de trein het station al uitgereden was.
He stayed on the platform, even though the train had already left the station.

Ik ga met uw plan akkoord, ofschoon ik het geen goed idee vind.
I will go along with your plan, even though I don't think it is a good idea.

Ondanks (het feit) dat Nico op de VVD stemt, vind ik hem een schappelijke kerel.
Despite the fact that Nico votes liberal, I think he is a decent chap.

De auto start niet, terwijl hij nota bene net een servicebeurt gehad heeft.
The car doesn't start, even though, mind you, it was just serviced.

Subordinating conjunctions expressing comparison

alsof	as though	**even/net zo . . . als**	just as	**zoals**	(just) as

Examples:

Jij kijkt alsof je een spook hebt gezien.
You look as though you've seen a ghost.

Peter kan net zo snel schrijven als hij denkt.
Peter can write as fast as he thinks.

Zoals mijn oma appeltaart maakt, kan niemand het.
Nobody can make an apple pie the way my grandmother does.

▶ For more on comparison, see **3.2** and **14.3**.

9.5 Indirect speech

Indirect speech is used to report what someone else said or asked or to repeat one's own statement or question. In indirect speech, the conjugated verb goes to the end of the sentence. Common verbs that introduce a sentence in indirect speech, are **zeggen** 'say,' **beweren** 'maintain,' **vertellen** 'tell,' **antwoorden** 'answer,' **denken** 'think,' **vinden** 'find,' **vragen** 'ask.'

De buurman zei dat onze kat de bloemen in z'n tuin omkrabt.
The neighbor said that our cat digs up the flowers in his yard.

Martin vond dat we dat aanbod niet moeten aannemen.
Martin thought we shouldn't accept that offer.

Indirect questions are introduced with **vragen** 'ask' or with phrases such as **ik wil weten** 'I want to know,' **kunt u me vertellen** 'can you tell me,' **mag ik vragen** 'may I ask.' Questions that do not have a question word, are introduced with **of** 'whether, if.'

De klant vroeg of de auto klaar was.
The customer asked if the car was ready.

Kunt u mij vertellen waar ik de tofu kan vinden?
Can you tell me where I can find the tofu?

As explained in the beginning of **9.4**, auxiliary verbs can be on either side of the infinitive or past participle. In a sentence with multiple infinitives, auxiliary verbs are placed before the verb group at the end of the sentence. Note that auxiliary verbs can separate the prefix from a separable verb. Examples:

Anna beweert dat ze het snoep van een vriendinnetje heeft gekregen/gekregen heeft.
Anna maintains she got the candy from a friend.

De dokter zei dat ik het medicijn tweemaal per dag moet innemen/in moet nemen.
The doctor said that I have to take the medication twice a day.

Hij vroeg of hij zijn koffer even bij de balie zou kunnen laten staan.
He asked whether he could leave his suitcase at the front desk for a little.

9.6 Relative clauses

Relative clauses are subordinated clauses, and so the word order rules as explained in **9.4** apply here as well. Some examples:

Ken jij de schrijver die de AKO-literatuurprijs heeft gewonnen/gewonnen heeft?
Do you know the writer who won the AKO-literature prize?

Wat je niet kunt opeten/op kunt eten, mag je wel laten staan.
You can leave whatever you cannot eat.

Hier is een foto van het nieuwe gebouw dat morgen geopend wordt/wordt geopend.
Here is a photo of the building that will be opened tomorrow.

Again, note how a relative pronoun with **waar** + preposition is often separated in the sentence.

Hier is het artikel waarover ik je heb verteld/waar ik je over verteld heb.
Here is the article I told you about.

In sentences that have a separable verb as well as a relative pronoun with **waar** + preposition, we can have a variety in word order options if the sentence is in the present or past perfect, or if there is an auxiliary verb in the sentence. In the sentence below, both the relative pronoun and the separable verb are separated.

Heb jij zo'n kabeltje waar je foto's mee op kunt laden?
Do you have a cable with which you can upload photos?

Examples in present and past perfect:

Dit is het boek waaruit ik de klas heb voorgelezen/waar ik de klas uit voor heb gelezen.
This is the book from which I read to the class.

Er stond een taart waarvan een stuk was afgesneden/waar een stuk van af was gesneden.
There was a cake from which a piece had been cut.

► See also **2.7** for relative pronouns.

9.7 Infinitive constructions

► For verbs with an infinitive construction (with or without **te**), see **6.2** and **6.3**.

This section gives examples of constructions with two or more infinitives. While the famous sentence **Jan zou Piet wel eens hebben willen zien durven blijven staan kijken** (English 'Jan would have liked to see Piet have the courage to keep standing there, looking') is an exception, a string of three or four infinitives at the end of a sentence is not uncommon in Dutch. A construction with two infinitives, for instance, is common in the present and past perfect of sentences with modal auxiliary verbs and those that can function as such.

Ik heb Bruce Springsteen twee keer zien spelen.
I saw Bruce Springsteen play two times.

We hadden dat huis moeten kopen toen de markt gunstig was.
We should have bought that house when the market was favorable.

In sentences with **zullen** that express future tense or the conditional with **zou**, two or more infinitives are also not uncommon.

Mijn schoonouders zullen drie dagen blijven logeren.
My parents-in-law will stay three nights.

Ik zou graag willen leren schaken.
I would like to learn to play chess.

► For more on the conditional, see **8.2**. For future tense, see **7.5**.

As mentioned before, in a string of infinitives, the modal auxiliary verb (**kunnen**, **mogen**, **moeten**, **willen**, **zullen**) comes first, then a verb that can function as such (**laten**, **komen**, **gaan**, **blijven**, **zien**, **horen**, **voelen**) and finally the main verb, which carries the main information.

Zou je hier even willen blijven wachten?
Would you please (stay and) wait here?

Also, in a string of infinitives, some of the verbs with **te** + infinitive (see also **6.3**) drop the **te**. This happens in sentences with **zitten**, **staan**, **liggen**, and **durven**. Note that such sentences are difficult to translate literally into English.

Hij zal wel weer de hele avond televisie blijven zitten kijken.
He is probably going to sit and watch TV all evening.

Ik heb m'n ouders niet om geld durven vragen.
I didn't have the courage to ask my parents for money.

Na de vergadering wilde Nico nog even blijven staan praten.
After the meeting, Nico wanted to stay around and talk for a while.

A string of four infinitives is possible in conditional sentences with **zou** in combination with two modal auxiliary verbs in the present perfect.

Ik zou Jessye Norman graag eens hebben willen horen zingen.
I would have liked to hear Jessye Norman sing some time.

Ik zou niet in dat huis hebben willen blijven wonen.
I wouldn't have wanted to stay living in that house.

However, sentences in the proper past perfect with three infinitives are more common.

Ik had Jessye Norman graag eens willen horen zingen.

and

Ik had niet in dat huis willen blijven wonen.

In subordinated sentences with multiple infinitives, the rules for word order in the verb group are the same as for coordinated sentences.

Hij zei dat hij graag zou blijven eten.
He said that he'd love to stay for dinner.

De directeur vroeg of ik voor hem zou willen komen werken.
The director asked if I'd like to come and work for him.

Het is jammer dat ze de kerk niet hebben kunnen laten restaureren.
It's too bad they couldn't have the church restored.

▶ See also **6.7** for word order in durative constructions.

9.8 The position of *niet*

Generally, if a whole clause or sentence is negated, the adverb **niet** is as far to the end of the sentence as possible. If only part of a sentence is negated, it will precede the negated element. Specifically, it follows the conjugated verb, time expressions, definite objects, and the adverbs **er**, **daar**, and **hier**. Examples:

De trein komt niet.
The train isn't coming.

Het voetbalteam speelt dit weekend niet.
The soccer team isn't playing this weekend.

De studenten hebben het boek niet gelezen.
The students have not read the book.

De krant ligt er/daar/hier niet.
The paper isn't there/here.

Maria is er niet geweest.
Maria has not been there.

Niet precedes prepositional phrases, adverbs, and predicate adjectives. Examples:

De sleutels zitten niet in de tas.
The keys are not in the bag.

Het team speelde vandaag niet slecht.
The team didn't play badly today.

Ik vind deze lamp niet mooi.
I don't think this lamp is beautiful.

▶ For more on predicate adjectives, see **3.1**.

The word order is sometimes different, depending on what part of the sentence one wants to negate, and where the emphasis (in *italics*) lies.

Karin gaat *niet vandaag* naar Amsterdam, maar *morgen*.
Karin isn't going to Amsterdam today, but tomorrow.

De studenten hebben *niet het boek* gelezen, maar *wel de film* gezien.
The students have not read the book, but they have seen the film.

In a sentence with an auxiliary verb, the position of **niet** is in front of the infinitive at the end of the sentence. However, when other sentence parts are added, the rules as explained above will apply.

Johan kan niet dansen.
Johan cannot dance.

Johan kan niet goed dansen.
Johan cannot dance well.

Johan wil vanavond niet in de disco dansen.
Johan doesn't want to dance in the disco tonight.

In subordinated sentences, **niet** generally precedes the conjugated verb or the verb group at the end of the sentence. When other sentence parts are added, the rules from above apply.

Hij zegt dat de vergadering niet lang duurt.
He says the meeting will not last long.

Mijn moeder zei dat ik m'n spruitjes niet mocht laten staan.
My mother said that I couldn't leave my Brussels sprouts untouched.

Hij was te laat, omdat hij het gebouw niet had kunnen vinden.
He was late, because he couldn't find the building.

When the subordinated sentence contains one of the pronominal adverbs **er**, **hier**, or **daar** with preposition, **niet** precedes the preposition.

Ik weet dat je er liever niet over praat.
I know you'd rather not talk about it.

Hij was in z'n nopjes omdat hij er niet voor heeft betaald.
He was happy because he didn't pay for it.

▶ For more on pronominal adverbs, see **3.7**.

When the sentence begins with a verb that expresses an opinion or hope (this includes verbs such as **denken** 'think,' **vinden** 'find,' **hopen** 'hope,' **geloven** 'believe'), the position of **niet** can be either in the main sentence with that verb, or it can be in the subordinated sentence.

Ik denk niet dat de wedstrijd doorgaat.
I don't think the game is on.

Ik denk dat de wedstrijd niet doorgaat.
I think the game isn't on/I don't think the game is on.

Ik hoop niet dat de storm onze kant op komt.
I hope the storm isn't coming our way.

Ik hoop dat de storm niet onze kant op komt/onze kant niet op komt.
I hope the storm isn't coming our way.

9.9 The position of *er*, *hier*, and *daar*

Er, **hier**, and **daar** can occur at the beginning or in the middle of a sentence, depending on their function and meaning. In a main sentence, as a place indicator, **er**, **hier**, and **daar** follow the verb.

Ik heb er (hier, daar) twee jaar gewoond.
I lived there (here) for two years.

We komen er (hier, daar) bijna nooit meer.
We almost never go there anymore.

▶ For **er** as place indicator, see **3.6**.

When the above sentences are subordinated sentences, **er**, **hier**, and **daar** follow the subject.

Ik zei dat ik er (hier, daar) twee jaar heb gewoond.
I said that I lived there for two years.

Het is raar dat we er (hier, daar) bijna nooit meer komen.
It is strange that we never go there anymore.

In this function, **er** cannot be at the beginning of the sentence. However, **hier** and **daar** can.

Hier heeft Bob Dylan gewoond.
Bob Dylan lived here.

Daar was vroeger een smederij.
There used to be a forge there.

As an indicator of a quantity, the position of **er** is the same as in the examples above.

Jij denkt dat ik maar één auto heb, maar ik heb er twee.
You think I have only one car, but I have two.

Wist jij dat ik er twee heb?
Did you know I have two?

▶ For **er** as an indicator of quantity, see **3.6**.

As part of a pronominal adverb with a preposition, **er**, **hier**, and **daar** follow the verb. When the pronominal adverb is separated by other sentence parts, the preposition stands at the very end or in front of the participle or infinitive at the end of the sentence. Examples:

De leerlingen praten erover (hierover, daarover).
The students talk about it (this, that).

De leerlingen praten er (hier, daar) graag over.
The students like to talk about it.

De leerlingen hebben er (hier, daar) met de leraar over gepraat.
The students have talked about it with the teacher.

▶ For more on pronominal adverbs, see **3.7**.

When the above sentences are subordinated sentences, the pronominal adverb follows the subject. Other parts of the sentence can separate the pronominal adverb. Note that the preposition in such sentences is in front of the verb group.

De leerlingen zeggen dat ze er (hier, daar) graag over praten.
The students say that they like to talk about it (this, that).

Ik hoorde dat de leerlingen er (hier, daar) met de leraar over hebben gepraat.
I heard that the students talked about it (this, that) with the teacher.

When **er** introduces an indefinite subject (with the verb **zijn**, we call it existential **er**), or when it is used in a passive sentence, it is at the beginning of a main sentence, except when a different sentence element such as a time expression takes the first position. In a subordinated sentence, it follows the subordinating conjunction or the question word.

Er is een nieuwe jongen bij ons in de klas.
There is a new boy in our class.

Vandaag is er een stuk appeltaart bij de koffie.
Today, there is a piece of apple pie with the coffee.

Er bloeien dit jaar maar weinig crocussen.
There are not many crocuses blooming this year.

Ik vind dat er te veel suiker in m'n koffie zit.
I think there is too much sugar in my coffee.

Er wordt veel over het multiculturele vraagstuk gepraat.
There's a lot of talk about the multicultural debate.

Hij vroeg of er vanavond nog gekaart wordt.
He asked whether they are playing cards tonight.

▶ For existential **er**, see **3.6**.

D

Letters and sounds

10

Pronunciation

10.1 Vowels

Dutch has both monophthongs (single vowel sounds) and diphthongs (double vowel sounds and glides). In the vowels, we distinguish between those that are pronounced with the tongue raised (so-called high vowels) and those that are pronounced without raising the tongue (low vowels). In addition, this raising of the tongue can be in the back of the mouth (back vowels) or in the front of the mouth (front vowels). Some are pronounced with the mouth rounded as if one wants to blow, some with a wide mouth as in a smile, and some with the mouth in a more neutral position. Another important distinction is between long and short vowels. The highest and widest vowels are those that occur in words such as **niet** 'not,' **zien** 'see,' **veel** 'much,' and **peer** 'pear.' A high, rounded vowel occurs in **duur** 'expensive,' **vuur** 'fire.' Wide vowels with the tongue in neutral position occur in **gek** 'crazy,' **ijs** 'ice,' **klein** 'small.' A rounded vowel with the tongue in neutral position occurs in **deur** 'door,' **zeuren** 'nag.' Rounded vowels with the tongue raised in the back of the mouth occur in **boek** 'book,' **pot** 'pot,' and **doos** 'box.' A low vowel with the lips in neutral position and the jaw slightly lowered occurs in words such as **kat** 'cat.' To make the long version of this, the mouth is widened slightly: **kaart** 'card.' The most neutral vowel in terms of position of the mouth is the *schwa* sound that occurs in words such as ***g*e*voel*** 'feeling,' **werk*e*n** 'work,' and **b*e*stellen** 'order.' In the following, I will treat the vowels one by one and include the phonetic symbol and examples. If it is possible to give similarities to English, I will do this in the notes.

Monophthongs

Spelling	*Symbol*	*Examples*	*Notes*
a	[ɑ]	**kat** cat, **kammen** comb, **zak** bag, **lappen** rags, **zand** sand	Short a-vowel, a bit similar to English *a* in *father*, *hard*, *car*.
aa (or a in open syllable)	[a:]	**raam** window, **ramen** windows, **staan** stand, **bananen** bananas	Pronounced a little further forward than English [æ], similar to Australian English *a* in *car*.
e	[ɛ]	**bel** bell, **stem** voice, **rennen** run	Very much like *e* in English *set* and *pet*.
ee (or e in open syllable)	[e:]	**veel** much, **geven** give, **eend** duck, **spelen** play	Very similar to English *ay* as in *play*.
e	[ə]	**g*e*voel** feeling, **v*e*rtellen** tell, **b*e*lov*e*n** promise	Sounds like English *uh*. Similar to *e* in English *water*.
ij	[ə]	**lelijk** ugly, **gevaarlijk** dangerous, **moeilijk** difficult	In the suffix -lijk, -ij- sounds like *schwa*.
i	[ɪ]	**kip** chicken, **zitten** sit, **vink** finch	Very similar to English *i*.
i	[ə]	**twint*i*g** twenty, **aard*i*g** nice	This unstressed -i- is pronounced as a *schwa*.
ie	[i]	**niet** not, **ziek** sick, **hier** here	Similar to English *ea* in *beat, steep, leek*.

Spelling	*Symbol*	*Examples*	*Notes*
o	[ɔ]	**pot** pot, **hond** dog, **rokken** skirts	Very short and rounded, tongue raised in the back of the mouth. Very similar to English *o* in *port*.
oo (o in an open syllable)	[o:]	**lopen** walk, **boom** tree, **doos** box, **rozen** roses, **voor** for	Similar to *o* in English *hope*. In front of -r, similar to English *door*.
u	[œ]	**hut** hut, **punt** point, **zussen** sisters	Very similar to English *u* in *hurt* (also similar to *short* German ö).
uu (u in an open syllable)	[ʏ]	**duur** expensive, **huren** rent, **buur** neighbor	Very similar to German ü. Lips are very rounded, as if to whistle. Begin to speak an [i:], then just round the lips. Raise the tongue in the front.
y	[i]	**lobby** lobby, **baby** baby	No difference to English.
oe	[u]	**boek** book, **schoen** shoe, **poetsen** polish, **boer** farmer	Similar to English *oo* as in *foot* or *root*. Sounding slightly longer in front of an -r.
eu	[ø:]	**neus** nose, **keuken** kitchen, **leuk** nice	Very similar to French *deux* and *jeu*. Lips are rounded, tongue moves from [ə] to [ʏ].
eu	[œ:]	**deur** door, **zeuren** nag, **kleur** color	In front of an -r, pronounced like [œ] but long.

Diphthongs

Dutch makes a lot of use of diphthongs (Dutch **tweeklanken**), combinations of two (or more) vowels. The most difficult sound for speakers of English to learn is the diphthong that occurs in words such as **huis** 'house,' **ruiken** 'smell,' because it begins with the mouth in a rounded position with the jaw slightly lowered as if to say *uh*, but then the lips become more rounded and the tongue is raised to *uu* (as in **vuur**). In the following, I will give the spelling, the symbol, examples, and, if possible, an English equivalent or description. I will do the same for the diphthongs that consist of three vowels.

Spelling	*Symbol*	*Examples*	*Notes*
au	[ɑu]	**blauw** blue, **pauw** peacock, **lauw** lukewarm	Similar to English *ou* as in *mouth*.
ou	[ɑu]	**vrouw** woman, **koud** cold, **gouden** golden	Dutch -au- and -ou- are pronounced the same.
ui	[œʏ]	**huis** house, **tuin** garden, **luisteren** listen	Lips are rounded, jaw and tongue lowered a little, then lips become puckered and tongue is raised.
ei or ij	[ɛi]	**dijk** dike, **lijn** line, **schrijven** write, **klein** small, **ei** egg	Similar to English *i* as in *pike*, but sounding more as æi than as ai. Note that -ij- is treated as one letter, it has its own key on a Dutch keyboard.
oei	[ui]	**moeite** effort, **groeien** grow	The lips go from rounded to wide, so from puckered to smile. Similar to English *buoy*.
ooi	[o:i]	**mooi** beautiful, **hooi** hay, **dooien** thaw	The -o- in front of the -i- is pronounced long, as if to stretch out *oy* in English *boy*.
aai	[a:i]	**aaien** pet, **haai** shark, **graaien** grab	The -a- in front of the -i- is pronounced long, as if to stretch out *y* in English *my*.
ieu	[iʏ]	**nieuw** new, **benieuwd** curious	The lips go from very wide to very rounded. The tongue is raised.
eeu	[e:ʏ]	**sneeuw** snow, **eeuw** century	The lips go from very wide to very rounded. The tongue is in a more neutral position.

10.2 Consonants

Most Dutch consonants are similar to English, while some, for instance the **g** and **ch** in words such as **groot** 'big' and **lachen** 'laugh' are entirely unfamiliar. As with the vowels, I will discuss each consonant, examples, pronunciation, regional differences, and also combinations of consonants.

Spelling	*Symbol*	*Examples*	*Notes*
b	[b] [p]	**baan** job, **hebben** have, **heb** have	Similar to English, but [b] is voiceless [p] at the end of a word.
c	[s] [k]	**cel** cell, **cultuur** culture, **proces** process	In front of a, o, u, c, l, and r, c is pronounced [k]. In front of e and i, c is pronounced [s].
d	[d] [t]	**doel** goal, **raden** guess, **had** had	Similar to English, but [d] is voiceless [t] at the end of a word.
f	[f]	**fiets** bike, **straffen** punish	Very similar to English.
g	[x] [ɣ]	**goed** good, **berg** mountain, **zeggen** say	A guttural fricative, voiced at the beginning of words and between vowels, voiceless at the end. In Flanders and the south of the Netherlands, it is a velar voiced fricative.
g	[ʒ]	**logies** lodging, **garage** garage, **beige** beige	In certain loan words, pronounced as in French *gendarm* or *beige*.
h	[h]	**huis** house, **horen** hear, **hand** hand	Very similar to English *h* as in *house*.
j	[j]	**jurk** dress, **jammer** too bad, **jong** young	Pronounced as in English *young*.
k	[k]	**koek** cake, **kopen** buy, **taak** task	A voiceless stop, unaspirated.
l	[l]	**lopen** walk, **bal** ball, **bellen** call	Similar to English, although less thick.
m	[m]	**maand** month, **kammen** comb	Similar to English.
n	[n]	**niet** not, **winnen** win, **lint** ribbon	Similar to English.
p	[p]	**pop** doll, **klappen** clap	A voiceless stop, unaspirated.
q	[kʋ]	**quota** quota, **querulant** trouble maker	Only in loan words.
r	[r] [ʀ]	**rollen** roll, **ver** far, **sarren** tease	Either rolled or guttural (similar to French).
s	[s]	**soort** kind, sort, **samen** together, **wassen** wash	Similar to English *s* in *sort*.
t	[t]	**tafel** table, **zetten** put, **nest** nest	A voiceless stop, unaspirated.
v	[v]	**veel** much, **zeven** seven	Pronounced with more voice than [f]. Similar to English *voice*, *voodoo*.
w	[ʋ]	**wie** who, **wonen** live, **waar** where	In the Netherlands, the upper teeth lightly touch the lower lip, not as much friction as in [v]. In some southern dialects, very similar to English *w* (bilabial).
x	[ks]	**xylofoon** xylophone	Only in certain loan words.
z	[z]	**zak** bag, **razen** rage, **lezen** read	Similar to English *z* as in *zoo*.

There are some difficult combinations of two or three consonants to pay special attention to.

Spelling	*Symbol*	*Examples*	*Notes*
ch	[x] [ʃ]	**acht** eight, **lachen** laugh, **machine** machine	Just like -g-. A guttural, voiceless fricative. In French loan words, it sounds like English *sh.*
ng	[ŋ]	**lang** long, **zingen** sing, **klank** sound	Spoken as one sound, not separated as in English *hunger*, but like *singer*.
nj	[ɲ]	**franje** frills, **oranje** orange, **champagne** sparkling wine	Spoken as in French *campagne*, *champagne*
sch	[sx] [s]	**schip** ship, **school** school, **scheren** shave, **logisch** logical	At the beginning of a word, spoken like [sx], but at the end, spoken like [s], so *fantastisch* is pronounced *fantasties*.
sj, ch	[ʃ]	**sjaal** scarf, **meisje** girl, **machine** machine, **chocola** chocolate	Very similar to English *sh* as in *show*.
tj	[tʃ]	**netje** small net, **deurtje** small door	Very similar to English *h* as in *huge* (net-je) or *ch* as in *chill* (deur-tje).

10.3 Stress

In general, in words with Dutch origin, the stress (Dutch **klemtoon**) falls on the first syllable of a word.

> ***huis*werk** homework, ***ta*fel** table, ***deur*knop** doorknob, ***boe*kenkast** bookcase

However, prefixes with the unstressed vowel *schwa* [ə], do not get stress.

> **ver*tel*len** tell, **be*lo*ven** promise, **ge*weer*** gun, **er*ken*nen** recognize, **her*in*neren** remember

This is also the case in words beginning with the unstressed prefix **ont-**.

> **ont*dek*ken** discover, **ont*moe*ten** meet, **ont*hul*len** reveal

Derivations of some words with Dutch origin have the stress on the last syllable.

> ***ko*ning – koning*in*** king – queen, ***le*raar – lerar*es*** teacher – female teacher

Loan words usually have a different pattern of stress than originally Dutch words.

> **fi*guur*** figure, **frag*ment*** fragment, **bac*te*rie** bacteria, **hu*maan*** humane, **finan*ciën*** finances
> **kabi*net*** cabinet, **seri*eus*** serious, **cam*pag*ne** campaign, **sympa*thie*** sympathy

Some word derivations with suffixes such as **-ig**, **-lijk**, **-isch**, and **-baar** also have a different stress pattern. A different syllable, but not the suffix, has the stress.

> ***aan*spraak – aan*spra*kelijk** claim – responsible, ***over*daad – over*da*dig** excess – excessive
> ***al*cohol – alco*ho*lisch** alcohol – alcoholic, ***aan*tonen – aan*toon*baar** prove – tangible

Note that the stress in many Dutch words differs from their English equivalent. In the following, I give the Dutch spelling first and then the English spelling, with the stress in italics.

> **con*cert*** *con*cert, **intelli*gent*** in*tel*ligent, **tele*foon*** *tele*phone, **mu*ziek*** *mu*sic,
> **sta*tion*** *sta*tion, **cul*tuur*** *cul*ture, **ca*ta*logus** *ca*talogue, **cata*stro*fe** ca*ta*strophe

For speakers of English, it is tempting to pronounce these cognates the English way, but do watch where the stress lies in Dutch.

11

Spelling

11.1 Closed and open syllables

Words are divided in syllables. Each syllable must contain a vowel. When a syllable ends in one or more consonants, we call it a closed syllable. For example, **kat** 'cat' and **dorst** 'thirst' are one syllable words, but the word **kattenbak** 'litterbox' has three syllables: **kat.ten.bak**. All of these are closed syllables. Open syllables, on the other hand, end in a vowel. Short words such as **zo** 'so,' **na** 'after,' and **mee** 'with' are one syllable words with an open syllable. Words such as **zo.ge.naamd** 'so-called,' **na.den.ken** 'ponder,' **mee.ne.men** 'take with' are longer words with open syllables.

We separate syllables between two of the same consonants or two different consonants.

> **kat.ten** cats, **bel.len** bells, **leg.gen** lay, **man.den** baskets, **dor.pen** villages, **fiet.sen** bike(s)

When there are more than two consonants, the consonants that form the beginning of a new word will go to the next syllable:

> **af.spre.ken** make an appointment, **deur.knop** doorknob, **op.schie.ten** hurry up

In derivations, prefixes and suffixes are separated from their ground word. However, when the suffix ends in a vowel (such as **-es**, **-aar**, **-in**, **-ig**), the syllable begins with a consonant.

> **ge.vaar.lijk** dangerous, **ver.trek.ken** depart, **boek.je** little book, **le.ra.res** female teacher, **moor.de.naar** murderer, **e.ze.lin** female donkey, **aar.dig** nice

Note that a syllable can never end in a double consonant or a double vowel. For instance, syllables ending in **-tt**, **-pp** or **-aa** are impossible. Exceptions are a few words that end in double **ee**: **twee** 'two,' **ree** 'deer,' **mee** 'with,' **zee** 'sea.'

Knowing the difference between open and closed syllables is important in pronunciation and in applying grammar rules. Single vowels in closed syllables, for instance, are pronounced short.

> **man** man, **kip** chicken, **bus** bus, **pop** doll, **hek** gate

When, for instance, the plural ending **-en** is added, the consonant at the end of the syllable must be doubled to ensure that the syllable remains closed and the vowel short.

> **man.nen** men, **kip.pen** chickens, **bus.sen** buses, **pop.pen** dolls, **hek.ken** gates

Similarly, in adjectives, when we add an adjective ending to a syllable with a short vowel, we double the consonant.

> **dik – dik.ke** fat, **net – net.te** neat, **los – los.se** loose, **ka.pot – kapot.te** broken

Double vowels in closed syllables are pronounced long.

> **maan** moon, **bier** beer, **vuur** fire, **doos** box, **veel** much

However, when we add a plural or adjective ending to a syllable with the double vowel, we drop one vowel and the syllable opens. The single vowel in the open syllable is pronounced long.

maan – ma.nen moon, **groot – gro.te** big, **duur – du.re** expensive,
steen – ste.nen stone

Notice the difference in verb stems with short vowels (closed syllable) and those with long vowels (open syllable). Verbs with short vowels drop one consonant in singular, and verbs with long vowels double the vowel in singular. Examples for first-person singular and plural:

	zitten	*leggen*	*bakken*	*praten*	*nemen*	*lopen*
singular 1st	zit	leg	bak	praat	neem	loop
plural 1st	zitten	leggen	bakken	praten	nemen	lopen

Note that the letters **v** and **z** become voiceless at the end of a syllable and in front of another consonant. So in verbs that have these consonants in the stem, **v** becomes **f** in singular, and **z** becomes **s**.

	schrijven	*leven*	*graven*	*lezen*	*reizen*	*wijzen*
singular 1st	schrijf	leef	graaf	lees	reis	wijs
plural 1st	schrijven	leven	graven	lezen	reizen	wijzen

When these voiceless consonants appear at the end of an adjective or a noun with a long vowel, they are voiced when the adjective or plural ending is added, because the ending adds a new syllable.

grijs – grijze grey, **stijf – stijve** stiff, **gaaf – gave** intact, **doos – dozen** box(es),
huis – huizen house(s), **druif – druiven** grape(s)

The change does not happen, however, in nouns that end in **-ps**, **-ts** and **-ks** and those that end in **-graaf** or **-soof**. Some examples:

fiets – fietsen bike(s), **heks – heksen** witch(es), **rups – rupsen** caterpillar(s),
filosoof – filosofen philospher(s), **fotograaf – fotografen** photographer(s)

Other nouns in which the change does not happen are **de mens** 'person,' **het kruis** 'cross,' **de eis** 'demand,' and **de dans** 'dance.'

11.2 Accents

Acute

Dutch uses the acute accent (accent aigu) in French loan words that have not been "dutchified" (Dutch **vernederlandst**) such as **café** 'café,' **coupé** 'train compartment,' **logé** 'overnight guest,' **paté** 'pate' to indicate that the **e** is pronounced long rather than as an unstressed *schwa*. Note that diminutives of such words drop the accent: **cafeetje**, **coupeetje**, **logeetje**.

▶ See **1.5** for more information on the diminutive.

We also put the acute accent over vowels in words that we want to give particular emphasis in a sentence. Note that when the word has two vowels, we put an accent on each.

Die jas is véél te duur.
That coat is *much* too expensive.

Ik wil dat je nú je kamer opruimt.
I want you to clean up your room *now*.

The accent is also used to distinguish between the indefinite article **een** [ən] 'a' and the number **één** [e:n] 'one.'

> **Je mag een koekje nemen.**
> You may take a biscuit.
>
> **Je mag één koekje nemen.**
> You may take one biscuit.

To distinguish between **voor** for and **vóór** in front of, we also use the acute accent.

> **De jongen vóór me in de bus stond op voor een oudere dame.**
> The boy in front of me in the bus got up for an elderly lady.

Grave

The grave accent is used for French loan words that have not been "dutchified" and in which the accent is used for pronunciation, i.e., to distinguish it from [e] or [ə]. Examples of such words are **scène** 'scene,' **première** 'premiere,' **etagère** 'cabinet,' **carrière** 'career.' This accent is also used on the word **à** in the phrases such as **twee à drie dagen** 'about two or three days.' Finally, it is used on the word **hè** [hɛ] to distinguish it from **hé** [he]. It can mean something like 'don't you agree?' or express annoyance such as 'oh no' or 'shoot,' 'darn,' or 'geez.' Examples:

> **Wat was dat een leuke film, hè?**
> That was a nice film, wasn't it?
>
> **Hè, wat laat het eten weer lang op zich wachten.**
> Man, the food is taking forever again.

Circumflex

This accent (Dutch **dakje**) is only used sporadically. It appears on **e** in some French loan words and occasionally on other vowels. Some common words with an accent circumflex are **enquête** 'survey,' **gêne** 'embarrassment,' **gênant** 'embarrassing,' **crêpe** 'crepe,' **fêteren** 'celebrate,' **maîtresse** 'mistress.'

Dieresis

In derivatives, we use a dieresis or Dutch **trema** to indicate where two vowels that are normally pronounced as one need to be separated in pronunciation, i.e., to distinguish it from a long vowel or diphthong. The dieresis is placed on the vowel with which the next syllable starts. Examples:

> ee – **tweeëntwintig** twenty two, **met ons drieën** three of us, **geëngageerd** engaged
> ei – **geïnteresseerd** interested, **beïnvloeden** influence
> eu – **reünie** reunion, **geüniformeerd** in uniform
> ie – **België** Belgium, **financiën** finances, **patiënt** patient
> oo – **coördinator** coordinator, **coöperatie** cooperation, **zoölogie** zoology
> oe – **poëzie** poetry
> oi – **egoïst** egoist, **taoïsme** Taoism
> ui – **ruïne** ruin, **druïde** druid, **continuïteit** continuity

When confusion about the pronunciation is not possible, for example in words such as **chaos** 'chaos,' **geadresseerd** 'addressed,' **eventueel** 'eventual,' a trema is not needed. Also, French words on **-ien** or **-ienne** do not have a trema: **electricien** 'electrician,' **comédienne** 'female comedian.' Finally, words with a completely foreign origin that keep their old spelling, do not need a trema, for example **museum** and **paella**. Many of these are from Latin origin. Note also that in some cases, recent spelling rules have replaced the dieresis with a hyphen: **zo-even** 'just now,' **mee-eten** 'join for dinner.' When in doubt, check a dictionary or the woordenlijst.nl for correct spelling.

Hyphen

The **koppelteken** or hyphen, on the other hand, is used when, in a compound word, two vowels need to be pronounced separately:

> **na-apen** mimic, **auto-ongeluk** car accident, **gala-avond** gala evening, **garage-eigenares** garage owner

Also words with prefixes of Latin or Greek origin such as **anti-**, **bi-**, **co-**, **duo-**, **loco-**, **micro-**, **neo-**, **pro-**, **re-**, **semi-**, **ultra-**, and **vice-** get a hyphen when combined with a word that starts with a vowel that could cause confusion in pronunciation. Examples:

> **co-ouder** co-parent, **de-escaleren** de-escalate

In compound words with **adjunct-**, **aspirant-**, **assistent-**, **bijna-**, **chef-**, **ex-**, **collega-**, **interim-**, **kandidaat-**, **leerling-**, **meester-**, **niet-**, **non-**, **oud-**, **stagiair-**, or **substituut-**, we also use a hyphen.

> **leerling-verpleger** student nurse, **kandidaat-notaris** notary candidate, **niet-roker** non-smoker, **oud-burgemeester** former mayor, **chef-kok** chef

Hyphens are also used as a mark of ellipsis when listing multiple compound nouns that share a component.

> **de voor- en nadelen** pros and cons, **een dag-, week- en een maandblad** a daily, weekly, and monthly paper

Also, derivatives with the suffix **-achtig** are hyphenated when the ground word ends in **-a**:

> **lila-achtig** like lilac, **opera-achtig** like an opera

Geographical names and their adjectives are also hyphenated.

> **Zuid-Holland** South Holland, **Noord-Brabant** North Brabant, **Centraal-Aziatisch** Central Asian, **trans-Europees** trans-European

In compound words with letters and digits, we also use hyphens.

> **tbc-patiënt** tuberculosis patient, **VWO-examen** VWO exam, **1-0-overwinning** 1-0 victory

Finally, hyphens are used in some fixed expressions.

> **kant-en-klaar** ready-made, **huis-tuin-en-keuken** simple, everyday, **twee-onder-een-kap** duplex

Apostrophe

The apostrophe is used in words where a letter is omitted. We often see this in pronouns.

> **'k = ik** I, **'t = het** it, **'n = een** a, **m'n = mijn** my, **z'n = zijn** his, **d'r = haar** her, **zo'n = zo een** such a, **'s morgens = des morgens** (old genitive case) in the morning, **'s winters** in winter

Next, it is used to indicate possession in names or words that end in **a**, **o**, **u**, **I**, and **y**. When a name ends in **-s**, we put an apostrophe after the **-s**. Similarly, the plural ending for nouns that end in **a**, **o**, **u**, **i**, and **y** is apostrophe **-s**.

> **Opa's sigarendoos** grandpa's cigar box, **Otto's kamer** Otto's room, **Harry's vrouw** Harry's wife, **Tini's nieuwe baan** Tini's new job, **Hans' fiets** Hans's bike, **auto's** cars, **parka's** parkas, **paraplu's** umbrellas, **taxi's** taxis, **baby's** babies.

11.3 Capital letters

The use of capital letters in Dutch is similar to English, but there are some notable differences to pay attention to. As in English, we use a capital letter to begin every new sentence; at the beginning of a text, after periods, question marks and exclamation marks, and in direct speech after a colon.

> **De man vroeg: "Waar kan ik hier een geldautomaat vinden?"**
> The man asked: "Where can I find a cash machine here?"

When the sentence begins with a word that is abbreviated with an apostrophe as explained in **11.2**, the next word is capitalized.

> **'s Winters is dit dorp uitgestorven.**
> In winter, this village is a ghost town.

> **'t Is merkwaardig dat Joost niet is komen opdagen.**
> It is strange that Joost hasn't shown up.

The first sentence in a letter also begins with a capital letter.

> **Beste Jan,**
> **We willen je graag voor een etentje uitnodigen.**
> Dear Jan,
> We want to invite you to a dinner party.

First and last names have capital letters. In names with **van**, **de(r/n)** and combinations thereof, these words are written in small letters (except in Flanders, where they are sometimes written with capital letters), unless the first name or the initials are not mentioned. The same rule applies to names of companies, organizations and institutions.

> **Karin van der Meer, Hans de Groot, mevrouw Van Vliet.**
> Karin van der Meer, Hans de Groot, Mrs. Van Vliet.

> **Ik praatte gisteren met De Bruyn.**
> I talked to De Bruyn yesterday.

> **De Nederlandse Taalunie ondersteunt het onderwijs Nederlands in het buitenland.**
> The Nederlandse Taalunie supports the teaching of Dutch abroad.

> **Ik ben al jaren klant bij de Rabobank.**
> I have been a customer with Rabobank for years.

Finally, geographical names and their derived nouns and adjectives have capital letters.

> **Ik kom uit Nederland, ben dus een Nederlander en spreek Nederlands.**
> I come from the Netherlands, so I am Dutch and I speak Dutch.

> **We maakten een tochtje op de Amsterdamse grachten.**
> We took a trip on the canals of Amsterdam.

> **Ik kocht een stukje Leidse kaas.**
> I bought a piece of cheese from Leiden.

Note that the names of the week days, the names of the months, the words for measures and weights, and also titles are not capitalized in Dutch.

> **Ik heb op maandag 5 februari een afspraak met de tandarts.**
> I have an appointment with the dentist on Monday, February 5.

> **Mijn kinderen rijden 15 km naar school.**
> My kids ride 15 kilometers to school.

> **Zou ik even met dr. Wolters kunnen spreken?**
> Could I speak with Dr. Wolters?

11.4 Comma

In Dutch, we place a comma when we address a person in a letter or in speech.

Geachte mevrouw De Boer,
Dear Mrs. De Boer,

Margo, heb jij mijn leesbril ergens gezien?
Margo, have you seen my reading glasses somewhere?

Leuk hè, Tommie?
Nice, isn't it, Tommie?

We place a comma between adjectives of equal value. Note that the comma may be dropped when there are only two adjectives preceding the noun. There is no comma before **en** 'and.' This is the same in summing up a string of objects.

een mooi oud huis
a beautiful old house

een lelijke, oude, stinkende schoen
an ugly, old, stinking shoe

voor slap, droog en futloos haar
for frail, dry, and washed-out hair

Er lagen druiven, bananen, sinasappels en noten in de fruitschaal.
There were grapes, bananas, oranges, and nuts in the fruit bowl.

We use a comma in appositions and subordinated sentences that expand on an antecedent.

Karel, de man van Bella, hield een leuke toespraak.
Karel, Bella's husband, gave a nice speech.

De leerlingen, die te laat waren, moesten een briefje halen.
The students, who were late, had to get a note.

However, before a limiting relative sentence beginning with **die** or **dat**, we don't use a comma.

De huizen die al jaren leegstonden, werden afgebroken.
The houses that had been vacant for years were torn down.

Het brood dat oud was gaven we aan de eenden.
The bread that was old we fed to the ducks.

A sub-clause that precedes a coordinated sentence is followed by a comma. The comma separates the two verbs.

Als je vanavond tijd hebt, kom dan even langs.
If you have time tonight, then stop by for a minute.

Voordat u het medicijn afhaalt, kunt u het beste bellen of het klaar is.
Before you pick up the medication, it is best to call us to see if it is ready.

Most of the time, sentences with subordinating conjunctions that follow a main sentence, are also separated by a comma.

Hij werd niet geholpen, hoewel hij een uur in de rij had gestaan.
He wasn't helped, even though he had been standing in line for an hour.

Karin liet de hond uit, terwijl Joop alvast met het eten begon.
Karin walked the dog while Joop began cooking dinner.

De trein had enkele uren vertraging, doordat er sneeuw op de rails lag.
The train was delayed by a few hours because there was snow on the tracks.

However, when the main sentence is short and flows into the subordinated sentence without a clear pause, we omit the comma.

Ik ga niet mee omdat ik hier nog wat werk te doen heb.
I'm not coming because I still have some work to do here.

We blijven thuis als het regent.
We'll stay at home if it rains.

Also, we don't put a comma before the conjunction **dat** 'that.'

Ik weet zeker dat ik die dossiers hier neergelegd heb.
I am sure I put those dossiers here.

Je gaat me toch niet vertellen dat je vrijdag niet meegaat.
You're not going to tell me that you are not going with us on Friday.

In English, particles such as 'however' and 'unfortunately' are separated with commas. In Dutch, they are not.

De soep was goed, het hoofdgerecht was echter te zout.
The soup was good. The main course, however, was too salty.

Deze broek is helaas uitverkocht.
Unfortunately, these pants are sold out.

In American English, adverbial expressions of time, manner and place at the beginning of a sentence are followed by a comma. In Dutch and British English, they are not.

Volgende week gaan we met de renovatie van ons huis beginnen.
Next week, we will start renovating our house.

In Parijs kun je heerlijke restaurantjes vinden.
In Paris, you can find delicious little restaurants.

Met de bus kom je veel sneller naar je werk.
By bus, you get to work much faster.

Part II

Functions in context

12

Social contact

12.1 Formal or informal: *u* or *je/jij*?

To address a person, speakers of Dutch use the pronoun **je** (emphasized **jij**) or **u**, depending on whether the situation is informal or formal. Generally they, in informal situations, they use **je/jij**, and in formal situations, the appropriate form is **u**. Age and status, and to a lesser extent gender and religion, play an important part in the decision whether the situation is formal or informal. **U** is an expression of respect and distance, while **je/jij** is all about solidarity and familiarity. Nevertheless, it is impossible to give exact rules for using **u** or **je/jij**. The choice depends a lot on one's relationship with the person addressed and on the situation. Regional differences also come into play.

The uses of *je/jij* and *u*

Informal **jij** and **je** are used when one speaks to a person whom one addresses by their first name. This includes relatives, close friends, and colleagues at work, especially among white-collar workers, where it is not uncommon to address one's direct supervisor by her/his first name. Note that the unstressed form **je** is much more widely used than emphasized **jij**, which is used primarily to express contrast with another word in the sentence (in italics).

> **Erik, kun je me even met deze kratjes bier helpen?**
> Erik, can you help me with these cases of beer?
>
> **Karin, heb je die offerte van Buisman al ontvangen?**
> Karin, have you received that bid from Buisman yet?
>
> **Doe *jij* vandaag de boodschappen of zal *ik* het maar even doen?**
> Are you doing the groceries today, or shall I just do it?

Jij or **je** are also used to address children and young people up to about 20 years old. Among each other, young people also use informal **jij** and **je**, even when they don't know each other.

> **Wat doe je hier? Waar is je moeder?**
> What are you doing here? Where is your mother?
>
> **Hé, weet jij misschien waar ik een geldautomaat kan vinden?**
> Hey, do you know where I might find an ATM?

Most of the time, children use informal **je** and **jij** to address their parents, grandparents, aunts, and uncles. In older generations, **u** is still used for aunts and uncles, but in younger generations, this is slowly disappearing. Young people who address their aunts and uncles with **je/jij** now will still do that when they are older.

> **Mama, kom je naast me zitten?**
> Mom, will you sit next to me?
>
> **Opa, kan je dit even voor me openmaken?**
> Grandpa, can you open this for me?

Service

In shops, banks, restaurants or when interacting with someone whose role it is to serve or assist (and that person is the same age or older), speakers of Dutch commonly use formal **u**, but young people (if both the customer and the person assisting are young) also use informal **je**.

> **Heeft u deze schoenen nog in maat 41?**
> Do you still have these shoes in size 41?
>
> **Kunt u hier even uw handtekening zetten?**
> Could you sign here, please?
>
> **Dag, kan ik je helpen? Wil je die jurk even passen?**
> Hi, can I help you? Would you like to try that dress on?
>
> **Mag ik nog een biertje van je?**
> Would you get me another beer?

School

In school, at the elementary level, pupils address their teachers with **juffrouw** or **juf** and **meester**, often followed by the teacher's first name: **juf Maaike** or **meester Wim**. The personal pronoun is therefore always **u**. At the secondary level, pupils use **mevrouw** and **meneer**, followed by the teacher's last name. Here, they also use the formal **u**. However, a young teacher might offer his teenage pupils the more informal **je** and **jij**, but this is certainly not the rule. In the north of the Netherlands, children often address their teachers in the third person, thus bypassing the choice between **je** and **u** and avoiding awkwardness.

> **Gaat juf ook mee op schoolreisje?**
> Is miss (name) also coming on the field trip?

At the post-secondary level, students address their professors with **u**. However, when there is not a huge difference in age between student and teacher, and if the teacher is a **docent** or **wetenschappelijk medewerker** (non-professorial staff), it is not uncommon to use informal **jij** and **je**.

> **Professor Visser, kunt u mij een datum voor het herexamen geven?**
> Professor Visser, can you give me a date for the makeup exam?
>
> **Karel, heb je die tests al nagekeken?**
> Karel, have you graded those tests yet?

The formal address pronoun **u** creates distance. It is used mostly in situations where age difference and difference in status or rank demand a certain respect or formality. The Dutch use **u**, therefore, when they address someone with **mevrouw** or **meneer**:

> **Pardon, meneer, bent u hier bekend?**
> Excuse me, sir, are you familiar here?

When one talks to someone in their professional or official function, one uses **u**:

> **Voorzitter, wilt u de vergadering openen?**
> Mister chairman, would you open the meeting?
>
> **Dokter De Bruyn, kunt u even naar zaal 2 komen?**
> Doctor De Bruyn, can you come to room 2?

Most of the time, if one is uncertain, it is appropriate to use **u** and wait until one is offered the **je/jij**. This usually happens with a variety of possible forms:

> **Zullen we elkaar tutoyeren?**
> Shall we say 'je' and 'jij' to each other?

Zeg maar je en jij hoor.
Please do say 'je' and 'jij' to me.

Zeg maar gewoon 'Kees' tegen me hoor.
Please just call me 'Kees.'

Changes in society have made the Dutch more informal. Just as **meneer** (sir, Mr.) and **mevrouw** (madam, Mrs.) have given way to the use of first names, **u** has less and less to do with age but more with distance and respectability. And while **je/jij** is used to express intimacy and familiarity, in contemporary Dutch it has more to do with equality and solidarity. However, one thing is sure: **u** is not out. In sum therefore, it is best to use **u** until one is offered the **je/jij**.

In the Flemish speaking part of Belgium, there is a distinction between **ge** (emphasized **gij**) and **u**. In informal situations, they use **ge** and **gij**, and **u** is for formal situations.

▶ For more information on personal pronouns, see **2.1**.

12.2 Greeting someone and conveying greetings

Greeting

To initiate social contact, speakers of Dutch use different forms of greetings (noun **de groet**, verb **groeten**) that often depend on the situation, the time of day, and the age and social standing of the people involved. In daily interactions in places such as school, the workplace, the neighborhood, the family, and services, it is common courtesy to greet someone one way or the other.

Formally, they greet someone with the form that is appropriate for the time of day:

Goedemorgen Good morning
Goedemiddag Good afternoon
Goedenavond Good evening

There are neutral standard forms that can be used throughout the day to greet acquaintances as well as strangers in all circumstances.

Dag (also **Daag**) Good day
Goede(n)dag (informal spelling: **Goeie(n)dag**) Good day

Informally, among friends, colleagues, and young people especially, people greet each other with the following most common forms:

Hallo hello
Hoi hi
Hé, Ha (very informal) Hey

Greetings are rituals that are culture-bound and regionally different. In the anonymity of the city, people on the street generally don't greet each other. But in the country, and in neighborhoods and small villages where one knows one another, people exchange informal pleasantries such as **Hallo** or **Goedemorgen**, often in the short form **Morgen**. In the same way, **Middag** might be short for **Goedemiddag** and **'n Avond** is short for **Goedenavond**.

Passing on greetings

In speech, there are a few different formal and informal ways in which speakers of Dutch pass on greetings (Dutch **de groeten doen**) through a third person.

De groeten aan je ouders.
Best wishes to your parents.

Doe de groeten aan Peter.
Say hello to Peter.

Wil je hem/haar van mij de groeten doen?
Would you say hello to him/her from me?

Groet je man van me.
Say hi to your husband for me.

Doet u uw man de hartelijke groeten (formal).
Give your husband my best regards.

Some appropriate ways to respond to someone's request to pass on greetings are:

Zal ik doen/Dat zal ik doen.
Will do.

Natuurlijk. Jij ook de groeten aan Mark.
Of course. And you say hello to Mark for me.

Dat doe ik graag.
I'll gladly do that.

Ja!/Jazeker.
You bet.

Ja hoor! Doe ik.
Of course I will.

When passing on someone else's formal or informal greetings, one can say:

De groeten van mijn ouders.
My parents say hello.

Je krijgt de groeten van Peter.
Peter says hi.

Ik moet je de groeten doen van Lies.
Lies asks me to say hello.

U krijgt de hartelijke groeten van professor Jansen (formal).
Professor Jansen sends kind regards.

A rather odd way to use **de groeten** is to express to someone that you absolutely don't like or don't want to do what that person suggests.

Hé Peter, ik ga even met de hond wandelen. Ga je mee?
Hey Peter, I'm going to go for a walk with the dog. Want to go?

Wandelen in dit weer? Ja zeg, de groeten.
Walk in this weather? Thanks but no thanks.

▶ For more information on declining requests and suggestions, see **16.8**.

Greeting in writing

In informal writing, such as a postcard or an informal email or letter, greetings such as the following are used:

Hartelijke groeten/Hartelijks van Kees en Nina.
Best wishes from Kees and Nina.

Groeten uit Davos!
Greetings from Davos!

Groetjes, (informal)
Cheers,

Liefs/Veel liefs, (between good friends, family members, in love relationships)
With love,

In more formal letters such as letters of application or business correspondence or any situation where formal speech is appropriate, one must use:

Met vriendelijke groet (abbreviated: **mvg**)/**Groeten** (more common in Flanders)
With kind regards,

Groet,
Greetings,

Hoogachtend,
Sincerely,

► See also **13.10** for more information about writing letters.

12.3 Introducing yourself and others

Asking for someone's name

Common formal (**u**) and informal (**je, jij**) questions to ask what someone's name is, are as follows.

Wat is uw/je naam? Wat is uw/je voornaam/achternaam/meisjesnaam?
What is your name? What is your first name/last name/maiden name?

Hoe heet u?/Hoe heet je?
What's your name?

Hoe was uw/de naam ook alweer?
And what was your name again?

Bent u mevrouw Achterberg?/Ben jij Martijn?/En wie ben *jij*?
Are you Mrs. Achterberg?/Are you Martijn?/And who are *you*?

► To ask for exact spelling, see **13.3**.

Geboortenaam versus *meisjesnaam*

Since the legalization of gay marriage, it is not uncommon for men to take their partner's name. Because it is embarrassing and inappropriate to ask a man for his **meisjesnaam**, the Nederlandse Taalunie has suggested using the gender neutral term **geboortenaam** 'birth name' instead.

Introducing oneself

People introduce themselves (**zich voorstellen**) by their first and last name, sometimes only the last name in a formal situation. This introduction is always accompanied by a handshake. Common verbs for informal introductions are **heten** 'to be called' and **zijn** 'to be.'

Mag ik me even voorstellen? Mijn naam is Kees Barends.
May I introduce myself? My name is Kees Barends.

Dag, Joop Admiraal.
Hi, Joop Admiraal.

Dag, Vanderwaal is de naam.
Hi, my name is Vanderwaal.

Miranda Eldersma.
Miranda Eldersma.

Van Heusden.
Van Heusden.

Hoi, ik ben Mirjam Wiersma.
Hi, I'm Mirjam Wiersma.

Dag, ik heet Lies.
Hi, my name is Lies.

Hallo, Arie Vermeer.
Hello, (I'm) Arie Vermeer.

Ik ben Ina. Mijn achternaam is Brinkman.
I'm Ina. My last name is Brinkman.

▶ For information on introducing oneself on the telephone, see **13.9**.

Introducing others

To introduce two people in a formal situation, one can say:

Dit is Lara Andersen.
This is Lara Andersen.

Mag ik u Lara Andersen voorstellen?
May I introduce to you Lara Andersen?

Mevrouw De Boer, kent u mevrouw Andersen?
Mrs. De Boer, do you know Mrs. Andersen?

Meneer Huisman, heeft u al met meneer Schippers kennisgemaakt?
Mr. Huisman, have you met Mr. Schippers?

To introduce a friend, a relative, an acquaintance, or a colleague in an informal setting, the following phrases are appropriate:

Dit is mijn man Gerard.
This is my husband Gerard.

Dit is Jonas, m'n oudste.
This is Jonas, my oldest (son).

Mag ik je mijn collega Simon voorstellen?
May I introduce my colleague Simon?

Kennen jullie elkaar? Dit is …
Do you know each other? This is …

Zij heet Jasperina, maar iedereen noemt haar Pien.
Her name is Jasperina, but everyone calls her Pien.

Formal responses to someone who is introducing him/herself to you are:

Prettig met u/je kennis te maken.
Nice to meet you.

Aangenaam kennis te maken/Aangenaam.
It's a pleasure to meet you/It's a pleasure.

An informal response is:

Leuk je te ontmoeten.
Nice to meet you.

The verb **ontmoeten**, as in the last example above, is used in the context of meeting someone for the first time. Other options are **tegenkomen**, **leren kennen**, while **kennen** is used when one has known a person for a longer time.

Hoe hebben jullie elkaar ontmoet?
How did you meet?

Wij zijn elkaar op een feest bij Chris tegengekomen.
We met at a party at Chris's.

Ik heb Johanna op de middelbare school leren kennen.
I met Johanna in high school.

Hoe lang kennen jullie elkaar al?
How long have you known each other?

Note that **tegenkomen** and **ontmoeten** are also used for coincidental meetings:

Ik kwam Rianne gisteren op de markt tegen.
I ran into Rianne at the market yesterday.

Toevallig ontmoette ik professor Jaspers bij die lezing van Van Geest.
I happened to meet Professor Jaspers at that lecture by Van Geest.

12.4 Asking people how they are

In Dutch, one uses the verb **gaan** 'to go' to ask how someone is doing. A more formal way is to use the verb **maken** 'to make,' and in another variation, Dutch uses **zijn** 'to be.'

Formal

Goedemorgen, mevrouw De Boer, hoe gaat het met u?
Good morning, Mrs. De Boer, how do you do? (*lit.* How goes it with you?)

Hoe maakt u het? (very formal)
How are you doing?

Hoe is het met u?
How are things with you?

Informal

Hé Jan, hoe gaat het met je?
Hey Jan, how are you doing?

Hallo Jaap, wat leuk, hoe gaat het ermee?
Hi Jaap, how nice, how are things going?

Karin, hoe is't?
Karin, how are you doing/what's up?

Hoi Ineke, hoe gaat-ie?
Hi Ineke, how are you/what's up?

To ask about the well-being of a third person, one can say the following:

En hoe gaat het met je man/uw vrouw/de kinderen?
And how is your husband/is your wife/are your children?

Alles goed thuis? Ook met de kinderen?
Everything fine at home? And the children as well?

Hoe is het met de gezondheid van uw vader?
How is your father's health?

Zijn de kinderen allemaal gezond en wel?
Are the kids all healthy and happy?

Responses

To appropriately respond, a brief answer is given, and in most cases, the question is returned.

Goed, dank u, en (hoe gaat het) met u?
Fine, thank you, and how are you?

Uitstekend/Prima/Heel goed, en met jou?
Very well, and you?

Ach, het gaat wel. En hoe gaat het met jou?
Oh, I'm doing okay. And how are you?

Het gaat niet zo best/niet goed/slecht. En met u/jou?
It's not going very well/not well/not well at all. And you?

Beroerd/Belabberd/Miserabel.
Lousy/Awful/Miserable.

Unlike in Anglophone countries, **Hoe gaat het met je?** is meant as a question to which the speaker expects an answer. In most cases, a few superficial pleasantries are exchanged, and the topic might be the weather, or a late bus, or prices that have gone up. Answers such as **Ach, het gaat wel** 'oh, okay' or **Niet zo best** 'not so great' will prompt the speaker to ask a follow-up question such as **Echt? Wat is er dan?** 'Really? What is the matter?' and this can then lead to a more serious exchange of situations, feelings, and experiences.

▶ For more information on sympathy and commiseration, see also **12.9**.

12.5 Coming and going: entering, welcoming, taking leave

Calling on someone

When calling on someone to enter their room or office, one can choose from different formal and informal things to say:

Mag ik even binnenkomen?
Can I come in for a minute?

Mag ik u/je even storen?
Can I disturb you for a minute?

Ik kom je even lastigvallen als je het goed vindt.
I'm coming to bother you for a minute if you don't mind.

Stoor ik?/Ik stoor toch niet?
Am I interrupting something?/I'm not disturbing you, am I?

Heeft u/Heb je even een moment tijd voor me?
Do you have a moment?

Kan ik u/je even spreken?
Can I talk to you for a minute?

Responses

There are a number of appropriate positive answers to these questions.

Natuurlijk/Geen probleem, kom binnen.
Of course/No problem, come in.

Komt u binnen. Neemt u plaats (formal).
Come in. Take a seat.

Welkom, ga even zitten.
Welcome, take a seat.

Kom binnen, ga zitten.
Come in, sit down.

Nee hoor, je stoort helemaal niet.
No, you're not interrupting at all.

Binnen.
Enter.

Some negative answers would be the following:

Sorry, maar ik heb nu even geen tijd.
I'm sorry, but I don't have time at the moment.

Het spijt me, maar ik ben nu even bezig.
I'm sorry, but I'm working on something right now.

Nee, sorry, het gaat nu even niet.
No, sorry, that won't work right now.

Het spijt me, maar ik ben in gesprek.
I'm sorry, but I am talking to someone.

▶ For more examples, see also Chapter **16**; for the use of **even**, see **3.9**.

The uses of *welkom*

The word **welkom** 'welcome' is used mostly in situations where a larger group of people is welcomed to a place or an event. When entering someone's house, the host might use it as well, but it is rather formal.

Welkom in Utrecht, de gezelligste stad van Nederland.
Welcome to Utrecht, the nicest city in the Netherlands.

Dames en heren, we heten u allen hartelijk welkom op deze jaarvergadering.
Ladies and gentlemen, we welcome all of you to this annual meeting.

Wees welkom. Doe alsof je thuis bent.
Welcome. Make yourself at home.

Je bent/U bent altijd welkom.
You're always welcome.

To welcome someone who has traveled a distance to see you, appropriate things to say would be:

Kom binnen. Heb je/Heeft u een goede reis gehad?
Come in. Did you have a good trip?

Kom erin. Hoe was de reis?
Come in. How was the trip?

Ben je/Bent u goed aangekomen?
Did you arrive safely?

Taking leave

To take leave, and say goodbye (**afscheid nemen**), the Dutch use the following:

Tot ziens/Tot kijk.
See you later.

Tot gauw/snel/later.
See you soon/later.

Later!
See you later!

Tot straks/Tot zo.
See you later/in a bit.

Tot de volgende keer.
See you next time.

Goeiedag/Daag/Dag.
Bye.

Doeg/Doei (very informal).
Bye.

Moi/Houdoe/Ajuus/Salut (regional dialects).
Bye.

De mazzel.
Cheers, see ya.

Tot straks

This expression means one will see the other person later, but *on the same day*. More specifically, one can determine a certain time when one will see the other person again.

Tot maandag/volgende week/volgend jaar.
See you Monday/next week/next year.

Tot over twee weken/tien dagen/een week.
See you in two weeks/ten days/a week.

When leaving late at night, or when wishing someone a good night, one can say:

Goedenacht.
Good night.

Welterusten.
Sleep well.

Slaap lekker.
Sleep tight.

Formal and informal ways to announce that one has to leave are the following:

Ik moet gaan/We moeten gaan.
I have to go/We have to go.

We gaan eens opstappen.
We should be going.

Ik moet ervandoor.
I have to dash.

Het wordt tijd om te gaan.
It's time to go.

To ask someone to stop by again, there are a variety of things one can say.

Kom gauw weer eens langs.
Stop by again soon.

Jullie zijn altijd welkom.
You are always welcome.

Wanneer zie ik je weer?
When shall I see you again?

Laten we gauw weer eens afspreken.
Let's meet again soon.

When saying goodbye on the phone, one can finish the phone call saying:

Tot horens.
Talk to you soon (*lit.* Until I hear you again).

Laat gauw weer eens iets van je horen.
Call me again soon.

We bellen wel weer.
We'll talk again soon.

Daag!
Bye!

▶ For more on telephone etiquette, see **13.9**.

12.6 Giving and receiving thanks, expressing gratitude

Expressing thanks

When offered something (food, drink, other objects, presents, help, assistance), one can say 'thank you' with simple short forms. **Dank je/u** and also **Bedankt** are the most common responses to **Alsjeblieft/Alstublieft**. For instance, in a restaurant, the following would be appropriate.

Alstublieft, een koffie en een appeltaart.
Here you are, coffee and apple pie.

Dank u/Bedankt.
Thank you/Thanks.

To express thanks more emphatically, one can use a variety of phrases.

Dank u wel/Dank je wel. (Also as one word: **Dankuwel/Dankjewel**)
Thanks so much.

Dank u zeer (formal).
Thank you so much.

Hartelijk bedankt/Hartelijk dank.
Sincere thanks.

Bedankt hoor! (very informal)
Thanks!

The verb **danken** and also **dank** and **bedankt** in combination with an object are used with the preposition **voor** 'for.' One can also use a subordinated sentence beginning with **dat** 'that.'

Wij danken u allen hartelijk voor uw aandacht.
We sincerely thank you for your attention.

Bedankt voor de uitnodiging, maar ik kan helaas niet komen.
Thanks for the invitation, but unfortunately I cannot come.

Hartelijk dank voor uw medewerking.
Sincere thanks for your cooperation.

Bedankt dat je me met die opgave hebt geholpen.
Thanks for helping me with that assignment.

▶ On prepositions, see Chapter **4**. On subordinated sentences, see **9.4**.

There are many other informal and formal ways to express gratitude. How one does this is a matter of preference, and it also depends on the relationship between the people involved and on the situation. Informally, one might say:

Fijn dat je me hebt geholpen.
It's great that you helped me.

We weten niet hoe we jullie moeten bedanken.
We don't know how to thank you.

Wat aardig van je dat je ook voor mij hebt gekookt.
How nice of you to also cook for me.

Dat had je niet hoeven doen.
You didn't have to do that.

Dankzij jouw handigheid werkt mijn computer nu weer.
Thanks to your handiness, my computer works again.

Some very formal expressions of gratitude and appreciation might include:

Ik ben u zeer erkentelijk dat u mijn boek wilt recenseren.
I am very grateful that you are willing to review my book.

Voor al uw steun en medeleven zijn wij zeer dankbaar.
We are very grateful for all your support and sympathy.

Wij willen onze dankbaarheid betuigen voor de goede samenwerking.
We want to express our gratitude for the excellent cooperation.

Wij weten uw hulpvaardigheid zeer te waarderen.
We value your helpfulness enormously.

Dat is erg vriendelijk van u.
That is very kind of you.

U hebt ons een grote dienst bewezen.
You have done us a great service.

Wij hebben ons succes aan u te danken.
We owe our success to you.

► To express thanks in a letter or email, see **13.10**.

Note that **danken** is also used to refuse politely, for example when one is offered something to eat or drink:

A: Wil je nog meer thee?
B: Nee, dank je/u.
A: Would you like more tea?
B: No, thanks.

Sometimes, **dank je** is used a little more sarcastically, as in 'thanks but no thanks,' often in combination with other words.

Vakantie op een Waddeneiland? Dank je lekker!
Vacation on a Wadden island? Thanks but no thanks!

Dank je de koekoek!
No way!

And finally, we often thank the Lord, although most of the time, religion doesn't have anything to do with it.

Godzijdank regent het niet meer. Kunnen we eindelijk gaan vissen.
Thank heavens it's no longer raining. We can finally go fishing.

Saying "you're welcome"

When one is the receiver of expressions of gratitude, one can choose from a variety of things to say.

> **Graag gedaan.**
> My pleasure.
>
> **Tot uw dienst/Tot je dienst.**
> At your service.
>
> **Geen probleem.**
> No problem.
>
> **Geen dank.**
> Don't mention it.
>
> **Het was niet de moeite.**
> It was nothing.
>
> **Ik heb het met plezier gedaan.**
> I enjoyed doing it.

12.7 Giving and receiving compliments

Giving a compliment on an object

Compliments often begin with **wat een** 'what a' with an adjective and noun. Examples:

> **Wat een leuke schoenen. Waar heb je die vandaan?**
> What nice shoes! Where did you get those?
>
> **Wat een heerlijke soep. Mag ik het recept?**
> What a delicious soup. Can I have the recipe?

Appropriate reactions might be to simply say **Dank je/u** or to respond saying something about the object.

> **Ja, vind je ze mooi? Ze komen van Manfield.**
> Yes, do you like them? They are from Manfield.
>
> **Lekker, hè? Ik heb het recept op Smulweb gevonden.**
> Delicious, isn't it? I found the recipe on Smulweb.

Giving a compliment on an action or appearance

If one wants to make a compliment on a performance or something someone has done well, one can also begin with **Wat** and the verb of the action, in present or past tense.

> **Wat speel je mooi!**
> How beautifully you play.
>
> **Wat doe je dat goed!/Wat heb je dat goed gedaan!**
> How well you do that!/How well you have done that!
>
> **Wat heb je lekker gekookt.**
> You cooked a delicious meal.

The same form can be used when giving compliments about one's appearance.

> **Wat staat die jurk je goed!**
> That dress looks really good on you!

Wat zit je haar leuk. Naar de kapper geweest?
Your hair looks great. Have you been to the hairdresser?

Wat zie je er vandaag leuk uit.
How nice you look today.

There are many other ways to express appreciation of a performance. Examples:

Bravo!
Bravo!

Uitstekend (gedaan).
Outstanding/Excellent.

Goed gedaan hoor!
Well done/Nice job!

Dat heb je heel goed gedaan.
You did that very well.

Dat kun jij goed, zeg!
You're very good at that!

Wat doet u dat goed!
How well you do that!

Or one can simply say that someone does a particular activity very well, either by using the verb with an adverb of appreciation, or by using the noun of the activity.

Je speelt geweldig goed piano.
You play the piano incredibly well.

Je bent een uitstekend leraar.
You are an outstanding teacher.

Note that the adjective does not get an ending **-e** when used this way.

▶ See also **3.1** for more on adjective endings.

12.8 Congratulations and condolences

Congratulations

Congratulations are usually expressed with the verb **feliciteren** 'congratulate.' We use the past participle in combination with the preposition **met** 'with.'

Gefeliciteerd met je verjaardag.
Congratulations on your birthday.

Hartelijk/Van harte gefeliciteerd.
Many happy returns.

Gelukkige verjaardag/Proficiat (Belgium).
Happy Birthday!

Note that the Dutch do not only congratulate the person whose actual birthday it is, but also the other family members present at the party.

Gefeliciteerd met de verjaardag van je moeder.
Congratulations on your mom's birthday.

Other than a birthday, one can congratulate someone on things such as getting a driver's license (**rijbewijs**), retirement (**pensionering**), a new job (**nieuwe baan**), a promotion or PhD (**promotie**), getting married (**huwelijk**), a wedding anniversary (**trouwdag**), the birth (**geboorte**) of a baby.

Gefeliciteerd met je havodiploma.
Congratulations on your high school diploma.

Gefeliciteerd met jullie nieuwe huis.
Congratulations on your new home.

Gefeliciteerd met de geboorte van jullie zoon.
Congratulations on the birth of your son.

Gefeliciteerd met jullie 40-jarig huwelijksfeest.
Congratulations on your 40th wedding anniversary.

Another verb used to convey congratulations and best wishes is **gelukwensen** (*lit.* wish someone luck). The past participle of this verb is used in more formal expressions:

Van harte gelukgewenst met de geboorte van Vincent.
Congratulations on the birth of Vincent.

Hartelijk gelukgewenst met jullie gouden bruiloft.
Congratulations on your golden wedding anniversary.

Condolences

To pass on condolences, one can simply say **Gecondoleerd** 'my condolences.' To express condolences on someone's passing, one can say:

Gecondoleerd met het overlijden van uw vader.
Condolences on your father's passing.

Gecondoleerd met uw verlies.
Condolences on your loss.

Met oprechte deelneming.
With sincere sympathy.

▶ For more on good wishes and commiseration, see **12.9**.

12.9 Expressing good wishes, sympathy, and commiseration

Good wishes

There are many reasons and occasions for expressing good wishes to someone (**iemand het beste wensen**). At the end of a letter, for instance, one can say:

Beste wensen/Met de beste wensen.
Best wishes.

Het beste/Het allerbeste.
Best/the very best wishes.

Holidays

During the holidays and at other celebrations, the Dutch send cards and express good wishes at parties. Examples:

Prettige Kerstdagen en een Gelukkig Nieuwjaar.
Merry Christmas and a Happy New Year.

Fijne feestdagen en een goed/gelukkig 2013.
Happy holidays and a good/happy 2013.

De beste wensen voor 2013.
Best wishes for 2013.

Veel geluk in het nieuwe jaar.
Best of luck in the new year.

Vrolijk Pasen!
Happy Easter!

Fijne Pinksterdagen.
Enjoy the holidays (this is during Pentecost when the Dutch get the Monday off).

Cheers

When they raise a glass to the new year, to someone's health, or other things, they say:

Proost!
Cheers!

Op het nieuwe jaar/de goede samenwerking/jullie gezondheid!
To the new year/a good collaboration/your health!

We nodigen u uit om samen het glas te heffen op het nieuwe jaar.
We invite you to raise a glass together to the new year.

Special situations

Newlyweds often get cards wishing them good luck. Also, people facing a new phase in their life or a difficult task get wishes for good luck or success. On stage, is it not 'break a leg,' but an expression originating in Yiddish.

Veel geluk samen.
Good luck together.

Veel geluk met de nieuwe woning.
Good luck with the new home.

Veel succes met je eindexamens.
Good luck with your final exams.

Toi toi toi.
Break a leg.

Have fun

At the start of an evening out, a vacation, a date or any event to look forward to, speakers of Dutch wish each other **veel plezier** 'have fun.' Even shopkeepers wish their customers fun times with what they just bought, a pair of shoes, a tool, anything.

Veel plezier vanavond!
Have fun tonight!

Veel plezier in Frankrijk, hè!
Enjoy France!

Veel plezier ermee.
Enjoy.

Leisure

It is also customary to wish someone a nice weekend, a nice day, or a nice vacation.

Prettig weekend.
Have a nice weekend.

Prettige/Fijne dag nog.
Enjoy the rest of the day.

Prettige vakantie/kerstvakantie/paasvakantie.
Enjoy your vacation/the Christmas break/the Easter break.

Work and school

When going to work, people wish each other a good workday. Similarly, parents might wish their children a good day at school.

Prettige/Fijne werkdag/Werk ze.
Have a good day at work.

Fijne dag op school.
Have a good day at school.

Sports

Players in a sports team also wish each other good luck, saying:

Zet hem op! (*short* **Zet 'm op!**)
Go for it!

Doe je best!
Do your best!

At the dining table

Before starting a meal, when wishing the guests or family members 'bon appetit,' the waiter, the host, or the person who has prepared the meal, will say:

Eet smakelijk/Smakelijk eten/Eet u smakelijk.
Enjoy your meal.

Laat het jullie smaken.
Enjoy your food.

Eet lekker/Eet ze.
Enjoy.

Tast toe.
Dig in.

An appropriate response to this is **Insgelijks** 'You too,' or **Van hetzelfde** 'Same to you.' This expression can be used in response to any good wish.

Sympathy and commiseration

When things don't go well, Dutch has many ways to express sympathy and commiseration. The Dutch word is **medelijden** (*lit.* suffering together), used with the verb **hebben**: **medelijden met iemand hebben** 'to feel sorry for someone.'

Ik heb medelijden met die arme zeehonden.
I feel sorry for those poor seals.

Het spijt me voor je dat je dat examen niet hebt gehaald.
I'm sorry you didn't pass that exam.

Wat jammer!/Wat jammer dat je niet mee kan naar het feest.
Too bad!/Too bad you can't come to the party.

Wat een pech/Wat heb jij een pech/Wat ben jij een pechvogel.
Such bad luck.

Ik vind het sneu/naar/rot/vervelend voor je dat je uit die flat moet (informal).
I think it sucks that you have to leave that apartment.

Jammer/Lullig/Balen voor je (very informal).
Wow, that sucks.

Ik heb met je te doen.
I feel bad for you.

Ik leef met u mee/Ik kan het me goed voorstellen (more formal).
I sympathize with you/I can imagine/relate.

Kan ik misschien iets voor u/je doen?
Is there anything I can do for you?

Ik heb alle begrip voor uw situatie (formal).
I completely understand your situation.

Ik denk aan je.
Thinking of you.

Sterkte.
(I wish you) strength.

When people are ill or don't feel well, one can use a variety of words to cheer them up. On get-well cards, one might find the following expressions:

Beterschap/Veel beterschap/Van harte beterschap.
Get well/From the bottom of my heart, get well.

Word gauw weer beter.
Get better soon.

Ik hoop dat je je gauw weer beter voelt.
I hope you feel better soon.

Consolation

To console someone (Dutch **troosten**, **opbeuren**, **opvrolijken**) and say that something doesn't matter or isn't really so bad, there are a variety of expressions. Note the verb **meevallen**, which means 'looking better than expected.' The opposite of this is **tegenvallen** 'looking worse than expected.'

Ach, wat geeft dat nou?
Oh, what does it matter?

Dat is toch helemaal niet zo erg.
That's not so bad at all.

Wat maakt dat nou uit? (informal)
What does it matter?

Het geeft echt niets.
It really doesn't matter.

Het had veel erger kunnen zijn.
It could have been much worse.

Het valt toch allemaal wel mee?
It's not as bad as it looks, is it?

Maak je/Maakt u zich nou maar geen zorgen.
Really, don't worry about it.

Wees maar niet verdrietig/Huil maar niet.
Don't be sad/Don't cry.

▶ For other uses of the imperative form, see **8.1**.

Responses

Appropriate responses to expressions of commiseration would be:

Dank je, dat is een hele troost.
Thank you, that is a big relief.

Dat is erg lief van je.
That is very sweet of you.

Hartelijk dank voor uw troostende woorden (formal).
Sincere thanks for your comforting words.

Hartelijk dank voor uw medeleven (very formal).
Sincere thanks for your sympathy.

12.10 Expressing apologies and regret

Apologies

As with everything, it depends on the situation and the relationship between the speakers, but in general, to express an apology for a mistake, speakers of Dutch say:

Sorry.
Sorry.

Het spijt me.
I'm sorry.

Note that Dutch people do not apologize as quickly and easily as British and Americans, who are usually more courteous. For bumping into someone or being in someone's way, common apologies are:

O, pardon.
Oh, I'm sorry.

O, neemt u mij niet kwalijk/O, neem me niet kwalijk.
Oh, I'm sorry (*lit.* Don't take it badly).

Excuseert u mij (very formal).
Excuse me.

Sorry hoor (more informal).
Sorry!

For mistakes or for things they regret, people apologize by saying **sorry** or **het spijt me** or **neem me/neemt u me niet kwalijk** with a subordinated sentence beginning with **dat**.

Sorry dat ik te laat ben.
Sorry I'm late.

Het spijt me dat ik je niet teruggebeld heb.
I'm sorry I didn't call you back.

Neemt u mij niet kwalijk dat ik die brieven nog niet klaar heb (more formal).
Please excuse me for not getting those letters ready.

A more formal way to apologize is with **mijn/onze excuses voor**, often combined with the verb **aanbieden** offer.

Mijn excuses voor de late reactie op je mail.
Excuse my late answer to your mail.

Onze excuses voor het ongemak.
Our apologies for the inconvenience.

Ik wil mijn excuses aanbieden voor die opmerking.
I want to apologize for that remark.

In very formal apologies, one uses the reflexive verb **zich verontschuldigen** or the noun **verontschuldiging** with the verb **aanbieden**.

Ik wil me voor de fout in de berekening verontschuldigen.
I want to apologize for the error in the estimate.

Wij willen onze verontschuldiging aanbieden voor het veroorzaakte ongemak.
We want to offer our apologies for the inconvenience we have caused you.

▶ For more on reflexive verbs, see **6.5**.

Taking the responsibility

Also, one can take the blame or responsibility (**de verantwoordelijkheid opnemen**) for something by saying:

Ik neem de schuld op me.
I take the blame.

Ik ben schuldig aan de brand in het magazijn.
I am guilty of the fire in the warehouse.

Ik neem de verantwoordelijkheid op voor die verkeerde bestelling.
I take the responsibility for that erroneous order.

Ik ben voor die verkeerde bestelling verantwoordelijk.
I am responsible for that erroneous order.

In formal apologies, the expression **tot mijn/onze spijt** also often occurs.

Tot onze spijt delen wij u mede dat de hoekbank Sigma niet meer in rood leverbaar is.
We regret to inform you that the corner sofa Sigma is no longer available in red.

Tot mijn spijt is die afdruk een beetje donker uitgevallen.
I regret that that print has turned out a bit dark.

Asking forgiveness

The verb **vergeven** 'forgive' is sometimes used to ask for forgiveness (**om vergeving vragen**) when serious offenses have been committed, and in religious contexts.

Vergeef me mijn stommiteit.
Forgive me my stupidity.

Kun je me vergeven?
Can you forgive me?

Vergeef ons onze zonden.
Forgive our sins.

Regrets

Furthermore, when expressing regrets and apologies, one can use the verb **moeten** 'must' or **mogen** 'may' in the past perfect with the negation **niet/geen/nooit**, as in English 'shouldn't have.'

Ik had dat nooit moeten doen.
I shouldn't have done that.

Ik had je geen hufter mogen noemen.
I shouldn't have called you a jerk.

Ik had u hier niet om mogen vragen.
I shouldn't have asked you for this.

▶ For more on modal verbs in the past tense, see **6.2**.

Responding to apologies

To respond to an apology, for example by accepting it and saying it doesn't matter, one can say a variety of things.

Het geeft niet hoor.
It doesn't matter.

Het is niet zo erg hoor.
It really isn't so bad.

Het hindert niet.
It doesn't matter.

Het doet er niet toe (less formal)**.**
It doesn't matter.

Maak je/Maakt u zich er geen zorgen over.
Don't worry about it.

Maak je er niet druk om (informal)**.**
Don't get worked up about it.

More formally, one can share in the blame and take some of the responsibility off someone's shoulders:

Het had mij ook kunnen overkomen.
It could have happened to me.

Dat kan iedereen gebeuren.
That could happen to anyone.

Is ook mijn fout hoor.
It is also my mistake/I am to blame too.

To reconcile, one can say:

Het is vergeven en vergeten.
Let's forget about it.

Zand erover.
Forget about it (*lit.* Cover it up with sand).

13

Basic communication strategies

13.1 Attracting attention and turning one's attention to someone

Attracting attention

There are numerous ways to attract a person's attention (**aandacht vragen/trekken**). Much of this depends on the situation, the location, the relationship between the speakers, and whether the situation is formal or informal.

To initiate a conversation, one can simply call the other person by their name (or relationship, function) or one can use a form of **luisteren** 'listen,' **horen** 'hear,' or **kijken** 'look.' Less polite variations would include interjections such as **hé** 'hey' or **hallo**.

> **Erik/Zeg, Erik/Hé, Erik . . .**
> Erik/Say, Erik/Hey, Erik . . .

> **Mama/Papa/Juf Linda/Meneer Jansen . . .**
> Mom/Dad/Miss Linda/Mr. Jansen . . .

> **Zeg, luister eens/Luister/Luister even . . .**
> Say, listen/Listen up/Just listen . . .

> **Wil je/Willen jullie even luisteren?**
> Can you listen up for a minute?

> **Hoor eens even/Moet je horen . . .**
> Hear this/Listen to this . . .

> **Kijk, je moet het natuurlijk zelf weten, maar ik vind die auto te duur.**
> Look, it's your decision, but I think that car is too expensive.

> **Hallo, is daar iemand?**
> Hello, anybody there?

> **Hé/Hé, jij daar/Hé, jij daar in dat rode shirt . . .**
> Hey, you/Hey, you in the red shirt . . .

Appropriate responses to such calls for attention could be:

> **Ja/Ja, wat is er?**
> Yes/Yes, what's up/what's the matter?

> **Ja, zeg het eens/vertel het eens.**
> Yes, tell me what's up.

Being irritated or not interested in talking, one could say:

> **Ja, wat wil je?/Wat moet je?** (rude)
> Yes, what do you want?

> **Ja, wat is er nou weer?**
> Yes, what is it this time?

Wat nou?
What?!

Jahaaaaa!
Yeahhh!

In formal situations, and depending on whether one simply needs someone's attention or one has a request for information, one can say a variety of things.

Pardon/Neemt u me niet kwalijk/Excuseert u me.
Pardon/Pardon me/Excuse me.

Pardon, mag ik u even storen/onderbreken?
Pardon, may I interrupt you?

Mag ik even uw aandacht?
May I have your attention, please?

Attentie, alstublieft.
Attention, please.

Mag ik u even iets vragen?/Ik heb even een vraag.
May I ask you something?/I just have a question.

Responses to such requests for attention could be:

Ja/Ja, natuurlijk.
Yes/Yes, of course.

Ja, wat kan ik voor u/je doen?
Yes, what can I do for you?

Waarmee kan ik u van dienst zijn? (very formal)
How can I assist you?

Ja, zegt u het maar.
Yes, go ahead.

Wat mag het zijn? (in a shop)
What would you like?

Wat is er van uw dienst? (very formal)
How can I be of service?

Negative answers to a call for attention would be the following:

Sorry, ik heb geen tijd.
Sorry, I don't have time.

Nu even niet.
Not right now.

Ik kan u niet helpen.
I can't help you.

Ik ben nu even bezig.
I am busy right now.

U bent bij mij aan het verkeerde adres.
I'm not the right person to ask.

Daar ga ik niet over.
That's not my department.

Dangerous situations

To attract someone's attention in a dangerous situation, one can say:

Help!
Help!

Pas op!
Watch out!

Kijk uit!
Watch out!

Brand!
Fire!

Non-verbal

There are also non-verbal ways to attract someone's attention. Restaurant guests raise their hand to a waiter, sometimes saying **Ober!** 'Waiter!', students raise their hand in class; waiving one's arms, nodding one's head or simply making eye contact can also draw attention, and then there are other non-verbal signs such as snapping fingers or whistling that would be considered inappropriate.

13.2 Asking for patience

When someone has drawn one's attention and one doesn't have time right away, there are various formal and informal ways to ask for patience or to ask someone to wait (**wachten**) for a few minutes. In informal situations, one can say:

Wacht (u) even/Kun je even wachten?/Kunt u even wachten?
Wait a minute/Can you wait a minute?

Wacht nou even! (informal, with irritation)
Wait!

Momentje/Een ogenblikje (alsjeblieft, alstublieft)
Just a moment (please).

Even geduld/Kunt u nog even geduld hebben?
Please be patient/Could you be patient for just a little longer?

Het duurt nog even.
It will take a little longer.

Ga/Gaat u (zolang) even zitten.
Sit down (while you wait).

Kun je/Kunt u over een uurtje terugkomen?
Can you come back in an hour?

Ik kom zo bij je/u.
I will be with you in a minute.

Kunt u even in de wachtkamer plaatsnemen?
Can you take a seat in the waiting room?

13.3 Asking for repetition, reformulation, and spelling

Repetition

There are many ways to ask someone for repetition (verb **herhalen**) of a word or sentence. To let someone know that one has not heard what was said, the following would be possible.

> **Pardon?** (neutral)
> Pardon?
>
> **Hè?** (only informal, rather rude)
> Huh?
>
> **Wat?** or **Wat zeg je/zegt u?** or **Wat zei je?/Zei je wat?**
> What?/What did you say?/Did you say something?
>
> **Zeg dat nog eens** or **Kun je/Kunt u dat nog een keer zeggen?**
> Could you say that again?
>
> **Ik kon je/u niet verstaan** or **Ik versta je/u niet** or **Ik verstond het niet.**
> I couldn't hear you/I can't hear you/I didn't hear you.
>
> **Kun je/Kunt u wat harder/langzamer praten?**
> Could you speak up?/Could you slow down?

Reformulation

To ask someone to say something in different words, one can say:

> **Kun je/Kunt u dat anders zeggen/formuleren?**
> Can you say that some other way?
>
> **Kun je/Kunt u dat een beetje duidelijker zeggen?**
> Can you say that a bit more clearly?
>
> **Kun je/Kunt u dat met andere woorden zeggen?**
> Can you say that in different words?

Translation

When one wants to know how exactly something is said in Dutch, one says:

> **Hoe zeg je 'tree' in het Nederlands?**
> How do you say 'tree' in Dutch?
>
> **Wat is het woord voor 'tree' in het Nederlands?**
> What is the Dutch word for 'tree?'
>
> **Hoe vertaal je 'I love apple pie' in het Nederlands?**
> How do you translate 'I love apple pie' in Dutch?

Spelling

To ask for the exact spelling of a name or a word, one can say:

> **Hoe spel je dat?/Hoe spelt u dat?**
> How does one spell that?
>
> **Kun je/Kunt u dat spellen?**
> Can you spell that?
>
> **Meier/Mijer met een korte of een lange ij?**
> Meier/Mijer with ei or ij?

Jansen met één of twee s'en?
Jansen with one or two s?

Eykhoff met E-Y- en dubbel f?
Eykhoff with E-Y- and double f?

To respond to questions about spelling, one can answer:

Kaspar met de K van kip.
Kaspar with K as in kip (chicken).

Dat spel je K-A-S-P-A-R.
You spell it K-A-S-P-A-R.

▶ For more on spelling and sounds, see Chapters **10** and **11**.

13.4 Understanding and misunderstanding

Understanding: *begrijpen* versus *verstaan*

To make sure someone has understood what you said, there are various things to ask. Note that there is a difference in Dutch between **verstaan** and **begrijpen**. While both mean 'understand,' **verstaan** is for understanding acoustically and for foreign languages, and **begrijpen** is to understand a concept. Other less formal expressions for **begrijpen** are **volgen** 'to follow,' **snappen** 'to get it,' **het door hebben** 'to get it.'

Versta je me?/Verstaat u mij?
Do you hear me?

Kunt u mij achterin de zaal verstaan?
Can you hear me in the back of the room?

Versta jij/Verstaat u Frans?
Do you understand French?

Begrijp je me?/Begrijpt u mij?
Do you understand me?

Hebben jullie het nu begrepen?
Do you understand it now?

Begrijp je/Begrijpt u wat ik bedoel?
Do you understand what I mean?

Kunnen jullie/Kunt u me volgen?
Are you following me?

Snap je het nu? (informal)
Do you get it now?

Heb je het door? (informal)
Do you get it?

To indicate that one does or does not understand a language, one can say:

Ja, ik versta Spaans.
Yes, I understand Spanish.

Nee, ik versta geen Russisch.
No, I don't understand Russian.

To indicate that one has understood a concept, one can say:

Ja, ik begrijp het/ik heb het begrepen.
Yes, I understand.

Ja, ik snap het/ik heb het door (informal).
Yes, I get it.

Ja, ik zie het.
Yes, I see.

Clarification: *bedoelen* versus *betekenen*

To ask for clarification, one can say a variety of things. Note the difference between **bedoelen** and **betekenen**. We use **bedoelen** in reference to people, and **betekenen** in reference to things.

Sorry, ik begrijp je niet/ik begrijp u niet/ik begrijp het niet.
Sorry, I don't understand you/it.

Kun je/Kunt u het nog een keer uitleggen?
Can you explain it again?

Wat bedoel je?/Wat bedoelt u (daarmee)?
What do you mean (by that)?

Hoe bedoel je dat?/Hoe bedoelt u dat?
How do you mean that?

Wat betekent dat?
What does that mean?

Wat wil je/Wat wilt u daarmee zeggen?
What are you trying to say by that?

Wat moet dat betekenen?/Wat heeft dat te betekenen? (with irritation)
What is that supposed to mean?

Some very informal ways to indicate that one has not understood, indeed that one has no clue, are as follows.

Ik begrijp er geen snars/geen bal/geen moer/geen donder van.
I don't understand any of it.

Ik snap er niks van/Ik snap er de ballen niet van.
I'm clueless.

Appropriate responses to such requests for clarification are:

Ik bedoel . . .
I mean . . .

Wat ik (ermee) wil zeggen, is . . .
What I want to say (by this), is . . .

Ik zal het nog een keer uitleggen.
I will explain it again.

Laat ik het anders/met andere woorden zeggen.
Let me say it differently/in other words.

Misunderstanding

To say that one has misunderstood someone or something, one can say:

Ik heb het/je/u verkeerd begrepen.
I misunderstood it/you.

Het is een misverstand.
It is a misunderstanding.

13.5 Giving and taking the floor

Giving the floor

There are endless possibilities to invite someone to speak (**iemand het woord geven, aan het woord laten**) or to wait one's turn in a conversation. A direct invitation is to simply ask an open question.

En wat hebben jullie op vakantie gedaan?
And what did you do while on vacation?

If one has a sense that the conversation partner wants to say something, one can nudge the person in various ways.

Ja?
Yes?

Ja? Wat wou je zeggen?/Je wilde wat zeggen.
Yes? What did you want to say? You wanted to say something.

Zeg het maar/Zegt u het maar.
Go ahead.

Ga je gang/Gaat u gang.
Go ahead.

Jij eerst.
You first.

Na u.
After you.

If the conversation was interrupted, and one wants to continue where it was halted, one can say, for example,

Waar hadden we het over?
What were we talking about?

Waar waren we gebleven?/Waar was ik gebleven?
Where were we/was I?

Formal ways to invite someone to speak (**het woord geven**) are:

Ik geef het woord aan de voorzitter.
I'm handing it over to the chairman.

Het woord is aan de voorzitter.
The chairman will say a few words now.

Taking the floor

To take the floor (**het woord nemen**), or to indicate that one wants to say something, one can choose from numerous varieties. A few informal examples are:

Mag ik even wat zeggen?/Ik wil even wat zeggen.
May I say something?/I want to say something.

Laat mij (nou) even wat zeggen.
Just let me say something.

Laat mij (nou) even aan het woord.
Let me speak please.

Ik wil even het woord hebben.
I want to have the floor for a minute.

Mag ik je even onderbreken?
May I interrupt you for a minute?

Note that **nou** 'now' is a particle that can indicate irritation or impatience. It can make a statement or a question less polite.

▶ For more information on particles, see **3.9** and **13.8**.

Interrupt

Formal requests to speak or polite ways to interrupt (**onderbreken, in de rede vallen**) someone are as follows:

Zou ik even iets mogen zeggen?
Could I say something?

Mag ik u even onderbreken?/Zou ik u even mogen onderbreken?
May I interrupt you for a minute?

Zou u mij even aan het woord willen laten?
Would you please let me speak for a moment?

Zou ik even het woord mogen hebben?/Mag ik even het woord?
Could I have the floor, please?

Note that the forms with **zou** are much more formal and polite than the sentences without. The use of the subjunctive (or conditional) generally makes statements more courteous, and therefore this form is quite common in very formal requests.

▶ For more information on the subjunctive and the conditional, see **8.2**.

There are less courteous versions of interruptions:

Hou(d) je mond/Hou(d) je kop, ik ben/was aan het woord.
Shut up, I am/was talking.

A very rude version of **Hou(d) je kop** 'Shut up' is **Hou(d) je bek** 'Shut your trap,' definitely to be avoided in courteous conversations. Other ways to tell or ask someone not to interrupt, informal and formal, are:

Onderbreek me niet!/Onderbreekt u mij niet!
Don't interrupt me!

Val me/Valt u mij niet in de rede!
Don't interrupt me!

Moment!
Just a moment.

Ik ben nog niet uitgepraat.
I have not finished yet.

Zou u mij niet willen onderbreken?
Would you please not interrupt me?

Laat (u) me even uitpraten/uitspreken (alstublieft).
Let me finish (please).

Ik ben/was aan het woord.
I am/was talking.

Addressing a group

To address a group of people in a formal situation, for example, when one is giving a talk, one can say:

Dames en heren . . .
Ladies and gentlemen . . .

Geachte toehoorders . . .
Dear listeners . . .

Geachte aanwezigen . . .
Dear attendees . . .

Beste collega's, vrienden . . .
Dear colleagues, friends . . .

Jongens en meisjes . . .
Boys and girls . . .

13.6 Refusing to talk about something

When one doesn't know or would rather not give the answer to a question, or when the topic is uncomfortable and the information is nobody's business, there are strategies to avoid the topic.

Not knowing the answer

When one doesn't know something, one can say:

Dat weet ik niet/Ik weet het niet.
I don't know that.

Ik zou het niet weten.
I wouldn't know.

Daar weet ik niets van.
I don't know anything about that.

Daar heb ik geen verstand van.
I'm not an expert on that.

Daar kan ik niets over zeggen.
I can't say anything about that.

Geen idee/Geen flauw idee.
No idea/Not a clue.

Hoe moet ik dat nou weten?
How should I know?

Vraag het maar aan iemand anders.
Ask someone else.

Uncomfortable questions

When someone asks an uncomfortable question, and one doesn't want to talk about the topic or doesn't want to divulge this information, one can say:

Dat zeg ik liever niet.
I'd rather not say that.

Daar praat ik liever niet over.
I'd rather not talk about that.

Daar wil ik niet over praten.
I don't want to talk about that.

Dat houd ik liever voor me.
I'd rather keep that to myself.

Nobody's business

When it is none of the other person's business, one can say:

Dat gaat je niets aan/Dat gaat u niets aan.
That's none of your business.

Dat zijn jouw zaken niet/Dat zijn uw zaken niet.
That's none of your business.

Daar heb je/heeft u niets mee te maken.
That's none of your concern.

Dat is voor jou/u een vraag en voor mij een weet.
(Something like) You ask it and I know it.

Some not so polite ways to say that something is nobody else's business are:

Dat ga ik je niet aan je neus hangen.
I'm not going to tell you that (*lit.* I am not going to hang that on your nose).

Bemoei je met je eigen zaken.
Mind your own business.

13.7 Changing the subject, resisting a change of subject

Changing the subject

To indicate that the topic is no longer, or never was, interesting, and to change the topic or propose a different topic, there are numerous things to say.

Ik wil hier niet meer over praten.
I don't want to talk about this anymore.

Laten we hier niet meer over praten.
Let us not talk about this anymore.

We hebben het er niet meer over.
We won't talk about this anymore.

Note that the verb **laten** in combination with the second-person plural pronoun **we** is typically used for suggestions such as these.

Laten we over iets anders praten.
Let's talk about something else.

Laten we het over iets anders hebben.
Let's talk about something else.

Laten we er een streep onder zetten.
Let's close the topic.

A more deliberate change of topic goes as follows:

Ander onderwerp!
Different topic!

Slightly more subtle is the use of **maar** 'but' to indicate a change of subject.

> **Ja, dat zijn leuke vakantieplannen. Maar wanneer ga je nou afstuderen?**
> Yes, those are nice vacation plans. But when do you plan to graduate?

If someone tries to continue to talk about the same topic or comes back to it, one can stop the conversation saying:

> **Begin er nou niet weer over.**
> Don't start that again.

> **We zouden er toch niet meer over praten?**
> (Didn't we say that) we wouldn't talk about it anymore?

Refusing to change the topic

On the other hand, if one is not interested in changing the topic, there are various ways to stay on it or come back to it.

> **Zoals ik al zei . . .**
> As I was saying . . .

> **Wat ik wilde zeggen, is . . .**
> What I wanted to say, is . . .

> **Waar hadden we het ook al weer over?**
> What were we talking about?

> **Je hebt me van m'n apropos gebracht.**
> You have distracted me.

> **Je probeert het gesprek af te leiden.**
> You are trying to change the conversation.

> **Om nog even op dat thema terug te komen . . .**
> To come back to that topic . . .

Postponing the discussion

If one is not successful in staying on track, a possibility is to announce that the topic will be discussed at a later time.

> **We zijn hier nog niet over uitgepraat.**
> We have not finished this discussion.

> **We komen er wel weer op terug.**
> We'll come back to this.

> **We hebben het er nog wel over.**
> We will talk about this later.

And something that could be said in similar situations:

> **Wacht maar, je bent nog niet van me af.**
> Just you wait, you are not rid of me yet.

13.8 Shaping a conversation with fillers, interjections, and particles

People use fillers and interjections to bridge a pause, to think about what they want to say, to engage the listener, to search for words, to change the topic, and many other things. The following is an overview of the most commonly used fillers, and special attention is devoted to particles: little, seemingly meaningless words that do, however, shape the tone and character of what one says.

To draw someone's attention, one can begin with **hé** 'hey' or **zeg** 'say.'

Hé, ik dacht dat jij in Canada zat.
Hey, I thought you were in Canada.

Zeg, heb jij nog aan die offerte voor Niemeyer kunnen werken?
Say, have you been able to work on that offer for Niemeyer?

Typical fillers to build bridges in one's thought process can be meaningless sounds or words one uses just to say something at all: **eh** 'uh,' **ehm** 'uhm,' **hmm**, **ja** 'yes/well,' **tja** 'oh well,' **nou ja** 'well,' **nou ja zeg** 'well darn it,' **zeg maar** 'like,' **als het ware** 'as it were,' **zogezegd** 'so to say,' **bij wijze van spreken** 'so to speak,' **min of meer** 'more or less,' **eigenlijk** 'actually,' **dus** 'so,' **weet je** 'you know,' **snap je** 'you see,' **zie je** 'you see,' **enne** 'and err,' and so on. Many of these go in and out of fashion, and overuse can be irritating, as is often the case with **dus** 'so' and **zeg maar** 'like.'

Gisteren ging ik dus even naar de markt, en toen, eh, kwam ik de ex van Inge tegen, weet je, enne, ja, ik vond dat eigenlijk heel vervelend, zeg maar, want, nou ja, hoe moet ik die nou onder ogen komen nu hij haar heeft laten zitten?
So I went to the market yesterday, and then, uh, I ran into Inge's ex, you know, and errr, I thought that was, like, really annoying, actually, because, well, how should I talk to him after he has dumped her?

Many fillers have actual meaning in the correct context and in the right position. The interjection **hè**, for instance, can be either at the beginning or at the end of a sentence. At the beginning, it expresses something similar to 'well,' 'gosh,' or 'geez,' or even 'argh,' and at the end, it means 'eh' or various forms of 'isn't it?'

Hè, gezellig is het hier.
Gosh, it's cozy here.

Hè, wat vervelend dat het regent.
Argh, what a pain it's raining.

Die man was aardig, hè?
That man was nice, wasn't he?

To use a certain expression or circumscribe something, or to indicate that something is not to be taken literally, we use **als het ware** 'as it were,' **zogezegd** 'so to say,' or **bij wijze van spreken** 'so to speak.'

Ik heb er zogezegd de balen van.
I'm fed up with it, so to say.

Je kunt de bomen als het ware zien groeien.
You can see the trees grow, as it were.

To express a certain resignation or disappointment, **tja** 'oh well' is used.

Wil Leo niet mee? Tja, dan moet ik iemand anders zoeken.
Leo doesn't want to go? Oh well, then I have to find someone else.

The word **eigenlijk** can mean 'actually' or 'by the way.'

Ik heb niet zoveel zin om naar dat feest te gaan, eigenlijk.
I don't really want to go to that party, actually.

Deze schoenen zitten heerlijk. Wat kosten ze eigenlijk?
These shoes are very comfortable. How much are they, by the way?

To check whether the listener is still following the conversation and to get some acknowledgement, we use fillers such as **zie je**, **snap je**, and **weet je.**

Weet je, ik zou wel eens naar Polen op vakantie willen.
You know, I'd love to go to Poland on vacation.

Hij had die auto allang verkocht, zie je.
He had already sold that car, you see.

It is much more difficult to give an exact meaning for **nou ja** and **nou ja zeg**. Depending on both context and intonation, they can mean resignation and indignation.

Zijn er geen vluchten meer? Nou ja, dan gaat het feest niet door.
There are no more flights? Well then, that means the party is off.

6 euro voor een doosje aardbeien? Nou ja (zeg), hoe vind je nou zoiets?
6 euros for a little box of strawberries? Well darn it, what do you think about that?

There are many ways to keep the conversation going with fillers and interjections at the end of a statement that ask the listener for some kind of acknowledgement or affirmation: **hè?** 'eh?', **nietwaar?** 'right?', **toch?** 'right?', **vind je niet?** 'don't you think?', **niet dan?** 'don't you agree?', **of niet (soms)?** 'or not?', **of wel (soms)?** 'or is it?' Note that fillers of this kind are not easy to translate literally.

Wat was dat een mooie film, hè?
Was that a beautiful film, or what?

Karel speelt mooi piano, nietwaar?
Karel plays the piano well, doesn't he?

Die jurk is uitverkocht, toch?
That dress is sold out, right?

Dit is nou een mooi schilderij, vind je niet?
This is a beautiful painting, don't you think?

Die nieuwe wet is toch complete waanzin, niet dan?
That new law is utter insanity, don't you agree?

Vakanties zijn zo duur, je kan net zo goed thuisblijven, of niet soms?
Vacations are so expensive, you might as well stay home, no?

Die man is geen geschikte troonopvolger, of wel soms?
That man is not a suitable heir to the throne, or is he?

The listener can signal verbally that he or she has heard the speaker, and can react accordingly with utterances such as **ja?** 'yes?', **ja ja** 'indeed,' **hm hm** 'hm hm,' **zo!** 'indeed,' **zo zo!** 'well now,' **goh** 'wow,' **jeetje** 'geez,' **sjonge** 'wow,' **ach** 'ah/oh,' **echt?** 'really?', **werkelijk?** 'really?', **meen je dat nou?** 'you're serious?', **wat?!** 'what?!', **jazeker** 'indeed/absolutely,' **natuurlijk** 'of course,' **klopt!** 'right,' **precies** 'precisely,' **nee toch?** 'no, really?', **ach welnee** 'nonsense,' **nee hoor** 'no no,' **ja(wel) hoor** 'oh yes,' **mooi niet** 'no way,' **ach wat** 'come off it.' With many of these, intonation can make a difference, for instance, the voice goes downward for affirmation and upward for questioning or doubt.

A: Ik ga volgende week naar Parijs.
B: Ja?/Echt?/Goh!/Wat?!/Zo zo!
A: I am going to Paris next week.
B: Yes?/Really?/Geez!/What?!/Well now!

A: Ik ga stoppen met roken.
B: Meen je dat nou?/Echt?/Sjonge!
A: I am going to quit smoking.
B: You're serious?/Really?/Wow!

A: Maat 34 is te klein voor jou.
B: Klopt/Precies/Ach welnee/Nee hoor.
A: Size 34 is too small for you.
B: Right/Precisely/Nonsense/No no.

A: Heb je de deur op slot gedaan?
B: Ja hoor/Jazeker/Natuurlijk/Hm hm/Ja ja.
A: Did you lock the door?
B: Yes/Certainly/Of course/Hm hm/Indeed.

A: Er is bij de buren ingebroken.
B: Nee toch?/Echt?/Ach!/Wat?!
A: Someone broke into the neighbors' house.
B: No, really?/Really?/Ah!/What?!

A: Ben je m'n verjaardag vergeten?
B: Nee hoor, mooi niet.
A: Did you forget my birthday?
B: No way, absolutely not.

When one is looking for a word, one can say things like **eh** 'uh,' **ehm** 'uhm,' **hoe zeg je dat** 'how do you say that,' **hoe noem je zoiets?** 'what is the name for that?', **hoe heet dat ook alweer?** 'how do you call that again?', **je weet wel, . . . zo'n . . .** 'you know, one of those . . . ,' **het ligt op het puntje van m'n tong** 'it's on the tip of my tongue,' **ik kom er even niet op** 'I can't think of it right now,' and many more. Examples:

Ik zag gisteren, eh, die nieuwe collega van Lydia. Hoe heet ze nou ook alweer?
Yesterday, I saw, uh, Lydia's new colleague. What is her name again?

Ik zoek zo'n, eh, hoe noem je zoiets, zo'n ding om mee te verven.
I'm looking for, uh, what is the name for that, the thing you use to paint.

Ik kan niet op dat woord komen, het ligt op het puntje van m'n tong.
I can't think of that word, it is on the tip of my tongue.

Particles

This section focuses on some of the most common particles that are used to structure a conversation. Note that particles carry little semantic value and are very difficult to translate literally.

To summarize or close off some previous thoughts, one can use **enfin** 'anyhow' or **kortom** 'in short.'

Enfin, je weet nu hoe het zit.
Anyhow, now you know what's going on.

Kortom, we laten de hele boel verbouwen.
In short, we are remodeling the whole thing.

The particle **hè?** 'right?' at the end of a sentence asks the listener to agree, whereas **hoor** 'mind/you know' resists contradiction.

Wat is het mooi weer, hè?
Beautiful weather, isn't it?

Je moet je jas dichtdoen, hoor, bij deze wind.
Mind you, you must close your coat in this wind.

The particle **hoor** has many other meanings. It very much depends on the tone and the context in which it is used. Meanings include 'sure,' 'alright/okay,' '(not) at all,' 'really.'

A: Mag ik een koekje?
B: Ja hoor.
A: May I have a cookie?
B: Yes, sure.

Laat die begroting maar tot morgen zitten hoor.
It's okay, leave that budget until tomorrow.

A: Ik dacht dat jullie gingen verhuizen.
B: Verhuizen? Nee hoor!
A: I thought you were going to move.
B: Move? No, not at all!

Goh, je hebt hartstikke mooi gespeeld hoor!
Gosh, you really did play beautifully!

To widen the context with a reason or an explanation, Dutch uses **namelijk** 'namely' and **immers** 'after all.' Other words that can be used in this context, are **althans** 'anyway/at any rate,' **toch** 'after all,' **tenslotte** 'after all,' **uiteindelijk** 'at the end of the day/after all.'

De bank is gesloten. Het is namelijk/immers zondag.
The bank is closed, because it is Sunday.

Koop die piano nou maar. Je hebt er tenslotte/immers jaren voor gespaard.
Just buy that piano. After all, you have saved money for it for years.

Je moet niet zoveel snoep eten, je bent toch veel te dik.
You shouldn't eat so much candy, you are too fat as it is.

We gaan dit jaar naar Frankrijk, althans, dat is de bedoeling.
We are going to France this year, at any rate, that's the plan.

Jij loopt maar met Fido. Je hebt hem uiteindelijk zelf gewild.
You should walk Fido. After all, you wanted him.

To emphasize a part of the sentence, or to single it out, one can use particles such as **met name** 'especially,' **vooral** 'especially/above all,' **zelfs** 'even,' **alleen** 'only,' **alleen maar** 'only,' **ook** 'also,' and **niet eens** 'not even.'

Het eten was erg lekker. Vooral/Met name de garnalencocktail was goed gelukt.
The food was delicious. Especially the shrimp cocktail turned out great.

Zelfs Maarten heeft ervan gegeten en die houdt eigenlijk niet van garnalen.
Even Maarten had some of it, and he doesn't actually like shrimps.

Alleen Ina liet het staan, maar die is allergisch voor schelpdieren.
Only Ina didn't touch it, but she is allergic to shellfish.

Die eet alleen maar witte vis en zalm.
She only eats white fish and salmon.

Er was ook een geweldige appeltaart gemaakt.
They had also made a fabulous apple pie.

Ik kook nooit. Ik kan niet eens een ei bakken.
I never cook. I can't even fry an egg.

To add something slightly less related or less relevant to a statement in the manner of a 'by the way,' 'for that matter,' or 'besides,' one can use **overigens**, **bovendien**, or **trouwens**.

Ik heb geen zin om naar de bioscoop te gaan. Bovendien heb ik geen geld.
I don't want to go to the movies. Besides, I have no money.

Trouwens, die film die je wilt zien, die draait allang niet meer.
By the way, that film that you want to see, it is not showing anymore.

Wist jij overigens dat er een nieuwe bioscoop in het winkelcentrum komt?
Did you know, by the way, that there will be a new cinema in the mall?

In questions, the words **niet** 'not' and **zeker** 'surely' can be used to confirm information that the speaker claims to have, but doesn't know for sure. Note that questions with **zeker** have inverted word order.

Is dat niet die nieuwe vriend van Karin?
Isn't that Karin's new boyfriend?

Jij wil vanavond zeker naar het voetbal kijken, hè?
You (do) want to watch the soccer game tonight, right?

▶ See also **9.2** and **14.1** for more information on asking questions.

Finally, many modal particles shape a conversation by giving statements, thoughts, commands, and questions a certain tone or quality: friendliness, politeness, patience, impatience, irritation, encouragement, and the like. The most common modal particles are **maar**, **eens**, **even**, **nou**, and **toch**.

With **maar**, one can express friendly encouragement, a general feeling that something is okay, no problem. This is often the case in sentences in the imperative, the command form. It can also express a subtle resignation, as if what the statement suggests is the only possible way.

Doe het raam maar dicht, het wordt koud.
(Just) close the window, it is getting cold.

Je moet die kaas maar weggooien, die is beschimmeld.
You should (just) throw that cheese out, it is moldy.

Similarly, **eens** makes a command friendlier. Note that literal translations are difficult.

Geef me dat kaasmes eens.
Give me that cheese slicer, would you?

Kom eens hier.
Come here for a sec.

Luister eens.
Listen, please.

Not unlike **eens**, and often in combination with it, **even** also expresses friendly encouragement and, when used in the command form, it suggests that the request is something that won't take a long time or a lot of effort.

We gaan even naar de bakker, ga je mee?
We're going to the baker, are you coming?

Wil jij even die stapel sollicitaties kopiëren?
Could you copy that stack of applications?

Kom eens even hier, ik wil je iets laten zien.
Come here for a minute, I want to show you something.

When there is a slight irritation or impatience involved then the Dutch use **nou** to modify a statement or a command. However, **nou** can also simply reinforce a sentence part.

Dat had ik nou eerder moeten weten, dan was ik thuisgebleven.
I really should have known that sooner. I would have stayed at home.

Boedapest, dat vind ik nou een leuke stad.
Budapest, now that's a fun city.

Eet je brood nou op, dan kunnen we weg.
Come on, finish your bread, then we can go.

Toe nou, pest die hond niet zo.
Come on, quit harassing that dog.

The function of **toch** is similar to **nou**, but it is more a strong encouragement than an expression of anger or impatience. However, used with the right intonation, it can also express anger. One of its other meanings is 'right?', used to verify information that one has but wants to know for sure.

Laat het stofzuigen toch tot volgende week zitten.
Just leave the vacuum cleaning until next week.

Hou toch op met die onzin.
For heaven's sake, stop that nonsense.

Jij ging toch naar de wintersport, of heb ik dat verkeerd?
Weren't you going on a ski vacation, or am I wrong?

These particles can also be used in combination. In fact, most of the time, at least two or three are combined. Combinations such as **maar even**, **eens even**, **nou even**, **maar eens**, **nou eens**, **toch maar even**, and others are quite common. Indeed, a sentence with all five of them is not out of the ordinary. It is impossible to translate such sentences literally into English.

Laat ik die rekeningen nou toch maar eens even betalen.
Well, I think I should really pay those bills now.

► For more on particles, see **3.9**.

13.9 The basics of telephone etiquette

This section focuses on basic communication strategies on the phone (**telefoneren**). How to answer, how to ask for someone, how to connect and be connected (**doorverbinden**), how to finish a call, and more.

Answering

When the telephone rings, speakers of Dutch answer with their name using the preposition **met**. Many people answer with both first and last name, some just say their last name, some (mostly young people) just the first name. A greeting is often added, especially in formal calls, for example a business call. Women often introduce themselves with **mevrouw**.

Met Jos (van Kampen).
This is Jos (van Kampen).

Met Van Kampen.
This is Van Kampen.

Van Kampen.
Van Kampen.

Van Kampen, goedemiddag.
Van Kampen, good afternoon.

Goedemorgen, Van Lier & Co, met Jos van Kampen, wat kan ik voor u doen?
Good morning, Van Lier & Co, this is Jos van Kampen, what can I do for you?

Met mevrouw De Jong.
This is Mrs. De Jong speaking.

Note that answering a call with just **hallo** 'hello' is out of the question. It will cause irritation and prompt the person on the other line to say things like **Ja, wie is dit?** 'Yes, who is this?' or **Wie bent u?** 'Who are you?' or **Met wie spreek ik?** 'Whom am I speaking to?' One must always identify oneself on the phone. Then, the caller will answer by saying, for instance:

Ja, dag, u spreekt met Flip Houtzager.
Yes, hi, this is Flip Houtzager (*lit.* You are speaking to Flip Houtzager).

Met Flip Houtzager.
This is Flip Houtzager.

In very informal situations, and when one knows the other person very well, some callers do not say their name, but instead they say:

Ja, hoi, met mij.
Yes, hi, it's me.

Asking to speak to someone

When the caller wants to speak to someone else than the person who answers the phone, he or she can say a number of things. If the situation is informal, one can say:

Is Jan/je moeder/je vader thuis?
Is Jan/your mom/your dad at home?

Mag ik even met Jan/je moeder/je vader spreken?
Can I speak to Jan/your mom/your dad?

In a formal situation, one can say:

Is meneer De Boer ook te spreken?
Is Mr. De Boer available?

Zou ik even met meneer De Boer kunnen spreken?
Could I speak to Mr. De Boer, please?

Possible answers, informal and formal, are:

Momentje, ik zal even kijken (of hij/zij thuis is).
Just a moment, I'll go and see (if he/she is at home).

Ik zal hem/haar even roepen.
I will get him/her.

Momentje, ik verbind u door.
Just a moment, I will connect you.

Call back or leave a message

When the person one asks for is not available, the speaker can say a variety of things, depending on the situation. One can ask the caller to call back (**terugbellen**) or leave a message (**een boodschap/berichtje achterlaten**).

Hij/zij is niet thuis. Kun je vanmiddag even terugbellen?
He/she is not at home. Can you call back this afternoon?

Hij/zij is er niet. Wil je een berichtje achterlaten?
He/she is not here. Do you want to leave a message?

Zal ik vragen of hij/zij jou terugbelt?
Shall I ask him/her to call you back?

In formal or business situations, it's more common to say that someone is on another line. Callers are often asked to leave a message or call back.

Het spijt me, meneer De Boer is niet aanwezig. Wilt u een boodschap achterlaten?
I'm sorry, Mr. De Boer is not here. Would you like to leave a message?

Meneer De Boer is in gesprek. Wilt u wachten of belt u terug?
Mr. De Boer is on another line. Would you like to wait, or do you want to call back?

Meneer De Boer neemt niet op. Ik zal zeggen dat u gebeld hebt.
Mr. De Boer is not answering the phone. I will tell him that you called.

In response, the caller can leave a message, promise to call back, ask for a more convenient time to call, or ask if the person can call back.

Kunt u een boodschap aan hem doorgeven?
Can you leave a message for him?

Kunt u zeggen dat ik gebeld heb?
Can you let him/her know that I called?

Kunt u vragen of hij mij terugbelt?
Can you ask him to call me back?

Wanneer denkt u dat ik hem kan bereiken?
When do you think I can reach him?

Kan ik op een geschikter moment terugbellen?
Can I call back at a more convenient time?

Ik probeer het later nog wel een keer.
I'll try again later.

Ending a call

At the end of a conversation, and to thank someone for their help, one can say:

Bedankt voor uw hulp/Bedankt voor de informatie.
Thanks for your help/Thanks for the information.

In response to that, one can say:

Graag gedaan/Tot uw dienst.
My pleasure/At your service.

Different greetings that work for both sides can be:

Goedemiddag/Dag/Tot ziens.
Good afternoon/Bye/See you later.

▶ For other ways to say goodbye on the phone, see **12.5**.

Bad line

Sometimes there are problems either with the phone or with the number one has dialed. When the phone line is bad, and one cannot hear much, one can say:

Kun je wat harder/langzamer praten, de lijn is zo slecht.
Can you speak up/speak slower, the line is quite bad.

Wrong number

When one has dialed the wrong number, and depending on who notices first, we say:

O pardon, ik heb een verkeerd nummer gedraaid/getoetst.
I'm sorry, I dialed the wrong number.

U heeft een verkeerd nummer gedraaid/getoetst.
You have dialed the wrong number.

Answering machine and voicemail

A formal/standard message on a Dutch answering machine might be as follows:

U bent verbonden met het automatisch antwoordapparaat van Henk en Lydia Visser. Wij zijn op dit moment niet te bereiken. Spreekt u een bericht in na de pieptoon.
You have reached Henk and Lydia Visser. We are not available at this time. Please leave a message after the beep.

Voicemail messages are similar:

Dit is de voicemail van Kees Barends. Momenteel ben ik niet bereikbaar. Als u een bericht/boodschap achterlaat met naam en telefoonnummer, bel ik u zo spoedig mogelijk terug.
This is Kees Barends's voicemail. I am not available at this time. If you leave a message with name and phone number, I will call you back as soon as possible.

Businesses may have a menu with different options to choose from. Example:

Welkom bij . . . U hoort nu een keuzemenu met vijf mogelijkheden. Voor . . . , toets 1. Voor . . . , toets 2. Voor . . . , toets 3. Toets 0 als u met een medewerker van . . . wilt spreken.
This is . . . Please listen to the following five options on our menu. For . . . , please press 1. For . . . , please press 2. For . . . , press 3. To speak with a staff member of . . . , press 0.

Businesses also may have automatic messages that ask the caller to stay on the line until someone is available to take their call. Example:

Welkom bij aannemersbedrijf Geertsema. Momenteel zijn al onze medewerkers in gesprek. U wordt zo snel mogelijk te woord gestaan. Blijft u aan de lijn?
You have reached Geertsema Construction. Currently, all our staff members are assisting other callers. Please stay on the line and your call will be answered as soon as possible.

Mobile phone and texting

For text messaging, the Dutch use the verb **sms'en** which means 'to text.' Cell phones used to be called **gsm'etje** (note that this is a diminutive) before **mobiel** or **mobieltje** 'mobile' took over. Examples from cyber communication:

Je kunt me ook mobiel bereiken.
You can also reach me on my cell phone.

Mijn mobiele nummer is . . .
My cell phone number is . . .

Stond je mobieltje uit?
Was your cell phone turned off?

Ik had je toch een sms gestuurd?
Didn't I send you a text message?

Sms me even wanneer je trein aankomt.
Text me when your train arrives.

Ik heb gisteren de hele avond met Jos zitten sms'en.
Last night, I was texting with Jos the whole evening.

Karel heeft me die treintijden even ge-sms't.
Karel has texted me those train times.

Note that indeed, **sms'en** can be conjugated just like any other verb.

13.10 The basics of letter writing

Beginning

A formal beginning of a letter can start with **Geachte** or **Beste**. In formal or business letters, one addresses the person with their last name. Examples:

Geachte heer Jansen,
Dear Mr. Jansen,

Geachte mevrouw De Boer,
Dear Ms./Mrs. De Boer,

Beste heer Van der Meer,
Dear Mr. Van der Meer,

Beste mevrouw Bartels,
Dear Ms./Mrs. Bartels,

If the name and/or gender of the addressee are not known, one can write:

Geachte heer/mevrouw,
Dear Sir/Madam,

Geachte heer, mevrouw,
Dear Sir, Madam,

Geachte dames en heren,
Dear Sirs, Madams,

If the addressee is someone with a title, a customer, a group of people such as a committee or a board or an organization, one can be more specific:

Geachte professor Haverman/Geachte Dr. Van Mering,
Dear Professor Haverman/Dear Dr. Van Mering,

Geachte klant/cliënt,
Dear customer/client,

Geachte abonnee,
Dear subscriber,

Geacht bestuur/Geachte bestuursleden,
Dear board members,

Geachte commissie/Geachte commissieleden,
Dear committee (members),

Geachte collega's,
Dear colleagues,

In less formal letters or emails to acquaintances, friends and colleagues, one uses **Beste** and that person's first and/or last name. One can also use **Dag** with someone's first name.

Beste Jaap van Zanden,
Dear Jaap van Zanden,

Beste Lidia,
Dear Lidia,

Dag Lidia,
Hi Lidia,

Beste collega's,
Dear colleagues,

Beste vrienden,
Dear friends,

Beste allemaal,
Dear all,

Letter text

After the comma in, for instance, **Beste Lidia**, the letter text begins with a capital letter. Some standard formulations and expressions are a reference to a previous letter, a request for something, something that one wishes to attach, thanking the addressee for their attention, saying that one is looking forward to an answer, and expressing hope that one has been able to be of assistance.

Referring back

One can refer to a previous letter saying:

In antwoord op uw schrijven van 25 maart . . .
In answer to your letter from March 25 . . .

Hartelijk dank/Bedankt voor uw brief van 25 maart . . .
Sincere thanks/Thanks for your letter from March 25 . . .

Naar aanleiding van uw brief van 25 maart . . .
In reference to your letter from March 25 . . .

Request

To ask the addressee to do (or send) something, one can use different expressions.

Gelieve ons . . . zo snel mogelijk te willen sturen.
Please send us . . . as soon as possible.

Zou u zo vriendelijk willen zijn . . . /Wilt u zo vriendelijk zijn . . .
Would you be so kind as to . . .

Wij zouden u vriendelijk willen vragen . . .
We would like to kindly ask you . . .

Attaching or enclosing something

To attach or enclose a document, one can say:

In de bijlage vindt u . . .
Enclosed you will find . . .

Ik sluit . . . hierbij in.
I enclose . . . in this letter.

Thanking the addressee

To thank the addressee (in advance) for their help or attention, one can say:

Met vriendelijk dank voor uw hulp.
With sincere thanks for your help.

Bedankt voor uw tijd en moeite.
Thanks for your time and effort.

Alvast bedankt voor de informatie.
Thanks in advance for the information.

Bij voorbaat dank voor uw medewerking.
Thanks in advance for your cooperation.

Ik dank u/Wij danken u bij voorbaat voor uw hulp.
I/We thank you in advance for your help.

U bij voorbaat (voor uw moeite) dankend,
With thanks in advance (for your effort),

Anticipating an answer

To say that one is looking forward to an answer, one can say:

Uw (spoedig) antwoord tegemoetziende,
In anticipation of a prompt reply,

Met belangstelling zie ik uw antwoord tegemoet.
Anxiously awaiting your reply.

Wij hopen spoedig van u te horen.
We hope to hear from you soon.

Ik hoor graag van u/je (less formal)**.**
I'm looking forward to hearing from you.

Assistance

To express hope that one has been able to help someone, one can say:

Wij hopen u hiermee van dienst te zijn geweest.
We hope that we have been able to assist you.

Ik hoop u hiermee voldoende geïnformeerd te hebben.
I hope I have been able to inform you adequately.

► To close a letter with a greeting, see **12.2**. To express good wishes, see **12.9**.

14

Giving and seeking factual information

14.1 Asking for and giving basic personal information

► To ask what someone's name is, and possible answers to that question, check **12.3**.

Date and place of birth

To ask what one's date and place of birth are, one can choose from different questions.

Wanneer en waar bent u/ben je geboren?
When and where were you born?

Wat is uw/je geboortedatum en geboorteplaats?
What is your date and place of birth?

Possible answers to this question are:

Ik ben op 5 mei 1982 in Utrecht geboren.
I was born on May 5, 1982, in Utrecht.

Mijn geboortedatum is 5 mei 1982. Mijn geboorteplaats is Utrecht.
My date of birth is May 5, 1982. My place of birth is Utrecht.

Birthday

To ask when someone's birthday is, one can say:

Wanneer is je/uw verjaardag?
When is your birthday?

Wanneer ben je/bent u jarig?
When is your birthday?

Possible answers to this question are:

Ik ben op 5 mei jarig/Mijn verjaardag is 5 mei.
My birthday is May 5.

Address

There are a variety of ways to ask where someone lives and to request more specific information such as a street address, a house number, a phone number, and an email address. Examples:

Waar woont u?/Waar woon je?/Wat is uw/je woonplaats?
Where do you live?

Wat is uw adres?/Wat is je adres?
What is your address?

In welke straat woont u/woon je? En op welk huisnummer?
In what street do you live? And at what number?

Wat is uw/je postcode?
What is your zip code?

U bent woonachtig in Maastricht? (very formal)
You reside in Maastricht?

Wat is uw/je telefoonnummer? Het netnummer en het abonneenummer?
What is your phone number? The area code and the home phone number?

Wat is uw/je mobiele telefoonnummer?
What is your cell phone number?

Kan ik u/je ook mobiel bereiken?
Can I reach you on your cell phone as well?

Wat is je/uw emailadres?
What is your email address?

In narrative form, the following summarizes the answers to these questions:

Ik woon in Utrecht, in de Bakkerstraat, op nummer 29. Mijn postcode is 3511 JV. Mijn telefoonnummer daar is 030-2675934. Mijn mobiele nummer is 06-8835920. Mijn emailadres is jansen@home.nl (jansen-apestaartje (at)-home-punt-nl).
I live in Utrecht, in the Bakkerstraat, at number 29. My zip code is 3511 JV. My phone number there is 030-2675934. My cell phone number is 06-8835920. My email address is jansen@home.nl.

Nationality

To ask about one's nationality or citizenship, one can say:

Welke nationaliteit heeft u?/Uit welk land komt u?
What is your nationality? What country are you from?

Van welk land heeft u het staatsburgerschap?
Of which country are you a citizen?

Possible answers to these questions are:

Ik ben Nederlander/Amerikaan/Duitser.
I'm Dutch/an American/a German.

Ik kom uit Amerika/Duitsland/Frankrijk.
I am from America/Germany/France.

Ik heb het Nederlandse staatsburgerschap.
I have Dutch citizenship.

Characteristics

In some situations, one may be asked about specific characteristics such as height, weight, color of one's eyes and hair, and eye sight.

Hoe lang bent u?/Wat is uw lengte?
How tall are you?

Wat is uw gewicht?
What is your weight?

Welke kleur hebben uw ogen?
What color are your eyes?

Wat is de kleur van uw haar?
What color is your hair?

Bent u verziend of bijziend?
Are you farsighted or nearsighted?

Note that the Dutch measure in the metric system. They measure weight in kilos rather than pounds, and they measure height in meters and centimeters. Note also that words like **kilo** and **meter** in this context are used in singular.

Ik weeg 62 kilo.
I weigh 62 kilos.

Ik ben 1.75 meter (1 meter 75) lang.
I am 1 meter and 75 centimeters tall.

▶ For more information on measurements, see also Chapter **5**.

Identification

To ask for someone's identification, one can say:

Heeft u een legitimatiebewijs?/Kunt u zich legitimeren?
Do you have an ID?

Heeft u een paspoort of rijbewijs?
Do you have a passport or driver's license?

Profession

Finally, to ask about and to give information about one's profession, one can say:

Wat bent u van beroep?/Wat voor werk doet u?
What is your profession?

Waar werkt u/Waar werk je?
Where do you work?

Karel is al weer drie jaar bij Philips werkzaam.
Karel has worked at Philips for three years now.

Joost is vorige week bij Leenman & Dijkstra aangesteld.
Joost was hired at Leenman & Dijkstra last week.

Hij is architect. Hij krijgt daar een vaste aanstelling.
He is an architect. He will be tenured there.

Note that, contrary to English, we leave the indefinite article out when we name someone's profession. We also leave the article out in combinations with **als** 'as.'

Jan is advocaat en zijn vrouw is lerares op een middelbare school.
Jan is a lawyer, and his wife is a teacher in high school.

Karin is sinds 2010 als fysiotherapeute in deze kliniek werkzaam.
Karin has worked as a physical therapist in this clinic since 2010.

▶ For more on articles, see **1.1**.

14.2 Describing people

Appearance, characteristics

To describe a person's outer appearance (Dutch **het uiterlijk**), we use the verb **eruitzien** 'look like.' This verb is separable, so it can be separated by other parts of the sentence.

Hoe ziet de nieuwe vrouw van Joost eruit?
What does Joost's new wife look like?

Goh, wat zie je er leuk uit vandaag!
Boy, you look nice today!

Je ziet eruit alsof je de hele nacht niet geslapen hebt.
You look like you didn't sleep all night.

Johan ziet er nog goed uit voor z'n leeftijd.
Johan looks good considering his age.

To describe that someone's appearance or character is similar to someone else's, we use the verb **lijken op** 'to resemble.'

Karel lijkt meer op z'n grootvader dan op z'n vader.
Karel looks more like his grandfather than his father.

Mieke en Sarah lijken erg op elkaar.
Mieke and Sarah really look like each other.

Je lijkt net op je broer. Die is ook zo verlegen.
You're just like your brother. He's also so shy.

To ask someone to describe or characterize a person, one can say:

Hoe zag die persoon eruit die iets uit uw auto stal?
What did the person who stole something from your car look like?

Kunt u die persoon beschrijven/identificeren?
Can you describe/identify that person?

Hoe zou jij de hoofdfiguur in dit boek karakteriseren?
How would you describe the main character in this book?

Wat voor iemand is Peter?
What kind of person is Peter?

To ask for or talk about specific features or characteristics, one can say:

Heeft hij bijzondere uiterlijke kenmerken?
Does he have special physical features?

Noem eens een paar typische eigenschappen van Kees.
Give me some typical characteristics of Kees.

Minnie is jaloers. Dat is een vervelende karaktertrek van haar.
Minnie is jealous. That's an annoying characteristic of hers.

To refer to someone, we typically use the demonstrative pronoun **die** or a relative sentence describing the person. We also give descriptions using the preposition **met** 'with' to sum up features.

Die man die met Karin praat, ken je die?
The man who is talking to Karin, you know him?

Wie is die vrouw op de foto met dat lange blonde haar en die rode jurk?
Who is the woman in the photo with that long blond hair in that red dress?

► For demonstrative pronouns, see **2.3**. For relative pronouns, see **2.7**.

Physical features

To find all possible physical features a person can have, it is best to refer to a dictionary. To stay within the scope of this book, here are just a few typical examples.

Tanja is blond/Tanja heeft blond haar, heeft blauwe ogen en een rond gezicht.
Tanja is blond, with blue eyes and a round face.

Ria heeft een lange, smalle neus en ronde lippen.
Ria has a long, thin nose and round lips.

Karel is vrij lang, slank en breedgeschouderd.
Karel is rather tall, slender, and broad-shouldered.

Anna is kort, mollig met brede heupen en smalle schouders.
Anna is short, chubby, with wide hips and narrow shoulders.

To talk about physical features in more general terms, here are some examples:

Zij is 75, maar fysiek nog heel fit.
She is 75, but physically very fit.

Deze jongen is lichamelijk gehandicapt.
This boy is physically disabled.

Menno heeft een knappe/aantrekkelijke vrouw.
Menno has a pretty/attractive wife.

Personality and character

A few common (positive) examples to describe someone's personality and character are:

Meneer Jansen is een aardige/vriendelijke/sympathieke man.
Mister Jansen is a nice/friendly/sympathetic man.

Jeroen is een lief en spontaan kind.
Jeroen is a sweet and spontaneous child.

Onze buren zijn zulke hulpvaardige mensen!
Our neighbors are such helpful people.

Joost is heel aangenaam in de omgang.
Joost is real easy to get along with.

We kunnen het goed met onze geschiedenisleraar vinden.
We really get along well with our history teacher.

Karin is echt een sociaal type.
Karin is a real social type.

Some not so positive ways to describe a person are the following:

Onze leraar wiskunde is een onaardige/gemene/onaangename vent.
Our math teacher is an unfriendly/mean/unpleasant guy.

Keesje zoekt altijd met iedereen ruzie.
Keesje always wants to pick a fight with someone.

Ik kan helemaal niet met m'n schoonmoeder overweg.
I don't get along with my mother-in-law at all.

Impressions

To describe what sort of impression a person makes on others, one can use a variety of words such as **eruitzien** 'look like,' **lijken** 'seem, appear,' **indruk maken** 'make an impression,' **voorkomen** 'appear' (also as noun: **het voorkomen** 'appearance').

Je ziet er vandaag moe uit.
You look tired today.

Die vriend van jou lijkt me maar een vreemde figuur.
That boyfriend of yours seems an odd character to me.

Hij heeft het voorkomen van een mafiabaas.
He looks like a mafia boss.

Martin maakte een goede indruk op z'n toekomstige schoonvader.
Martin made a good impression on his future father-in-law.

Het publiek was erg onder de indruk van de schrijfster.
The audience was very impressed by the writer.

Habits

To describe a person's good or bad habits, the Dutch use the word **gewoonte** 'habit.'

Nagelbijten is een slechte gewoonte.
Nail biting is a bad habit.

Het is al jaren zijn gewoonte om 's morgens te joggen.
He has been jogging in the mornings for years.

Naar gewoonte gingen we na aankomst eerst even naar het strand.
Like we always do, we went to the beach right after arrival.

Dispositions

To describe someone's (genetic) dispositions, we use the word **aanleg** 'predisposition.' To describe certain tendencies, we use the words **neiging** 'inclination' or **drang** 'urge.'

Erik heeft totaal geen aanleg voor muziek.
Eric is not musically gifted.

Met jouw aanleg om dik te worden zou ik maar niet zoveel snoepen.
With your predisposition to get fat, I wouldn't snack so much if I were you.

Mia heeft de neiging tot dweperigheid.
Mia is inclined to idolatry.

Hij heeft voordurend de drang om z'n handen te wassen.
He has a constant urge to wash his hands.

► For people's talents and capabilities, see **15.8**.

Relationships

For basic family relationships, consult a dictionary. Note that the Dutch have different words for nuclear family (**het gezin**) and extended family (**de familie**).

Ik woon met mijn gezin in Haarlem.
I live in Haarlem with my family (= father, mother, and children).

De rest van de familie woont vooral in de noordelijke provincies.
The rest of the family live primarily in the northern provinces.

Ik heb ook nog een paar verwanten in het buitenland.
I also have a few relatives abroad.

Er kwamen 32 familieleden naar de bruiloft.
32 relatives came to the wedding.

Step family members receive the prefix **stief-**, similar to English.

stiefmoeder stepmother, **stiefvader** stepfather, **stiefouders** stepparents, **stiefkinderen** stepchildren, **stiefbroer** stepbrother, **stiefzus** stepsister, **stiefoma** stepgrandmother, **stiefopa** stepgrandfather.

For adoptive and foster arrangements, we have words with **adoptief-** and **pleeg-**:

Joost en Hanna hebben een adoptiefzoon, Michael.
Joost and Hanna have an adoptive son, Michael.

In dit gezin leven twee pleegkinderen.
In this family, there are two foster children.

Bert en Minnie hebben een kindje uit Vietnam geadopteerd.
Bert and Minnie have adopted a child from Vietnam.

In-laws and people related by marriage are described as follows. Note that all in-laws have the prefix **schoon-**, except brother-in-law, which is **zwager**. In Belgium, **schoon-** is also used for brother-in-law, **schoonbroer**.

Mijn schoonouders komen dit weekend op bezoek.
My parents-in-law are visiting this weekend.

Peter is een aangetrouwde neef van me.
Peter is a cousin by marriage.

Note also the different words for grandparents and grandchildren.

Grootouders geven hun kleinkinderen vaak dure cadeau's.
Grandparents often give their grandchildren expensive presents.

With newer, more open forms of family relationships in Dutch society, 'partner' is quite common aside from 'husband' and 'wife.'

Ik heb mijn man op vakantie in Engeland leren kennen.
I met my husband while on vacation in England.

Mijn vrouw en ik houden van een goed glas wijn.
My wife and I like a good glass of wine.

Joop en zijn partner gaan een kind adopteren.
Joop and his partner are going to adopt a child.

Note the verbs for different forms of relationships such as marriage, engagement, divorce, and living together.

Mijn ouders zijn in 1959 getrouwd.
My parents got married in 1959.

In die tijd was het nog de gewoonte om je eerst te verloven.
In those days it was customary to get engaged first.

Veel jonge paren opteren ook voor een geregistreerd partnerschap.
Many young couples opt for a registered partnership.

Uit zo'n partnerschap kan je makkelijker weer scheiden.
It is easier to dissolve such a partnership.

Karin en Menno willen eerst een jaar samenwonen.
Karin and Menno want to live together for a year first.

Tinus en Miriam hebben al tien jaar een lat-relatie.
Tinus and Miriam have been 'living apart together' for ten years.

Erik is alleenstaand en voelt zich daar prima bij.
Eric is single and is quite fine with that.

There are several ways to talk about dating, crushes and casual relationships.

Peter gaat al twee maanden met Tineke.
Peter has been going out with Tineke for two months.

Hoe moet je iemand verkering vragen? (very old-fashioned)
How do you ask someone to date you?

Pim is verliefd op Mia, maar zij is op Bert.
Pim is in love with Mia, but she's after Bert.

Karin heeft vanavond een afpraakje met de nieuwe klasgenoot.
Karin has a date with the new classmate tonight.

Johan heeft de date afgezegd, vind je dat niet lullig?
Johan has cancelled the date, don't you think that's crap?

Note that **afspraakje** 'date' is different from **afspraak** 'appointment' (in a general sense). The diminutive ending brings it into the realm of dating.

14.3 Describing objects

To ask for and to give a definition of an object, one can say:

Wat is een papaya?
What is a papaya?

Een papaya is een soort fruit.
A papaya is a type of fruit.

Function

To describe the function of an object, Dutch often uses a relative sentence or an infinitive construction with **om te** 'in order to, for the purpose of.' Another possibility is to use the preposition **voor** with an infinitive as noun.

Een garde is een keukengereedchap waarmee je een ei los kan kloppen.
A whisk is a kitchen tool with which you can beat an egg.

Je gebruikt een hamer om een spijker in de muur te slaan.
You use a hammer to hit a nail into the wall.

Deze platte bakvorm is niet geschikt voor het bakken van een cake.
This flat baking dish is not suitable for baking a cake.

As with describing people, one can ask for a more detailed description of an object, using the verb **eruitzien** 'look like.'

Hoe ziet uw tas eruit? Kunt u hem nader beschrijven?
What does your bag look like? Can you describe it in more detail?

Similarity

To describe similarity between objects, we also use the verb **lijken op** 'look just like, resemble' or **eruitzien als** 'look similar to.'

Die abstracte schilderijen van Mondriaan lijken allemaal op elkaar, vind je niet?
Those abstract paintings by Mondriaan all look like each other, don't you think?

De nieuwe Volkswagen Golf ziet er net zo uit als het model van vorig jaar.
The new Volkswagen Golf looks just like last year's model.

Difference

To ask about and describe the 'difference' (**het verschil**) between objects, Dutch uses verbs such as **verschillen** 'to differ' and adjectives such as **verschillend, anders** 'different, other.' Also, one can use **eruitzien** with **niet zo . . . als** 'not as . . . as.'

Wat is het verschil tussen groene kool en boerenkool?
What's the difference between green cabbage and kale?

Wit brood ziet er niet zo gezond uit als bruin brood.
White bread doesn't look as healthy as brown bread.

Ik doe verschillende soorten kaas in mijn kaasfondue.
I put different kinds of cheese in my cheese fondue.

De nieuwe Audi A4 ziet er heel anders uit dan het model van vorig jaar.
The new Audi A4 looks very different from last year's model.

Size, shape, color

The words for size (**maat/grootte**), weight (**gewicht**), shape (**vorm**), and color (**kleur**) of an object are as follows:

Geef me even de breedte, de hoogte en de diepte van die koelkast.
Please give me the width, the height, and the depth of that fridge.

De lengte van het zwembad is 25 meter.
The length of the pool is 25 meters.

De driehoek, de cirkel, de rechthoek en het vierkant zijn geometrische vormen.
The triangle, the circle, the rectangle, and the square are geometric forms.

Zwart, wit, rood, geel en blauw zijn primaire kleuren.
Black, white, red, yellow, and blue are primary colors.

Het gewicht bepaalt de prijs van een stuk kaas.
The weight determines the price of a piece of cheese.

Metrics

When talking about size, the Dutch use the metric system: **meter**, **centimeter**, **millimeter**, **kubieke meter**. Adjectives to describe sizes and dimensions are **lang** 'long,' **breed** 'wide,' **hoog** 'high,' **diep** 'deep.' Note that after a numeral, **-meter** is singular.

Onze woonkamer is 5 bij 6 meter, dus 30 vierkante meter/m^2.
Our living room is 5 by 6 meters, so it is 30 square meters.

Bij de hoge duikplank is het zwembad 2,5m diep.
At the high diving board, the pool is 2.5 meters deep.

Dit stuk hout is 15 bij 30 centimeter lang en 2 centimeter dik.
This piece of wood is 15 by 30 centimeters long and 2 centimeters thick.

Larger areas are measured in **vierkante kilometers** 'square kilometers' and (farm) land is measured in **hectares** 'acres.'

Op een oppervlakte van ongeveer 6 km^2 worden hier nieuwe woningen gebouwd.
On a surface of approximately 6 km^2, they are building new housing.

Mijn opa heeft er in 1980 vier hectare bouwland bijgekocht.
My grandfather bought an additional four acres of farmland in 1980.

The Dutch also use the metric system to talk about the weight of objects. Note that after a numeral, words such as **kilo**, **pond**, and **gram** appear in singular.

Dit stuk kaas weegt anderhalf pond.
This piece of cheese weighs a pound and a half.

Ik mocht de koffer niet inchecken, want hij was drie kilo te zwaar.
They didn't let me check in my suitcase, because it was three kilos overweight.

▶ For more information on weights and measurements, see Chapter **5**.

Surfaces, shapes, material

To describe the surfaces and shapes of objects, we use words such as **lijn** 'line,' **vlak** 'surface, side,' **hoek** 'corner, angle,' and adjectives such as **recht** 'straight,' **schuin** 'slanting,' **rond** 'round,' **strak** 'straight, tight.' To describe the material of which objects are made, we use adjectives derived from the material with the ending **-en**: **houten** 'wooden,' **metalen** 'metal,' **glazen** 'glass,' etc. Note that adjectives derived from loan words do not get the ending -en: **nylon**, **rayon**, etc.

In de hoek van de kamer stond een ronde houten eettafel.
In the corner of the room, there was a round, wooden dining table.

Veel schilderijen van Mondriaan hebben strakke lijnen en fel gekleurde vlakken.
Many paintings by Mondriaan have straight lines and brightly colored shapes.

Patterns

The most common words for patterns on clothes and furniture are as follows:

Ik trek vandaag mijn gestippelde jurk (stippeltjesjurk) aan.
I'm putting my dotted dress on today.

Er lag een geruit/geblokt tafelkleed op de tuintafel.
There was a checkered tablecloth on the garden table.

Wie loopt er nou in zo'n achterlijke gestreepte broek (streepjesbroek)!
Who would run around in such a stupid striped pair of pants!

Leuk, die gebloemde gordijnen!
Nice, those flowered curtains!

▶ For more information on adjectives, see Chapter **3**.

The verb **passen** 'fit' is used to describe whether the size of an object is right or whether it matches another object in shape and color.

Die bank past niet in onze woonkamer, hij is veel te groot.
That sofa doesn't fit in our living room, it's much too big.

Mag ik deze jurk even passen?
Can I try on this dress?

Die bruine rok past niet bij die blauwe bloes.
That brown skirt doesn't match that blue shirt.

Alteration

When objects don't have the right dimension or quality, we use a variety of verbs (many of them beginning with the prefix **ver-**) to express alteration: **verlengen** 'lengthen, extend,' **verkorten** 'shorten,' **innemen** 'take in,' **uitleggen** 'let out, tailor,' **veranderen** 'alter, change,'

vernieuwen 'renew, renovate,' **vergroten** 'enlarge,' **verkleinen** 'reduce,' **verdubbelen** 'double,' **halveren** 'divide in two.'

> **Ik moet mijn abonnement op Fit for Life verlengen.**
> I have to extend my subscription to Fit for Life.
>
> **Bezoek onze geheel vernieuwde website.**
> Visit our entirely renewed website.
>
> **Ik ga deze foto vergroten en inlijsten.**
> I'm going to enlarge this picture and frame it.

Condition, substance

To talk about the state, condition, or substance of an object, we use the following common verbs: **smelten '**melt,' **bevriezen** 'freeze,' **koken** 'boil,' **verdampen** 'evaporate,' **stollen** 'solidify,' **drogen** 'dry,' **opwarmen/verwarmen** 'warm up,' **afkoelen** 'cool down.' Note that temperature is measured in degrees Celsius.

> **Het water kookt. Zet jij even thee?**
> The water is boiling. Can you make some tea?
>
> **Rond de kandelaar lag een plas stollend kaarsvet.**
> There was a puddle of solidifying candle wax around the candle holder.
>
> **We kunnen de taart pas uit de vorm halen als hij wat afgekoeld is.**
> We can take the cake out of the tin when it has cooled down a bit.
>
> **De was droogt buiten aan de lijn.**
> The laundry is drying outside on the line.
>
> **Water bevriest bij nul graden Celcius/0°C.**
> Water freezes at zero degrees Celsius.

Quantity, number

When one wants to be precise about the quantity (**de hoeveelheid**) and number (**het aantal**) of objects, one uses cardinal numbers.

> **Er zitten 23 leerlingen in deze klas.**
> There are 23 students in this class.
>
> **In dit pak gevulde koeken zitten zes stuks.**
> This packet of 'gevulde koeken' (type of Dutch cookie) contains eight pieces.

When one cannot be precise, the Dutch use words such as **ongeveer** 'approximately,' **een stuk of** 'about, around,' **een paar** 'a few,' **een aantal** 'a number of,' **een (hele)boel** 'quite a few,' **talloze** 'numerous,' **massa's** 'masses of.' Note also even more vague descriptions with **rond** 'around,' **in de** 'about,' and **zo'n** 'about,' followed by a numeral.

> **Er zitten ongeveer vier appels in een pond.**
> There are approximately four apples in a pound.
>
> **Ik heb nog een stuk of zes kerstkaarten over.**
> I have six or so Christmas cards left over.
>
> **Er stonden talloze mensen op de metro te wachten.**
> There were numerous people waiting for the subway.
>
> **Jan heeft in de veertig verschillende fuchsiasoorten.**
> Jan has about forty different types of fuchsia.
>
> **Er waren zo'n zestig mensen op de begrafenis.**
> There were about sixty people at the funeral.

Fractions

Words for most common fractions are as follows. Note that the form for fractions is the same as ordinal numbers, using the suffixes **-ste** and **-de**. We also use a form in which the ending **-en** is added to a lower numeral: **in vieren verdelen** 'to divide in four parts.'

Wil jij de helft van mijn reep chocola?
Do you want half of my chocolate bar?

Een kwart van de studenten ontbrak in het college.
A quarter of the students in the class was missing.

Een derde van de studenten zakte voor het examen.
A third of the students failed the exam.

De moeder sneed de pizza in zessen.
The mother cut the pizza into six parts.

► For more on numerals with **-en**, see Chapter **5**.

Note that when we talk about quantities of objects with words that express weight or the container that holds the object, we do not use the Dutch equivalent of English 'of' as in 'a pound of tomatoes.'

Ik wil graag een kilo bananen.
I would like a kilo of bananas.

Breng je even een doosje eieren van de supermarkt mee?
Can you bring a box of eggs from the supermarket?

Quality

To refer to the quality of objects, there are numerous ways to express excellence, durability and good looks. Useful vocabulary: **de topkwaliteit** 'top quality,' **het topniveau** 'top quality,' **het merk** 'brand,' **het huismerk** 'house brand,' **de duurzaamheid** 'durability, sustainability,' **aanbevelen** 'recommend.'

Wij verkopen slaapzakken van hoogste kwaliteit/van topkwaliteit.
We sell sleeping bags of the highest quality/top quality.

Dit is een uitstekend merk.
This is an outstanding brand.

Laten we die wijn van het huismerk nemen.
Let's have the house-brand wine.

Onze kinderen willen alleen nog maar merkschoenen.
Our kids only want brand gear shoes these days.

Onze firma produceert hagelwit, duurzaam papier voor uw printer.
Our company produces snow white, durable paper for your printer.

Ik kan u deze DVD-speler aanbevelen.
I can recommend this DVD-player.

To refer to the quality of older or second-hand objects, one can say:

Deze fiets is tien jaar oud maar nog in goede staat.
This bike is ten years old but in decent shape.

Dit paar ski's is zo goed als nieuw, één keer gebruikt.
This pair of skis is as good as new, used only once.

Deze auto is tweedehands, maar hij rijdt heerlijk.
This car is used, but it's a great ride.

Price

In that context, there are numerous words to ask for and talk about the price of objects.

De tomaten zijn duur dit jaar.
The tomatoes are expensive this year.

Ik heb goedkope vliegtickets naar Athene op de kop getikt.
I scored cheap flights to Athens.

Een tientje voor die trui? Jemig, wat een koopje!
Ten bucks for that sweater? Geez, what a sweet deal!

Ik heb hem in de uitverkoop gekocht, vandaar.
I bought it on sale, that's why.

Alles bij elkaar kost 6,50 euro (zes euro vijftig), mevrouw.
All of that makes 6.50 euros, madam.

15 euro per kilo?! Goedkoop is anders!
15 euros per kilo?! That is not cheap!

Wat/Hoeveel kost die televisie?/Hoe duur is die televisie?
How much is that television?

Hoe lang is de garantie?
How long is the warranty?

Contents

To list the contents of an object, or to talk about the materials that things are made of, one can say a variety of things.

Dit product bevat natuurlijke kleur- en smaakstoffen.
This product contains natural food dye and flavoring.

Giet de inhoud van dit zakje in de kokende melk.
Pour the contents of this bag into the boiling milk.

Eiwitten en vitaminen zijn belangrijke bestanddelen van melk.
Protein and vitamins are important components of milk.

Heb je alle ingrediënten voor dat recept in huis?
Do you have all the ingredients for that recipe in the house?

Bier bestaat uit gerst, hop, gist en water.
Beer consists of barley, hops, yeast, and water.

Waar is dit van gemaakt? Van bamboe.
What's this made of? Bamboo.

Statistics

To give statistical information, the Dutch use nouns such as **de statistiek** 'statistics,' **de grafiek** 'graph,' verbs such as **groeien** 'grow,' **toenemen** 'increase,' **afnemen** 'decrease,' **stijgen** 'rise,' **dalen** 'sink,' and phrases such as **in verhouding tot** 'in proportion to,' **naar verhouding** 'proportionally,' **in vergelijking met** 'compared to.'

In deze grafiek zie je de bevolkingsgroei van de laatste tien jaar.
In this graph, you see the population growth in the last decade.

Het aantal immigranten is sinds 2007 weer afgenomen.
The number of immigrants has decreased since 2007.

Karels salaris is erg hoog in verhouding tot het werk dat hij doet.
Karel's salary is very high in proportion to the work that he does.

Het aantal schoolverlaters is het laatste jaar weer gestegen.
The number of dropouts has increased in the last year.

In vergelijking met Zwitserland is Oostenrijk een goedkoper vakantieland.
Compared to Switzerland, Austria is a cheaper vacation destination.

Naar verhouding verdienen vrouwen nog steeds te weinig.
Proportionally, women still don't make enough money.

We use the word **procent** 'percent' to describe percentages. Another way to say 25 percent would be **één op de vier** 'one in four.' Note that after **procent**, the conjugated verb is in singular, even when a group of people or objects is meant.

Tien procent van de studenten slaagt niet voor dit examen.
Ten percent of the students don't pass this exam.

Eén op de vier kinderen in deze klas is allochtoon.
One in four children in this class is foreign.

Amount

Finally, to talk about the amount or constellation of something, we use verbs such as **bedragen** 'amount to,' **belopen** 'amount to,' and **uitmaken** 'form.'

De huur voor dit appartement bedraagt 450 euro per maand.
The rent for this apartment amounts to 450 euros per month.

De brandschade beliep twee miljoen euro/liep in de miljoenen.
The fire damage amounted to two million euros/millions.

Dit werkboek maakt deel uit van de leergang *Contact*.
This workbook is part of the textbook *Contact*.

14.4 Talking about the weather

The weather is always a welcome topic of conversation. Dutch people often use the weather in informal greetings and pleasantries such as the following.

Dag buurman. Mooi weertje, niet waar?
Hello neighbor. Nice day, isn't it?

Wat een hondeweer, hè?
Isn't this weather terrible?

Lekker weer, hè?
Lovely weather, isn't it?

Some common verbs of weather types are **regenen** 'rain,' **sneeuwen** 'snow,' **hagelen** 'hail,' **dooien** 'thaw,' **ijzelen** 'sleet.' When the sun shines, we use the verb **schijnen**, and when the wind blows, we say **waaien**. Some examples:

Het regende tien minuten pijpestelen en toen scheen de zon alweer.
It rained cats and dogs for ten minutes and then the sunshine came back already.

De wind waait vandaag uit het oosten.
The wind blows from the east today.

Wind directions have the article **het** and end in **-en**: **het oosten** 'east,' **het westen** 'west,' **het noorden** 'north,' **het zuiden** 'south.' They are used to form combinations with **wind**. The wind directions themselves can also be combined.

De westenwind van vanmorgen is naar het noordwesten gedraaid.
This morning's west wind turned northeast.

Many nouns describing the weather are used to form corresponding adjectives: **de zon – zonnig** 'sun – sunny,' **de wolk – bewolkt** 'cloud – cloudy,' **de regen – regenachtig** 'rain – rainy,' **de mist – mistig** 'fog – foggy,' **de wind – winderig** 'wind – windy,' **de storm – stormachtig** 'storm – stormy,' **de bui – buiig** 'shower – showery.'

We hebben een regenachtige lente achter de rug.
We have a rainy spring behind us.

Als het mistig is, kun je de misthoorn horen loeien.
When it is foggy, you can hear the sounding of a fog horn.

A typical weather forecast in the Netherlands might go like this (temperatures are measured in degrees Celsius, and wind is measured by force, not by mph):

De weersverwachting voor morgen: Half tot zwaar bewolkt met een minimum temperatuur van 14 graden en een maximum temperatuur van 21 graden, aan de kust en op de Waddeneilanden iets koeler. In de avond kans op een bui. Zwakke tot matige zuidwestenwind, kracht 3. De verwachting voor het weekend: Opklaringen en geleidelijk warmere temperaturen.
The weather forecast for tomorrow: Partly cloudy to overcast with a minimum temperature of 14 degrees and a maximum temperature of 21 degrees, a little cooler on the coast and on the Wadden Islands. A possible shower in the evening. Mild to moderate wind out of the southwest at 3mph. The forecast for the weekend: Partly cloudy and gradually warmer temperatures.

For idioms, expressions and proverbs that have to do with weather, Google "spreekwoorden en gezegdes met het weer."

14.5 Describing actions and processes

Verbs for 'to act'

The two main verbs to describe actions are **doen** 'to do' and **handelen** 'to act.' The verb **handelen**, however, must be used in more formal contexts. Examples with **doen**:

Wat doe je daar?/Wat ben je daar aan het doen?
What are you doing there?

Is er vanavond iets te doen in de stad?
Is there something going on in the city tonight?

Hè, ik heb niks te doen. Weet jij iets?
Geez, I've got nothing to do. Do you have an idea?

The verb **handelen** is used in more formal situations. The derived noun from **handelen** is **de handeling** 'act.'

De arts heeft in alle opzichten correct gehandeld.
The physician has acted correctly in every respect.

Wat heeft deze handeling voor zin?
What is the purpose of this action?

Note in this context also the two verbs **behandelen** 'treat' and **onderhandelen** 'negotiate' with their nouns **behandeling** 'treatment' and **onderhandeling** 'negotiation.'

Hier worden de klanten met respect behandeld.
Customers are treated with respect here.

Wenst u een volledige behandeling?
Would you like a complete treatment?

We moesten nog wel even over de prijs onderhandelen.
We did have to negotiate the price.

De vredesonderhandelingen in het Midden-Oosten zijn goed verlopen.
The peace process in the Middle East went well.

Other verbs to describe an action are **verrichten** 'execute, carry out' and **uitvoeren** 'perform.'

Aan deze universiteit wordt veel onderzoek verricht.
At this university, they do a lot of research.

Wat voeren jullie eigenlijk de hele dag uit op dat kantoor?
What exactly are you doing the whole day in that office?

Het orkest heeft die sonate heel mooi uitgevoerd.
The orchestra performed the sonata very well.

Verbs for 'to happen'

Verbs and expressions for 'to happen' are **gebeuren** 'happen,' **plaatsvinden** 'take place,' **doorgaan** 'take place,' and **aan de hand zijn** 'going on.' Stories or plots such as in movies and novels take the verb **zich afspelen**.

Wat een vervelende film. Er gebeurt helemaal niets!
What a boring movie. Nothing happens!

Wat is er gebeurd?
What happened?

Waar vindt het festival dit jaar plaats?
Where does the festival take place this year?

Vanwege de regen gaat het openluchtconcert niet door.
Because of the rain, the open air concert will not take place.

Wat is hier aan de hand?
What's going on here?

Het verhaal speelt zich af in een klein kustplaatsje.
The story takes place in a little village on the coast.

The verb **lopen** 'walk, run' and its derivations with prefixes such as **ver-** and **af-** and **samen-** is also used to describe actions and processes.

Het programma loopt van juni tot september.
The program runs from June to September.

Deze klok loopt op batterijen.
This clock runs on batteries.

Mijn paspoort is verlopen.
My passport is invalid.

Na verloop van tijd/In de loop van de tijd ging de pijn vanzelf over.
In the course of time, the pain went away on its own.

Na afloop is er gelegenheid het bruidspaar te feliciteren.
Afterwards, there is time to congratulate the bride and groom.

Door een gunstige samenloop van omstandigheden kon de voorstelling doorgaan.
Because of a favorable course of events, the show could go on.

The verb **draaien** 'turn' is used to say that a film is running.

De film draait nog tot zondag.
The film runs until Sunday.

Work and operate

The verb **werken** 'to work' and its derivations with **ver-** and **be-** are also used to describe processes. In the context of 'operate,' one can also use **bedienen** or **omgaan met** 'handle.'

> **Weet jij hoe deze boormachine werkt?**
> Do you know how this drill works?

> **Hoe moet je deze boormachine bedienen?**
> How does one operate this drill?

> **Kun jij met deze boormachine omgaan?**
> Can you handle this drill?

> **Ik verwerk restjes gegrilde kip in een kipsalade.**
> I use leftover grilled chicken to make a chicken salad.

> **De designer bewerkt het ontwerp verder op zijn computer.**
> The designer continues to edit the draft on his computer.

Make and produce

To describe how things are made, speakers of Dutch use the verbs **maken** 'make,' **vervaardigen** 'make,' and **produceren** 'produce.'

> **In deze firma wordt tuingereedschap gemaakt.**
> In this company, they make garden tools.

> **Deze appelstroop wordt volgens een oud recept vervaardigd** (very formal)**.**
> This apple treacle is produced according to an old recipe.

> **Nederland produceert veel kaas voor de exportmarkt.**
> The Netherlands produces a lot of cheese for the export market.

Corresponding nouns to describe the way something is done or made are **methode** 'method,' **wijze** 'way, manner,' **manier** 'way, manner,' **procedure** 'procedure.'

> **Welke methode gebruiken jullie in je taalcursussen?**
> What method do you use in your language courses?

> **Als je 't niet erg vindt maak ik die wijnsaus liever op mijn eigen manier/wijze.**
> If you don't mind, I'd prefer to make that wine sauce my own way.

> **De taken in dit bedrijf worden volgens standaardprocedures uitgevoerd.**
> The tasks in this company are fulfilled according to standard procedures.

Turning on and off

To start a machine, a car or an electrical device, we use the verbs **starten**, **aandoen**, or **inschakelen**. To turn them off, we use **uitdoen**, **uitschakelen**, or **afzetten**.

> **Mijn auto wil in de winter soms niet starten.**
> My car sometimes doesn't want to start in the winter.

> **Doe je even het licht aan/uit?**
> Can you turn the light on/off?

> **U moet de monitor apart inschakelen/uitschakelen.**
> You have to switch on/off the monitor separately.

> **Wilt u bij de benzinepomp de motor afzetten?**
> Could you turn the engine off at the gas pump?

Beginning of action

The verbs and expressions we use to describe the beginning of an action or process are **beginnen** 'begin,' **een begin maken '**make a start,' **ontstaan** 'occur, originate,' **van start gaan** 'to start,' **aan de slag gaan** 'get to work,' **aan het werk gaan** 'start working.'

De les begint om vier uur.
The lesson begins at four o'clock.

Laten we van de week een begin maken met die bestellingen.
Let's make a start with those orders this week.

Hoe is die fout in de berekening ontstaan?
How did the mistake in the calculation occur?

Volgende week gaan de nieuwe cursussen Nederlands van start.
Next week, the new courses in Dutch will start.

Ik ben vanmorgen lekker vroeg aan de slag/aan het werk gegaan.
I started working really early this morning.

Note also the various expressions with **gang** 'course,' derived from **gaan** 'to go,' to describe actions and processes.

We hebben het productieproces in gang gezet.
We have started the production process.

Joost komt 's morgens maar langzaam op gang.
Joost doesn't get going quickly in the mornings.

Alles gaat zijn gangetje.
Business as usual.

Dat is niet de normale gang van zaken.
That is not the normal procedure.

Hoe lang is die ruzie bij de buren nu al aan de gang?
How long has that fight at the neighbors been going on?

Duration

To describe the duration of an action or process, we use **duren** 'to last' or **in gang zijn/bezig zijn**.

Het college van professor Jansen duurt anderhalf uur.
Professor Jansen's lecture lasts an hour and a half.

Het semester is in volle gang.
The semester is in full swing.

De vergadering is nog bezig.
The meeting is still in progress.

Also, durative constructions are used to describe that an action is ongoing.

Het bestuur is al drie uur aan het vergaderen.
The board has been in the meeting for three hours already.

De kinderen zijn in de tuin aan het spelen.
The children are playing in the yard.

Peter zit een boek te lezen.
Peter is reading a book.

De studenten stonden buiten een sigaretje te roken.
The students were smoking a cigarette outside.

► For the grammar of durative constructions, see **6.7**.

Interruption

To describe the interruption of an action or process, we use verbs such as **onderbreken** or **pauzeren**, and to describe the continuation of the action, we use verbs such as **verdergaan**, **doorgaan**, **voortzetten**, and **vervolgen**.

We gaan even pauzeren en dan gaan we door met oefening 8 in het werkboek.
We are going to take a break and then we continue with exercise 8 in the workbook.

Goed werk, ga zo door!
Good work, keep it up!

We onderbreken deze uitzending met een speciaal bericht.
We interrupt this program with a special message.

Zullen we verdergaan of wil je liever stoppen voor vandaag?
Shall we continue, or would you rather call it a day?

Maarten wil zijn studie volgend jaar in Singapore voortzetten.
Maarten wants to continue his studies in Singapore next year.

De professor nam een slok water en vervolgde zijn betoog.
The professor took a sip of water and continued his lecture.

Note also that adverbs such as **(nog) steeds** 'still, ever,' **almaar/aldoor** 'continuously,' **weer** 'again,' **voortdurend** 'permanently,' and **ononderbroken** 'uninterruptedly' also describe the continuation of a process or action.

Zijn jullie nog steeds aan het werk?
Are you still working?

Het kind achter mij schopte aldoor tegen mijn stoel.
The child behind me kept kicking my chair.

De pianist begon weer te spelen.
The pianist started playing again.

Hij zit me voortdurend te jennen.
He is teasing me all the time.

Er werd ononderbroken wijn en frisdrank geserveerd.
There was continuous service of wine and soft drinks.

Consecutive actions

To describe actions and processes following each other, we use verbs such as **volgen** 'follow,' prepositions such as **voor** 'before' and **na** 'after,' and adverbs such as **eerst** 'first,' **dan/toen** 'then,' **daarna** 'after that,' **vervolgens** 'further,' **tenslotte** 'finally.' We also use expressions such as **om de beurt** 'taking turns' and **aan de beurt** 'being next.'

Op de bruiloft volgde nog een receptie.
The wedding was followed by a reception.

Na het eten gingen we een blokje om.
After dinner, we took a stroll around the neighborhood.

Je moet eerst de HAVO doen en daarna kan je een vervolgopleiding doen.
You have to do HAVO first, and afterwards you can continue your education.

Jan en Minnie koken om de beurt.
Jan and Minnie take turns cooking.

Na de toespraak van de burgemeester kwam de voorzitter aan de beurt.
After the mayor's speech, it was the chairman's turn.

Simultaneous actions

When actions and processes take place simultaneously, we use verbs such as **samenvallen** 'coincide' and prepositions and conjunctions such as **tijdens** 'during' and **terwijl** 'while.' One can also use a verb as a noun with the preposition **bij** 'in doing so.'

Het bezoek van de president viel samen met een hittegolf.
The presidential visit coincided with a heatwave.

Tijdens het wereldkampioenschap voetballen waren de kijkcijfers heel hoog.
During the world championship soccer, the viewing ratings were very high.

Terwijl in het hele land de klokken luidden, braken overal de dijken door.
As the bells were ringing in the whole country, the dikes were breaking everywhere.

Bij het koken van risotto moet je voortdurend blijven roeren.
When cooking risotto, you have to stir continuously.

Repeated actions

When actions or processes are repeated, we use verbs such as **herhalen** 'repeat' or **overdoen** 'repeat' and expressions with **nog een keer** 'once again,' **opnieuw** 'again,' and **nogmaals** 'again.' Actions that take place on a regular basis will get adverbs such as **regelmatig** 'regularly' or **dagelijks** 'daily' and **wekelijks** 'weekly.'

Kunt u die laatste woorden herhalen?
Can you repeat those last words?

Kunt u dat nog een keer zeggen?
Can you say that again?

Een derde van de studenten moest het examen overdoen.
A third of the students had to take the exam again.

Ik werd opnieuw gevraagd of ik de introductie kon doen.
I was asked again if I could do the introductions.

Ik zeg u nogmaals: Die man is geen goede fractievoorzitter.
I tell you again: That man is not a good party leader.

Het afval wordt wekelijks opgehaald.
The trash is collected weekly.

Change

To denote a change or a difference in an action or a process, we use the verb **veranderen** 'change' and its noun **de verandering** 'change.'

Goh, wat is die buurt hier veranderd!
Gosh, how much this neighborhood has changed!

Kees wilde rechten studeren, maar hij is van gedachten veranderd.
Kees wanted to study law, but he has changed his mind.

De klimaatverandering geeft aanleiding tot bezorgdheid.
The climate change is a reason to be worried.

We also use verbs such as **verschillen** 'differ' with its noun **het verschil** 'difference,' **(zich) aanpassen** 'adapt,' **afwisselen/omwisselen** 'interchange' with **de afwisseling, de omwisseling** 'change,' **wijzigen** 'change' with **de wijziging** 'change,' **omslaan** 'suddenly change' and other nouns such as **de omschakeling** 'change,' **de transformatie** 'transformation.' Also note the words for 'improve,' **verbeteren**, and for 'worsen' **verslechteren**.

Smaken verschillen!
Tastes differ!

Ik moest me erg aan mijn nieuwe omgeving aanpassen.
I really had to adapt to my new surroundings.

Laten we voor de afwisseling de wandeling in de omgekeerde richting doen.
Let's do the walk in the opposite direction for a change.

Mag ik u erop attent maken dat het programma licht gewijzigd is?
May I draw your attention to a slight change in the program?

De acteurs moesten in vliegende vaart hun kostuums omwisselen.
The actors had to rapidly change their costumes.

Jongens, het weer slaat om. We kunnen maar beter inpakken.
Guys, the weather's changing. We'd better pack up.

Het was zeker een hele omschakeling, die verhuizing naar Australië.
That must have been a huge change, moving to Australia.

De toestand van de patiënt is in de afgelopen nacht verslechterd.
The patient's condition has deteriorated overnight.

Ik wil deze zomer mijn kennis van het Italiaans verbeteren.
I want to improve my knowledge of Italian this summer.

▶ See also the verbs to express alteration of objects in **14.3**.

End of an action

To denote the end of an action or process, the Dutch use the verb **eindigen** 'to end' with its corresponding noun **het eind** 'end.' Note also the verb **beëindigen**, which is transitive. Other ways to say that something is ending are **afgelopen** or **voorbij zijn** 'to be finished.'

De voorstelling eindigt ongeveer om half tien.
The show ends at around nine thirty.

We beëindigen het feestmaal met een voortreffelijk glas cognac.
We finish the banquet with an excellent glass of cognac.

Om twee uur in de morgen was het feest bij de buren nog niet afgelopen.
At two in the morning, the party next door had not yet finished.

De lentevakantie is alweer bijna voorbij.
Spring break is already almost over.

To stop an action or process, the Dutch use verbs such as **ophouden** 'stop,' **stoppen** 'stop,' **stopzetten** 'put to a stop,' and **uitscheiden** 'stop.' Or expressions such as **er een punt achter zetten** 'stop' (*lit.* put a period behind it).

We gaan stoppen/ophouden, het is genoeg voor vandaag.
We'll quit, it's enough for today.

Hou op/Schei uit met dat getrommel op de tafel.
Stop drumming on the table.

De fabriek heeft het productieproces stopgezet.
The factory has put the production process to a stop.

Het is goed. Laten we er een punt achter zetten.
It's good. Let's finish it off.

Another meaning of **ophouden** is to hinder, to keep someone from doing something.

Ik wil je niet langer ophouden. Laten we een keer een afspraak maken.
I don't want to keep you any longer. Let's get together some time.

Graduate

The words for finishing one's education are **afstuderen** 'graduate' or **een opleiding afsluiten/afronden** 'finish an education.'

Karel is van plan volgend jaar af te studeren.
Karel plans to graduate next year.

Nino heeft zijn opleiding met de bachelor afgesloten/afgerond.
Nino has finished his education with the bachelor.

Retirement

To talk about (early) retirement, the Dutch use the expression **met (vervroegd) pensioen gaan** or **pensioneren**.

Wanneer ga jij met pensioen?
When do you plan to retire?

Naast ons woont een gepensioneerde notaris.
A retired notary lived next door to us.

For machines that have stopped running, we use verbs such as **stilstaan** or expressions such as **het niet meer doen**, **niet meer werken**.

Mijn horloge is stil blijven staan.
My watch stopped running.

Mijn elektrische tandenborstel doet het niet meer.
My electric toothbrush doesn't work anymore.

To stop a person

Finally, to stop someone in the street, we use the verb **aanhouden** 'stop.'

Een voorbijganger hield me aan en vroeg waar de Sarphatistraat is.
A passer-by stopped me and asked where the Sarphatistreet is.

De politie heeft zaterdag tientallen dronken automobilisten aangehouden.
The police pulled over dozens of drunk drivers on Saturday.

Note that a common grammatical feature in describing actions is the passive voice. When the agent of the action is not there or not important, the verb of the action is put into the passive mode, often in combination with **er**.

Volgend jaar wordt hier de nieuwe supermarkt geopend.
Next year, the new supermarket will be opened here.

Er werd op het feest erg veel gedronken.
There was a lot of drinking going on at the party.

► For an explanation of the passive voice, see **8.3**.

14.6 Talking about existence and availability, presence and absence

Existence

The main verbs and expressions the Dutch use to talk about existence are **bestaan** 'to exist,' **er zijn** 'to be there,' and **leven** 'live.' Corresponding nouns are **het bestaan, het leven**. Note the negation of **nog** with an indefinite subject or object: **geen . . . meer** 'no more.'

Kabouters bestaan niet.
Gnomes don't exist.

Mensen in de sloppenwijken van Calcutta hebben een moeilijk bestaan.
People in the slum neighborhoods of Calcutta have a difficult existence.

Er zijn tientallen verschillende soorten tulpen.
There are dozens of different types of tulips.

Is er nog koffie/Zijn er nog eieren?
Is there any coffee left/Are there any eggs left?

Er is geen koffie meer/Er zijn geen eieren meer.
There is no more coffee/There are no more eggs.

Er leven geen mensen op de maan.
There are no people living on the moon.

► See also **1.7**, **3.4**, and **9.8** for more information about negation.

Presence

More concretely, the words for 'to be present' are **aanwezig zijn** and **er zijn**. In the negation, we add **niet** 'not' or we use the words **afwezig zijn**. The corresponding nouns are **de aanwezigheid** 'presence,' **het bijzijn** 'presence,' and **afwezigheid** 'absence.'

Bij het emeritaat van professor Vermeer waren alle studenten aanwezig.
All students were present at Professor Vermeer's retirement.

Is Carla er ook?
Is Carla here?

Carla is er vandaag niet/Carla is vandaag niet aanwezig/Carla is vandaag afwezig.
Carla isn't here today/Carla is not present today/Carla is absent today.

Dit formulier moet in het bijzijn van een notaris ondertekend worden.
This form has to be signed in the presence of a notary.

Occurance

Earlier in this chapter, we saw the words for 'to happen,' **gebeuren** and **plaatsvinden**. Here, I would like to add ***voor*komen** 'to occur.' Note that the emphasis in this separable verb is on **voor-**, so as not to confuse it with inseparable **voor*komen*** 'to prevent.'

Aardbevingen komen hier niet voor.
Earthquakes do not happen here.

Het komt vaak voor dat Rob moet overwerken.
It occurs often that Rob has to work late.

Zulke fouten mogen in een opstel niet voorkomen.
Such mistakes should not happen in an essay.

In de roman komt een paar keer een sterfgeval voor.
Death occurs a few times in the novel.

Hoe voorkom je een verkoudheid?
How do you prevent a cold?

Cancel

When things fail to happen or are cancelled, we use verbs such as **afgelasten** 'cancel,' **afzeggen** 'cancel,' **niet doorgaan** 'not take place,' **uitvallen** 'to fail,' **vervallen** 'be cancelled.'

Door de regen moest de voetbalwedstrijd afgelast worden.
Because of the rain, the soccer game had to be cancelled.

Nico heeft onze afspraak afgezegd.
Nico cancelled our date.

Sorry jongens, maar het feest gaat niet door.
Sorry guys, but the party is off.

Door de storm viel overal de stroom uit.
Because of the storm, there were power outages everywhere.

Het college van professor Jansen komt te vervallen.
Professor Jansen's seminar has been cancelled.

Missing

When people or things are missing, we use words such as **vermist** 'missing,' **weg** 'gone,' **kwijt** 'lost,' and verbs such as **verliezen** 'lose' and **ontbreken** 'be missing.'

Een klasgenoot van Dirk is sinds eergisteren vermist.
One of Dirk's classmates has been missing since the day before yesterday.

Ik heb even bij de buren gebeld, maar ze zijn weg.
Ik rang the neighbors' doorbell, but they are gone.

Ik ben m'n sleutels kwijt/Ik heb mijn sleutels verloren. Heb jij ze ergens gezien?
I lost my keys. Have you seen them somewhere?

Ach, wat jammer. Er ontbreken twee letters in ons Scrabblespel.
Ah, too bad. Two letters are missing in our Scrabble game.

Note the different meanings of **missen**: 'to miss someone or something, to miss an event.'

Ik mis m'n familie/m'n oude racefiets.
I miss my family/my old road bike.

Ik heb de bus/de vergadering gemist.
I missed the bus/the meeting.

Lack

When there is lack or not enough of something, we use expressions such as **gebrek aan** 'lack of,' **te kort komen** 'have lack of, be short,' **te weinig** 'too little/few,' **niet genoeg** 'not enough,' **krap** 'barely enough,' **nauwelijks** 'barely.'

In dit land is er groot gebrek aan goede medicijnen.
There is a great lack of good medicines in this country.

Jongens, ik kom drie euro te kort, wie springt even bij?
Guys, I'm three euros short, who can help out?

Ik heb deze maand te weinig/niet genoeg geld om uit te gaan.
I don't have enough money to go out this month.

Ik ben krap bij kas; kun je me wat geld lenen?
I'm pretty much broke; can you lend me some money?

We hebben nauwelijks eten in huis.
We hardly have any food in the house.

Finished

When something or someone is finished, spent or used up, speakers of Dutch use **op**. They also combine verbs with this separable prefix to form **opeten** 'finish,' **opdrinken** 'drink up,' **opgebruiken** 'use up.'

Ik ben op. Ik ben hard aan vakantie toe.
I'm exhausted. I really need a vacation.

De koffie is op. Haal jij even nieuwe?
The coffee is finished. Can you get some more?

Drink je melk op. We moeten weg.
Finish your milk. We have to go.

Hebben jullie alle suiker opgebruikt?
Did you use up all the sugar?

Dutch has some suffixes to indicate lack or absence of something: **-loos** 'less,' **-vrij** 'free,' and **-arm** 'low in.'

Menno is sinds drie jaar werkloos.
Menno has been unemployed for three years.

Steeds meer mensen gaan over op cafeïnevrije koffie.
More and more people move to decaf coffee.

Mijn oma is op een zoutarm dieet.
My grandma is on a low-salt diet.

The word **af** 'off' and combinations of **af-** with verbs are used to say that something is no longer there, discontinued, or dismantled.

Na de storm waren er tien pannen van het dak af.
After the storm, ten roof tiles were off.

Ze hebben de bingo-avonden in het buurthuis afgeschaft.
They have discontinued the bingo nights in the community center.

De oude fabriek wordt afgebroken.
The old factory will be dismantled.

Disappearance

When things or people disappear, we use the verb **verdwijnen** 'disappear.' When they leave or move, we use **vertrekken** 'leave,' **verlaten** 'leave,' and **verhuizen** 'move.' Note that **verlaten** needs an object.

De sneeuw van gisteren is alweer verdwenen.
Yesterday's snow has already disappeared.

De trein naar Utrecht is een minuut geleden vertrokken.
The train for Utrecht left a minute ago.

Karin heeft haar man en haar huis verlaten.
Karin has left her husband and her home.

Joop en Alie zijn vorig jaar naar Alkmaar verhuisd.
Joop and Alie moved to Alkmaar last year.

Decease

When things or people cease to exist, die, or die out, we use verbs such as **verdwijnen** 'disappear,' **sterven** 'die,' **overlijden** 'pass away,' **doodgaan** 'die,' **uitsterven** 'become extinct.'

> **De Solex is in Nederland helemaal uit het zicht verdwenen.**
> In the Netherlands, the Solex has disappeared out of sight.
>
> **Mijn opa stierf in 1990.**
> My grandfather died in 1990.
>
> **De patiënt is twee dagen geleden overleden.**
> The patient passed away two days ago.
>
> **Drie van mijn mooiste lelies zijn in de droogte doodgegaan.**
> Three of my most beautiful lilies died in the drought.
>
> **De Bengaalse tijger wordt met uitsterven bedreigd.**
> The Bengal tiger is in danger of becoming extinct.

Availability

Many of the verbs and expressions above are also used when we talk about availability. For example, **er zijn** is used to inquire about availability in the following questions:

> **Zijn er nog boontjes?**
> Are there any beans left?
>
> **Is er al thee?**
> Is there tea yet?

To ask whether a store item is still available for purchase, we use the verb **krijgen** 'to get' and words derived from it such as **verkrijgbaar** 'available.' Alternatively, one can use a simple question with **hebben**. Another expression is **komen aan** 'get.'

> **Kan ik hier verse kabeljauw krijgen?**
> Can I get fresh cod here?
>
> **Is de laatste roman van Saskia Noort nog verkrijgbaar?**
> Is Saskia Noort's last novel still available?
>
> **Heeft u deze schoen nog in maat 40?**
> Do you still have this shoe in size 40?
>
> **Hoe kom ik aan een goedkope tweedehands fiets?**
> How do I get a cheap used bicycle?

To say that something is in stock, we use **in voorraad**, **voorradig**, derived from the noun **de voorraad** 'inventory, stock.' To say that something is not available, we use **niet verkrijgbaar** or **niet leverbaar** (from **leveren** 'to deliver'). To say that something is sold out, we use **uitverkocht** or, for hotels and planes, **volgeboekt** 'booked up.' If something is on sale, it is **in de uitverkoop**.

> **De roman van Saskia Noort is niet meer verkrijgbaar/leverbaar.**
> Saskia Noort's novel is no longer available.
>
> **We hebben die slaapzakken niet meer in voorraad.**
> We don't have those sleeping bags in stock anymore.
>
> **Ik heb nog genoeg macaroni voorradig.**
> I still have a good supply of macaroni.
>
> **Jammer, de kaarten voor het concert waren al uitverkocht.**
> Too bad, the tickets for the concert were already sold out.

Jammer meneer, maar we zijn dit weekend volgeboekt.
Unfortunately, sir, we are booked solid this weekend.

Ik heb dit shirt voor een tientje in de uitverkoop gekocht.
I bought this shirt on sale for ten euros.

To inquire or talk about having something handy, we use phrases such as **bij je hebben** 'have with/on you,' **bij de hand hebben** 'have something to hand,' **paraat hebben** 'to have ready,' and **klaarstaan** 'be readily available.'

Heb jij een pen bij je?
Do you have a pen?

Ik heb geen zakdoek bij de hand.
I don't have a handkerchief to hand.

Voor het geval de situatie escaleert houden ze de mobiele eenheid paraat.
Just in case the situation escalates, they have the riot police ready.

Ik heb even geen antwoord paraat.
I don't have an answer ready.

Als jullie straks thuiskomen, staat de koffie klaar.
When you come home later, coffee will be ready.

Borrow and lend

To ask whether one can borrow something or whether something is available, and to make something available to someone, speakers of Dutch use verbs and expressions such as **lenen** 'borrow, lend,' **in bruikleen geven** 'lend,' **beschikbaar stellen** 'make available,' **ter beschikking stellen** 'make available,' **beschikken over** 'have at one's disposal.'

Mag ik even je pen lenen?
May I borrow your pen for a moment?

Ik geef je graag mijn auto een week in bruikleen.
I'm happy to lend you my car for a week.

Het hotel stelt u gratis badhanddoeken en strandstoelen beschikbaar.
The hotel offers you towels and beach chairs at no fee.

Voor studenten zijn er concertkaarten met korting beschikbaar.
For students, there are concert tickets at a reduced price available.

Ik stel mijn diensten graag tot uw beschikking.
I gladly put my services at your disposal.

Ik stel mijn lichaam ter beschikking van de wetenschap.
I donate my body to medical science.

We hebben de hele week beschikking over het vakantiehuisje van Nico.
Nico's vacation home is at our disposal the entire week.

When lending or borrowing money, we use **lenen** 'lend, borrow,' **een lening afsluiten** 'borrow money from the bank.' A less formal word for lending money is **voorschieten** 'pay in advance.' For spending money, we use the verb **uitgeven,** and when one is broke, we use the word **blut**. The more official word for bankruptcy is **failliet** or **bankroet**.

Mag ik 10 euro van je lenen?
Will you lend me 10 euros?

Corrie en Nick hebben een lening bij de bank afgesloten.
Corrie and Nick got a loan from the bank.

Kun je me het geld voor de bioscoop even voorschieten?
Can you lend me the money for the cinema?

Siem heeft al z'n geld op de kermis uitgegeven. Hij is blut.
Siem has spent all his money at the fair. He's broke.

Ons loodgietersbedrijf is vorige maand failliet gegaan.
Our plumbing company filed for bankruptcy last month.

Purchase and rent

When something is available for purchase, it is **te koop**. When something is available for rent, it is **te huur** (from the verb **huren** 'rent'). The verb **verhuren** is 'to rent to someone.' Similarly, **verkopen** is 'to sell.'

Dit huis staat al acht maanden te koop/te huur.
This house has been for sale/for rent for eight months.

Ik ga mijn kamer verhuren.
I'm going to rent out my room.

Ik heb mijn oude racefiets voor 100 euro verkocht.
I sold my old road bike for 100 euros.

To ask if something is free to use or if someone is free to do something, one can use **vrij** 'free' or, when it is a person, **tijd hebben** 'be free, have time.'

Is deze stoel nog vrij?
Is this chair free?

Ben je vanmiddag vrij/Heb je vanmiddag tijd?
Are you free this afternoon/Do you have time this afternoon?

► See also **13.9** on how to ask for someone's availability.

To say that an object is not available for use, we use words such as **bezet** 'busy,' **niet vrij** 'not free,' or **in gebruik** 'in use.' In colloquial Dutch, we also use **bezet** to say that someone is spoken for.

Sorry, deze stoel is bezet/niet vrij.
Sorry, this chair is taken.

Alle huurbootjes zijn op dit moment in gebruik.
All rental boats are in use at the moment.

Jij valt op Susanne, hè? Nou, die is al bezet hoor!
You have a crush on Susanne, right? Well, she is spoken for!

When persons are busy or not available, we use **bezig** 'busy,' **geen tijd hebben** 'have no time,' and **verhinderd zijn** 'to be unable to make it.'

Meneer Jansen is even (met iets anders) bezig.
Mr. Jansen is busy (doing something else) at the moment.

Mevrouw De Graaf heeft nu geen tijd/is op dit moment verhinderd.
Ms. De Graaf doesn't have time now/is busy at the moment.

14.7 Asking for and giving information about location and distance

Location

To ask for the location of an object or a person, one uses a question with **waar** 'where.'

Pardon meneer, waar is het toilet?
Excuse me sir, where is the restroom?

Weet u waar ik hier een postkantoor kan vinden?
Do you know where I can find a post office here?

Waar bevindt zich het regeringsgebouw?
Where is the government building located?

Waar is Peter?
Where is Peter?

To ask where someone or something is from, we use **waar . . . vandaan** 'where . . . from.'

Waar komt u vandaan?
Where are you from?

Waar kom jij zo laat vandaan?
Where are you coming from this late?

Waar komt die mooie zijden sjaal vandaan?
Where does that beautiful silk scarf come from?

To ask where someone or something is going, we use **waar . . . naartoe/heen** 'where . . . to.'

Waar gaan jullie op vakantie naartoe?
Where are you going for vacation?

Waar gaat deze trein naartoe?
Where is this train going?

Directions

To ask for directions to a certain place, we use questions with **waar** 'where' and **hoe** 'how.' Asking for specific metro or bus lines, we use questions with **welke** 'which.'

Pardon, weet u waar de Molenstraat is?
Pardon me, do you know where the Molenstraat is?

Hoe kom ik van hier naar het Rijksmuseum?
How do I get from here to the Rijksmuseum?

Welke buslijn rijdt naar het Centraal Station?
Which bus line goes to the Central Station?

To give someone directions to a place, one uses words such as **rechtdoor** 'straight,' **rechtsaf** 'turn right,' **linksaf** 'turn left,' and expressions such as **de eerste straat rechts** 'the first street to your right.' Note also prepositions such as **langs** 'past, by,' **over** 'over,' **door** 'through,' **(rond) om** 'around.' Europeans don't think in terms of north–south, east–west oppositions when they give directions, and they don't think blocks but rather streets. Locations close by are **dichtbij** or **vlakbij**, and locations far away are **ver (weg)**. Example:

De Molenstraat? Die is dichtbij. U loopt hier rechtdoor. Bij de stoplichten steekt u over. Dan is het de tweede straat links.
The Molenstreet? That is close. You go straight here. You cross at the traffic lights. Then it is the second street on your left.

Common prepositions in giving directions are:

Je gaat hier de hoek om, langs de supermarkt, over de brug, door het park met het verzetsmonument en dan kom je vanzelf bij het museum.
You go around the corner here, past the supermarket, over the bridge, through the park with the resistance monument, and then you automatically get to the museum.

To talk about directions where things or people are coming from or going to, we use words such as **richting** 'direction,' **links** 'left,' and **rechts** 'right,' the four wind directions and their adjectives, the prepositions **van** 'from,' **uit** 'out,' **naar** 'to,' and adverbs describing location as explained in section **3.3**.

Hij kwam me uit de richting van het station tegemoet.
He came towards me from the direction of the station.

De auto die de fietser aanreed kwam van links.
The car that hit the cyclist came from the left.

De wind waait vandaag uit zuidelijke richting.
The wind blows from the south today.

Laten we maar naar binnen gaan, het wordt koel.
Let's go inside, it's getting cool.

Peter kwam in vliegende vaart naar beneden rennen.
Peter came flying downstairs.

▶ See also **4.2** on prepositions describing place.

Distance

To ask for and to give information about distances and how quickly one can reach them (note the verb **bereiken** 'reach'), one uses prepositions such as **van . . . naar** 'from . . . to' and **tussen** 'between.' The word for distance is **afstand**.

Hoe ver is het/Hoe groot is de afstand van hier naar Breda?
How far is it from here to Breda?

Tussen Groningen en Delfzijl ligt een spoorlijn van 38 kilometer.
There is a 38 kilometer rail line between Groningen and Delfzijl.

Hoe lang duurt de rit van Parijs naar Nice?
How long is the ride from Paris to Nice?

Van hier uit kunnen we de kust in anderhalf uur bereiken.
From here, we can reach the coast in an hour and a half.

Is de bioscoop op loopafstand of moeten we een bus nemen?
Is the cinema within walking distance, or should we take a bus?

Order

Note the words for following and preceding: **volgen** 'follow,' **achternagaan** 'go after,' **vooruitgaan** 'go ahead.' Note also the words we use to indicate a certain spatial order or sequence: **eerst . . . dan** 'first . . . then,' **de volgorde** 'sequence,' **één voor één** 'one by one.'

De Duitser volgde de Nederlander over de finishlijn.
The German followed the Dutch over the finish line.

Mijn hond loopt me de hele tijd achterna.
My dog follows me all the time.

Gaan jullie maar vast vooruit, wij komen zo.
You guys go ahead, we'll be there in a minute.

Eerst zie je de kerk en dan een oude molen.
First, you see the church, and then an old windmill.

De namen staan in alfabetische volgorde.
The names are listed in alphabetical order.

De kinderen sprongen één voor één in het zwembad.
One by one, the children jumped into the pool.

14.8

Asking for and giving information about time

To ask for exact clock time, we use **hoe laat?** 'what time?' and for other questions regarding time, we use **wanneer** 'when.'

Hoe laat begint de les?
What time does the class start?

Wanneer heb je tijd om eens naar de film te gaan?
When do you have time to go to the movies?

▶ For information about clock time, see **5.4**.

To ask about the beginning, the duration and the end of an event, we use the verbs **beginnen** 'begin,' **duren** 'last,' and **eindigen** 'end' or **afgelopen zijn** 'be finished.'

Hoe laat begint de les?
What time does the class start?

Hoe lang duurt de les?
How long does the class last?

Hoe laat eindigt de les?/Hoe laat is de les afgelopen?
What time does the class end?

Present

For talking about the present, we use words such as **nu** 'now,' **op dit moment** 'at the moment,' **momenteel** 'at the moment,' **tegenwoordig** 'current, contemporary,' and **huidig** 'current, present.' Note also more general notions of the present with **jaar**, **week**, **maand**.

Doe je huiswerk weg, we gaan nu aan tafel.
Put your homework away, we're sitting down for dinner now.

Op dit moment/Momenteel zijn alle roeibootjes verhuurd.
At the moment, all rowing boats are rented out.

Tegenwoordig heeft iedereen een mobiele telefoon.
These days, everyone has a cell phone.

De huidige situatie in het Midden-Oosten is zorgwekkend.
The present situation in the Middle East is worrisome.

Ik wil dit jaar/deze maand/deze week een nieuwe fiets kopen.
I want to buy a new bike this year/this month/this week.

Recent past

Talking about the very recent past, one needs words and expressions such as **(daar)net/zojuist**, 'just,' **een moment/minuut geleden** 'a moment/minute ago,' **zo-even** 'a moment ago.'

Sorry, maar meneer de Boer is net weggegaan.
Sorry, but Mr de Boer just left.

De regen is zo-even opgehouden.
It stopped raining a moment ago.

To talk about the recent past, we use words and expressions such as **onlangs** 'recently,' **kortgeleden/een tijdje geleden** 'a short while ago,' **recentelijk** 'recently,' **pas (nog)** 'recently,' and **laatst** 'recently.'

Hij is onlangs/kortgeleden/pas vrijgelaten.
He was released recently.

Ik heb laatst zo'n goeie film gezien!
I recently saw such a good movie!

Note the uses of **al** 'already' and **pas** 'only.' To express that something has been a while, we use **al** with the appropriate period of time. To say that something has not been long at all, we use **pas**.

Ik werk hier al tien jaar, maar Johan werkt hier pas twee maanden.
I have worked here for ten years, but Johan has only worked here for two months.

Past

To go back even further in the past, we use expressions such as **vroeger** 'in the old days,' **voormalig** 'former,' **toen** 'then,' **eens** 'once,' **een (hele) tijd geleden/lang geleden** 'long time ago,' expressions with **vorig(e)/verleden** 'last,' and other expressions with **geleden** 'ago.'

Vroeger was hier een heel mooi station.
There used to be a beautiful station here.

Maar dat is heel lang geleden.
But that is a very long time ago.

De voormalige bewoner heeft het huis behoorlijk verwaarloosd.
The former tenant really neglected the house.

Ik ben eens vreselijk door een hond gebeten. Ik was toen zes.
I was once bitten badly by a dog. I was six years old then.

Vorige/Verleden week hebben we geschaatst.
Last week, we skated.

Twintig jaar geleden heb ik mijn vrouw leren kennen.
Twenty years ago, I met my wife.

When talking about a certain time period, century, or decade, we say:

In de zeventiger jaren had je van die verschrikkelijke kapsels.
In the seventies, you had these terrible hairdos.

Ik ging in de jaren zeventig naar de middelbare school.
I went to high school in the seventies.

Dit schilderij stamt uit de zeventiende eeuw.
This painting is from the seventeenth century.

Immediate future

To talk about the immediate future, we use words and expressions such as **onmiddellijk** 'immediately,' **direct/per direct** 'immediately,' **van nu af aan** 'from now on.'

Je moet onmiddellijk bij de conrector komen.
You have to come to the vice-principal immediately.

Henk heeft per direct ontslag gekregen.
Henk was fired with immediate effect.

Van nu af aan eet ik geen vlees meer.
From now on, I won't eat meat anymore.

Near future

To talk about the very near future (within the hour or at least on the same day), we use expressions such as **zo/zo meteen** 'in a minute,' **straks** 'later (on the same day),' **dadelijk** 'in a moment,' **aanstonds** 'in a moment,' **over een paar minuten** 'in a few moments.'

Ik kom zo (meteen) bij u, mevrouw.
I will be right with you, madam.

Zullen we straks even naar Albert Heijn gaan?
Shall we go to Albert Heijn later?

We gaan dadelijk/aanstonds/over een paar minuten weg.
We are leaving in a few minutes.

Distant future

To talk about events at a more distant or not clearly defined moment in the future, we use words and expressions such as **over een paar dagen/weken** 'in a few days/weeks,' **een keer** 'some time,' **ooit** 'some time,' **spoedig** 'soon,' **gauw** 'soon,' **over een tijdje** 'in a while,' and combinations thereof. Time expressions with **ergens** 'somewhere' are more vague.

Over een paar dagen komen de kinderen thuis van vakantie.
In a few days, the kids will come home from vacation.

Zullen we gauw een keer samen naar Amsterdam gaan?
Shall we go to Amsterdam some time soon?

Ooit wil ik een keer in een luchtballon varen.
I want to fly in a hot-air balloon some day.

Over een tijdje zie je niets meer van dat litteken.
Soon, you won't notice that scar anymore.

Die afspraak is geloof ik ergens in januari.
That appointment is sometime in January, I believe.

Note, however, that **ooit** and **een keer** can also be used in the past.

Heb jij ooit zo'n mooie pioenroos gezien?
Have you ever seen such a beautiful peony?

Ik ben een keer door een Volkswagen Kever aangereden.
I was hit by a Volkswagen Beetle once.

There are, of course, many ways to be more precise and give a specified time in the future, for example with days of the week, parts of the day, dates, and clock time.

Die afspraak met Jansen is op dinsdag 21 januari om 16 uur.
That appointment with Jansen is on Tuesday, January 21, at 4pm.

Zullen we vanmiddag even naar een nieuwe wasmachine gaan kijken?
Shall we go look at a new washing machine this afternoon?

Over twee weken is het semester afgelopen.
In two weeks, the semester is finished.

Things that are yet to happen are denoted with **nog** 'still, yet,' **nog steeds** 'still,' and **nog (steeds) niet** 'not yet.'

Die bestelling moet nog gedaan worden.
That order has yet to be placed.

Ben je nog steeds aan het werk?
Are you still working?

Heb je de hamsterkooi nog (steeds) niet schoongemaakt?
Have you not yet cleaned the hamster cage?

Things that cannot happen anymore are denoted with **niet meer** 'no longer,' **allang niet meer** 'not for a long time,' **nooit meer** 'never again.'

Ik ga nooit meer naar Schotland op vakantie.
I'm never going to Scotland on vacation anymore.

Dat model is allang niet meer verkrijgbaar.
That model hasn't been available for a long time.

Simultaneous events

For things happening simultaneously, we use words such as **tegelijk**, **gelijktijdig**, **tegelijkertijd**, **op hetzelfde moment**; they all mean 'at the same time.'

De twee schaatsers kwamen precies tegelijk over de finish.
The two skaters crossed the finish at the exact same time.

We hoorden een knal en op hetzelfde moment ging het licht uit.
We heard a bang, and at the same time, the lights went out.

Before and after

To denote the before and after of events, we use words such as **voor** 'before,' **(van) tevoren** 'before, earlier,' **alvorens** 'previous to,' **eerder** 'earlier,' and **na** 'after,' **naderhand** 'afterwards,' **na afloop (van)** 'afterwards,' **later** 'later.'

Zullen we voor of na het eten even met de hond uit?
Shall we walk the dog before or after dinner?

We moeten onze bagage twee uur van tevoren inchecken.
We have to check in our luggage two hours ahead of time.

Lees de instructies alvorens het formulier in te vullen.
Read the instructions before filling out the form.

Ik zet nu vast de koffie klaar want naderhand is er geen tijd meer voor.
I'm setting up the coffee now because there is no time afterwards.

Na afloop van de dienst is er koffie in het bijgebouw.
After the service, there is coffee in the social hall.

Kom, we doen die afwas later wel.
Come on, let's do those dishes later.

Frequency

We have many words to describe the frequency of events. On a spectrum from **altijd** 'always' to **nooit** 'never,' we have **vaak** 'often,' **regelmatig** 'regularly,' **af en toe** 'off and on,' **soms** 'sometimes,' and **zelden** 'rarely.'

Ik ga soms/af en toe/zelden naar een disco.
I sometimes/sporadically/rarely go to a disco.

Voor advies kunt u altijd bij ons terecht.
You can always count on us for advice.

Regularity

Other ways to express regularity of events are expressions with **elk(e)** 'each,' adverbs with **-(e)lijks** such as **jaarlijks** 'each year,' expressions with **om de twee/andere** 'every two,' and expressions with **keer per** 'times per.'

Ik ga elke dinsdag en donderdag/twee keer per week volleyballen.
I play volleyball Tuesdays and Thursdays/twice a week.

We geven de hond z'n wekelijkse borstelbeurt.
We give the dog his weekly brush.

Je moet deze plant om de twee dagen water geven.
You must water this plant every two days.

Timeliness

To describe punctuality, being on time and meeting deadlines, we use words and expressions such as **stipt/punctueel** 'punctual,' **(precies) op tijd** '(exactly) on time,' **net op tijd** 'just in time,' and **tijdig** 'timely.' To give someone a deadline, one can use **binnen** 'within' with a number of days/weeks, or one can use **uiterlijk/op z'n laatst** 'at the latest' with a date.

Mijn baas is heel stipt. Hij komt nooit te laat.
My boss is really punctual. He's never late.

De student had zijn scriptie net op tijd ingeleverd.
The student had handed in his thesis just in time.

Je moet je tijdig voor het examen aanmelden.
You have to register for the exam in a timely manner.

Ruilen kan alleen binnen acht dagen met de bon.
An exchange is only possible within eight days with the receipt.

Het essay moet uiterlijk op 15 december ingeleverd worden.
The essay needs to be handed in no later than December 15.

Untimeliness

To describe untimeliness or delay, we use words such as **niet op tijd** 'not in time,' **te laat** 'too late,' **met vertraging** 'with a delay,' **vertraging hebben** 'be delayed,' **vertraagd** 'delayed,' **het oponthoud** 'delay,' **het uitstel** 'postponement.'

Deze student komt altijd te laat naar college.
This student is always late to class.

Nederlandse treinen hebben heel vaak vertraging/zijn vaak vertraagd.
Dutch trains are often delayed.

De journalisten veroorzaakten enig oponthoud bij de uitgang.
The journalists caused some delay at the exit.

De student vroeg uitstel van het mondelinge examen aan.
The student requested a postponement of the oral exam.

▶ See also Chapter **7** for verb tenses.

14.9 Expressing ownership

To inquire about and express ownership, one can use questions with the possessive pronoun or constructions with **van** 'of.'

Is dat jouw/uw paraplu?
Is that your umbrella?

Is die paraplu van jou/u?
Is that umbrella yours?

Dat is de moeder van Nico.
That is Nico's mother.

▶ See **2.4** for a list of possessive pronouns.

Ownership is also denoted with the possessive **-s**. Note the apostrophe after a, i, o, u, y.

Ik ga even op Tanja's fiets naar de bakker.
I'm taking Tanja's bike to the bakery.

Another way to express the possessive is to use **van** in combination with **die** or **dat**.

Gaan we met jouw auto de stad in of die van mij?
Are we taking your car to town or mine?

Mag ik even je woordenboek? Dat van mij ligt thuis.
Can I have your dictionary? Mine is at home.

Yet another, less commonly used form of the possessive takes the articles **de** and **het** and the possessive pronoun (except **jullie**) with the ending **-e**.

Wat hou jij je boek netjes. Het mijne zit vol vlekken.
You keep your book very neat. Mine is full of stains.

Het huis van de buren is groot maar het onze is veel mooier.
The neighbor's house is bigger, but ours is much prettier.

Informal, colloquial expressions of the possessive use the abbreviated forms of the possessive pronoun: **m'n**, **z'n**, **d'r**.

Piet z'n fiets heeft een lekke band.
Piet's bike has a flat tire.

Annie d'r schoenveters zijn los.
Annie's shoelaces are undone.

Wie z'n uitsmijter staat hier koud te worden?
Whose egg and ham sandwich is getting cold here?

The Dutch word for owner is **eigenaar**. Derived from this is **eigen** 'own.'

Bent u de eigenaar van deze auto?
Are you the owner of this car?

Ik heb in mijn studentenflat mijn eigen badkamer.
In my dorm, I have my own bathroom.

Lastly, we use the verb **bezitten** 'possess' with its derivations **de bezitter** 'owner,' **het bezit** 'possession.'

Mijn grootouders bezitten nog enkele hectares land.
My grandparents own several acres of land.

De bezitter van deze kaart heeft recht op 50% korting.
The owner of this card is entitled to 50% reduction.

Wij zijn in het bezit van uw brief (formal).
We are in receipt of your letter.

14.10 Talking about origins and provenance

Provenance

There are many ways to describe origin and provenance, using nouns such as **de herkomst** 'origin,' **de oorsprong** 'origin,' **het uitgangspunt** 'starting point,' **de basis** 'basis' and verbs such as **ontstaan** 'originate' and **vandaan komen** 'come from.'

Waar komen deze appels vandaan?
Where are these apples from?

De emigrant ging weer terug naar zijn land van herkomst.
The emigrant returned to his country of origin.

Wat is de oorsprong van dit woord?
What is the origin of this word?

Mijn familie komt oorspronkelijk uit Duitsland.
My family is originally from Germany.

Het uitgangspunt van deze wandeling is de oude molen.
The old mill is the beginning of this hike.

Vertrouwen is de basis voor een goed huwelijk.
Trust is the basis of a good marriage.

De brand is door kortsluiting ontstaan.
The fire was caused by a short circuit.

Descent

Origin by descent is denoted with the verb **stammen** 'derive' or **afstammen van** 'descend from.' Note also the nouns **de afstamming** 'descent' and **de stamboom** 'family tree.'

Zijn voorouders stammen van een oud adellijk geslacht af.
His ancestors descend from an old noble family.

Marja werkt al jaren aan de stamboom van haar familie.
Marja has been working on her family tree for years.

Foundation

Origin by foundation is denoted with the verbs **stichten** 'found' and **oprichten** 'found.'

Dit klooster werd in 1145 door benedictijnse monniken gesticht.
This monastery was founded by Benedictine monks in 1145.

De studenten hebben een debatclub opgericht.
The students have organized a debate club.

▶ See **14.1** and **14.7** on asking about someone's origin by birth and nationality.

15

Putting things into a wider context

15.1 Talking about cause and effect

Cause

The most important words to describe the cause of an event are **de oorzaak** 'cause' with its verb **veroorzaken** 'to cause,' **de reden** 'reason,' and **de aanleiding** 'cause, reason.'

> **De oorzaak van de brand is nog niet bekend.**
> The cause of the fire is not yet known.
>
> **De storm veroorzaakte veel schade aan daken.**
> The storm caused a lot of roof damage.
>
> **Mag ik vragen naar de reden van je absentie?**
> May I ask about the reason for your absence?
>
> **Wat was de aanleiding van die ruzie?**
> What was the reason for that argument?

Effect

To describe the effect of an action or an event, we use words such as **het gevolg** 'consequence, effect,' **het resultaat** 'result,' **het effect** 'effect,' **de consequentie** 'consequence,' **de werking** 'effect.' When we talk about side effects, we use **de bijwerkingen**.

> **De longkanker was het gevolg van jarenlang kettingroken.**
> The lung cancer was the consequence of years of chain-smoking.
>
> **Het resultaat van een ochtend in de keuken staan was een mislukte cake.**
> The result of a morning in the kitchen was a cake that didn't turn out well.
>
> **De nieuwe regelingen tegen schoolverzuim hadden totaal geen effect.**
> The new policies against school absence didn't have any effect at all.
>
> **Als jij zo brutaal tegen je leraar bent, moet je de consequenties accepteren.**
> If you are so rude to your teacher, you have to accept the consequences.
>
> **Dit medicijn heeft een langdurige werking.**
> This medication works for a long time.
>
> **De bijwerkingen van dit medicijn zijn gelukkig minimaal.**
> Fortunately, this medication has only minimal side effects.

Cause and effect are linked with conjunctions such as **als . . . dan . . .** 'if . . . then . . . ,' **hoe . . . des te . . .** 'the more . . . the more,' **zo . . . dat . . .** 'so . . . that . . .' and **te . . . om te** 'too . . . to . . .'

Other conjunctions and conjunctional adverbs are **daarom** 'therefore,' **daardoor** 'because of that,' **dus** 'so.'

> **Als je zo om snoep blijft zeuren, krijg je helemaal niets.**
> If you continue to beg for candy like this, you won't get anything at all.
>
> **Hoe harder je rijdt, des te groter de kans op een bekeuring.**
> The faster you drive, the more chance to get a ticket.
>
> **Het boek was zo saai, dat ik het niet uitlas.**
> The book was so boring that I didn't finish it.
>
> **Dit kopje is te vies om uit te drinken.**
> This cup is too dirty to drink from.
>
> **Het hout was verrot. Daardoor/Daarom stortte het dak in.**
> The wood was rotten. That's why the roof collapsed.
>
> **Het gaat regenen, dus neem een paraplu mee.**
> It's going to rain, so take an umbrella.

▶ See **3.5** and **4.4** for adverbs and prepositions expressing cause and reason.

Interdependence

To express interdependence between events or occurrences, we use words such as **liggen aan (het ligt aan)** 'the reason is' and **afhangen van** 'depend on.'

> **Waar ligt het aan dat ik me zo moe voel?**
> What is the reason for my tiredness?
>
> **Het ligt aan het warme weer.**
> It is because of the warm weather.
>
> **A: Gaan we naar het strand?**
> **B: Dat hang van het weer af.**
> A: Are we going to the beach?
> B: That depends on the weather.
>
> **A: Ga je mee uit eten?**
> **B: Dat hangt ervan af of ik moet overwerken.**
> A: Are you coming for dinner?
> B: It depends on whether I have to work late.

Conclusions

Finally, when drawing conclusions from facts, events and research, we use the words **het resultaat** 'result,' **de uitkomst** 'result, outcome,' **het bewijs** 'proof,' **bewijzen** 'prove,' **de diagnose** 'diagnosis,' **concluderen** 'conclude,' **vaststellen** 'conclude,' **blijken (uit)** 'appear.'

> **Wat was het resultaat/de uitkomst van die enquete?**
> What was the result of that survey?
>
> **Uit dat rapport stel ik vast/concludeer ik dat het onderzoek geen succes had.**
> From the report I conclude that the research project was unsuccessful.
>
> **Het sporenonderzoek heeft nog geen bewijs opgeleverd.**
> The criminal investigation has not yet yielded any proof.
>
> **Na een grondig onderzoek was de diagnose niet zorgwekkend.**
> After a thorough examination, the diagnosis was not worrisome.
>
> **Uit onderzoek blijkt dat het aantal jeugdige rokers weer is gestegen.**
> Research shows that the number of young smokers has risen again.

15.2 Asking for and giving reasons and purpose

Reasons

To ask why something is happening, we use the question word **waarom** 'why.' We also use the word **de reden** 'reason' to ask more formally.

> **Waarom is Karin vandaag afwezig?**
> Why is Karin absent today?
>
> **Wat is de reden voor uw verzoek?/Om welke reden vraagt u dit?**
> What is the reason for your request?

To ask how something happened, we use questions beginning with **hoe** 'how.'

> **Ober, hoe komt die knoop in m'n soep?**
> Waiter, how did that button get into my soup?
>
> **Hoe heb je je been gebroken?**
> How did you break your leg?
>
> **Hoe komt het dat er alweer een fout in de afrekening staat?**
> How come there is a mistake in the account again?

Purpose

To ask for the purpose of an action or an event, we use words such as **het doel** 'purpose,' **de bedoeling** 'purpose, intention,' and question words such as **waarom** and **waarvoor** 'what for.'

> **Wat is het doel/de bedoeling van dit project?**
> What is the purpose of this project?
>
> **Waarom doe je dat?**
> Why are you doing that?

Explanation

To ask for a specific (and more formal) explanation, we use words such as **de verklaring** 'explanation,' **verklaren** 'explain,' and **uitleggen** 'explain.'

> **Heb jij hier een verklaring voor?**
> Do you have an explanation for this?
>
> **Kunt u deze gegevens nader verklaren?**
> Can you clarify these data?
>
> **Meneer, kunt u die laatste zin uitleggen?**
> Sir, can you explain that last sentence?

For giving reasons and explaining why, we use conjunctions such as **omdat** 'because,' **want** 'because,' and **daarom** 'that's why.'

> **Ik ben te laat omdat ik de bus gemist heb.**
> I'm too late because I missed the bus.
>
> **Haal even wat lekkers in huis want ik heb de buren uitgenodigd.**
> Get some nice snacks to eat because I have invited the neighbors.
>
> **Die plant heeft water nodig. Daarom hangen de bladeren slap.**
> That plant needs water. That's why the leaves are hanging down.

▶ For conjunctions and word order, see Chapter **9**.

The prepositions **wegens** 'because of' and **vanwege** 'because of' also give a reason.

Wegens een technische storing was het treinverkeer ontregeld.
Because of a technical problem, the train traffic was disturbed.

Vanwege de regen werd het feestje binnen gehouden.
Because of the rain, they had the party inside.

▶ For prepositions, see also Chapter **4**.

The adverbs **namelijk** 'actually, you see' and **immers** 'after all' further explain a statement.

Neem je paspoort mee. Je gaat namelijk een paar keer de grens over.
Take your passport along. You're crossing borders a few times, you see.

Dat moet jij toch weten. Jij hebt immers geschiedenis gestudeerd.
You should know that. After all, you studied history.

To explain the purpose of an action or object, we use conjunctions such as **zodat** 'so that' and an infinitive construction with **om . . . te . . .** 'in order to.'

Leg een stevige knoop in dat touw zodat de boot niet los kan schieten.
Tie that rope tightly so that the boat can't break away.

Ik drink veel water om fit te blijven.
I drink a lot of water to stay fit.

▶ See **9.9** for more on infinitive constructions.

Use, purpose

To ask about and explain the particular use of an object, we use questions with **waarvoor** 'what for' and verbs such as **dienen** 'serve' and **gebruiken** 'use.' We respond with the infinitive construction **om . . . te . . .** 'in order to.'

Waarvoor dient dit apparaat?/Waar gebruik je dit apparaat voor?
What do you use that tool for?

Je gebruikt een hamer om een spijker in de muur te slaan.
You use a hammer to hit a nail in the wall.

Intention

To explain one's intentions, we use words such as **de bedoeling** 'intention,' **van plan zijn** 'intend,' **zich voornemen** 'intend,' **het voornemen** 'intention,' **de opzet** 'intention,' **met opzet/expres** 'intentionally, on purpose.'

Het is de bedoeling dat we allemaal om 4 uur hier terug zijn.
We are all supposed to be back here at 4.

Ik ben van plan/Ik heb me voorgenomen met roken te stoppen.
I'm planning to quit smoking.

Je hebt die band met opzet lekgestoken.
You punctured that tire intentionally.

To explain that something happened unintentionally, we use words such as **niet met opzet/niet expres** 'unintentionally,' **per ongeluk** 'by accident.'

Sorry, ik heb dat niet met opzet/niet expres gedaan.
Sorry, I didn't do that intentionally.

Ik heb dat kopje per ongeluk gebroken.
I broke that cup by accident.

▶ To talk about responsibility, see **17.8**.

15.3 Expressing necessity, obligation, and duty

Necessity

To express necessity and needs, we use words such as **de noodzaak** 'necessity,' **noodzakelijk** 'necessary,' **nodig** 'necessary.' The adverbs are negated with **niet** 'not.'

Winterbanden zijn hier strikt noodzakelijk/een absolute noodzaak.
Winter tires are strictly necessary here.

Een handtekening is niet nodig.
A signature is not necessary.

To talk about what one needs, we use the words **nodig hebben** 'need' or **moeten hebben** 'must have, need.'

Ik heb een nieuwe winterjas nodig.
I need a new winter coat.

Carla moet nodig eens een nieuwe bril hebben.
Carla really needs new glasses.

▶ For more on modal verbs, see **6.2**.

Requirement

To express what is mandatory or required, we use words such as **verplicht** 'mandatory' or **vereist** 'essential.'

Het dragen van een motorhelm is in Nederland verplicht.
Wearing a motorcycle helmet is mandatory in the Netherlands.

Voor deze studierichting is kennis van het Nederlands vereist.
For this course of study, knowledge of Dutch is required.

Such requirements or necessary actions can also be expressed with the imperative, the command form.

Motor afstellen.
Turn the engine off.

Stempel hier uw kaartje af.
Validate your ticket here.

▶ For more information on the imperative, see **8.1**.

Another common way of expressing what needs to be done or is necessary, is to use the modal verb **moeten** 'must.' To express the necessity of an action (when the agent is not important or irrelevant), this is often used in the passive voice. Note the difference:

Jullie moeten je huiswerk aan het eind van de les inleveren.
You must hand in your homework at the end of class.

De ramen moeten weer eens gewassen worden.
The windows should be cleaned again.

▶ See **8.3** for more information on the passive.

Obligation, duty

To talk about obligation and duty in a narrower sense, we use words such as **de plicht** 'duty,' **de verplichting** 'commitment, obligation,' **zijn plicht doen** 'do one's duty,' **een plicht vervullen** 'fulfill one's duty.' The noun **plicht** takes the preposition **tegenover** 'towards.'

Mag ik je aan je plicht herinneren?
May I remind you of your duty?

De verpleegster vervulde haar plichten met toewijding.
The nurse carried out her duties with devotion.

Doe je plicht!
Do your duty!

Je hebt bepaalde plichten tegenover je superieuren.
You have certain duties towards your superiors.

Ik wil graag komen, maar ik heb verplichtingen elders op die dag.
I would like to come, but I have other commitments on that day.

To talk about the obligation to do something, we use the word **verplicht** 'obligated.' When it is a legal or contractual obligation, we add **wettelijk** 'according to the law' or **contractueel**. When something is legally binding, we also use the participle **gebonden**, from the verb **(zich) binden** 'bind (oneself').

In dit college is aanwezigheid verplicht.
In this class, presence is mandatory.

U bent wettelijk verplicht zich aan de grens te legitimeren.
The law requires you to show an ID at the border.

Dat ben je aan je broer verplicht.
You owe it to your brother.

Ik voelde me verplicht hem financieel te ondersteunen.
I felt obligated to support him financially.

U bent contractueel gebonden dit werk af te maken.
You have a contractual obligation to finish this job.

To express that someone is not fulfilling their duty or is acting contrary to (legal) obligation, we use expressions such as **zich niet houden aan** 'not obey, not keep to,' **z'n plicht verwaarlozen** 'neglect one's duty,' **tegen de wet in/illegaal handelen** 'act against the law.'

De verkoper hield zich niet aan het contract.
The seller didn't keep to the contract.

Je hebt je niet aan je plicht gehouden/Je hebt je plicht verwaarloosd.
You didn't stick to your duty.

Hij heeft tegen de wet in/illegaal gehandeld.
He acted against the law.

To say that someone doesn't have to do something, we use the infinitive construction **niet hoeven te** 'don't have to.' This is the negative answer to a question that begins with **Moet ik . . . ?** 'Do I have to . . . ?' or **Moeten we . . . ?** 'Do we have to . . . ?.' Another way to express absence of obligation is by negating the verb **dwingen** 'to force.'

Je hoeft je spruitjes niet op te eten.
You do not have to eat your sprouts.

U hoeft dit deel van het formulier niet in te vullen.
You don't have to fill out this part of the form.

Ik wil je niet dwingen, nog langer hier te blijven.
I don't want to force you to stay any longer.

To express that someone is not obligated to do something or doesn't have to commit to anything, we use words such as **niet verplicht** 'not obligatory' and **niet bindend** 'not binding.'

U bent niet verplicht, deze waren aan te geven.
You are not obligated to declare these goods.

Deze mondelinge overeenkomst verplicht u tot niets.
This oral agreement doesn't commit you to anything.

Dit contract is niet bindend.
This contract is not binding.

To say that someone is completely free of an obligation, we use the verb **vrijstellen** 'relieve' and its noun **de vrijstelling** 'exemption.'

Hij werd van de dienstplicht vrijgesteld.
He was exempted from military service.

U hebt recht op vrijstelling van het examen Nederlands.
You are entitled to an exemption from the Dutch language exam.

15.4 Referring to sources of information

Referring

The most common way to refer to sources of information is with the preposition **volgens** 'according to.'

Volgens het rapport staan de zaken redelijk goed.
According to the report, business is going reasonably well.

Volgens getuigenverklaringen reed de automobilist na het ongeluk door.
According to witness statements, the driver hit and ran.

To refer to written texts, we also use the verb **staan** 'stand' with the preposition **in** 'in.'

De voetbaluitslagen stonden vanmorgen in de krant.
The soccer results were in the paper today.

Zo staat het in de tekst/de bijbel/de grondwet.
It says so in the text/the Bible/the constitution.

Quote

To quote a text, we use the verb **citeren** 'cite' (noun **citaat**) or **aanhalen** 'cite.'

In zijn opstel citeerde de student een tekst van Vondel.
In his essay, the student cited a text by Vondel.

De schrijver haalde een aantal regels van Marcuse aan.
The writer quoted a few lines from Marcuse.

Heb je de bronnen voor al je citaten nauwkeurig aangegeven?
Did you clearly indicate the sources for your quotes?

Invoke authority

To invoke an authority we use **verwijzen naar** 'refer to,' **zich beroepen op** 'refer to,' and **onderbouwen** 'substantiate.'

In zijn betoog verwees de professor een paar keer naar Multatuli.
In his lecture, the professor referred to Multatuli a few times.

De spreker beriep zich op Marx en Engels.
The speaker invoked Marx and Engels.

De voorzitter onderbouwde zijn argument met cijfers uit een rapport.
The chairman substantiated his argument with numbers from a report.

15.5 Reporting other people's words and claims

Report

As in the examples in section **15.4**, one can use **volgens** 'according to' to report someone else's speech. Another form commonly used in newspaper language is **aldus** 'according to.' Note that **aldus** always follows the statement.

Volgens Nico was dit de heetste zomer ooit.
According to Nico, this was the hottest summer ever.

Er zal nog meer op cultuur bezuinigd moeten worden, aldus de minister.
There will have to be more budget cuts in the arts, the minister said.

To report a direct statement, we use introducing verbs such as **zeggen** 'say,' **vertellen** 'tell,' **beweren** 'maintain,' and the actual statement is turned into a subordinated sentence beginning with **dat** 'that' with the verb at the end.

Karin zegt dat ze een nieuwe computer gekocht heeft.
Karin says that she has bought a new computer.

Ze vertelden dat ze naar Alaska op vakantie zijn geweest.
They told us that they went to Alaska on vacation.

Direct questions are turned into indirect questions with introducing verbs such as **vragen** 'ask,' **willen weten** 'want to know,' **zich afvragen** 'ask oneself,' etc.

De studenten vragen/willen weten of het examen uitgesteld kan worden.
The students are asking/want to know if the exam can be postponed.

Je moeder vraagt zich af wanneer je nou eens thuiskomt.
Your mom is wondering when you're finally coming home.

▶ For more on indirect speech, see **9.5**.

If one questions the truth of what someone said, we use the verb **beweren** 'maintain' to express a certain doubt.

Hij beweert dat hij dat geld van een overleden oom heeft geërfd.
He maintains that he inherited that money from a deceased uncle.

Rumor

To report a rumor, we use expressions such as **men zegt** 'they say' or **het gerucht gaat** 'rumor has it' or also **van horen zeggen** 'from hearsay.' In situations such as these, we also like to use the passive voice to hide the source of information.

Men zegt/Er wordt beweerd dat er twee bioscopen in de binnenstad gaan sluiten.
They say that two cinemas downtown will close down.

Het gerucht gaat dat de burgemeester een buitenechtelijke relatie heeft.
Rumor has it that the mayor has been having an extramarital affair.

Ik heb het maar van horen zeggen hoor, het zal wel niet waar zijn.
I only have this from hearsay, it's probably not true.

▶ For more on passive, see **8.3**.

When one doesn't want to say the source of the information, the following expression can be used.

Ik heb me laten vertellen, dat jij je schoolopleiding niet afmaakt.
I have heard that you are not finishing your education.

News reporters often use the conditional **zou** 'would' in the present perfect to express that the information they have is second hand. In English we would say 'allegedly.'

Bij de passagiers zou twee kilo heroïne gevonden zijn.
Allegedly, two kilos of heroin were found on the passengers.

De brand zou door een gaslek zijn ontstaan.
Apparently, the fire started because of a gas leak.

▶ For more on the conditional, see **8.2**.

To ask someone to report what someone else said exactly (in a formal context), we use the verb **weergeven** 'quote, reproduce':

Kunt u precies weergeven, wat de verdachte tegen u zei?
Can you repeat exactly what the suspect said to you?

And finally, to ask someone to pass on a message, we use the verb **doorgeven** 'pass on.'

Kun je even een berichtje aan Karina doorgeven?
Can you pass on a message to Karina?

15.6 Making assumptions, expressing probability and possibility

Assumptions

There are many verbs we use to make assumptions. The most common are **geloven** 'believe,' **aannemen** 'assume,' **veronderstellen** 'assume,' **uitgaan van** 'assume,' and **menen** 'mean.'

De film begint om kwart over negen, geloof ik.
The film starts at quarter past nine, I believe.

Ik neem aan dat jij vanavond kookt?
I assume you will do the cooking tonight?

Ik veronderstel dat jij van deze affaire niets afwist?
I assume you didn't know about this affair?

We gaan ervan uit dat we deze zomer gewoon op vakantie gaan.
We assume that we will go on vacation this summer as normal.

Ik meen dat we die nog in uw maat hebben.
I think we still have that in your size.

We also use the modal verb **moeten** 'must' to make assumptions.

Er moet toch iets over in de krant staan.
There must be something about it in the paper.

In a more formal or scientific context, we use a form of **aannemen** 'assume' or **ervan uitgaan** 'assume.' In a less formal context, one can use **zich voorstellen** 'imagine' in the imperative.

Laten we aannemen/Laten we ervan uitgaan dat uw theorie klopt.
Let's assume your theory is correct.

Aangenomen dat u gelijk heeft . . .
Supposing that you are right . . .

Stel je voor dat de bruidsjurk niet op tijd klaar is.
Imagine the wedding gown not being ready in time.

Possibility

To express possibility, we use the adverbs **mogelijk** 'possible' and **waarschijnlijk** 'probable' and the noun **de kans** 'chance.'

> **Het is mogelijk dat ik vanavond iets later kom.**
> It's possible I will be coming a little later this evening.
>
> **Waarschijnlijk komt de hoofdpijn van de warmte.**
> Probably the heat is causing the headache.
>
> **Er is kans op een bui.**
> There is a chance of showers.
>
> **Er bestaat een kans dat het feest niet doorgaat.**
> There is a chance that the party will be cancelled.

The verb **kunnen** 'can' is also used to express possibility, often in the conditional with **zou** 'would/could.'

> **Het kan zijn dat ik vanavond iets later kom.**
> It's possible I'll be coming a little later this evening.
>
> **Het zou kunnen dat we die vergadering moeten verschuiven.**
> There's a possibility that we may have to postpone that meeting.
>
> **Het zou kunnen.**
> Could be.

A very common way to express possibility and assumptions is with the verb **zullen** 'shall/will' in the future or future perfect tense. To add to the degree of certainty, we insert adverbs and particles such as **zeker** 'surely,' **toch** 'indeed,' **wel** 'surely,' and so on. Note that these are difficult to translate literally.

> **Hij zal zo wel komen.**
> He will probably be here in a minute.
>
> **Hij zal toch wel komen?**
> He will come, won't he?
>
> **Hij zal de trein wel gemist hebben.**
> He has probably missed the train.
>
> **Je zult er wel iets over gelezen hebben.**
> You've probably read something about it.

▶ For more on modal auxiliary verbs, see **6.2**.

15.7 Discussing conditions

To express a condition, we begin the sentence with a conjunction such as **als** 'if, when,' **tenzij** 'unless,' or **mits** 'as long as.' Sentences with these conjunctions are subordinated and thus have the verb at the end. In the following situations, the condition is likely to be fulfilled.

> **Als het mooi weer is, kunnen we het feest buiten houden.**
> If the weather is nice, we can have the party outside.
>
> **We gaan vanmiddag de stad in, tenzij het regent.**
> We are going to town this afternoon, unless it rains.
>
> **U kunt het artikel ruilen, mits u de bon nog heeft.**
> You can change the item, as long as you still have the receipt.

If we are talking about a situation in which the condition is less likely to be fulfilled (fantasy or dream), we change the sentences to the simple past tense or the simple past of the verb **zullen**, **zou**, in combination with an infinitive.

Als ik jou was, kocht ik die auto niet/zou ik die auto niet kopen.
If I were you, I wouldn't buy that car.

Als ik genoeg geld had, ging ik op reis/zou ik op reis gaan.
If I had enough money, I would travel.

If the speaker is looking back on a situation in which the condition was not fulfilled and is not likely to ever be fulfilled, the sentence is changed to past perfect.

Als ik dat had geweten, dan had ik je daarvoor geen toestemming gegeven.
If I had known that, I would not have given you permission for that.

Als ik niet zo moe was geweest, had ik het boek nog uitgelezen.
If I hadn't been so tired, I would have finished the book.

► For more on the conditional, see **8.2**.

15.8 Expressing the ability to do something

To express ability to do something, we use the verb **kunnen** 'can.'

Peter kan pianospelen.
Peter can play the piano.

Kun jij tango dansen?
Can you dance the tango?

To express that one can do something because one has learned or studied it, we use **kennen** 'to know.' This, therefore, has more to do with being familiar with something. When one has memorized something, we add **van buiten** or **uit het hoofd**.

Ik denk dat ik het hoofdstuk geschiedenis nu wel ken.
I think I know the history chapter now.

Hij kent veel gedichten van Slauerhoff van buiten/uit zijn hoofd.
He knows a lot of Slauerhoff's poems by heart.

One can also use **in staat zijn** 'be able to' to express ability to do something.

De automobilist was nog in staat zelf uit het wrak te kruipen.
The driver was able to crawl out of the wreck by himself.

Wij zijn niet in staat die hypotheek te betalen.
We are not able to pay for that mortgage.

When something is difficult or takes a lot of effort, we use verbs such as **lukken** 'succeed' or expressions such as **het voor elkaar krijgen** 'manage to do.'

Het lukte hem de marathon af te maken.
He managed to finish the marathon.

Johan kreeg het voor elkaar, de hele woonkamer zelf te behangen.
Johan managed to hang wallpaper in the entire living room.

Gefeliciteerd, je hebt het voor elkaar gekregen!
Congratulations, you did it!

When we talk about mental and physical abilities in a more formal context, we use the word **het vermogen** 'ability.' This can also be a verb, **vermogen**.

Ik vermag daar de humor niet van in te zien (very formal).
I'm not able to see the humor in that.

Ik heb die taak naar m'n beste vermogen vervuld.
I have completed that task to the best of my abilities.

De baas verliest zijn vermogen om belangrijke beslissingen te nemen.
The boss is losing his ability to make important decisions.

Door de tumor verloor hij zijn reukvermogen.
Because of the tumor, he lost his sense of smell.

Finally, to talk about someone's talents and capabilities, we use words such as **talent** 'talent,' **gave** 'gift,' **vermogen** 'ability,' **vaardigheid** 'skill,' **bekwaamheid** 'ability,' **handigheid** 'handiness,' and their related adjectives and adverbs.

Dat is een getalenteerde/begaafde pianist.
That is a talented/gifted pianist.

Gert heeft totaal geen improvisatievermogen.
Gert doesn't have any ability to improvise.

Mijn zoon is ontzettend handig met mijn pastamachine.
My son is quite handy with my pasta maker.

Welke vaardigheden heb jij op je CV staan?
What skills do you have listed on your CV?

Dat wil zeggen: Waar ben jij goed in?
That is to say: What are you good at?

Deze meubelmaker is een bekwaam vakman.
This cabinetmaker is an accomplished professional.

15.9 Expressing knowledge

The two main verbs to express knowledge are **weten** 'to know' and **kennen** 'to know' but they differ in the way they are used. The verb **weten** is used to say that one has certain factual information.

Weet u waar de Beethovenstraat is?
Do you know where Beethoven Street is?

Ik weet niet hoe laat het is.
I don't know what time it is.

Weet jij hoeveel eieren je voor dit recept nodig hebt?
Do you know how many eggs you need for this recipe?

The verb **kennen** is used to say that one is familiar with someone or something.

Ik ken Amsterdam niet zo goed.
I don't know Amsterdam very well.

Ken jij de baas van Nico? Een aardige vent.
Do you know Nico's boss? A nice chap.

Ik oefen Für Elise nu al weken, maar ik ken het nog niet goed.
I've been practicing Für Elise for weeks, but I don't yet know it very well.

Two other common ways to express knowledge are **verstand hebben van** 'know something about' and **inzicht hebben in** 'have an insight into.'

> **Heb jij verstand van computers?**
> Do you know something about computers?
>
> **Door dit onderzoek krijgen we meer inzicht in het gedrag van pinguins.**
> Through this research, we will gain more insight into the behavior of penguins.

Two important nouns denoting knowledge are **de wetenschap** 'science' (adjective **wetenschappelijk** 'scientific, scholarly') and **de kennis** 'knowledge.'

> **De medische wetenschap is behoorlijk ver gevorderd.**
> Medical science has made considerable advances.
>
> **Irma leest veel wetenschappelijke artikelen over sociale vraagstukken.**
> Irma reads a lot of scholarly articles about social issues.
>
> **Kennis van minstens één vreemde taal is voor deze baan van groot belang.**
> Knowledge of at least one foreign language is crucial for this position.

16

Communication in transactions

16.1 Giving orders and commands

To give an order, we use the command form, the imperative. In its shortest, most basic form, this is just the stem of the verb. Examples:

> **Kijk uit/Kom hier/Kom binnen/Ga weg/Laat staan/Laat maar.**
> Watch out/Come here/Come in/Go away/Leave it/Forget about it.

Of course, other sentence elements can be added to the imperative.

> **Geef me even de krant.**
> Give me the newspaper please.

> **Maak je huiswerk voor het eten.**
> Do your homework before dinner.

The examples above use the imperative without a subject. In second person plural, and when we want to emphasize the subject, it is added. In a formal sentence, the subject **u** must be added.

> **Neem jij maar een lekker koekje.**
> You take a nice cookie.

> **Gaan jullie je maar gauw omkleden.**
> You all go and change quickly.

> **Blijft u hier maar even wachten.**
> Please stay here and wait for a minute.

Particles such as **even**, **maar**, **nou**, and **toch** can modify a command, making it friendlier (**even**, **maar**) or more impatient or harsh (**nou**, **toch**).

> **Kijk even of er nog genoeg melk is.**
> Go see if there is enough milk yet.

> **Ruim die rommel nou op, ik wil de tafel dekken.**
> Clear away that stuff, will you, I want to set the table.

> **Zeg dan toch dat je niet mee wilt!**
> Just say that you don't want to come along!

► For more on particles, see **3.9** and **13.8**.

Formal commands are made with the formal personal pronoun **u** and the corresponding verb form, with the word order inverted.

> **Komt u maar even binnen.**
> Please come in for a moment.

> **Geeft u mij maar twee ons champignons.**
> Please give me two ounces of mushrooms.

It is customary for sales persons and waiters to ask their customers to say what they want in the manner below.

Zegt u het maar.
What will it be/How may I help you?

A very curt form of the imperative is to simply use only the infinitive of the verb.

Ophouden!
Stop it!

Doorrijden.
Keep driving.

Afblijven!
Hands off!

In the negative form with **niet**, this form of the imperative is used to tell people what not to do.

Niet roken.
No smoking.

Niet fotograferen.
Do not take photographs.

Niet doen.
Don't do that.

In recipes, one may find the informal command form or the form with the infinitive.

Schil de aardappels, snijd ze in plakjes en bak ze in olie goudbruin.
Peel the potatoes, cut them in slices, and fry them in oil until golden brown.

De spinazie wassen, aan de kook brengen, afgieten en met boter op smaak maken.
Wash the spinach, boil it, drain it, and add butter to taste.

Finally, a more unusual command form is the use of the past participle or a participle construction.

Opgelet, het spel gaat beginnen.
Pay attention, the game is starting.

Niet getreurd, misschien winnen we volgende keer.
Don't be sad, maybe we will win next time.

Opgehoepeld/Ingerukt!
Get lost!

► See also **8.1**.

16.2 Asking for and offering help and advice

Help

There are several different words for help and assistance: **hulp** 'help,' **assistentie** 'assistance,' **steun** 'help, support,' and **bijstand** '(legal) aid.' To ask for help (Dutch **om hulp vragen**), we use a variety of questions with the verb **helpen** 'help,' from simple commands to more elaborate ways using the conditional with **zou**. Inserting **alsjeblieft** or **alstublieft** helps to make the request more polite and urgent.

Help me even met die dozen (alsjeblieft).
Help me with those boxes please.

Kun je/Kunt u me even helpen?
Can you help me please?

Zou je/Zou u me willen helpen dit formulier in te vullen?
Would you be willing to help me fill out this form?

In very formal situations, one might say:

Zou u zo vriendelijk willen zijn mijn koffers naar boven te dragen?
Would you be so kind as to help me carry the suitcases upstairs?

Another, more formal way uses the phrase **iemand behulpzaam zijn** 'help someone.'

Zou u me met deze papieren behulpzaam willen zijn?
Would you be willing to help me with these papers?

Very informal ways to ask a favor use phrases such as **een plezier doen**, **een lol doen** 'do a favor.'

Doe me een plezier en zet die vuilnisbak even buiten.
Do me a favor and put that trash can outside.

Doe me een lol en zeg het niet tegen mijn ouders!
Do me a favor and don't tell my parents!

Support

Asking for support, financial or otherwise, one uses words such as **bijdrage** 'contribution' and **steun** 'support.' Note that **bijdrage** is used with the verb **leveren** '*lit.* deliver.'

Zou u een financiële bijdrage aan dit project willen leveren?
May we ask you to make a financial contribution to this project?

Zou u dit project met een financiële bijdrage willen steunen?
Would you be willing to support this project with a financial contribution?

Mogen wij om uw steun vragen?
May we ask for your support?

Wij vragen u dringend steun te geven aan het rampgebied.
We urge you to give your support to the disaster area.

Martin kwam naar de wedstrijd om morele steun te geven.
Martin came to the match to give moral support.

Also, when we receive governmental or legal aid, we use the word **uitkering** and **bijstand**. They are both forms of the Dutch welfare system.

Nadat Marco zijn baan verloren had, kreeg hij een (werkloosheids)uitkering.
When Marco lost his job, he received (unemployment) benefits.

Veel alleenstaande moeders komen in de bijstand.
Many single mothers get into the welfare system.

To appeal to the other person's willingness to help, even if it is inconvenient, one can use a variety of polite questions:

Vind je het erg/vervelend/lastig om vanavond te koken?
Do you mind cooking tonight?

Heb je er iets op tegen het gras even te maaien?
Would it bother you to mow the grass?

Maakt het je wat uit morgen iets vroeger met werk te beginnen?
Would it be inconvenient to start working a little earlier tomorrow?

Responses

There are many ways to respond to requests for help. Positive short answers would be:

Natuurlijk.
Of course.

Graag.
With pleasure.

Geen probleem.
No problem.

Ja, zo meteen.
Yes, right away.

Ja, momentje.
Yes, just a second.

Ja, ik kom zo.
Yes, I'll be with you in a minute.

In reply to a request asking whether you'd mind doing something, one can say:

Nee hoor, geen probleem.
No, that's no problem.

Nee hoor, dat doe ik graag.
No, it's my pleasure.

Als ik je/u daarmee een plezier kan doen.
If I can do you a favor.

Nee hoor, ik vind het niet erg/vervelend/lastig.
No, I don't mind.

Het maakt me niets uit.
It makes no difference to me.

Ik heb er niets op tegen.
I don't mind at all.

If one cannot or doesn't want to help, or when it is inconvenient, there are many ways to express this.

Ik kan je/u (nu) niet helpen.
I can't help you (right now).

Ik ben nu even met iets anders bezig.
I'm busy doing something else right now.

Ik heb op het moment geen tijd.
I have no time right now.

Het komt me op het moment slecht uit.
It is inconvenient at the moment.

If one feels unable or inadequate to help, one can say:

Sorry/Het spijt me, maar dat is mijn afdeling niet/daar heb ik geen ervaring mee.
I'm sorry, but that is not my department/that's not my area of expertise.

Daar weet ik zelf ook niets van/Daar heb ik zelf ook geen verstand van.
I don't know anything about that myself.

To offer help and assistance, one can use phrases with **helpen** 'help' or **van dienst zijn** 'to be of service' (more formal) or simply **doen** 'do.'

Kan ik je/u (ergens mee) helpen?
Can I help you with something?

Kan ik u ergens mee van dienst zijn?
Can I be of any service to you?

Wat kan ik voor je/u doen?
What can I do for you?

Heb je/Heeft u hulp nodig?
Do you need help?

Advice

To ask for advice, we use phrases with **advies geven** 'give advice,' **adviseren** 'advise,' **raad geven** 'recommend,' **aanraden** 'recommend, suggest.'

Ik heb advies/raad nodig.
I need advice.

Kun je/Kunt u me advies/raad geven?
Can you give me advice?

Wat zou jij/zou u in dit geval adviseren?
What would you suggest in this case?

Wat zou jij/zou u me aanraden om te doen?
What would you advise me to do?

To offer advice, we use the same words in the following phrases:

Mijn advies is: Koop die tweedehands auto.
My advice is: Buy that used car.

Ik adviseer je/raad je aan een advocaat in te schakelen.
I advise you to bring in a lawyer.

Or we simply use the conditional with **zou**:

Als ik jou was, zou ik die auto niet kopen.
If I were you, I wouldn't buy that car.

Je zou eens wat meer moeten sporten en minder moeten roken.
You should do more sport and smoke less.

Recommendation

The word **aanbevelen** is used when one wants to recommend something/someone.

Ik kan u deze Miele wasmachine zeer aanbevelen.
I can strongly recommend this Miele washing machine.

Ik kan je mijn trainer aanbevelen, een prima vent.
I can recommend my trainer, a really nice chap.

Heeding advice

The words **een advies opvolgen** 'heed advice' are used to indicate that the advice is taken seriously.

Karel volgde het advies van zijn vader op.
Karel followed his father's advice.

Heeding advice, one can say a variety of things:

Je hebt gelijk. Dat zal ik doen.
You are right. I'll do that.

Goed idee. Dat ga ik proberen.
Good idea. I'll try that.

Ja, dat zal wel het beste zijn.
Yes, that's probably best.

Bedankt voor de tip. Daar had ik zelf niet aan gedacht.
Thanks for the tip. I hadn't thought of that myself.

Daar zou ik zelf nooit op gekomen zijn.
I would never have thought of that myself.

Not following or turning down advice

When the advice is not taken seriously, we use the idiom **in de wind slaan** 'ignore' or the verb **negeren** 'ignore.'

Erik sloeg het advies van zijn mentor in de wind.
Erik ignored his mentor's advice.

Annie negeerde de goede raad van haar vriendin.
Annie ignored her friend's good advice.

To decline or turn down advice, one might say:

Dat lijkt me niet zo'n goed idee.
That doesn't seem like such a good idea.

Dat doe ik toch maar liever niet.
I would rather not do that.

Dank je, maar ik beslis daar liever zelf over.
Thanks, but I'd rather decide for myself.

16.3 Expressing needs, wishes, and desires

Need

As explained in **15.3**, the Dutch word for 'to need' is **nodig hebben**. The verb **hebben** takes second position, and **nodig** is placed at the end of the sentence. One adds the desired object.

Ik heb een nieuwe bril nodig.
I need new glasses.

Heb je nu alweer nieuwe voetbalschoenen nodig?
Do you need new soccer shoes again?

When we talk about a certain need, we use the word **de behoefte** 'need' with the preposition **aan**.

We hebben behoefte aan vakantie.
We need a vacation.

Met deze medicijnen voorzien we in dit land in een behoefte.
With these medications, we supply a want in this country.

► To talk about lack, see **14.6**.

To express the need for something to be done, we use the modal verb **moeten** and a passive construction.

De hond moet nodig weer eens geborsteld worden.
The dog really needs a brush again.

Het gras moet dit weekend gemaaid worden.
The grass needs to be mowed this weekend.

▶ For more on passive, see **8.3**.

For needs to which one is entitled by contract or by law, we use words such as **recht hebben op** 'have a right to' and **aanspraak maken op** 'claim.'

Ik heb dit jaar nog recht op vier vakantiedagen.
I'm entitled to four more vacation days this year.

De gedupeerde klant maakte aanspraak op een schadevergoeding.
The aggrieved customer claimed damages.

Demand

For wishes and needs that are more like demands, we use words such as **eisen** 'demand' and its noun **de eis** 'demand,' often with the verb **stellen**. The adjective we use with this noun is **veeleisend** 'demanding.'

De klant eiste haar geld terug.
The customer demanded her money back.

Deze manager stelt hoge eisen aan zijn personeel.
This manager makes high demands on his staff.

Het orkest werkte met een veeleisende dirigent.
The orchestra worked with a demanding conductor.

Wish

To express a wish, one can use constructions with the verb **wensen** 'wish' and its noun **de wens**.

Vakantie op de Bahamas, dat is nou al jaren een grote wens van me.
A vacation in the Bahamas, I have wanted that for years.

Heb je speciale wensen voor je verjaardag?
Do you have special wishes for your birthday?

Jij bent de beste opa die ik me kan wensen.
You are the best grandpa I could wish for.

Nou, de bediening hier laat veel te wensen over.
Well, the service here leaves much to be desired.

Note that one can also use **wensen** to wish something for someone.

Ik wens je het allerbeste.
I wish you the best.

We wensen u een prettig verblijf in ons hotel.
We wish you a pleasant stay in our hotel.

To express wishes, one can also use the verb **willen** 'want' with its conditional form **wou**. In the context of shopping or dining out, one adds **graag** for politeness.

Ik wil een nieuwe fiets voor m'n verjaardag.
I want a new bike for my birthday.

Ik wil graag een auto huren.
I would like to rent a car.

Ik wou graag de tonijn, alstublieft.
I would like the tuna, please.

Ik wou dat het niet zo heet was.
I wish it wasn't so hot.

Another very common way to express wishes and daydreams is to use the conditional with **zou** in combination with **(graag) willen** + infinitive.

Ik zou zo graag weer eens een week naar de Antillen gaan.
I would really love to go to the Antilles again for a week.

Ik zou assertiever willen zijn.
I would like to be more assertive.

Ik zou graag beter willen kunnen skiën.
I wish I could be a better skier.

Desire

When it comes to really strong desires (or demands), we use words such as **verlangen naar** 'desire for,' **het verlangen** 'desire,' or **snakken naar** 'crave.'

Na drie weken vakantie verlangden de kinderen naar huis.
After three weeks of vacation, the children were homesick.

Dat kun je niet van haar verlangen.
You can't ask that of her.

Op verlangen moesten we onze paspoorten laten zien.
On demand, we had to show our passports.

Ik snak naar een kop koffie.
I'm craving a cup of coffee.

Finally, to enquire after needs and desires, one can ask a variety of things, depending on the situation and context:

Heeft u verder nog iets nodig?/Laat maar weten of je nog iets nodig hebt.
Anything else you need?/Let me know if you need anything else.

Is er verder nog iets van uw dienst?
Anything else I can do for you?

16.4 Expressing objections and complaints

Objections, complaints

The Dutch are fairly direct in expressing objections and complaints. They are not exactly champions of diplomacy, they like to come straight to the point. They may come across as offensive, but most of the time it is not meant that way, it's just a cultural difference.

Pardon, maar hier klopt iets niet.
Pardon, but something's wrong here.

Pardon, maar ik geloof dat hier een fout is gemaakt.
Pardon me, but I believe a mistake was made here.

Neemt u me niet kwalijk, maar hier is iets misgegaan.
Don't take me wrong, but something's amiss here.

Ik denk dat u zich/je je vergist hebt.
I think you made a mistake.

Kun je/Kunt u dat nog even nakijken/controleren?
Can you check that again?

When they see a reason to actually complain, they will use words such as **klagen** 'complain,' **zijn beklag doen** 'complain,' **een klacht indienen** 'file a complaint,' and in very informal contexts, **mekkeren** 'bleat, complain.' Note that **klagen** is also used for physical or mental pain.

Ik ging bij de buurman klagen over z'n harde muziek.
I went to complain at the neighbor's about his loud music.

Mijn zoon klaagt al weken over hoofdpijn.
My son has been complaining about headaches for weeks.

De leerling ging zijn beklag doen nadat de leraar hem ten onrechte had gestraft.
The student went to complain after the teacher had punished him unfairly.

We hebben een klacht bij de gemeente ingediend vanwege overlast door hangjongeren.
We have filed a complaint with the city because of harassment by loitering youth.

Mekker toch niet de hele tijd over het weer.
Don't moan about the weather the whole time.

When it gets really ugly, the Dutch might use phrases and expressions involving words such as **schandalig** 'scandalous,' **onbeschoft** 'extremely rude,' **smeerlapperij** 'crap,' **oplichterij** 'swindling,' **zootje** 'mess,' and others.

Wat een schandalige manier van doen/ Dat is een grof schandaal!
What a scandalous/outrageous behavior/It's a bloody disgrace!

Wat een onbeschofte hufter/klootzak.
What a rude jerk/complete asshole.

Wat een smeerlapperij/oplichterij.
This is such crap/swindling.

Wat een zootje is dat hier.
What a bloody mess this is.

Dit slaat toch nergens op!
What bullshit!

There are a few slightly less offensive ways to express one's chagrin. Examples:

Hier neem ik geen genoegen mee.
I don't accept this.

Hier hoort u nog van.
You will hear from me again.

Dit slaat alles/Dit is het toppunt!
This is the limit!

Lawsuit

To sue or to file a lawsuit, the Dutch use words such as **iemand/iets aangeven** 'to report something/someone,' **aangifte doen** 'report,' **iemand aanklagen** 'sue someone,' **iemand beschuldigen** 'accuse someone,' **iemand schuldig verklaren** 'convict a person,' **een aanklacht indienen** 'file a charge,' **een proces/rechtszaak aanspannen** 'prosecute.'

Ik kom een inbraak aangeven/Ik kom aangifte doen van een inbraak.
I'm coming to report a robbery.

Joost heeft z'n buurman aangeklaagd wegens huisvredebreuk.
Joost sued his neighbor for trespassing.

De verdachte werd beschuldigd van poging tot doodslag.
The suspect was accused of attempted homicide.

De rechter heeft hem schuldig verklaard.
The judge convicted him.

Er werd een aanklacht ingediend tegen de caféhouder die het rookverbod negeerde.
A complaint was filed against the pub owner who ignored the smoking ban.

Vier weken later werd er tegen hem een proces/rechtszaak aangespannen.
Four weeks later, a lawsuit was filed against him.

16.5 How to issue and respond to invitations and offers

Invitation

A simple, informal invitation to an activity usually involves phrases with **zin hebben om te** 'would like to' or the modal verb **zullen** 'shall.'

Zullen we dit weekend iets leuks doen?
Shall we do something nice this weekend?

Heb je zin om zaterdag naar de film te gaan?
Would you like to go to the movies this Saturday?

In an informal invitation to drinks or dinner, we would use similar expressions.

Hebben jullie zin om vanavond even op de borrel te komen?
Would you like to come over for drinks tonight?

We willen jullie graag voor een etentje uitnodigen.
We would like to invite you to dinner.

Komen jullie zondag (gezellig) bij ons eten?
Would you like to come over for dinner on Sunday?

Laten we een afspraak maken om een keer samen te eten.
Let's set up an appointment to have dinner together.

Note that **borrel** means 'drinks,' usually alcoholic drinks, i.e., wine or spirits.

There are many ways to invite someone to an event or a party. Informal written invitations via email or a card might include the following phrases:

Ik vier op 12 november mijn verjaardag. Heb je/Hebben jullie zin om te komen?
I'm celebrating my birthday on November 12. Would you like to come?

Je bent van harte uitgenodigd op mijn eindexamenfeest op dinsdag 15 juni.
You are cordially invited to my graduation party on Tuesday, June 15.

An invitation to a slightly more formal occasion (**de vijftigste verjaardag** '50th birthday,' **een 25-jarig jubileum** '25 years of service,' **het 40-jarig huwelijksfeest** '40th wedding anniversary' etc.) might look like this:

Op zaterdag 3 mei zijn we 25 jaar getrouwd. Dat willen we graag met vrienden en familie vieren in . . . Jullie zijn van harte welkom vanaf 6 uur voor een hapje en een drankje . . .
On Saturday, May 3, it is our 25th wedding anniversary. We would like to celebrate this with family and friends at . . . Starting at 6pm, you are very welcome for snacks and drinks . . .

RSVP

To informally ask for an RSVP, one might say:

Bel of mail even of je komt/Laat me even weten of je komt.
Call or mail me to say whether you are coming.

Laten jullie ons even weten of jullie kunnen komen.
Please let us know if you can come.

And then there are many formal invitations to work related or other events. An invitation to such a formal occasion might look like this:

U bent allen hartelijk uitgenodigd op de nieuwjaarsborrel op 5 januari 2014 . . .
You are all cordially invited to raise a glass to the new year on January 5, 2014 . . .

The Dutch are familiar with the letters RSVP, but people often prefer to write a sentence requesting an RSVP. An example of this would be:

Wilt u alstublieft laten weten of wij op u mogen rekenen en zo ja, met hoeveel personen u komt?
Would you please let us know if we can count on you and if yes, with how many persons you are coming?

To respond to an invitation when one plans to accept, one can write or say:

Bedankt voor de uitnodiging. Ik kom/we komen graag.
Thanks for the invitation. I/we would love to come.

Hartelijk dank voor de uitnodiging. We komen met ons tweeën/vieren.
Thanks so much for the invitation. There will be two/four of us.

Decline invitation

If one cannot accept the invitation, one can write or say:

Bedankt voor de uitnodiging, maar ik kan/we kunnen helaas niet komen.
Thanks for the invitation, but unfortunately I/we cannot make it.

Bedankt voor de uitnodiging, maar ik ben/we zijn op die dag helaas verhinderd.
Thanks for the invitation, but unfortunately I/we already have an engagement that day.

Hartelijk dank voor de uitnodiging, maar ik heb/we hebben die dag al een afspraak.
Thanks for the invitation, but I/we already have an appointment on that day.

Het spijt me dat ik niet op je feestje kan komen. Hopelijk een andere keer.
I'm sorry I can't make your party. Hopefully some other time.

Offer

To make an offer, we use words such as **aanbieden** 'to offer' and **het aanbod** 'offer.' A special offer is **de aanbieding**.

Mag ik je een drankje aanbieden?
May I offer you a drink?

Ik kan u dit model van vorig jaar voor een zacht prijsje aanbieden.
I can offer you last year's model for a nice price.

Ik kan u een gunstig aanbod doen.
I can make you a favorable offer.

Dit aanbod geldt tot 31 augustus.
This offer is open until August 31.

De jong belegen kaas is deze week in de aanbieding.
The slightly aged cheese is on special offer this week.

To accept an offer, one can say:

Ik neem je/uw aanbod graag aan.
I gladly accept your offer.

To turn it down, one says:

Het spijt me, maar ik kan je/uw aanbod niet aannemen.
I'm sorry, but I cannot accept your offer.

16.6 Seeking and making promises and assurances

Promise

To seek and make promises, one needs the verb **beloven** 'promise.'

Beloof je me dat je me elke avond zult bellen?
Promise me that you will call me every evening.

Ik beloof (je) dat ik de garage dit weekend zal opruimen.
I promise that I'll clean up the garage this weekend.

Beloofd is beloofd.
A promise is a promise.

Another way to seek and make a promise is to use a form of the verb **zullen** 'will, shall.'

Zul je geen ruzie meer met Karin maken?
Promise me to not fight with Karin anymore.

Ik zal het nooit meer doen.
I won't do it ever again.

Assurance

Another verb that gives more of an assurance than a promise is **verzekeren** 'assure.' Note in this context the noun **de verzekering** 'insurance.' Similarly, one could use **garanderen**, which is sometimes used as a synonym for **beloven** or **verzekeren**.

Ik verzeker u dat u van die deuk niets meer zult zien.
I assure you that you won't notice that dent anymore.

Ik verzeker je dat ik er op tijd zal zijn.
I assure you that I will be there on time.

Ik garandeer u dat deze stof in de wasmachine niet krimpt.
I guarantee you that this material doesn't shrink in the washing machine.

De verzekering vergoedde de schade aan mijn auto.
The insurance paid for the damage to my car.

Count on someone/something

There are also some other expressions one can use to seek and give promises and assurances. Examples are **op iemand/iets kunnen rekenen** 'be able to count on someone,' **ergens van op aan kunnen** 'be able to count on something.'

Kan ik erop rekenen dat de reparatie morgen klaar is?
Can I count on it that the repair is finished tomorrow?

We hebben een keeper nodig. Kunnen we op jou rekenen?
We need a goalie. Can we count on you?

Ik haal je van het station. Daar kun je van op aan.
I'll fetch you from the station. You can count on that.

Word of honor

An expression that is often used with making a promise is **je erewoord geven** 'give one's word of honor' and also in that context **op mijn erewoord** 'by word of honor.' To 'keep a promise' is **je aan je woord/belofte houden**.

Op mijn erewoord; ik heb die laatste biertjes niet opgedronken.
I promise; I didn't drink those last beers.

Je zei dat je me zou helpen maar je hebt je niet aan je woord gehouden.
You said you'd help me but you didn't keep your promise.

16.7 Asking for, granting, and denying permission

Permission

The most common (modal) verb we use to ask for permission is **mogen** 'may.'

Mag ik even naar de wc?
May I go to the bathroom?

Mogen we een tent in de tuin opzetten?
May we set up a tent in the garden?

One can also use **kunnen** 'can,' but the preferred form is with **mogen**.

Kan ik hier telefoneren?
Can I make a phone call here?

Kan ik vanavond jouw auto lenen?
Can I borrow your car tonight?

To make these questions even more friendly and polite, we add the conditional form of **zullen**, **zou** to the modal verb **mogen** or **kunnen**.

Zou ik je pen even mogen lenen?
Could I borrow your pen?

Zou ik hier even kunnen telefoneren?
Could I use the phone here?

Zou ik even van uw toilet gebruik mogen maken?
Could I use your bathroom please?

There is an infinite number of possible responses, positive (left) and negative (right).

Ja hoor, dat mag. Yes, you may.	**Nee, dat mag niet.** No, you may not.
Ja, dat mag wel hoor. Yes, that's okay.	**Nee, dat heb ik liever niet.** No, I'd rather you didn't.
Ja, dat is goed. Yes, that's fine.	**Nee, dat gaat niet.** No, that won't work.
Ja, natuurlijk. Yes, of course.	**Nee, in geen geval.** No way.

Ja, ga je gang/gaat uw gang.
Yes, go ahead.

Ja, doe maar (hoor).
Yes, go right ahead.

Nou, goed dan.
Well, alright.

Ja, dat lijkt me geen probleem.
Yes, that should be no problem.

Dat is best.
That's fine.

Okee.
Okay.

(Daar) komt niks van in.
No way.

Dat wil ik niet hebben.
I won't have it.

Geen sprake van.
Out of the question.

Daar kunnen we niet aan beginnen.
We can't do that.

Dat lijkt me geen goed idee.
That doesn't sound like a good idea.

Liever niet.
Rather not.

Besides **mogen** and **kunnen**, other verbs and expressions we use to grant permission are, for example, **toestaan/toelaten** 'allow,' **toestemmen** or **toestemming geven** 'allow permission,' **dulden** 'tolerate,' the modal verb **laten** 'let' and **goedvinden** 'allow.' Some are used in more formal contexts. Examples:

Staat u mij toe u met die bagage te helpen.
Please allow me to help you with that luggage.

Zulk brutaal gedrag kan ik niet toelaten.
I can't allow such impertinent behavior.

Nick bleef maar om een hond vragen, en uiteindelijk stemden z'n ouders toe.
Nick kept asking for a dog and in the end his parents conceded.

Erik kreeg geen toestemming om op schoolreis mee te gaan.
Erik didn't get permission to go on the school field trip.

Ik duld geen tegenspraak.
I won't stand for back talk.

Some are more appropriate in informal contexts.

Ik wil graag alleen op vakantie, maar m'n ouders vinden het niet goed.
I'd like to go on vacation by myself, but my parents won't allow it.

Mijn ouders laten me 's avonds niet alleen over straat gaan.
My parents won't let me be out on the street alone at night.

Note that **mogen** is often used with the preposition **van**, to indicate who gives or doesn't give permission.

Ik mag van mijn ouders niet alleen op vakantie.
My parents will not allow me to go on vacation by myself.

Het mocht van papa, waarom vind jij het dan niet goed?
Dad said it was okay, why don't you?

▶ For more examples of this, see **6.2**.

Formal permissions

Formal permitting or empowering is expressed with the words **toestemming geven** 'allow permission,' **een vergunning geven** 'give a permit,' **een machtiging verlenen** 'give an authorization' or **machtigen** 'authorize' and **een volmacht geven** 'empower.'

We kregen toestemming van de gemeente om een demonstratie te houden.
The city granted us permission to organize a demonstration.

Straatmuzikanten hebben een vergunning nodig om op te treden.
Street musicians need a license to perform.

Hij machtigde zijn advocaat tijdens zijn afwezigheid zijn bankzaken te regelen.
He authorized his lawyer to take care of his financial affairs during his absence.

Deny permission

To deny permission, one can use any of the expressions above in the negative form with **niet** or **geen**, or one can use the verb **verbieden** 'forbid.'

Ik had jou geen toestemming gegeven de hele middag te computeren.
I didn't give you permission to spend the whole day on the computer.

We moeten het roken op het schoolplein gaan verbieden.
We should forbid smoking in the schoolyard.

Het is verboden in het museum te fotograferen.
Taking photographs in the museum is prohibited.

16.8 Making, accepting, and declining suggestions

To make a suggestion, we use the expression **een voorstel doen** 'make a suggestion.' The (separable) verb is **voorstellen** 'propose.'

Mag ik een voorstel doen?
May I make a suggestion?

Ik stel voor dat we de vergadering tot volgende week uitstellen.
I suggest we postpone the meeting until next week.

To accept or decline the proposal, one can use expressions with **het voorstel (niet) aannemen** 'accept (or not) the proposal,' **(niet) op het voorstel ingaan** 'agree (or not) to a proposal' or with the prepositions **voor** 'for' or **tegen** 'against':

Laten we het voorstel van de voorzitter aannemen.
Let's accept the chairman's proposal.

Het hele bestuur ging op het voorstel van de voorzitter in.
The entire board agreed to the chairman's proposal.

Zijn jullie voor of tegen het voorstel van Karel?
Are you for or against Karel's proposal?

Ik neem/We nemen je voorstel graag aan.
I/We gladly accept your proposal.

The verbs **zullen** and **laten** are also used to make suggestions:

Zullen we dit jaar naar Ameland op vakantie gaan?
Shall we go to Ameland for vacation this year?

Laten we de vergadering tot volgende week uitstellen.
Let's postpone the meeting until next week.

Many times, a first proposal with **zullen** is countered with a second one with **laten**, as follows:

Zullen we vanavond bij Atrium gaan eten?
Shall we go out for dinner at Atrium tonight?

Ach nee, laten we toch lekker thuis iets koken.
Ah no, let's just fix something nice at home.

The modal verb **moeten** 'must' can also be used to make a suggestion, if it is something that needs to be done. Note that these are negative questions with **niet**.

> **Moeten we je moeder niet weer eens op de koffie vragen?**
> Shouldn't we ask your mother over for coffee again?

> **Moet je niet eens aan je huiswerk gaan?**
> Shouldn't you be getting on with your homework now?

Other ways to make a suggestion are with expressions such as **Wat dacht je van . . . ?** 'How about . . . /What would you say . . . ?' or **Wat vind je van . . . ?** 'What do you think about . . . ?'

> **Wat dacht je ervan als we dit jaar eens niet op wintersport gaan?**
> What would you say if we didn't go skiing this year?

> **Wat vind je van lichtblauw voor die tegels voor de badkamer?**
> How do you like pale blue for those tiles for the bathroom?

These can be made even more polite (or cautious) with the conditional form **zou**.

> **Wat zou je ervan vinden als ik de Rover voor een BMW inruilde?**
> What would you say if I were to swap the Rover for a BMW?

Finally, one can also ask a question using the expression **er iets op tegen hebben** 'object to.'

> **Heb je er iets op tegen als we vanavond rond acht uur pas eten?**
> Would you object if we didn't eat until 8pm tonight?

To accept such suggestions, one can say:

> **Ja, lijkt me een goed idee/Ja, geen probleem.**
> Yes, that seems like a good idea/Yes, that's no problem.

> **Nee, daar heb ik niets op tegen/Ja, daar ben ik helemaal voor.**
> No, I don't have a problem with that/Yes, I'm all for that.

To decline, one can say:

> **Nou, dat lijkt me niet zo'n goed idee/Nou, daar heb ik wel een probleem mee.**
> Well, that doesn't seem such a good idea/Well, I do have a problem with that.

> **Ja, daar heb ik wel iets op tegen/Nee, daar ben ik op tegen.**
> Yes, I do have a problem with that/No, I am against that.

16.9 Using persuasion

The most common verb we use for persuasion is **overtuigen** 'persuade, convince.'

> **Hij probeerde me ervan te overtuigen dat zijn idee beter was dan het mijne.**
> He tried to convince me that his idea was better than mine.

> **Overtuig me maar eens van het tegendeel.**
> Convince me to the contrary.

> **Okee, je hebt me overtuigd.**
> Okay, you convinced me.

Other, more colloquial, informal verbs are **overhalen** 'persuade, convince' and **ompraten** 'persuade, bring around.'

> **Johan haalde me over om te stoppen met roken.**
> Johan persuaded me to stop smoking.

> **Maarten had eerst geen zin om te kaarten, maar hij liet zich ompraten.**
> At first, Maarten had no desire to play cards, but then he was brought around.

Lots of fillers and particles can be used to produce a convincing tone. Examples are **toch**, **nou**, **gewoon**, and expressions such as **kom op** 'come on' and **toe nou** 'come on.' Most of these are used to modify an imperative (command form).

Koop die jas toch, het is een koopje!
Do buy that coat, it's a steal!

Ach, doe het gewoon, we zien wel wat ervan komt.
Ah, just do it, we'll see what happens.

Ga nou toch gezellig mee vanavond.
Just come along tonight, alright?

Kom op, neem er nog een van me.
Come on, have another one on me.

Ah, toe nou, laat die jongen nou z'n gang gaan.
Ah, come on, just let the kid do what he wants.

Finally, forms with **moeten** 'must' (also with **niet**) and **zullen** (here in the conditional with **zou**) are also used to persuade someone to do or not do something.

Je moet een hond niet slaan, zo'n beest weet niet beter.
You shouldn't hit a dog, an animal doesn't know any better.

Een promotiekans? Moet je doen, joh!
An opportunity for promotion? You should take it!

Ik zou van de gelegenheid gebruik maken als ik jou was.
I would use the opportunity if I were you.

16.10 Issuing and responding to warnings

The most commonly used verb for issuing warnings is **waarschuwen** 'warn, notify' with the preposition **voor** 'for.' The corresponding noun is **de waarschuwing** 'warning.'

Je bent gewaarschuwd/Ik heb je nog zo gewaarschuwd.
You've been warned/I warned you about that (I told you so).

We hebben meteen de politie gewaarschuwd.
We immediately notified the police.

Ik waarschuw je maar één keer.
I warn you only once.

Waarschuw even als de film begint.
Give me a shout when the film starts.

In de kranten werd er voor overstromingsgevaar gewaarschuwd.
The papers issued flood warnings.

De fietser die zonder licht reed kwam er met een waarschuwing van af.
The cyclist who didn't have lights on his bike got away with a warning.

Admonish

Other possible words for issuing warnings are **manen** 'admonish, warn,' **vermanen** 'admonish, warn,' **aanmanen** 'urge, demand for payment' with the noun **de aanmaning** 'reminder, summons.'

Dit maant tot voorzichtigheid.
This calls for caution.

De leraar maande tot orde in de klas.
The teacher urged the class to be orderly.

De leraar sprak de rumoerige klas vermanend toe.
The teacher berated the rowdy class.

Ik heb een aanmaning van de balastingsdienst gekregen.
I received a summons from the IRS.

In situations of danger or in an emergency, we also use the words **alarmeren** 'alarm,' and **het alarm** 'alarm.'

Na het ongeval werd een arts gealarmeerd.
After the accident, they called a doctor.

Het brandalarm ging af en iedereen moest het gebouw verlaten.
The fire alarm came on, and everyone had to leave the building.

Another way to issue a warning or tell someone to be prepared for a situation is by using the expression **rekening houden met** 'take into account.'

Door werkzaamheden op het spoor moet u rekening houden met vertraging.
Because of work on the tracks, you need to be prepared for delays.

Houdt u er rekening mee dat het weer hier plotseling kan omslaan.
Please be aware that the weather here can suddenly change.

Caution

To tell someone to be careful, we use the adverb **voorzichtig** 'careful' with an imperative or the verbs **oppassen** 'pay attention, watch out' and **uitkijken** 'watch out.'

Wees voorzichtig als je de straat oversteekt.
Be careful when you cross the street.

Weest u voorzichtig bij het openen van het bagagecompartiment.
Be careful opening the overhead compartment.

Je gaat in de sneeuw de weg op? Voorzichtig dan maar.
You're going out on the road in this snow? Just be careful.

Pas op! Er komt een auto van links.
Watch out! There's a car coming from the left.

Kijk toch uit waar je loopt!
Watch where you're going!

Danger

To warn in a dangerous situation, we use the word **gevaar** 'danger,' often as a compound noun attached to the word that actually forms the danger.

Er bestaat altijd gevaar dat de dijken doorbreken.
There is always the danger that the dikes will break.

Slipgevaar! Minder uw vaart.
Danger of skidding! Slow down.

In droge hete zomers waarschuwen ze vaker voor bosbrandgevaar.
In dry hot summers, there are more forest fire alerts.

Threat

When the warning takes the form of a threat, we use the word **dreigen** 'threaten' and its nouns **de dreiging** 'threat,' **het dreigement** 'threat,' and **de bedreiging** 'threat.' We also use the conditional with **als** 'if.'

Hij dreigde de politie te bellen.
He threatened to call the cops.

De bewoners op dit eiland leven met de constante dreiging van een natuurramp.
The inhabitants of this island live with the permanent threat of a natural disaster.

Hij werd onder bedreiging van een pistool beroofd.
He was robbed at gunpoint.

Is dat een dreigement?
Are you threatening me?

Als je nu niet ophoudt, dan zwaait er wat!
If you don't stop now, you'll be in big trouble!

Heed warnings

To heed warnings, we use words such as **luisteren naar** 'listen to,' **gehoor geven aan** 'pay attention to,' **serieus nemen** 'take seriously.' When the warning or threat are not taken seriously, we use the words **niet serieus nemen** 'to not take seriously,' **in de wind slaan** 'ignore,' **geen acht slaan op** 'to not pay attention to,' **tegenin gaan** 'act against.'

Johan luistert altijd naar de waarschuwingen voor de scheepvaart.
Johan always listens to the shipping forecast.

Je kunt maar beter gehoor geven aan de waarschuwingen van je vader.
You'd better listen to your father's warnings.

De bewoners namen de waarschuwing voor overstromingsgevaar niet serieus.
The inhabitants didn't take the flood warning seriously.

Joop sloeg de waarschuwingen van zijn vrienden in de wind.
Joop ignored the warnings of his friends.

De zwemmers sloegen geen acht op de borden met "gevaarlijke branding".
The swimmers paid no attention to the signs with "dangerous surf."

Tegen alle waarschuwingen in ging de schaatser toch het ijs op.
Against all warnings, the skater went on the ice.

17

Expressing attitudes and mental states

17.1 Asserting and denying the truth of something

To assert the truth of something, one can use the following expressions:

Dat klopt/Dat is juist.
That's correct.

Dat is waar.
That is true.

Ja, dat is zo.
Yes, that's right.

Inderdaad.
Indeed.

Note that **Dat klopt** is to confirm the truth of facts. Example:

A: Simon is toch medewerker bij Philips?
B: Ja, dat klopt.
A: Simon is an employee with Philips, right?
B: Yes, that's right.

To assert the truth of someone's statement, one can say:

Ja, je hebt gelijk.
Yes, you are right.

Ja, daar heb je gelijk in.
Yes, you are right in that.

To deny the truth of something, one can use the following expressions:

Dat klopt niet/Daar klopt niets van/Daar klopt geen bal van.
That's not right/wrong/completely wrong.

Dat is (helemaal) niet waar/Dat is niet helemaal waar.
That's not true (at all)/That's not quite true.

Dat is (complete) onzin.
That's (complete) nonsense.

Dat slaat nergens op (idiomatic expression)**.**
That's hogwash.

Dat is gelogen/Dat is een leugen.
That's a lie.

Gelul/Lulkoek/Larie (rather vulgar).
Bollocks/Bullshit.

We also use the word **geloven** 'believe' and adjectives such as **geloofwaardig** 'believable' and **ongelofelijk** 'unbelievable' to assert or deny the truth of something.

Geloof jij wat ze in de krant over die moordzaak zeggen?
Do you believe what they say in the paper about that murder case?

Ik geloof er niets van/Ik geloof er geen woord (or **geen bal) van.**
I don't believe a word of it.

Ik vind dat verhaal van die koe op de weg niet erg geloofwaardig.
I don't find that story about the cow in the road very credible.

Karel was op de top van Everest? Ongelofelijk.
Karel summited Everest? Unbelievable.

To express that something is only half the truth or neither true nor untrue, one can say:

Dat is maar de halve waarheid.
That's only half the truth.

Dat verhaal klopt maar ten dele.
That story is only partially true.

Dat verhaal komt niet overeen met de feiten.
That story doesn't correspond to the facts.

Jouw verhaal klinkt uit de lucht gegrepen.
Your story sounds far-fetched.

To declare solemnly the truth of something, one can use expressions with **zweren** 'swear' or **een eed afleggen** 'swear an oath.'

Ik zweer dat ik hem sinds dinsdag niet meer gezien heb.
I swear I have not seen him since Tuesday.

De aangeklaagde legde een eed af niets dan de waarheid te zeggen.
The defendant swore an oath to say nothing but the truth.

► See **6.3** and **9.7** for infinitive constructions with **te**.

In a less formal context, we also use **bij hoog en bij laag beweren** 'pretend, maintain.'

Hij beweerde bij hoog en bij laag dat hij het geld gevonden had.
He pretended that he found the money.

17.2 Expressing certainty, uncertainty, and doubt

Certainty

To express certainty, we use words such as **zeker weten** 'know for sure,' **er zeker van zijn** 'be sure,' and **ervan overtuigd zijn** 'be convinced.' These can be reinforced with adverbs such as **absoluut** 'absolutely,' **pertinent** 'definitely,' and **helemaal** 'completely.'

Ik weet het zeker.
I'm sure.

Ik weet pertinent zeker dat ik die schaar teruggelegd heb.
I'm absolutely sure I put those scissors back.

Ik ben er zeker van dat het weer vandaag goed blijft.
I'm sure the weather will stay nice today.

Ik ben ervan overtuigd dat Maarten voor dat examen gaat slagen.
I'm convinced that Maarten is going to pass that exam.

A: Knip het maar kort.
B: Zeker weten?
A: Cut it short.
B: You sure?

One can also simply use certain adverbs (**absoluut** 'absolutely,' **heus** 'surely,' **beslist** 'decidedly') and adverbial expressions (**vast en zeker** 'most certainly,' **met zekerheid** 'with certainty,' **in elk/ieder geval** 'definitely,' **in geen geval** 'no way') to express certainty.

Ik kan met zekerheid zeggen dat die deur gisteravond op slot zat.
I can say with certainty that that door was locked yesterday.

Maarten komt absoluut/beslist naar het feest.
Maarten will definitely come to the party.

Sinterklaas komt heus wel, wacht nou maar af.
Santa Claus will really come; just you wait.

Het wordt vast en zeker een succesvolle avond.
It will most certainly be a successful evening.

Je kunt in elk geval blijven slapen.
You can stay the night no matter what.

We gaan in geen geval nieuwe computers aanschaffen.
We will definitely not purchase new computers.

Uncertainty

To express uncertainty, one can simply negate the statements from above with **niet** 'not' or use other expressions with **denken** 'think,' **geloven** 'believe,' **zich afvragen** 'wonder,' **aannemen** 'assume.'

Ik weet het niet (helemaal) zeker.
I'm not (entirely) sure.

Ik denk niet/Ik geloof niet dat Piet en Mia dat huis gaan kopen.
I don't think Piet and Mia will buy that house.

Ik vraag me af of ik het gas wel uitgedraaid heb.
I wonder if I turned off the gas.

Ik neem aan dat Frans en Hanna deze zomer weer naar Ameland gaan.
I assume Frans and Hanna will go to Ameland again this summer.

The word **zeker** 'surely' is also used when one assumes, but is not certain.

Jij gaat zeker niet naar dat feest van Monica, hè?
I assume you are not going to that party at Monica's?

Jij hebt zeker heel wat werk als voorzitter van de tennisvereniging.
You must have quite a bit of work as chairman of the tennis club.

One can also express uncertainty with adverbs (**misschien** 'maybe,' **waarschijnlijk** 'probably,' **mogelijk** 'possibly') and expressions such as **voor zover ik weet** 'as far as I know.'

Het gaat misschien regenen/Mogelijk komt er onweer.
Maybe it's going to rain/It's possible there will be a thunderstorm.

Je hebt waarschijnlijk te lang in de zon gezeten.
You probably have been sitting in the sun for too long.

Voor zover ik weet zijn alle dossiers compleet.
As far as I know, all files are complete.

Doubt

To express doubt, we use words such as **twijfelen aan** 'doubt,' **betwijfelen** (with a direct object) or **twijfelen** with an indirect question.

Ik twijfel aan de waarheid van dat bericht.
I doubt the truth of that message.

Ik betwijfel de echtheid van die edelsteen.
I doubt the authenticity of that gem.

Ik twijfel nog of ik die studiebeurs zal aannemen.
I'm still in doubt about whether to accept that scholarship.

► See also **9.5** for indirect speech.

Adjectives of **twijfelen** are **twijfelachtig** 'doubtful, dubious' and **ongetwijfeld** 'doubtless, no doubt.'

Dit restaurant heeft een nogal twijfelachtige reputatie.
This restaurant has a rather doubtful reputation.

Bij de Hema krijg je zulke dingen ongetwijfeld veel goedkoper.
At the Hema, you get such things much cheaper, no doubt.

17.3 Expressing likes and dislikes

Likes

In Dutch, the verbs **houden van** 'like, love,' **mogen** 'like,' and **bevallen** 'please, satisfy' all express likes, but are not interchangeable. Less common is **aanstaan** 'appeal, please.'

To say that one likes a person, one can use **vinden** 'find' with any adjective that gives a positive description of that person, one can use **mogen** 'like' or, when it is love, one uses **houden van**. In certain contexts, for example when someone's performance is satisfactory, one can also use **bevallen** 'please, satisfy' or **tevreden zijn met** 'be satisfied/pleased with.'

Ik vind Johan aardig/een aardige vent.
I think Johan is kind/a nice guy.

Ik mag Van Houten wel/Ik mag Van Houten graag.
I quite like Van Houten/I really like Van Houten.

Ik hou van m'n neefjes en nichtjes/Karin houdt van Joost.
I love my nephews and nieces/Karin loves Joost.

Onze nieuwe dirigent bevalt ons heel goed.
We are very pleased with our new conductor.

We zijn heel tevreden met de nieuwe stagiaire.
We are very satisfied with our new intern.

To say that one likes a thing, one can again use **vinden** with some adjective that describes the object (note, however, that **lekker** 'tasty, nice' is used almost exclusively for food and drink), one can use **houden van** 'like,' and one can use **bevallen** 'please, satisfy,' **aanstaan** 'appeal, please' or **tevreden zijn met** 'be satisfied/pleased with.'

Ik vind de muziek van Mozart mooi.
I think Mozart's music is beautiful.

Ik vind appeltaart lekker.
I think apple pie is tasty.

Frank houdt van een goed glas cognac.
Frank likes a good glass of brandy.

Ik hou van het strand bij zonsondergang.
I love the beach at sunset.

Mijn kamer in de studentenflat bevalt me goed.
I like my room in the dorm.

De reis naar Turkije is ons goed bevallen.
We enjoyed our trip to Turkey.

Hoe bevalt jouw tennisracket je?
How do you like your tennis racket?

Jouw vakantieplan staat me wel aan.
I quite like your vacation plan.

Ik ben heel tevreden met m'n nieuwe auto.
I'm really pleased with my new car.

To say that one likes certain activities (including eating and drinking), one can use the verb for that activity with **graag** 'like to' or one can use the verb as noun with **houden van** 'like, love.'

Peter gaat graag hardlopen.
Peter likes to run.

De buren eten graag in een restaurant.
The neighbors like to eat in a restaurant.

De jongens houden van voetballen.
The boys like to play soccer.

Mijn oma hield van breien.
My grandma loved knitting.

A colloquial way to express likes is to use the expression **gek/dol zijn op** 'be crazy/nuts about.' This can be used for people, things and situations.

Miriam is gek op haar oma.
Miriam adores her grandma.

Joop en Annelies zijn dol op bergwandelen.
Joop and Annelies love to hike in the mountains.

Vincent is gek op zoute drop.
Vincent is nuts about salty licorice.

Dislikes

To express dislikes, many of the expressions above can simply be negated with **niet** or **geen**, but the Dutch have a few more ways to say they don't like something or someone. In reference to people, they also use the verbs **aanstaan** 'appeal' and **uitstaan** 'bear, stand' in the negative form. And they use the expressions **een hekel hebben aan** 'dislike,' or **haten** 'hate.'

Ik vind Benno niet aardig.
I don't think Benno is nice.

We vinden onze wiskundeleraar geen aangename vent.
We think our math teacher is not an agreeable guy.

Ik mag die man helemaal niet.
I don't like that guy at all.

Sarah houdt niet van mensen die aan tafel roken.
Sarah doesn't like people who smoke at the dinner table.

Jouw gezicht staat me niet aan.
I don't like your face (or better: I don't like you).

Ik kan die nieuwe vriend van Marion niet uitstaan.
I can't stand Marion's new boyfriend.

Onze hond heeft zo'n hekel aan de buurman.
Our dog really hates the neighbor.

Johanna haat haar stiefmoeder.
Johanna hates her stepmother.

In reference to things, we negate **vinden** + adjective, **houden van**, **bevallen**, and **aanstaan**. We also use **een hekel hebben aan** 'dislike' or **haten** 'hate.'

Ik vind het nieuwe huis van Nico en Liesbeth niet mooi.
I don't think Nico and Liesbeth's new house is beautiful.

Marja houdt niet van schoenen met hoge hakken.
Marja doesn't like shoes with high heels.

M'n nieuwe koffiezetapparaat bevalt me helemaal niet.
I don't like my new coffee maker at all.

Die bank is groot genoeg, maar de kleur staat me niet aan.
That sofa is big enough, but I don't like the color.

Ik heb zo'n hekel aan hiphopmuziek.
I can't stand hip hop music.

Ik haat de files op de A2.
I hate the traffic jams on the A2.

In reference to activities, we negate **graag** and **houden van**, and we use **een hekel hebben aan** and **haten** here as well. Or we say **het is niet zo mijn ding** 'it's not my thing.'

Ik luister niet graag naar jazz.
I don't like listening to jazz.

Joris houdt niet van koken.
Joris doesn't like to cook.

Karin heeft een vreselijke hekel aan strijken.
Karin hates ironing.

Ik haat het om naar de tandarts te moeten.
I hate having to go to the dentist.

Breien is niet zo mijn ding.
Knitting isn't really my thing.

The expression **gek/dol zijn op** can also be negated.

Ik eet wel kikkererwten, maar ik ben er niet gek op.
I do eat chickpeas, but I'm not crazy about them.

Erik is niet zo dol op strandwandelingen.
Eric isn't so crazy about walking on the beach.

17.4 Expressing preference and indifference

Preference

One way of expressing preference in Dutch is by using the adverb **graag** 'gladly, readily' and its comparative and superlative forms **liever** and **het liefst**.

Miranda drinkt graag koffie, maar ze drinkt liever thee.
Miranda likes to drink coffee, but she prefers tea.

Van alle soorten drop eet ik het liefst muntendrop.
Of all the different kinds of licorice, I like coin licorice best.

Ik wil wel naar de bioscoop, maar ik zou liever gaan dansen.
I'd like to go to the movies, but I'd rather go dancing.

Wat heb je liever bij de vis, wortelen of spinazie?
What would you prefer with your fish, carrots, or spinach?

These forms can also be used in negation:

Ik ga niet graag naar een museum en nog minder graag naar pretparken.
I don't like going to a museum and even less to amusement parks.

Ik houd niet van rode kool en ik eet het minst graag spruitjes.
I don't like red cabbage and I like sprouts the least.

To express preference with the verb **houden van** 'like, love,' we use **meer** 'more' and **meest** 'most.'

Jacob houdt van zwemmen, maar hij houdt meer van hardlopen.
Jacob likes to swim, but he likes running more.

Jasmine zegt dat ze het meest van wielrennen houdt.
Jasmine says she likes cycling best.

M'n favoriete groente? Nou, ik houd het meest van sperziebonen.
My favorite vegetable? Well, I like green beans most.

To express preference by comparison, we use expressions with **liever dan** 'more than,' **het liefst** 'most,' **niet zo . . . als** 'not as . . . as,' **net zo . . . als** 'just as . . . as.'

Karin gaat liever naar een theatervoorstelling dan naar een film.
Karin likes to go to a theater show more than to a movie.

Maar ze gaat het liefst naar popconcerten.
But she likes pop concerts the most.

Ik sport liever buiten dan in een studio.
I prefer to do sport outside rather than in a gym.

Ik hou niet zo veel van Haydn als van Mozart.
I don't like Haydn as much as Mozart.

Peter gaat net zo graag met de trein naar werk als met de auto.
Peter likes to go to work by train as much as by car.

Instead of **net zo graag**, we also use **net zo lief**.

Ik eet net zo lief een stukje vlees als een visje van de markt.
I like eating a piece of meat just as much as fish from the market.

Note that **net zo lief** can also be used in a rather ironic way, with a bit of sarcasm, in a manner that is not possible with **net zo graag**.

Je wilt kamperen? Dan ga ik net zo lief drie weken doorwerken.
You want to camp? Then I might as well continue to work for three weeks.

▶ For more information on comparison, see **3.2**.

There are a number of expressions with **voorkeur** 'preference' to indicate preference. A less common expression is with **voorliefde** 'predilection.'

Rode of witte wijn bij de vis? Hm, ik geef de voorkeur aan witte.
Red or white wine with the fish? Hm, I prefer white.

Die bank met die blauwe bekleding heeft mijn voorkeur.
That sofa with the blue cover has my preference.

Je wilt kamperen? Nou, ik vind dat een huisje aan zee de voorkeur verdient.
You want to camp? Well, I think a house at the sea deserves our preference.

Mijn voorkeur gaat uit naar een wandelvakantie in de bergen.
My preference would be a hiking vacation in the mountains.

Zij heeft een voorliefde voor oudere mannen.
She has a predilection for older men.

Mijn vader had een voorliefde voor Franse componisten.
My father had a predilection for French composers.

When someone is given preferential treatment, we use the word **voorkeursbehandeling**. In a less formal context, we use the word **voortrekken**.

Ze kreeg een voorkeursbehandeling omdat ze de dochter van de rector was.
She received preferential treatment because she was the daughter of the headmaster.

Mama trekt Joris altijd voor omdat hij de jongste is.
Mom always favors Joris because he is the youngest.

Indifference

To denote indifference, one can use many different expressions. Some neutral ones are:

Dat maakt mij niet(s) uit.
That doesn't make any difference to me.

Dat kan mij niet(s) schelen.
That makes no difference to me.

Dat is mij om het even.
That's all the same to me.

Others are rather rude or vulgar:

Dat is mij worst/Dat zal mij worst wezen.
I couldn't care less.

Dat interesseert me geen moer/bal/hol.
I don't give a damn.

Dat gaat me niet(s) aan.
That doesn't concern me.

If one wants to leave the decision to someone else, one can say:

Zoals je wilt/Doe maar wat je wilt/Doet u maar wat u het beste lijkt.
As you wish/Just do what you want/Please do what seems best to you.

Dat laat ik aan jou/u over/Ik laat het helemaal aan jou/u over.
I leave that (entirely) up to you.

Beslis jij maar.
You decide.

17.5 Asking for and voicing an opinion

To ask for someone's opinion (**mening**, **opinie**) about something, one can say in Dutch:

Wat vind je/vindt u van het nieuwe museum voor moderne kunst?
What do you think about the new museum for modern art?

Ik vind dat we groen voor de tegels moeten nemen. Wat denk jij?
I think we should take green for the tiles. What do you think?

Wat is uw mening over het probleem van jeugdcriminaliteit?
What is your opinion about the problem with youth crime?

We hebben een aantal mensen naar hun opinie over schaliegas gevraagd.
We have asked a number of people for their opinion about shale gas.

To express an opinion (Dutch **je mening uitdrukken**), one can say a number of things, using verbs like **vinden** 'find,' **denken** 'think,' **geloven** 'believe,' expressions with **mening** 'opinion' and **volgens** 'according to.'

Ik vind/denk dat het energieprobleem met windmolens alleen niet op te lossen is.
I think that the energy crisis cannot be solved with wind turbines alone.

Ik geloof dat de HAVO de beste vooropleiding voor jou is.
I believe HAVO is the best preparatory education for you.

Jasper is van mening dat we de jaarlijkse contributie moeten verhogen.
Jasper thinks we should raise the annual dues.

Naar mijn mening moet je een puppie heel goed trainen.
In my opinion, you really have to train a puppy well.

Volgens opiniepeilingen gaat de PvdA in deze verkiezingen fors winnen.
According to opinion polls, the PvdA will gain enormously in these elections.

Volgens mij gaat het regenen.
I think it's going to rain.

Change one's opinion

To change one's opinion (Dutch **van mening veranderen**) on something, one can say:

Ik ben van mening veranderd.
I've changed my opinion.

Na het politiek debat is Karel van gedachten veranderd.
After the political debate, Karel changed his mind.

Door de nieuwe bewijsmaterialen hebben we een heel andere kijk op de zaak.
Because of the new evidence, we have a completely different perspective on the case.

Ik was voor een verhoging van de maximumsnelheid, maar ik denk daar nu anders over.
I was for raising the speed limit, but I have changed my mind about that.

▶ See **3.7** for more on pronominal adverbs such as **daarover**.

When one doesn't want to change one's mind, one can use **van mening/gedachten veranderen** with the negation **niet**, or say:

Ik blijf erbij dat die bezuinigingsmaatregel ons niets zal opleveren.
I still think that that budget cut will not bring us anything.

We probeerden hem te overtuigen, maar hij bleef bij zijn mening.
We tried to convince him, but he stuck with his opinion.

Firm convictions

When one has firm convictions, they can be expressed with derivations of the verb **overtuigen**:

Zijn politieke overtuiging speelde geen rol in die beslissing.
His political convictions didn't matter in that decision.

Ze was ervan overtuigd dat ze haar biologische moeder zou vinden.
She was convinced that she would find her biological mother.

Uit overtuiging weigerde mijn broer in dienst te gaan.
From conviction, my brother refused to go into military service.

No opinion

When one has no or little opinion at all, one can say:

Daar heb ik geen mening over.
I have no opinion on that.

Sorry, geen mening.
Sorry, no opinion.

Daar kan ik niets over zeggen.
I can't say anything about that.

Geen idee.
No idea.

Different opinion

When people have different opinions, they say:

Jij en ik verschillen van mening over dit thema.
You and I have different opinions about this topic.

Ik wil graag een schutting, maar mijn buurman denkt daar heel anders over.
I would like a fence, but my neighbor has a different view on that.

Er bestond een ernstig meningsverschil dat uitgepraat moest worden.
There was a serious difference in opinion that needed to be discussed.

De meningen over het immigratiebeleid waren verdeeld.
People's opinions about immigration policies differed.

▶ For more on agreeing and disagreeing, see **17.7**.

Prejudice

When one is prejudiced, speakers of Dutch use forms of the word **vooroordeel** 'prejudice.'

Er bestaan veel onterechte vooroordelen over allochtonen.
There are many unjustified prejudices against foreigners.

Je moet nooit bevooroordeeld aan een onderzoek beginnen.
Don't be partial when you start a research project.

17.6 Expressing belief and disbelief

As explained in **17.1**, the verb **geloven** 'believe' and adjectives such as **geloofwaardig** 'believable' and **ongelofelijk** 'unbelievable' are used to assert or deny the truth of something, or to express disbelief at something very surprising.

Hij zegt dat hij de tango kan dansen, maar ik geloof er niks van.
He says he can dance tango, but I don't believe a word of it.

Hij kwam met een ongeloofwaardig excuus te laat naar het examen.
He arrived late to the exam with an implausible excuse.

Dat geloof je toch zelf niet!
You don't believe that yourself, do you?

Ongelofelijk/Niet te geloven!/Hoe is het mogelijk?
Unbelievable!/How is it possible?

A: Ik had een fantastische vakantie.
B: Dat geloof ik graag!
A: I had a fantastic break.
B: I'm sure you did!

To express one's belief in something or someone, we use the verb **geloven in/aan** 'believe in.'

Geloof jij in God?
Do you believe in God?

Wie gelooft er nou aan spoken?
Who believes in ghosts?

Mijn achtjarige neefje gelooft nog in Sinterklaas.
My eight-year-old nephew still believes in Santa Claus.

Karina gelooft in de werking van homeopathische medicijnen.
Karina believes in the effect of homeopathic medicine.

Note that **geloven in** is more common than **geloven aan**, even though there is only a slight difference in meaning.

► See also **4.7** for more information on verbs with prepositions.

17.7 Agreement and disagreement

Agreement

As in section **17.1** on asserting the truth, one can use the following expressions to say that one agrees with someone.

Dat is waar/Dat is zo/Dat klopt.
That's true/right/correct.

Je hebt gelijk/Daar heb je gelijk in.
You're right/You're right in that.

Or one can use an expression with **vinden** 'find' or **denken** 'think.' These sentences are negated with **niet**.

Dat vind/denk ik ook.
I agree/I think so too.

Dat vind/denk ik niet.
I don't think so.

Less similar to English are expressions with **het eens zijn met** 'agree with.' One can agree with a person or with a statement. These expressions are negated with **niet**.

Ik ben het (niet) met je eens.
I agree (don't agree) with you.

Ik ben het helemaal met Joost eens.
I totally agree with Joost.

Ik ben het ermee eens/er niet mee eens.
I agree (don't agree) with it.

Daar zijn wij het (niet) mee eens.
We agree (don't agree) with that.

A simple way to express agreement is with the preposition **voor** 'for,' often used with the verb **stemmen** 'vote.' To disagree, we use the preposition **tegen**.

Veel mensen zijn voor/tegen de invoering van de zogenaamde wietpas.
Many people are for/against the introduction of the so-called weed pass.

De gemeenteraad stemde voor/tegen het voorstel van de wethouder.
The City Council voted for/against the proposal of the alderman.

Ik ben ervoor/ertegen dat we het aanbod van Janssen & Co aannemen.
I am for/against accepting the offer from Janssen & Co.

Other verbs to express agreement are **overeenstemmen met** 'agree with' (from the verb **stemmen** 'to vote') and **akkoord gaan met** 'agree.' There are, however, subtle differences. Both of these are not used so much to agree with someone's opinion, but rather in the context of plans, intentions and actions. Corresponding nouns are **de overeenstemming** 'agreement' and **het akkoord** 'agreement.'

Iedereen stemde met het plan overeen om de contributie te verhogen.
Everybody agreed with the plan to raise the annual dues.

Het bestuur kon niet tot een overeenstemming komen.
The board couldn't reach an agreement.

Ik ga met jullie plan akkoord, op één voorwaarde.
I agree with your plan, on one condition.

Gaan jullie ermee akkoord dat we vandaag buiten trainen?
Are you okay with training outside today?

De strijdende partijen gooiden het op een akkoord.
The quarreling parties reached a compromise.

Another verb that can be used to express agreement is **toestemmen** 'agree, approve.'

We willen het clubhuis renoveren, maar jullie moeten er allemaal in toestemmen.
We want to renovate the clubhouse, but you all have to agree with it.

The expressions with **akkoord gaan**, **overeenstemmen**, and **toestemmen** are negated with **niet** or **geen**. Indefinite nouns are negated with **geen**.

Ik ga niet met jullie plan akkoord.
I don't agree with your plan.

Na drie uur vergaderen was er nog geen overeenstemming bereikt.
After a three-hour meeting, an agreement had not been reached.

Julia vond dat ze recht had op een extra vakantiedag, maar de baas stemde er niet in toe.
Julia thought she was entitled to an extra day of vacation, but her boss didn't agree.

▶ See also **17.5** for differences of opinion. For negation, see **1.7**, **3.4**, and **9.8**.

Concession

To express that an agreement has been reached through concession, we use expressions such as **het eens worden** 'come to an agreement,' **overeenkomen** 'agree,' **concessie doen** 'concede,' **toegeven** 'concede, admit.'

De handelspartners konden het over de prijs maar moeilijk eens worden.
The trading partners had a hard time reaching an agreement about the price.

Uiteindelijk moest de verkoper concessie doen.
In the end, the seller had to concede.

We zijn met elkaar overeengekomen dat we de contributie pas volgend jaar verhogen.
We have come to an agreement that we don't raise the dues until next year.

De kinderen zeurden om ijs, en uiteindelijk gaf de moeder toe.
The children whined for ice cream, and eventually the mother conceded.

Ze gaf toe dat ik gelijk had.
She admitted that I was right.

17.8 Guilt and responsibility

Guilt

To talk about guilt, speakers of Dutch use the words **de schuld** 'guilt' and the adjective **schuldig (aan)** 'guilty (of),' the negation of which is **onschuldig** 'innocent.' The noun of this adjective is **de onschuld** 'innocence.' Someone who is guilty is **de schuldige**. When one incriminates oneself, we use the expression **zich schuldig maken aan**. Examples:

Ik kreeg er de schuld van dat de tentstokken ontbraken.
I was blamed for the missing tent poles.

Het ongeluk was de schuld van de automobilist die geen voorrang verleende.
The driver who didn't yield was to blame for the accident.

De winkelier was zelf schuldig aan de brand in z'n winkel.
The shopkeeper himself was to blame for the fire.

Jaap heeft het niet gedaan; hem treft geen schuld.
Jaap didn't do it; he's not to blame.

Kijk maar niet zo schuldig, het kan wel weer gerepareerd worden.
Don't look so guilty, it can be fixed.

De misdadiger werd schuldig bevonden/verklaard.
The criminal was found guilty/convicted.

Je moet een dier niet slaan, het zijn maar onschuldige wezens.
You shouldn't hit an animal; they are only innocent beings.

Probeer je onschuld maar eens te bewijzen.
Try to prove your innocence.

De eigenaar van dit bedrijf heeft zich schuldig gemaakt aan fraude.
The owner of this company committed fraud.

Iemand heeft een ruit gebroken. Wie is de schuldige?
Someone broke a window. Who's the culprit?

Note that **de schuld** and **schuldig** can also mean 'debt' and 'being indebted to, owe.'

Joop heeft zich met gokken in de schulden gestoken/heeft met gokken schulden gemaakt.
Joop has made a lot of gambling debts.

Ik ben jou nog een tientje schuldig.
I still owe you ten euros.

To admit one's guilt, we use expressions such as **(schuld) bekennen** 'confess,' **een bekentenis afleggen** 'confess,' **toegeven** 'admit.'

De leerling bekende dat hij de portemonnee van een klasgenoot gestolen had.
The student confessed that he had stolen a classmate's wallet.

De verdachte heeft een volledige bekentenis afgelegd.
The suspect made a full confession.

Hij gaf toe dat hij de situatie verkeerd beoordeeld had.
He admitted that he misjudged the situation.

Responsibility

To talk about responsibility, we use words such as **de verantwoordelijkheid** or **de verantwoording** 'responsibility' and **verantwoordelijk** 'responsible, accountable' with the preposition **voor** 'for', derived from the verb **verantwoorden** 'justify, account for'. For (financial) liability, we use the word **de aansprakelijkheid** and the adjective **aansprakelijk**.

In haar werk is Linda verantwoordelijk voor de boekhouding.
In her job, Linda is responsible for the bookkeeping.

Ouders zijn verantwoordelijk voor hun kinderen.
Parents are responsible for their children.

Ik neem de verantwoordelijkheid voor het ongeluk op me.
I take responsibility for the accident.

Jij schuift de verantwoordelijkheid voor je eigen fouten altijd op een ander.
You always shove the responsibility for your own mistakes onto someone else.

Onderteken maar, op mijn verantwoording.
Just sign it, I'll take the responsibility.

De leerling moest zich wegens plagiaat verantwoorden.
The student stood accused of plagiarism.

De automobilist werd voor het ongeluk aansprakelijk gesteld.
The driver was held liable for the accident.

17.9 Remembering and forgetting

Remembering

The verb **herinneren** 'remind' and **zich herinneren** 'remember' are used in different ways to talk about things one recalls. The noun is **de herinnering** 'memory.' Our ability to remember things is **het geheugen** 'memory.'

Ik herinner me niet veel van mijn lagere schooltijd.
I don't remember much of my grade school years.

Herinner je je die keer dat we met de zeilboot omsloegen?
Do you remember that day we capsized with the sailboat?

Die foto herinnert me aan een vakantie in Engeland, jaren geleden.
That photo reminds me of a vacation in England, years ago.

Kun je me eraan herinneren dat ik morgen die afspraak heb?
Can you remind me that I have that appointment tomorrow?

Gisteren hebben Jannie en ik leuke herinneringen uit onze studietijd opgehaald.
Yesterday, Jannie and I dug up old memories of our college days.

Jeetje, weet jij dat nog? Wat heb jij dan een goed geheugen.
Geez, you remember that? You have a real good memory.

Dat uit de hand gelopen feest ligt mij nog vers in het geheugen.
That party that got out of hand is still fresh in my memory.

Note in the last example the verb **onthouden** 'remember, retain information.' This verb is used primarily for facts and concrete or important information.

Melk, boter, havermout, eieren en tomaten; kun je dat allemaal onthouden?
Milk, butter, oatmeal, eggs, and tomatoes; can you remember all that?

Help me onthouden dat ik de kat van de buren even eten moet geven.
Remind me to feed the neighbors' cat.

Remind

The expression **doen denken aan** 'make one think of' is used when something or someone reminds one of something or someone else.

Dit nummer doet me denken aan m'n eerste jaar aan de universiteit.
This song reminds me of my first year at the university.

Some idiomatic expressions for remembering something are **paraat hebben** 'have information at hand,' **te binnen schieten** 'come to mind,' **uit het hoofd kennen** 'know from memory.'

Hij had alle telefoonnummers van de afdeling paraat.
He had all phone numbers in the department at hand.

Hoe heet die plant nou? Wacht, het schiet me wel weer te binnen.
What's the name of that plant? Wait, it'll come back to me in a minute.

Maarten kent tientallen gedichten uit z'n hoofd.
Maarten has memorized dozens of poems.

Commemorate

In commemoration of people or things, we use the verb **gedenken** 'remember, commemorate' or **herdenken** 'commemorate, celebrate.'

We gedenken hen die in het afgelopen jaar gestorven zijn.
We remember those who passed away last year.

Op 4 mei herdenken de Nederlanders de slachtoffers van oorlogen.
On May 4, the Dutch remember war victims (May 4 is the Dutch Memorial Day).

Forget

The main verb for talking about forgetting is **vergeten** 'forget' with its derivative **vergeetachtig** 'forgetful.' Note that the present perfect of **vergeten** can be with **hebben** or **zijn**. With **hebben**, it means one has forgotten an object, with **zijn**, it means one has forgotten information.

Vergeet niet de deur af te sluiten als je weggaat.
Don't forget to lock the door when you leave.

Ik heb m'n leesbril vergeten.
I forgot my reading glasses.

Karina heeft een nieuwe vriend, maar ik ben z'n naam even vergeten.
Karina has a new boyfriend, but his name has slipped my mind.

Wat ben jij toch vergeetachtig de laatste tijd.
You are so forgetful these days.

Other expressions are **niet meer weten** 'not know anymore,' **ontgaan** 'escape, slip one's mind,' **ontschieten** 'slip one's memory,' and **verleren** 'forget, unlearn.'

Ik weet niet meer waar ik dit gekocht heb.
I don't remember where I bought this.

De grap van dat verhaal is mij ontgaan.
The joke in that story escaped me.

Zijn mobiele telefoonnummer is me ontschoten.
His mobile phone number has slipped my memory.

Fietsen verleer je nooit.
You never forget how to bike.

17.10 Talking about physical and mental well-being

See section **12.4** for inquiries about one's well-being in general. To ask about how someone is feeling, for example after an illness or surgery or something, we use the verb **voelen** 'feel,' which is a reflexive verb in this context.

Hoe voel je je?/Hoe voelt u zich?
How are you feeling?

▶ See also **6.5** for reflexive verbs.

When someone looks unwell or seems to have problems, people ask:

Wat is er?/Wat is er aan de hand?/Is er iets?
What's the matter?

Wat scheelt eraan?
What's wrong?

Wat mankeert je? (can come across as rather rude)
What's the matter with you?

Je ziet er moe/slecht uit. Is er iets?
You look tired/bad. Is something wrong?

Possible positive (or neutral) answers to these questions are:

Ik voel me uitstekend/prima/goed.
I feel great.

Er is niets aan de hand/Ik mankeer niets.
Nothing's the matter with me.

Ik voel me naar omstandigheden goed.
I feel good, considering the circumstances.

Possible negative answers would be:

Ik voel me niet zo goed/niet zo best/ellendig.
I don't feel well/I feel lousy.

Health

To ask specifically about one's health, one can say the following, using words such as **gezond** 'healthy' and **de gezondheid** 'health':

Hoe gaat het met je gezondheid?
How's your health?

Iedereen gezond en wel?
Everybody doing well?

Ben je weer helemaal gezond?
Are you all well again?

To talk about health in a general way, one can say:

Je ziet er goed/gezond uit.
You look good/healthy.

De baby blaakt van gezondheid.
The baby is very healthy.

Mijn opa was ver in de tachtig, maar hij was kerngezond.
My grandfather was in his late eighties, but he was fit as a fiddle.

Frisse zeelucht is goed voor je gezondheid.
Fresh sea air is good for your health.

Op je gezondheid!
To your health!

Lifestyle

There are numerous ways to talk about a healthy lifestyle, and these are just a few examples.

Wat doe jij om zo slank te blijven?
What do you do to stay so thin?

Ik doe regelmatig fitness/Ik sport drie keer per week/Ik ga 's morgens hardlopen.
I go to fitness regularly/I work out three times a week/I run in the mornings.

Als je veel beweging krijgt en gezond eet, blijf je fit.
If you get enough exercise and eat healthy, you stay fit.

Ik rook niet en ik drink met mate.
I don't smoke and I drink in moderation.

Weight

To discuss weight, we use words like **het gewicht** 'weight,' **aankomen** 'gain weight,' **afvallen** 'lose weight,' and **op dieet gaan** 'go on a diet.'

Mijn gewicht is de laatste jaren stabiel gebleven.
My weight hasn't changed in the last few years.

Ik ben met de kerstdagen twee kilo aangekomen.
I gained two kilos over the holidays.

Door een stevige griep was Harmen een paar pond afgevallen.
Because of a hefty flu, Harmen lost a few pounds.

Ga je nu alweer op dieet? Het maakt toch nooit wat uit?!
Are you going on a diet again? It never makes a difference, does it?!

Stress and relaxation

To talk about stress and relaxation, we use words such as **gestrest** (also **gestressed**) 'stressed,' **nerveus** 'nervous,' **gespannen** 'tense,' **overspannen** 'overworked,' **(zich) ontspannen/relaxen** 'relax,' **chillen** 'chill out,' **uitrusten** 'get rest,' and different forms of **slapen** 'sleep' such as **in slaap vallen/komen** 'go to sleep,' **uitslapen** 'sleep in,' **slapeloos** 'sleepless,' **slaperig** 'sleepy,' **de slaap** 'sleep.'

Doe niet zo gestrest, we komen heus wel op tijd.
Don't be so stressed, we will get there on time.

Je kon zien hoe nerveus de studenten voor het examen waren.
You could see how nervous the students were for the exam.

Wat ben jij gespannen de laatste tijd. Is er iets?
You're so tense these days. Is something wrong?

Leraren raken vaak overspannen.
Teachers often get overworked.

Ik ontspan me graag met een goed boek of een film.
I like to relax with a good book or a film.

Jij maakt een heel ontspannen indruk.
You seem to be really relaxed.

Rust maar eens goed uit, dat heb je wel verdiend.
Get some rest; you have deserved it.

Slaap je wel genoeg/Krijg je wel genoeg slaap?
Do you sleep enough/Do you get enough sleep?

Na een lange film val ik niet makkelijk in slaap/kom ik niet makkelijk in slaap.
After a long film, I have a hard time falling asleep.

Ik slaap op zaterdag uit.
I sleep in on Saturdays.

Toen Kees in Afghanistan was, had Lydia veel slapeloze nachten.
When Kees was in Afghanistan, Lydia had many sleepless nights.

Een bijwerking van dit medicijn is dat je er slaperig van wordt.
A side effect of this medication is drowsiness.

► See also **6.5** for reflexive verbs.

Note also the verb **inslapen** 'go to sleep' which is primarily used in the context of dying and euthanasia. Do not confuse it with English 'sleep in' which is **uitslapen** in Dutch.

De patiënt is vredig ingeslapen.
The patient died peacefully.

We hebben onze hond moeten laten inslapen.
We had to put our dog to sleep.

Habits, addiction

To talk about habits and addictions, we use words such as **de gewoonte** 'habit,' **de verslaving** 'addiction,' **verslaafd (raken) aan** 'get addicted to.'

Nagelbijten is een slechte gewoonte.
Nail-biting is a bad habit.

Drugsverslaving is in toenemende mate een probleem.
Drug addiction is an increasing problem.

Sommige mensen raken verslaafd aan pijnstillers.
Some people get addicted to painkillers.

Illness, disease

To talk about illness and disease in general, we use words such as **ziek** 'sick, ill,' **de ziekte** 'illness, disease,' **lijden aan** 'suffer from,' **genezen** 'heal,' and **beter worden** 'get better.' A get well wish is expressed with **Beterschap!**

We hebben geen wiskunde, want meneer Blankers is ziek.
We have no math, because Mr. Blankers is ill.

De griep was vroeger een gevaarlijke ziekte.
The flu used to be a dangerous disease.

Op deze school is veel ziekteverzuim.
There is a lot of absence through illness at this school.

Een collega van mij lijdt al twee jaar aan kanker.
A colleague of mine has been suffering from cancer for two years now.

De schaafwond op Piet z'n knie is al helemaal genezen.
The scratch on Piet's knee has healed completely.

Ik hoop dat je gauw weer beter wordt.
I hope you get better soon.

Beterschap!/Ik wens u van harte beterschap/Ik wens je/u een spoedig herstel.
Get well!/I hope you get well soon/I wish you a speedy recovery.

When one attracts a disease, the Dutch use the word **oplopen** 'attract,' when one passes it on or when the disease is contagious, they say **aansteken** 'infect' or **besmettelijk** 'contagious,' and for preventing the disease, the word is **voorkomen** (with the emphasis on **-komen**).

Johan heeft in Afrika malaria opgelopen.
Johan attracted malaria in Africa.

Bah, Katja heeft me met haar verkoudheid aangestoken.
Bah, Katja gave me her cold.

Dit virus is heel besmettelijk.
This virus is very contagious.

Wat doe jij om ziekte te voorkomen?
What do you do to prevent illness?

Voorkomen is beter dan genezen.
Prevention is better than a cure.

Cold and flu

Consult a dictionary for different types of diseases. For common diseases such as a cold, we use the words **verkouden zijn** and **de verkoudheid**, and for the flu, we use the word **de griep**. The words for nausea are **misselijk zijn** 'be nauseated' and **overgeven** 'throw up,' and dizziness is **duizeligheid** with the adjective **duizelig**. When one has a temperature, we use the word **de koorts** 'fever,' and when one feels cold (or hot), we say **het koud (warm) hebben**.

Ben je nu al weer verkouden?
Do you have a cold again?

Ach, wat is nou een verkoudheid. Gaat zo weer over.
Ah, what is a little cold. It'll be over soon.

Veel mensen halen tegenwoordig een griepprik.
Many people these days get a flu shot.

Toen het kind uit de achtbaan kwam, was het misselijk en moest overgeven.
When the child came out of the roller coaster, he was nauseated and threw up.

Als Peter in een afgrond kijkt, wordt hij duizelig.
When Peter looks into an abyss, he gets dizzy.

Chris kwam ziek naar huis maar hij had geen koorts.
Chris came home ill but he didn't have a fever.

Ik ga een trui aantrekken, ik heb het zo koud.
I'm going to put on a sweater. I'm so cold.

Pain

To talk about pain in general, we use words such as **de pijn** 'pain,' **pijn hebben (in)** 'have pain (in),' nouns that can form a compound noun with **pijn** such as **rugpijn** 'backache,' **hoofdpijn** 'headache,' **pijn lijden** 'suffer pain,' **pijn doen** 'hurt' **zeer (doen)** 'hurt' and **last hebben van** 'be bothered by.'

Ik heb pijn in m'n buik.
My stomach hurts.

Joop heeft vaak last van hoofdpijn.
Joop often suffers from headaches.

Au! Mijn knie doet ineens pijn.
Ouch! My knee suddenly hurts.

Waar doet het pijn?
Where does it hurt?

De patiënt heeft niet veel pijn geleden.
The patient didn't suffer much pain.

Mama, mijn vinger doet zeer.
Mom, my finger hurts.

Ik heb al een paar dagen last van m'n rug.
My back has been bothering me for a few days.

Death

To talk about death and dying, we use the words **de dood** 'death,' **dood zijn** 'be dead,' **doodgaan** 'die,' **sterven** 'to die,' **overlijden** 'to die,' **omkomen** 'die,' **om het leven komen** 'die,' **verongelukken** 'die in an accident.'

De dood is een belangrijk thema in de literatuur.
Death is an important topic in literature.

"Oma is dood." Zo begint een bekend kinderboek van Guus Kuijer.
"Grandma is dead." Thus begins a famous children's book by Guus Kuijer.

Onze poes is vorige week doodgegaan.
Our cat died last week.

Goethe stierf in 1832.
Goethe died in 1832.

De patiënt is gisteravond overleden.
The patient died yesterday evening.

De fietser is door een ongeluk omgekomen.
The cyclist died in an accident.

Care, treatment, insurance

To talk about doctors, treatment and insurance, we use vocabulary such as **de arts** 'physician' with the verb **raadplegen** 'consult,' **de huisarts** general practitioner, **het spreekuur** 'office hours,' **de specialist** 'specialist,' **verwijzen** 'refer' and **het verwijsbriefje** 'referral,' **de dokter** 'doctor,' **de (poli)kliniek** 'clinic,' **EHBO (Eerste Hulp bij Ongeluk)** 'ER,' **het ziekenhuis** 'hospital,' **de behandeling** 'treatment,' **behandelen** 'treat,' **de kuur** 'cure, treatment,' **de ziekte(kosten)verzekering** 'health insurance.'

Het lijkt me verstandig in dit geval een arts te raadplegen.
I think it is best to consult a doctor in this case.

Onze huisarts heeft op woensdag geen spreekuur.
Our family physician doesn't have surgery hours on Wednesdays.

De dokter verwees me naar een specialist.
The doctor referred me to a specialist.

Ik geef u een verwijsbriefje mee.
I'll give you a referral.

In deze polikliniek doen ze veel ambulante operaties.
In this outpatient's center, they do a lot of same-day surgeries.

Karin heeft een week in het ziekenhuis gelegen.
Karin spent a week in the hospital.

Linda geeft de voorkeur aan een homeopathische behandeling.
Linda prefers a homeopathic treatment.

Hier worden alleen psychiatrische patiënten behandeld.
They only treat psychiatric patients here.

U moet deze kuur helemaal afmaken.
You have to finish this entire treatment.

Harry besloot met een ontwenningskuur te beginnen.
Harry decided to go into detox.

De premie van mijn ziektekostenverzekering is gestegen.
My health insurance premium has gone up.

Medicine

To talk about prescribing and taking medicine, we use words such as **het medicijn** 'medicine,' **het geneesmiddel** 'medicine, remedy,' **de pil** 'pill,' **de tablet** 'pill,' **pillen slikken** 'take pills,' **een medicijn innemen** 'take a medication,' **een medicijn voorschrijven** 'prescribe a medication,' **de bijsluiter** 'instructions for use,' **de bijwerking** 'side effect,' **het recept** 'prescription,' **de apotheek** 'pharmacy.'

In veel derde wereldlanden is groot gebrek aan medicijnen.
Many third world countries suffer great lack of medications.

Deze arts werkt met homeopathische geneesmiddelen.
This doctor works with homeopathic medicine.

Dit medicijn is verkrijgbaar in pillen van 50 of van 100 mg.
This medication is available in 50 or 100mg pills.

Johan neemt zijn medicijnen 's avonds in.
Johan takes his medications in the evening.

Onze huisarts schrijft heel weinig antibiotica voor.
Our family doctor prescribes very few antibiotics.

Lees voordat u dit medicijn inneemt eerst de bijsluiter.
Before you take this medication, read the instructions for use.

Heeft dit medicijn vervelende bijwerkingen?
Does this medication have unpleasant side effects?

Ik kan u een recept voor een pijnstiller geven.
I can give you a prescription for a painkiller.

U kunt het medicijn na 3 uur bij de apotheek ophalen.
You can pick up the medication at the pharmacy after 3 o'clock.

18

Expressing emotions

The word for emotion is **de emotie**, or also **het gevoelen** 'feeling' (used mostly in the plural).

Hij kon zijn emoties niet in bedwang houden.
He couldn't keep his emotions in check.

Wat voor gevoelens roept die film bij jou op?
What sort of feelings does that film trigger with you?

To talk about someone's mood in general, we use the words **de stemming** 'mood, atmosphere' and **het humeur** 'mood' with its corresponding adjective **humeurig** 'moody.' A colloquial word for mood is **de bui** 'mood, fit.'

Ik ben vandaag in een opperbeste stemming.
I'm in a jolly good mood today.

Als hij in een slecht humeur is, kun je hem maar beter met rust laten.
If he's in a bad mood, it's better to leave him alone.

Karel heeft een ochtendhumeur.
Karel is moody in the morning.

Niks ergers dan drie uur in de auto met humeurige kinderen.
Nothing worse than three hours in the car with moody kids.

Wat heb jij een pestbui zeg!
Geez, you're in a rotten mood!

18.1 Wishes, hopes, and disappointment

Wishes

The most commonly used verbs to express wishes are **wensen** 'wish' and **willen** 'want.' The verb **wensen** is used to express a wish for oneself or for someone else, in which case we also use the verb **toewensen**. The corresponding noun is **de wens** 'wish.'

Die meneer wenst een eenpersoonskamer met uitzicht op zee.
That gentleman would like a single room with an ocean view.

Wenst u gebruik te maken van draadloos internet?
Would you like to use the wireless internet?

Ik wens u een prettig verblijf in ons hotel.
I wish you a pleasant stay in our hotel.

Fijne vakantie toegewenst.
Have a great vacation.

We wensen u een prettige jaarwisseling en een gelukkig nieuwjaar.
We wish you a pleasant New Year's Eve and a happy New Year.

Heb je nog speciale wensen voor het etentje op je verjaardag?
Do you have any special requests for your birthday dinner?

Als er een ster valt mag je een wens doen.
When a star falls, you may make a wish.

Much more common, however, are the various forms of the verb **willen** 'want,' modified with particles such as **graag** and **wel (eens)**, and used in the subjunctive **wou** or with the helping verb **zou**.

Ik wil een nieuwe fiets voor m'n verjaardag.
I want a new bike for my birthday.

We willen graag bestellen, kan dat?
We'd like to order. Is that possible?

Ik wou graag een bos wortelen (alstublieft).
I'd like a bunch of carrots (please).

Als je toch thee zet, wil ik wel een kopje.
If you're making tea anyway, I'd like a cup.

Ik wil wel eens wat anders dan de traditionele kalkoen met kerst.
I'd like something different for a change than the traditional turkey for Christmas.

Ik zou graag willen dat jullie dit keer de kaartjes voor de veerboot betalen.
I would like you to pay for the tickets for the ferry this time.

Ik wou dat het niet zo koud was.
I wish it weren't so cold.

When shopping or placing any kind of order, other forms are possible as well.

Mag ik een kilo bananen?
May I have a kilo of bananas?

Een gesneden bruin en 12 kadetjes, alstublieft.
A loaf of brown bread, sliced, and 12 rolls, please.

Een pilsje, graag.
A beer, please.

A less common verb to express a wish is **verlangen** 'long for, demand, desire,' often used with the preposition **naar**. A more colloquial form of this is **snakken naar** 'crave, die for.'

De glazenwasser verlangde z'n geld en ging er zonder groet vandoor.
The window-cleaner asked for his money and left without saying goodbye.

Dat kun je niet van hem verlangen.
You can't ask that of him.

De kinderen verlangen naar de zomervakantie.
The children are longing for the summer break.

Ik snak naar een kop koffie.
I'm dying for a cup of coffee.

Wishful thinking can also be expressed by simply using the simple past or past perfect tense in reverse order of subject and verb, modified with particles such as **maar**, **nou** and **toch**.

Was ik maar niet zo slecht in wiskunde.
If only I were not so bad at math.

Had ik maar een snellere computer.
If only I had a faster computer.

Kwam hij nou maar.
I wish he'd show up.

Was ik toch maar thuisgebleven.
If only I'd stayed home.

Had ik die nieuwe auto toch maar niet gekocht.
If only I hadn't bought that new car.

▶ See **3.9** for more on particles and Chapter **7** for verb tenses.

Hopes

The most commonly used verb to express hope is **hopen** 'hope.' When used with the preposition **op**, it is followed by a noun. Otherwise, it is used with a subordinated sentence with **dat** 'that.' The corresponding noun is **de hoop**, and the adverb is **hopelijk** 'hopefully.'

We hopen op iets beter weer.
We're hoping for somewhat better weather.

Laten we hopen dat de koersen weer stijgen.
Let's hope the rates will go up again.

Ik hoop dat je gauw beter wordt.
I hope you get better soon.

Hopelijk drijft het onweer over.
Hopefully, the storm will pass us by.

Disappointment

When hopes and wishes don't come true, and one is disappointed, we use the words **teleurstellen** 'disappoint,' **teleurgesteld** 'disappointed,' and **de teleurstelling** 'disappointment.'

Het uitzicht vanaf de top van die berg zal u niet teleurstellen.
You won't be disappointed by the view from the top of that mountain.

Hanna was vreselijk teleurgesteld toen ze niet door de voorronde kwam.
Hanna was terribly disappointed when she didn't make it through the first round.

Ze kon haar teleurstelling niet bedwingen.
She could not control her disappointment.

When something is disappointing or not as expected, we also use the verb **tegenvallen** 'disappoint.' The opposite of **tegenvallen** is **meevallen**.

Ik had online een jurk besteld, maar de kleur viel een beetje tegen.
I ordered a dress online, but the color was not quite as expected.

Johan dacht dat hij zijn pols gebroken had, maar het viel gelukkig mee.
Johan thought he had broken his wrist, but it wasn't as bad as he expected.

18.2 Expectation and anticipation

To express expectation, we use the verb **verwachten** 'expect' and its corresponding noun **de verwachting** 'expectation.'

Minnie verwacht/is in verwachting van een tweeling.
Minnie's expecting twins.

Ik verwacht om elf uur thuis te zijn.
I expect to be at home at eleven.

Dat had ik niet van hem verwacht.
I didn't expect that of him.

Wat verwacht jij van de toekomst?
What do you expect of the future?

Kijk even naar de weersverwachting voor morgen.
Look at the weather forecast for tomorrow.

We also use the verb **uitkijken** (or **uitzien**) **naar** to express joyful anticipation.

We kijken uit naar de zomervakantie.
We look forward to the summer vacation.

Similarly, the reflexive verb **zich verheugen op** 'look forward to' is used to express joyful anticipation.

Ik verheug me op de reis naar Rome.
I'm looking forward to the trip to Rome.

We verheugen ons op jullie komst.
We are looking forward to your visit.

Fearful anticipation, on the other hand, is expressed with the verb **opzien tegen** 'not look forward to, dread.'

Ik zie tegen het examen op.
I'm dreading the exam.

De kinderen zien er tegenop, naar de tandarts te moeten.
The children dread having to go to the dentist.

If anticipation is almost certainty, we use the expression **ervan uitgaan** 'assume.'

Mag ik ervan uitgaan dat jullie blijven eten?
May I assume that you'll stay for dinner?

Ik ga ervan uit dat ik dit jaar een salarisverhoging krijg.
I assume I'll get a pay raise this year.

18.3 Fear, anxiety, and tension

Fear

Fear is expressed first and foremost with the word **bang** 'afraid.' Most of the time, it is used with the preposition **voor**, but **van** is also accepted, although it is seen as more colloquial.

Ben jij bang voor spinnen?
Are you afraid of spiders?

Onze Kees is zo bang van grote honden!
Our Kees is so afraid of big dogs!

Je moet wel doodsbang zijn geweest alleen in dat enge huis.
You must have been terrified alone in that creepy house.

Ik ben bang dat we niet op tijd gaan komen.
I'm afraid we're not going to be on time.

A noun for fear is **de angst**, with the corresponding adjective **angstig** 'afraid.'

Uit angst voor de blaffende hond durfde het kind niet naar binnen.
For fear of the barking dog, the child didn't want to come in.

De moeder zat in angst over het vermiste kind.
The mother was anxious about the missing child.

Wat kijk jij angstig; ben je soms bang voor kwallen?
You look scared; do you happen to be afraid of jellyfish?

Shock

Anxiety from shock, fright, or sudden alarm is expressed with the verb **schrikken** 'be startled.' It can be reflexive and non-reflexive. The corresponding noun is **de schrik** 'scare, fright.' Corresponding adjectives are **schrikaanjagend**, **schrikbarend** 'frightening, dreadful.'

Het kind schrok toen de ballon kapotknalde.
The child was scared when the balloon burst.

We schrokken ons rot toen de boot ineens begon te slingeren.
We were scared to death when the boat began swerving all of a sudden.

We zijn met de schrik vrijgekomen.
We got off with a fright (or: We had a narrow escape).

Hè, je laat me schrikken.
Hey, you scared me.

Het aantal werklozen in deze stad is schrikbarend.
The number of unemployed in this city is astounding.

Nervousness

To express nervousness, we use the adjective **zenuwachtig**, which stems from the noun **de zenuw** 'nerve.' Another word is **nerveus** 'nervous.'

Voordat de jongen het toneel op moest, was hij vreselijk zenuwachtig/nerveus.
Before the boy had to go on stage, he was terribly nervous.

De moeder van het vermiste kind was op van de zenuwen.
The mother of the missing child was scared out of her mind.

Die blaffende hond van de buurman werkt op m'n zenuwen.
My neighbor's barking dog gets on my nerves.

A similar kind of tension is expressed with the word **gespannen** 'nervous, tense' from the noun **de spanning** 'tension.'

Je ziet er gespannen uit. Probeer aan iets anders te denken.
You look tense. Try to think of something else.

De sfeer in het klaslokaal was gespannen.
The atmosphere in the classroom was tense.

Je kon de spanning tussen hen beiden snijden met een mes.
The tension between the two of them could be cut with a knife.

The opposite of **gespannen** is **ontspannen**. Note that the verb **zich ontspannen** is reflexive.

Ik kom altijd helemaal ontspannen van mijn koorrepetitie vandaan.
I always come back from my choir rehearsal totally relaxed.

Wat doe jij graag om je te ontspannen?
What do you like to do to relax?

When someone is completely stressed or burnt out, we use the word **overspannen**.

Toen Joost overspannen raakte, kwam hij in de ziektewet terecht.
When Joost was overworked, he went on sick leave.

18.4 Happiness, sadness, and worry

Happiness

The main word for happiness is **het geluk** 'luck, felicity, bliss' with its corresponding adjective **gelukkig** 'happy, fortunate.'

De bruid en bruidegom straalden van geluk.
The bride and groom radiated with joy.

Kees en Minnie zijn al tien jaar gelukkig getrouwd.
Kees and Minnie have been happily married for ten years.

Ben je wel gelukkig in je nieuwe huis?
Are you really happy in your new house?

Wat een geluk dat ik m'n sleutels terugvond in de sneeuw.
I was so lucky to find my keys in the snow.

We hebben geluk gehad.
We were lucky.

Gelukkig Nieuwjaar!
Happy New Year!

The most commonly used word to express happiness is **blij** 'happy, glad.' It is used with the preposition **met** 'with' or with a subordinated sentence with **dat**. Corresponding nouns are **de blijdschap** and **de blijheid** 'happiness.'

Karin is erg blij met haar nieuwe huis.
Karin is very happy with her new house.

Ik ben dolblij met m'n nieuwe baan.
I'm overjoyed with my new job.

We zijn blij dat de feestdagen weer achter de rug zijn.
We're glad the holidays are behind us.

De moeder huilde van blijdschap toen ze haar kind weer zag.
The mother cried with joy when she saw her child again.

Met grote blijdschap geven we u kennis van de geboorte van onze zoon (very formal).
It is with great joy that we announce the birth of our son.

Van blijheid schreeuwde hij het uit.
He screamed with joy.

More formal are words such as **de vreugde** 'happiness' and **verheugd** 'delighted, pleased.'

Tot onze grote vreugde konden we een week eerder in ons nieuwe huis (rather formal).
To our great satisfaction, we could move into our new house a week early.

We zijn zeer verheugd over het resultaat van de onderhandelingen (formal).
We are very pleased with the result of the negotiations.

The word **vrolijk** 'merry, cheerful, gay' is used more for a mood, an atmosphere, or a character trait. The corresponding verb is **opvrolijken** 'cheer up.'

Jeroen is een vrolijk en intelligent kind.
Jeroen is a cheerful, intelligent child.

Er kwamen vrolijke geluiden van het terras.
Cheerful sounds came from the patio.

Ze hadden de zaal met bloemen en slingers opgevrolijkt.
They had made the hall more cheerful with flowers and garlands.

When someone is overjoyed, we use the expressions **opgetogen** 'elated' or **door het dolle heen** 'ecstatic.'

> **De winnaars van de wedstrijd kwamen opgetogen van het veld.**
> The winners of the match were overjoyed when they left the field.

> **De fans van het winnende team waren door het dolle heen.**
> The fans of the winning team were ecstatic.

Lastly, when people express happiness or joy in laughter, we use the verb **lachen** 'laugh' and **glimlachen** 'smile' with its corresponding noun **de glimlach** 'smile.'

> **We hebben gisteren zo gelachen op het feest van Johan.**
> We laughed a lot at Johan's party yesterday.

> **Lach even naar de camera.**
> Smile for the camera.

> **Robert trok zijn gezicht in een brede glimlach.**
> Robert pulled a broad smile.

Sadness

To talk about sadness, we use the word **het verdriet** 'sadness' with its corresponding adjective **verdrietig** 'sad.' The word for 'to cry' is **huilen**.

> **Het kind huilde van verdriet om haar dode poes.**
> The child cried with grief over her dead cat.

> **Er kwamen allemaal verdrietige berichten van het front.**
> Lots of sad messages came from the front.

> **Die jongen doet zijn moeder veel verdriet met zijn eeuwige spijbelen.**
> That boy causes his mother a lot of trouble playing hooky all the time.

There are many other words that express sadness. Less common than **verdriet** and **verdrietig** are **droefheid** 'sorrow,' **droevig** 'sad' and **bedroefd** 'sad,' **treuren** 'lament,' **treurnis** 'sadness' and **treurig** 'sad,' **verslagenheid** 'defeat' and **verslagen** 'defeated,' **triestheid** 'gloom' and **triest** 'somber.'

> **Er was grote droefheid/treurnis na het overlijden van Nelson Mandela.**
> There was great sorrow after Nelson Mandela's death.

> **De situatie in het rampgebied is bedroefd.**
> The situation in the disaster area is distressing.

> **Het toneelstuk had een treurig/triest/droevig einde.**
> The play ended sadly.

> **Treur niet om die verloren tol, we kopen weer een nieuwe.**
> Don't be sad about the lost top. We'll buy another one.

> **Met verslagenheid/Verslagen keken de bewoners naar de ravage na de storm.**
> Utterly dismayed, the inhabitants looked at the damage after the storm.

Note that **triest**, **treurig**, and **bedroefd** are also used to talk about the dismal state of something, and this can sometimes come across as irony or sarcasm.

> **Het is treurig/droevig wat een rotzooi jij van je kamer maakt.**
> It's sad to see the mess you have turned your room into.

When one is terribly upset about something, we use the words **overstuur** 'upset,' **ondersteboven** 'upset,' and **ontdaan** 'upset, disconcerted.'

> **Anne was helemaal overstuur/ondersteboven/ontdaan toen haar baas haar ontsloeg.**
> Anne was really upset when her boss fired her.

Mourning

Mourning is expressed with the words **rouwen/in de rouw zijn** 'grieve, mourn.' The corresponding adjective, **rouwig** 'sad, sorry,' is used mostly to actually say that one is not sorry.

> **Het land rouwt om de dood van hun leider.**
> The country is grieving the death of their leader.
>
> **Er was vandaag een rouwkaart in de post.**
> There was a funeral card in the mail today.
>
> **Ik ben er niet rouwig om.**
> I'm not sorry for it/I couldn't care less about it.

Missing someone/something

Sadness because one is missing something or someone is expressed with the words **missen** 'miss,' **het gemis** 'lack,' **het heimwee** 'homesickness.'

> **Toen ik in het buitenland studeerde, miste ik mijn familie.**
> When I studied abroad, I missed my family.
>
> **Dat ik hier geen oven heb, is een groot gemis.**
> It is very inconvenient not having an oven here.
>
> **Na drie dagen vakantie hadden de kinderen al heimwee.**
> After three days of vacation, the children were already homesick.

Depression

When someone is generally depressed or sad, we use the words **de depressie** or **de neerslachtigheid** 'depression.' Corresponding adjectives are **depressief** 'depressive,' **gedeprimeerd** 'depressed,' **deprimerend** 'depressing,' **neerslachtig** 'depressed.'

> **Depressie in tieners komt steeds vaker voor.**
> Depression in teenagers is becoming more and more common.
>
> **Karel was de hele dag in een neerslachtige bui.**
> Karel was feeling depressed all day.
>
> **Ik word helemaal depressief van dit druilerige weer.**
> I get all depressed from this rainy weather.

Suffering

The verb for 'to suffer' is **lijden**. It is used with the preposition **aan** or **onder**. The preposition **aan** is used for diseases, while **onder** is more for moods, circumstances or situations.

> **Veel mensen in dit land lijden aan aids.**
> Many people in this country suffer from AIDS.
>
> **Joost lijdt onder zijn depressies.**
> Joost suffers from depression.

Worry

To express worry, we use the expressions **zich zorgen maken over** or **bezorgd zijn om/over** 'worry about.' Another expression is **in de zorgen zitten** 'be worried.' A more colloquial expression is **zich druk maken** 'make a fuss' or **drukte maken** 'make a fuss.' And lastly, we also use the word **ongerust** 'worried.'

> **Henk maakt zich zorgen over zijn zieke moeder.**
> Henk worries about his sick mother.

Maak je geen zorgen, het komt echt wel goed.
Don't worry. It will be alright.

Het ministerie is bezorgd over de toenemende werkeloosheid.
The State Department is worried about the increase in unemployment.

We hebben in de zorgen gezeten om jou, waar was je?
We've been worried about you. Where were you?

Maak je toch niet zo druk om een paar euro.
Don't make such a fuss about a few euros.

Wat maak je een drukte. Er komen toch maar vier gasten?
You're making such a fuss. Aren't there only four guests coming?

Nick is nog steeds niet thuis. Ik word nu langzaam ongerust.
Nick isn't home yet. I'm beginning to get worried now.

18.5 Satisfaction and dissatisfaction

The most important word to use to express one's satisfaction is **tevreden** 'satisfied, pleased.' The corresponding noun is **de tevredenheid** 'satisfaction.' The negation is **ontevreden(heid)**.

Ik ben heel tevreden met m'n nieuwe racefiets, hij rijdt fantastisch.
I'm very pleased with my new road bike. It's a fantastic ride.

De tevredenheid van onze klanten gaat boven alles.
Customer satisfaction is our priority.

Wat kijk je nou ontevreden! Is het weer niet goed genoeg?
You look so displeased! Isn't it good enough again?

Another word for satisfaction is **het genoegen**. The negation is **het ongenoegen**.

Is de kamer naar genoegen?
Is the room to your satisfaction?

Het doet me genoegen dat het zo goed met je gaat.
I'm pleased you are doing so well.

Daar neem ik geen genoegen mee.
I will not put up with that.

Ik gooi met genoegen die ouwe spullen van je op het grofvuil.
I'd be delighted to throw all that old stuff of yours in the garbage.

De toeschouwers stampten op de vloer om hun ongenoegen te tonen.
The audience stamped their feet on the floor to show their discontent.

Another, less commonly used word is **de voldoening** 'pleasure, satisfaction.' The corresponding adjective is **voldaan**. The verb is **voldoen (aan)** 'satisfy.'

Ik kijk met veel voldoening op m'n carrière terug (rather formal).
I look back on my career with much satisfaction.

Het schept voldoening als je iemand kan helpen.
It is a pleasure to help someone.

Moe maar voldaan gingen we in onze slaapzakken liggen.
Tired but satisfied, we got into our sleeping bags.

Deze nieuwe stofzuiger voldoet niet aan de verwachtingen.
This new vacuum cleaner does not meet the expectations.

When one is satisfied at the dinner table, one can use the word **verzadigd** 'satisfied' or simply say that one has had enough.

Geen tweede bord voor mij, ik ben verzadigd/ik heb genoeg gehad.
No seconds for me. I am satisfied/I have had enough to eat.

18.6 Surprise, wonder, and curiosity

Surprise

To express surprise, we use the word **de verrassing** 'surprise' and the corresponding verb **verrassen** 'surprise.' The adjective is **verrast** 'surprised.'

Ik heb een verrassing voor je.
I have a surprise for you.

Zullen we moeder met een bos bloemen verrassen?
Shall we surprise mom with a bunch of flowers?

Marieke keek heel verrast toen Jaap haar een klein zwart doosje voorhield.
Marieke looked very surprised when Jaap showed her a small black box.

Astonishment

To express that one is surprised or astonished about something, we use the verb **verbazen** 'astonish,' the noun **de verbazing** 'astonishment' and the adjective **verbaasd** 'astonished.'

We waren heel verbaasd toen Mick met een voldoende voor wiskunde naar huis kwam.
We were really surprised when Mick came home with a passing grade for math.

Hun monden vielen open van verbazing toen er een paard het toneel op kwam.
They were flabbergasted when a horse entered the stage.

Ik ben in één keer voor m'n rijbewijs geslaagd. Verbaast je dat?
I passed my driver's exam in one try. Does that surprise you?

Other, less commonly used words expressing astonishment are **verwonderen** 'astonish' and **verwonderd** 'staggered, amazed,' **verbijsteren** 'astonish, alarm,' **verbijsterd** 'flabbergasted,' **sprakeloos** 'speechless,' and **verstomd** 'speechless.' A colloquial expression is **paf staan** 'be flabbergasted.'

Het zou me niets verwonderen als Anke dit jaar niet meer meeging op vakantie.
I would not be surprised if Anke didn't go with us on vacation this year.

Voorbijgangers stonden verbijsterd bij het huis dat in vlammen opging.
Passersby stood aghast at the house that went up in flames.

Ik was sprakeloos toen Hans zei dat hij ontslag zou nemen.
I was speechless when Hans said that he'd quit his job.

Karin kon niet geloven dat ze geslaagd was. Ze stond er verstomd van.
Karin couldn't believe she had passed. It took her breath away.

Het volkorenbrood is nu al uitverkocht? Nou, ik sta paf.
The wholegrain bread is already sold out? Well, beats me.

Bewilderment

Shock and dismay can be expressed with words such as **geschokt** 'shocked,' **onthutst** 'dismayed,' and **ontsteld** 'bewildered.'

De buurt was geschokt over de ontvoering van het kind.
The neighborhood was shocked at the kidnapping of the child.

De schoonmaakster keek onthutst/ontsteld naar de gebroken vaas op de grond.
The cleaner was upset by the broken vase on the floor.

When one can hardly believe something, we use different expressions with **geloven** 'believe.' A corresponding adjective is **ongelofelijk** 'unbelievable.'

Je gelooft niet wie ik vandaag in de stad tegenkwam.
You won't believe whom I ran into in town today.

4 euro voor een pond tomaten? Niet te geloven!
4 euros for a pound of tomatoes? Unbelievable!

Ongelofelijk, wat is Joris snel gegroeid.
Unbelievable, how much Joris has grown.

When something unexpected happens, we use words such as **onverwacht** 'unexpected' and expressions with **rekenen op** or **voorzien/voorspellen** 'count on, expect, foresee.'

Marianne kwam onverwacht met een appeltaart aanzetten.
Marianne unexpectedly showed up with an apple pie.

We hadden er niet op gerekend dat de zaak verkocht zou worden.
We had not foreseen that the business would be sold.

Ik had nooit kunnen voorspellen dat de voorstelling een flop zou worden.
I couldn't have predicted that the show would be a failure.

When someone is caught doing something, we use words such as **betrappen** or **snappen** 'catch someone doing something.'

Ik betrapte mezelf erop dat ik alweer een leugen stond te vertellen.
I caught myself telling another lie.

Ze hebben de dief op heterdaad betrapt.
They caught the thief in the act.

De fietsendief werd door een voorbijgaande agent gesnapt.
The bicycle thief was caught by a passing police officer.

Wonder

When one is wondering about something, we use the reflexive verb **zich afvragen** 'ask oneself.'

Ik vraag me af hoe duur een ticket naar Parijs is.
I wonder how much a ticket to Paris costs.

Curiosity

Curiosity is expressed with words such as **nieuwsgierig** 'curious,' **benieuwen** 'wonder if,' **benieuwd zijn** 'be curious,' and **willen weten** 'want to know.'

Karel was heel nieuwsgierig naar de voetbaluitslagen.
Karel was very curious about the soccer results.

Wat ben jij een nieuwsgierig aagje!
You are so nosy!

Het zal me benieuwen (expression) **wie de verkiezingen gaan winnen.**
I'm dying to know who is going to win the elections.

Ik ben benieuwd wat je van ons nieuwe huis zult vinden.
I'm curious to know what you think of our new home.

Ik zou willen weten wie dit jaar het boekenweekgeschenk schrijft.
I'd like to know who will write this year's book week gift.

18.7 Enjoyment and pleasure

Enjoyment

To talk about and express enjoyment, we use the verb **genieten van** 'enjoy' with its corresponding noun **het genot** 'pleasure.' Other words are the reflexive verb **zich amuseren** 'enjoy oneself' and various expressions with the noun **het plezier** 'fun, pleasure.' The adjective for this noun is **plezierig** 'enjoyable.'

Jaap zit lekker van z'n glas whiskey te genieten.
Jaap is enjoying a glass of whiskey.

Geniet maar lekker van je vakantie!
Enjoy your vacation!

Het is een genot om de kinderen zo te zien spelen.
It's such a joy to see the kids playing like that.

Hebben jullie je geamuseerd op het feestje?
Did you enjoy yourselves at the party?

Ik heb zo'n plezier van die wandelkaarten die je me hebt gegeven.
I'm having so much fun with those hiking maps that you gave me.

Het doet me plezier dat je het zo leuk vindt op school.
I'm so pleased that you are enjoying school.

Je zou ons een groot plezier doen.
You'd do us a great favor.

Veel plezier vanavond!
Have fun tonight!

We hebben een plezierig contact met onze buren.
We have a pleasant relationship with our neighbors.

We also use various expressions with **leuk** 'nice' and **fijn** 'fine, good.'

Heb je het leuk gehad op schoolreis?
Did you enjoy the school trip?

Ik wens u allemaal fijne feestdagen.
I wish you all happy holidays.

Fijne dag nog!
Enjoy the rest of your day!

A treat

To treat oneself or someone else to something enjoyable, we use words such as **gunnen** 'allow, grant,' **permitteren** or **veroorloven** 'allow, afford' and **verwennen** 'spoil, pamper.'

Ik gun mezelf vandaag een bezoekje bij de schoonheidsspecialiste.
I'm treating myself to a visit with the beautician.

Jij gunt hem zijn succes niet.
You envy him his success.

Ik kan me deze dure jas niet permitteren/veroorloven.
I can't afford this expensive coat.

We gaan mama op haar verjaardag eens lekker verwennen.
We're going to pamper mom on her birthday.

Cozy

The Dutch word **gezellig** 'cozy, enjoyable, nice' is used in many situations that evoke feelings of joy and pleasure. It has a strong social connotation.

We zijn gezellig naar de stad geweest.
We had fun going into town.

Zijn jullie er ook? Wat gezellig!
Are you here too? How nice!

We hadden een gezellige middag bij Tina thuis.
We had a pleasant afternoon at Tina's.

It is negated with **on-** or **niet**.

Wat een ongezellige kamer!
What an uninviting/cheerless room!

Ga je vanavond niet mee uit eten? Wat ongezellig nou!
Aren't you going out to dinner with us tonight? What a shame!

Fun

More colloquial is the word **de lol** 'fun' with its adjective **lollig** 'fun, funny, absurd.' In the context of joking, one can use the words **de grap** 'joke,' **grappig** 'funny,' and **de mop** 'joke.'

We hebben vandaag zo'n lol gehad in de scheikundeles.
We had so much fun today in the chemistry class.

A: Waarom doe je dat nou?
B: Gewoon, voor de lol.
A: Why are you doing that?
B: Just for fun.

Doe me een lol en ruim die rotzooi in je kamer op.
Do me a favor and clean up the mess in your room.

Doe niet zo lollig zeg.
Don't be funny/absurd, please.

Ik zei dat ik m'n portemonnee verloren had, maar het was maar een grapje.
I said I lost my wallet, but it was only a joke.

Wat een grappige foto.
What a funny picture.

Simon is de grappenmaker in de klas.
Simon is the jokester in the class.

Hij vertelde een mop en de hele klas lachte, de leraar ook.
He told a joke, and the whole class laughed, the teacher too.

Another word for 'fun' is **de pret** with its adjective **prettig**. It is often used as a synonym for **lol**. Note that it can also be used in situations that are not fun at all!

Met Joost kan je veel pret/lol hebben.
You can have a lot of fun with Joost.

Ga jij graag naar een pretpark?
Do you like going to an amusement park?

Ik had gisteren een wortelkanaalbehandeling. Dolle pret hoor!
I had a root canal yesterday. Loads of fun!

Karel is een prettig contact. Je kan met hem zo lekker over het onderwijs kankeren.
It is fun knowing Karel. I enjoy bitching and moaning about education with him.

Prettige feestdagen.
Happy holidays.

Prettige dag nog.
Enjoy the rest of your day.

Asking someone if they'd like to do something (or eat/drink something, for that matter), one can use expressions with **zin hebben in** or **om te** 'fancy, have desire for, would like to.' **Zin hebben in** is used for food and drink, while **zin hebben om te** is used for activities.

Heb je zin in een kopje koffie?
Would you like a cup of coffee?

Heb je zin om vanavond naar de film te gaan?
Would you like to go to the movies tonight?

Enjoying food

Finally, to ask if or to say that one has enjoyed the taste of something, for instance a meal in a restaurant, one can use expressions with the verb **smaken** 'taste' and its derivations **de smaak** 'taste,' **smakelijk** 'tasty.' The word **de smaak** 'taste' is used to talk about taste in general, not just when talking about food.

De kip smaakt heerlijk.
The chicken is delicious.

Heeft het gesmaakt?
How was your meal?

Eet smakelijk.
Enjoy your food.

Ik heb heerlijk gegeten.
I really enjoyed my food.

Jullie hebben je huis met smaak ingericht.
You have tastefully furnished your house.

18.8 Love, hate, and disgust

Love

To say that we love someone or something, we use the verb **houden van** 'like, love.' This verb is negated with **niet**.

Erik houdt van Karin.
Erik loves Karin.

Ik hou van jou.
I love you.

Wij houden van lange boswandelingen.
We like long walks in the forest.

Hou jij van bieten met spek?
Do you like beets with bacon?

Ik hou van de pianoconcerten van Mozart.
I love Mozart's piano concertos.

Mijn zoon houdt niet van pannenkoeken, gek hè?
My son doesn't like pancakes. Funny, isn't it?

Note that **houden van** is not as frequently used as English 'to love.' In English, the verb 'to love' can be used for almost anything. In Dutch, **houden van** is not as ubiquitous. It is used for relationships, food and drink, things one loves to do, and objects in a more general sense. For example, in a shoe store, one can say that one loves high heels, but one could not say that one loves the pair of shoes that one has just tried on. Or one can say that one loves romantic movies, but in Dutch, one can't say that one loves the film *Love Actually*. See examples:

Ik hou van hoge hakken.
I love high heels.

Ik vind deze schoenen heel mooi.
I like these shoes a lot.

Ik hou van romantische films.
I love romantic movies.

Ik vind *Love Actually* geweldig.
I find *Love Actually* marvelous.

Other words to talk about love are **de liefde** 'love,' **lief** 'lovable, sweet,' and **verliefd** 'in love.'

De liefde is een belangrijk thema in de literatuur.
Love is an important theme in literature.

Ik vind Joris zo lief!
I find Joris so sweet!

Wat lief van je om dat groentebed om te spitten.
How nice of you to plough up that vegetable patch.

Mijn zoon is verliefd op een meisje uit zijn klas.
My son is in love with a girl in his class.

Hate

The opposite, hate, is expressed with the verb **haten** 'hate,' the noun **de haat** 'hate,' and expressions such as **de pest hebben aan** 'hate, loathe,' **een hekel hebben aan** 'hate, loathe.' There is also the expression **niet kunnen uitstaan** 'can't stand.'

Peter haat z'n wiskundeleraar.
Peter hates his math teacher.

Ik wil geen grind op de oprijlaan, ik haat grind.
I don't want gravel on the driveway, I hate gravel.

Ik heb de pest aan rokers.
I loathe/hate smokers.

Frans heeft een vreselijke hekel aan honden.
Frans absolutely hates dogs.

Margo kan haar schoonmoeder niet uitstaan.
Margo can't stand her mother-in-law.

Die vrouw koestert haat tegen alle mannen.
That woman has nothing but hatred against men.

Er heerst een sfeer van haat en nijd in die familie.
There is an atmosphere of hatred and envy in that family.

▶ See also **17.3** for more on likes and dislikes.

Jealousy

Finally, an emotion that is related to love and hate is jealousy. In English, there is a difference between jealousy and envy, but in Dutch, we use the words **jaloers** 'jealous, envious' and **jaloersheid** 'jealousy, envy' for both. We also use the word **benijden** 'to envy,' which is used in situations where one envies someone for what that person has or can do.

Barend is met een heel jaloerse vrouw getrouwd.
Barend is married to a very jealous wife.

Ik ben jaloers op die mooie auto van jou.
I'm envious of that beautiful car of yours.

Jaloersheid is een verschrikkelijke karaktertrek.
Jealousy is a terrible character trait.

Ik benijd hem om zijn geweldige conditie.
I envy him for his excellent condition.

Disgust

There are many words for disgust. To express disgust with expletives, one can say:

Getverderrie, die kat heeft poep aan z'n poten.
Yuck, that cat has poo on his paws.

Gadver(damme), die wijn is niet te drinken.
Yuck/Eek, that wine is undrinkable.

Bah, kom hier en was meteen je handen.
Yuck, come here and wash your hands immediately.

Things that we find disgusting are called **vies** 'dirty,' **smerig** 'filthy,' **walgelijk** 'disgusting,' **onsmakelijk** 'repulsive,' or **afschuwelijk** 'repellent, horrific.'

Doe die vieze kleren maar meteen in de was.
Put those dirty clothes in the wash right away.

Wat rij jij in een smerige auto. Komt die wel eens in de wasstraat?
You really drive a filthy car. Do you ever go to the carwash?

Jan Wolkers kan de meest walgelijke dingen prachtig beschrijven.
Jan Wolkers can describe the most disgusting things beautifully.

Hou eens op met die onsmakelijke moppen van je.
Just stop telling those dirty jokes of yours.

Er hangt hier een afschuwelijke stank.
There is a repellent stench here.

The adjective **walgelijk** is derived from the verb **walgen van** 'abhor.' Other expressions are **misselijk worden van** 'get sick of' and **een afkeer hebben van** 'have an aversion to.'

Ik walg van die sigarettenstank die hier hangt.
I am sick of that cigarette smell here.

Ik hoef het maar te ruiken en ik word misselijk van Nutella.
I only have to smell it and I get sick of Nutella.

Peter heeft een afkeer van schelpdieren.
Peter doesn't like shellfish.

18.9 Anger, frustration, and insult

Anger

To say that one is angry, one can use the adjectives **boos** 'angry' or **kwaad** 'angry.' The words **woedend** 'livid' (from **de woede** 'anger'), **ziedend** 'irate' and **razend** 'raging' express even stronger feelings of anger. Other, less commonly used words are **nijdig** (with variations such as **spinnijdig** and **pisnijdig**) 'envious, furious,' **woest** 'furious,' and **pissig** 'pissed off.'

De juf was boos op ons omdat we te lang op het schoolplein bleven hangen.
The teacher was angry with us because we lingered in the schoolyard too long.

Ik was zo kwaad toen m'n zoveelste fiets gestolen was.
I was so mad when yet another bike of mine was stolen.

Met zulke opmerkingen kun je hem woedend/razend maken.
With such remarks, you can make him furious.

Hij was buiten zichzelf van woede.
He was beside himself with anger.

Hij stond me ziedend op te wachten toen ik eindelijk aankwam.
He awaited me furiously when I finally arrived.

Peter is spinnijdig omdat ik die prijsvraag gewonnen heb.
Peter is furious because I won that contest.

Pa was woest toen ik hem vertelde dat ik met m'n studie ga stoppen.
Dad was really cross when I told him I'm quitting college.

Waarom ben je nou zo pissig?
Why are you so pissed off?

Outrage

In a situation where one is indignant, outraged or upset about something, we use the word **verontwaardigd**.

De vakbonden reageerden verontwaardigd op het bezuinigingsplan van de minister.
The unions were outraged about the minister's budget cuts.

Grudge, revenge

When one has a grudge against someone, or wants revenge, we use the words **de wrok** 'grudge,' **op wraak zinnen** 'to want revenge,' **wraak nemen** 'take revenge.'

Maarten koesterde geen wrok toen zijn collega de promotie kreeg en niet hijzelf.
Maarten didn't hold a grudge when his colleague got the promotion and he did not.

Joris heeft Nico's meisje afgepakt en nu zint Nico op wraak.
Joris stole Nico's girlfriend, and now Nico wants revenge.

Hij zit al dagen te bedenken hoe hij wraak op hem kan nemen.
He's been pondering for days how to take revenge on him.

Frustration

To talk about or express frustration, one can use the word **de frustratie** 'frustration' and its adjectives **gefrustreerd** 'frustrated' and **frustrerend** 'frustrating.'

Hij heeft die frustratie aan z'n moeilijke jeugd overgehouden.
That frustration hails back to his difficult childhood.

Het is heel frustrerend als je na uren oefenen nog steeds fouten maakt.
It's very frustrating when you still make mistakes after hours of practicing.

Hoe ga je met een gefrustreerd kind om?
How do you handle a frustrated child?

Annoyance

When one is annoyed or irritated, one can use the word **de ergernis** 'annoyance.' This comes from the reflexive verb **zich ergeren** 'be irritated, annoyed.' Adjectives are **ergerlijk** 'irritating' and **geërgerd** 'irritated.' We also use **balen van** 'hate.'

Fietsendiefstal is een bron van ergernis in deze stad.
Bike theft is a source of annoyance in this city.

Erger jij je ook zo aan de treinvertragingen?
Are you also so annoyed by the train delays?

Ik heb zo'n hekel aan die ergerlijke vergaderingen.
I can't stand those tedious meetings.

De leraar keek heel geërgerd toen Jeroen tien minuten te laat binnenkwam.
The teacher looked very annoyed when Jeroen came in ten minutes late.

Ik baal van die eeuwige reclame.
I hate those constant commercials.

In a similar context, one can use the word **vervelend** 'annoying.'

Vervelend hè, dat de boot net weg is.
Annoying, isn't it, that the ferry has just left.

Moeten we nu een uur wachten? Wat vervelend.
Do we have to wait for an hour now? How annoying.

Insult

To talk about and express insult, we use the word **beledigd** 'insulted, offended' and the verb **beledigen** 'to insult.' The noun is **de belediging** 'insult.'

Johan is niet voor de catering gevraagd en nu is hij beledigd.
They didn't ask Johan to do the catering, and now he is offended.

Als je iemand beledigd hebt moet je je excuses aanbieden.
If you have offended someone, you must say you are sorry.

Hij heeft die opmerking als belediging opgevat, maar het was niet zo bedoeld.
He took that remark as an insult, but it wasn't meant that way.

Two other, less commonly used words to express insult are **krenken** 'hurt, offend' and **kwetsen** 'hurt, offend.'

Karin was heel gekwetst toen ik haar vroeg of ze aangekomen was.
Karin was really hurt when I asked her if she'd gained weight.

Als je kritiek op zijn werk uit, is hij meteen gekrenkt.
When you criticize his work, he is offended right away.

18.10 Shame, embarrassment, and shyness

Shame, embarrassment

To talk about and express shame, we use the verb **zich schamen** 'be ashamed.' The noun is **de schaamte** 'shame, embarrassment,' and corresponding adjectives are **beschamend** 'embarrassing, shameful' and **schaamteloos/onbeschaamd** 'shameless.'

> **Ik schaamde me dood toen ik een grote vlek op het smetteloze witte tafelkleed maakte.**
> I was terribly ashamed when I made a big stain on the spotless white tablecloth.
>
> **Marco kreeg een rood hoofd van schaamte toen hij de klas uit gestuurd werd.**
> Marco turned red with shame when he was sent out of the classroom.
>
> **Het team speelde een beschamend slechte wedstrijd.**
> The team played an embarrassingly bad game.
>
> **Dat is een schaamteloze/onbeschaamde leugen.**
> That's a shameless lie.

We also use the word **zich generen** 'be embarrassed' with the adjectives **gênant** 'embarrassing' and **ongegeneerd** 'shameless.'

> **Vind je het heet? Nou, als je wat uit wilt trekken, geneer je niet hoor.**
> You think it's hot? Well, if you want to take something off, don't be ashamed.
>
> **Ik vind het nogal gênant om ongevraagd op een feest te komen aanzetten.**
> I find it rather embarrassing to show up at a party uninvited.
>
> **Hij bediende zich ongegeneerd van een glas whiskey.**
> He shamelessly helped himself to a glass of whiskey.

Finally, the word **pijnlijk** 'embarrassing' can be used as a synonym for **beschamend**.

> **Hij bracht zichzelf in een pijnlijke situatie door op Facebook iets over z'n baas te zeggen.**
> He got himself into a painful situation by saying something about his boss on Facebook.

Shyness

To say one is shy, we use the word **verlegen** 'shy.' The corresponding noun is **de verlegenheid** 'abashment, embarrassment.'

> **Simon is vreselijk verlegen. Hij zegt nooit een woord in de les.**
> Simon is terribly shy. He doesn't ever speak up in class.
>
> **Ik bracht mezelf in verlegenheid door met te weinig geld op zak een rondje aan te bieden.**
> I made rather a fool of myself by offering everyone drinks while not having enough money.

18.11 Tiredness and boredom

Tiredness

To say that one is tired, we use the word **moe** 'tired.' The corresponding noun is **de moeheid** 'fatigue.'

> **Ik ben moe, ik ga maar eens naar bed.**
> I'm tired, I'll just go to bed.

Hij zat te knikkebollen van moeheid.
His head was nodding with fatigue.

To say that one is exhausted, we use the words **doodmoe** or **uitgeput** 'exhausted.'

Na een dag strand vielen we doodmoe in onze slaapzakken.
After a day at the beach, we fell into our sleeping bags exhausted.

Gerard kwam uitgeput van z'n werk thuis.
Gerard came home from work exhausted.

Boredom

To express boredom, we use the reflexive verb **zich vervelen** 'be bored.' Adjectives are **verveeld** 'bored' and **vervelend** 'annoying, boring.' The corresponding noun is **de verveling** 'boredom.' We also use the word **saai** for something that is boring.

Ik verveel me!
I'm bored!

De kinderen klieren al de hele dag, ze zijn verveeld.
The kids have been nagging all day. They are bored.

Uit verveling gingen de jongens met elkaar op de vuist.
The boys started fighting because they were bored.

Dit is een vervelend videospelletje.
This is a boring/annoying video game.

Wat een saaie film!
What a boring movie!

Appendix

Common strong and irregular verbs

The following is a list of commonly used strong and irregular verbs. The strong verbs are organized according to the way they change their stem vowel in simple past and present perfect tense.

a – oe – a			
dragen	droeg	gedragen	*carry, wear*
ervaren	ervoer	ervaren	*experience*
graven	groef	gegraven	*dig*
slaan	sloeg	geslagen	*hit, strike*
varen	voer	gevaren	*float, sail*
a – ie/i – a			
bevallen	beviel	bevallen	*please, give birth*
blazen	blies	geblazen	*blow*
laten	liet	gelaten	*let*
slapen	sliep	geslapen	*sleep*
vallen	viel	gevallen	*fall*
hangen	hing	gehangen	*hang*
vangen	ving	gevangen	*catch*
e – a – e			
eten	at	gegeten	*eat*
genezen	genas	genezen	*heal*
geven	gaf	gegeven	*give*
lezen	las	gelezen	*read*
meten	mat	gemeten	*measure*
treden	trad	getreden	*step, move*
vergeten	vergat	vergeten	*forget*
vreten	vrat	gevreten	*devour, gobble*
e – a – o			
bevelen	beval	bevolen	*order, command*
breken	brak	gebroken	*break*
nemen	nam	genomen	*take*
spreken	sprak	gesproken	*speak*
steken	stak	gestoken	*stick, sting, prick*
stelen	stal	gestolen	*steal*
e – ie – a			
scheppen	schiep	geschapen	*create*
e – ie – e			
heffen	hief	geheven	*lift, heave*
e – ie – o			
bederven	bedierf	bedorven	*spoil, rot*
helpen	hielp	geholpen	*help*
sterven	stierf	gestorven	*die*
ontwerpen	ontwierp	ontworpen	*design*
werpen	wierp	geworpen	*throw*

werven	wierf	geworven	*recruit*
zwerven	zwierf	gezworven	*wander, roam*
e – o – o			
bedelven	bedolf	bedolven	*overwhelm, bury*
bergen	borg	geborgen	*store, save*
bewegen	bewoog	bewogen	*move*
delven	dolf	gedolven	*dig, unearth*
gelden	gold	gegolden	*apply, count*
melken	molk	gemolken	*milk*
schelden	schold	gescholden	*scoff, scold*
schenden	schond	geschonden	*violate*
schenken	schonk	geschonken	*give, donate*
scheren	schoor	geschoren	*shave*
smelten	smolt	gesmolten	*melt*
treffen	trof	getroffen	*meet, strike*
trekken	trok	getrokken	*pull*
vechten	vocht	gevochten	*fight*
vertrekken	vertrok	vertrokken	*depart*
vlechten	vlocht	gevlochten	*braid, twine*
wegen	woog	gewogen	*weigh*
zenden	zond	gezonden	*send*
zwellen	zwol	gezwollen	*swell*
zwemmen	zwom	gezwommen	*swim*
e – oe – o			
zweren	zwoer	gezworen	*swear*
i – a – e			
bidden	bad	gebeden	*pray*
liggen	lag	gelegen	*lie (down)*
zitten	zat	gezeten	*sit*
i – o – o			
beginnen	begon	begonnen	*begin*
bezinnen (zich)	bezon	bezonnen	*ponder*
binden	bond	gebonden	*bind*
blinken	blonk	geblonken	*gleam, glitter*
dingen	dong	gedongen	*haggle, bargain*
dringen	drong	gedrongen	*push forward*
drinken	dronk	gedronken	*drink*
dwingen	dwong	gedwongen	*force*
glimmen	glom	geglommen	*shine, gleam*
klimmen	klom	geklommen	*climb*
klinken	klonk	geklonken	*sound, hammer*
krimpen	kromp	gekrompen	*shrink*
opwinden	wond op	opgewonden	*wind up, excite*
schrikken	schrok	geschrokken	*be scared, startled*
slinken	slonk	geslonken	*decrease*
spinnen	spon	gesponnen	*spin, purr*
springen	sprong	gesprongen	*jump, spring*
stinken	stonk	gestonken	*stink*
verzinnen	verzon	verzonnen	*contrive, make up*
vinden	vond	gevonden	*find*
winden	wond	gewonden	*wind*
winnen	won	gewonnen	*win*

wringen	wrong	gewrongen	*wrench, wring out*
zingen	zong	gezongen	*sing*
zinken	zonk	gezonken	*sink*
ie – o – o			
bedriegen	bedroog	bedrogen	*cheat*
bieden	bood	geboden	*offer*
gieten	goot	gegoten	*pour*
kiezen	koos	gekozen	*choose*
liegen	loog	gelogen	*lie*
opschieten	schoot op	opgeschoten	*hurry up*
schieten	schoot	geschoten	*shoot*
verbieden	verbood	verboden	*forbid*
verliezen	verloor	verloren	*lose*
vliegen	vloog	gevlogen	*fly*
vriezen	vroor	gevroren	*freeze*
ij – e – e			
begrijpen	begreep	begrepen	*understand*
bijten	beet	gebeten	*bite*
blijken	bleek	gebleken	*appear*
blijven	bleef	gebleven	*stay*
drijven	dreef	gedreven	*float, drive (push)*
glijden	gleed	gegleden	*slide, glide*
grijpen	greep	gegrepen	*seize, grab*
hijsen	hees	gehesen	*raise, hoist*
kijken	keek	gekeken	*look*
knijpen	kneep	geknepen	*pinch*
krijgen	kreeg	gekregen	*get, receive*
lijden	leed	geleden	*suffer*
lijken	leek	geleken	*appear*
mijden	meed	gemeden	*avoid, shun*
overlijden	overleed	overleden	*pass away*
prijzen	prees	geprezen	*praise, price*
rijden	reed	gereden	*drive*
rijgen	reeg	geregen	*tie, string*
rijzen	rees	gerezen	*rise*
schijnen	scheen	geschenen	*shine, appear*
schrijven	schreef	geschreven	*write*
slijpen	sleep	geslepen	*sharpen*
slijten	sleet	gesleten	*wear out, spend, sell*
smijten	smeet	gesmeten	*throw, toss*
snijden	sneed	gesneden	*cut*
spijten	speet	gespeten	*regret, be sorry*
splijten	spleet	gespleten	*split, crack*
stijgen	steeg	gestegen	*rise, increase*
strijden	streed	gestreden	*fight, struggle*
strijken	streek	gestreken	*iron, brush*
verdwijnen	verdween	verdwenen	*disappear*
vergelijken	vergeleek	vergeleken	*compare*
verwijten	verweet	verweten	*blame*
wijken	week	geweken	*make way for*
wijzen	wees	gewezen	*point*
wrijven	wreef	gewreven	*rub, buff*
zwijgen	zweeg	gezwegen	*be silent*

ui – o – o

buigen	boog	gebogen	*bend, bow*
druipen	droop	gedropen	*drip*
duiken	dook	gedoken	*dive*
fluiten	floot	gefloten	*whistle*
kluiven	kloof	gekloven	*nibble, gnaw*
kruipen	kroop	gekropen	*crawl*
ruiken	rook	geroken	*smell*
schuiven	schoof	geschoven	*push, shove*
sluipen	sloop	geslopen	*sneak, creep*
sluiten	sloot	gesloten	*close, lock*
snuiten	snoot	gesnoten	*blow nose, snuff*
snuiven	snoof	gesnoven	*sniff, snort*
spuiten	spoot	gespoten	*spout, gush, inject*
stuiven	stoof	gestoven	*blow, dust*
verschuilen	verschool	verscholen	*hide*
zuigen	zoog	gezogen	*suck*
zuipen	zoop	gezopen	*drink, booze*

The following is a list of strong verbs that don't seem to follow a clear pattern such as the ones above or are alone in their pattern. They are organized here in alphabetical order.

doen	deed	gedaan	*do*
gaan	ging	gegaan	*go*
houden	hield	gehouden	*hold*
komen	kwam	gekomen	*come*
lopen	liep	gelopen	*walk*
roepen	riep	geroepen	*call*
staan	stond	gestaan	*stand*
weten	wist	geweten	*know*
worden	werd	geworden	*become*
zien	zag	gezien	*see*

The following is a list of irregular verbs. They are irregular because one of their past tense forms is strong, and one is regular, or their past tense forms seem to follow the rules for regular verbs. They are organized in alphabetical order.

bakken	bakte	gebakken	*bake*
barsten	barstte	gebarsten	*burst*
bezoeken	bezocht	bezocht	*visit*
braden	braadde	gebraden	*fry, sauté*
brengen	bracht	gebracht	*bring*
denken	dacht	gedacht	*think*
hebben	had	gehad	*have*
heten	heette	geheten	*be called*
jagen	joeg	gejaagd	*hunt*
kopen	kocht	gekocht	*buy*
lachen	lachte	gelachen	*laugh*
laden	laadde	geladen	*load*
malen	maalde	gemalen	*grind, ground*
raden	raadde	geraden	*guess*
scheiden	scheidde	gescheiden	*separate*
spannen	spande	gespannen	*stretch, tighten*
stoten	stootte	gestoten	*bump, knock*
verraden	verraadde	verraden	*cheat, betray*
vouwen	vouwde	gevouwen	*fold*
vragen	vroeg	gevraagd	*ask*

waaien	woei/waaide	gewaaid	*blow*
wassen	waste	gewassen	*wash*
weven	weefde	geweven	*weave*
zeggen	zei, zeiden	gezegd	*say*
zijn	was, waren	geweest	*be*
zoeken	zocht	gezocht	*look for*
zouten	zoutte	gezouten	*salt, pickle*

Index of grammatical terms

References are to sections, not to pages.

Index of functions

References are to sections, not to pages.